Democracy and Democratization in the Gulf

Democracy and Democratization in the Gulf

Edited by

Gulshan Dietl

SHIPRA

Price: Rs. 895 (US$ 45)

ISBN: 978-81-7541-563-8

First Published in India in 2010

Democracy and Democratization in the Gulf

SHIPRA PUBLICATIONS
H.O.: LG 18-19, Pankaj Central Market, Patparganj,
I.P. Ext., Delhi-110092, Tel: 91-11-2223 5152, 2223 6152
Br.Off.: 4617/18, Ansari Road, Darya Ganj,
New Delhi-110002, Tel: 6594 6453, 9810522367
E-mail: info@shiprapublications.com
www.shiprapublications.com

Contents

Part 3
Saudi Arabia: Opposition and Human Rights in a Liberalizing Autocracy

Part 4
Iran and Iraq: Ethnicity and Gender, Economy and Occupation

Part 5
Kuwait, Oman, Bahrain, Qatar and the UAE

Introduction

Gulshan Dietl

The origins of democracy go far back in time. It long preceded and was wider-spread than the ancient Greece in the sixth century BC—as is commonly understood. Through various stages of its growth, democracy has exerted a powerful influence on people's minds and motivated them for better management of their community living. It has sought to ensure the widest possible participation of common people in the decision-making as well as in their implementation.

Is it possible to sum up democracy in terms of elections at regular intervals, universal suffrage, individual freedom, multiple political parties, independent media, majority rule and minority rights? The man's highest ends are not necessarily or exclusively political. Democracy, though, enhances his chances of attaining his ends to the best of his ability and attempts. Is democracy, then, a means to the ideal or is it an ideal in itself?

Samuel Huntington's thesis on democracy envisages its progression in waves. The third and the most recent wave made advances in the seventies. If one accepts this theory, then the third wave did not wash the shores of the Arab world; more so the Gulf region. Is it possible, instead, to understand democracy as a process that goes on continuously in various places, at varied paces, all over the world? Such a conception of democracy guards against the all-or-none division of states into democratic or otherwise. Imagining democracy as a process also permits monitoring its moves sometimes progressing and consolidating its gains, sometimes regressing into authoritarian tendencies. The process never ends; there is no perfect democracy. It is, and must always remain, an ideal that humans must constantly strive for.

Is there a positive relationship between democracy and development; or does the former hinder economic growth, and therefore, development? Should democracy wait till the economic, social and cultural sub-structures are sufficiently developed? Is civil society a prerequisite and social stratification a hindrance in a country's path to an open society? Noise and chaos of democracy provide a peaceful route to change; lack thereof may lead to violent changes or attempted changes. Questions and assumptions like these belong in the common toolbox in attempting a diagnosis of the democratic failure in the Gulf.

The patriarchal social order and rentier economies have impacted domestic political systems in the Gulf. Genuine leaders of yesterday have become hereditary rulers; spoils of power have been retained within small elite groups; co-optation and corruption of opponents and suppression of dissent have become routine. In addition, the states in the Gulf region are vulnerable to supra-state ideologies of Arabism and Islamism as also to the sub-state sectarian and ethnic affiliations. The uneven spread of natural resources, the uneven distribution of national wealth, domestic conflicts, the role of military and police, etc. have posed further challenges to the progress of democracy.

The external influences in this region need to be closely scrutinised for a better appreciation of the situation. The Gulf is the most penetrated region in the world. The US-sponsored democracy-promotion project was short-lived and resulted in a war on Iraq. Today, it is mostly replaced by utter indifference on the matter; except when it is invoked to threaten the political system in Iran. Will external intervention/indifference encourage/discourage democratic forces inside a state?

What would be the implications of democracy or a lack of it beyond the region? According to Kantian theory of perpetual peace, the democracies are less inclined to go to war. According to Thomas Friedman's Big Mac Theory, no two countries having a McDonald's have ever fought a war against each other. Taken together, the American soft power and commercial interests would spell democracy and that, in turn, would bring about a peaceful world. The assertions beg more questions than they offer prescriptions. The linkage between internal democracy, regional stability and international security is still to be established.

The most pertinent question in this context would be: must democracies stop at the national borders or should there be initiatives towards a more democratic international order? The Westphalian state exercised comprehensive, supreme, unqualified and exclusive sovereignty over its territorial domain. That state is undergoing transformation for more than four centuries. The international system, simultaneously, has been going through multipolarity to bipolarity to unipolarity; and evolving towards a yet undefined future order. Should the democracies insist on a democratic global order? Would a democratic global order be conducive to democratic political entities?

Hussein Solomon provides the theoretical underpinning and methodological rigour to the analysis of the term 'Democracy". He seeks to contextualize democratization in a time of great upheaval where change is the only constant. Three of the most important forces driving such change are globalization, regionalization and democratization. In the Gulf, like everywhere else, histories, cultural and religious practice, economic development, demographic composition, geographical peculiarities all impact on the form and nature of democracy in a particular country. No two countries in the Gulf have gone through the exact same experience and therefore we need to speak of broad principles of democratic practice rather than scientific certainties, he concludes.

Dietrich Jung maintains that the conceptual apparatus of historical sociology can still serve as our core tool-kit for the analysis of contemporary state formation and for an assessment of the prospects of democracy in the Gulf. Identifying the rentier aspect of economy as the reason, he observes that the states in the Gulf have been able to build up an enormously high level of regime security while holding societal demand for more participation at bay. His conclusion: state formation is an ongoing process with an open end characterized by state formation and state decay in the Gulf as also in the West.

Gulshan Dietl traces the US project of democratization in the Gulf from its original propozal of the Greater Middle East Initiative to its evolution into the Broader Middle East Partnership and assesses its impact on the Gulf states. Whereas the rulers feared a Helsinki-type fate for themselves, the reaction of the people went all the way from eager expectation to total disbelief. The political evolution in the Gulf predates the democratization from afar and has continued even after the US banner of democracy has been folded and shelved. The entire episode has given a new impetus to the issue of democracy in the disciplines of political science and international relations in the meanwhile.

Rushda Siddiqui examines the dynamics of change in the Arab Gulf on two counts. The first is regarding the role of religion in shaping the challenges of change and the state responses to it, and the second is the changing political power equations in the strategic environment of the region. Though the two are inter-related changes, she makes a distinction between the role of the state and the role of the external forces in the situation. The role of the Western world to ensure that the existing state and social formations do not undergo any significant change unless it is economically beneficial and provides a strategic base for an outreach to the rest of Asia is the biggest hurdle to change in the Arab Gulf.

Omair Anas provides a broad overview of the situation of media in the GCC states. In the absence of political institutions and civil society, the media have to deal with existing institutions like religion, tribes and the undemocratic ruling class that controls and finances them. Noting the utter failure of American-sponsored Arabic TV channel *al-Hurra,* he believes that the media in the GCC states have sufficient potential to engage with and advance the debate on democracy.

M.H. Ilias takes a hard look at the Special Economic Zones (SEZs), which he prefers to call "sacred spaces of capitalism"—not meant for ordinary people and beyond the rules of the land where they are located. Like the original sacred spaces, the SEZs are seldom concerned with the serious threats they pose to the politico-legal sovereignty of the states.

There are four papers on Saudi Arabia; each with a distinct perspective. Jajati Pattnaik explains the process of democratization in the Kingdom of Saudi Arabia by designing a graph that takes in the variables of electoral democracy, civil society and culture. The Sauds have introduced a set of reforms in the form of Majlis as-Shura, a partially elected municipal council, professional organizations and syndicates; and have instituted national dialogues between the rulers and the people. The cultural ingredient is included in the process of consolidation of reform.

Ajish Joy could not disagree more! The institution of the Consultative Assembly, promulgation of the Basic Laws, the setting up of the Allegiance Institution, the Municipal elections, the initiation of the National Dialogue and some key changes in the cabinet and other important bodies are only steps towards a liberalized autocracy. The House of Saud will never permit democratization because it will mean the end of *Saudi Arabia—Arabia of the Sauds*. So what we are witnessing is House of Saud's attempts to perpetuate their reign. They have decided that permitting limited and tightly controlled political and social openings are the best means to go about it, he concludes.

Stanly Johny treads a middle path in his assessment of the Saudi domestic politics. The Islamists and the liberal democrats have been pursuing different agendas of reform in the country; empowering the rulers to balance each other out at times. At present, the democrats are given a sympathetic hearing. It would be illogical to expect sudden changes or democratization of polity in view of the hold of the conservative values and religious establishment. Like their rulers, the Saudi population also seem to believe in gradualism.

Prasanta Kumar Pradhan acknowledges the moves by the Saudi government regarding the education and employment of women, talking to the dissident Shia leadership, reforming the judiciary, giving some rights to the labourers, initiating press freedom, forming a national body to deal with the human rights abuses and also signing some international treaties etc. They do not satisfy the aspirations of the people nor do they conform to the established international human rights standards. He explains that the government is trying to strike a balance between demands for more liberal human rights, the Islamic responsibility of the government and the pressure from the conservative elements of the society.

The papers on Iran deal with three crucial issues: the situation of women in the country, the oil-based economy and freedom of expression. Beryl Anand explains how the strand of Marxist feminist discourse has been suppressed in Iran since the Islamic Revolution of 1979. The Iranian women have developed a distinct Islamic discourse that is within the Islamic context but still leaves them political space. Even though its etymology is questioned by the feminists worldwide, it still is a commendable advancement towards gender equality and has accomplished some significant changes in law and customs. The past few years have witnessed a recrudescence of conservatism, she regrets.

Elected on the platform of political and economic reforms, President Khatami ushered in a period of freedom for the press unknown in Iran since the Islamic Revolution. After eight years of his presidency, there was very little advancement on the ground. Sujata Ashwarya Cheema calls the exercise a "flicker of democracy" and passes a rather harsh verdict: Khatami's governing style of taking one step forward and two steps backward left him with an empty coffer on democratic reforms which he tended to blame on 'systemic' forces, like all indecisive and unsuccessful politicians.

Sameena Hameed scrutinizes the Iranian economy with a special emphasis on large-scale subsidies that the government has been doling out since the Revolution. She establishes, with the help of Iranian government statistics, that the subsidies have restricted growth, fuelled inflation and increased disparities. Eliminating inefficient and distorting subsidies would create economic space to allow greater participation and skill generation in the society.

There are two papers on Iraq: one critiquing the parliamentary elections held under the American military occupation and the other on democratic experiment in the Kurdish region of Iraq. Angela Gangmei traces the democratization process in Iraq under the US military occupation. The process culminated in the parliamentary elections in January 2005. The US needed a client regime as a cover for its continuing occupation. The elections took place in conditions of extreme insecurity and political turmoil. The umbrella group of Shia candidates and the Kurdish list were the winners. More than an exercise in electing a government, the elections proved to be an ethnic/identity referendum, in the circumstances.

LungthuiYang Riamei holds that since the creation of the modern state of Iraq, the history of Iraqi Kurdistan has been one of underdevelopment, political and cultural repression, destruction, ethnic cleansing and genocide. After the Gulf War of 1991, the Kurds were autonomous in their region, where they successfully experimented with multi-party democracy. Besides Kurds, the Assyrians, Chaldeans and Turkomans within the region preserved their respective ethno-linguistic identities, while simultaneously establishing a wider sense of collective identity based on three key factors: first, common geography; second, the ongoing experiment in self rule, democratization and cultural tolerance; and last, their shared experience as non-Arab Iraqis who have all known repression and marginalization within the modern state of Iraq.

There is a paper each on each of the five remaining states: Kuwait, Oman, Bahrain, Qatar and the UAE. Anwar Alam examines the trajectory of democracy in Kuwait. He maintains that the history of parliamentary democracy in Kuwait has defied the dominant western paradigms of 'Middle East exceptionalism' and 'thesis of rentier economy' that sought to explain the absence of democratic rule in Muslim West Asian countries, particularly in the Gulf. Except for a two short breaks—1976-1981 and 1986-1992—Kuwait has been a functioning democracy since 1961. His prognosis is cautious, however. The possibility of regression remains as Amirs of Kuwait have, on several occasions, used their power to dissolve the Assembly when it aggressively challenged the government.

Shelly Johny charts the course of Oman's attempts to introduce political liberalization and also to identify the major factors that influence this process and make Oman's experience unique in the Gulf region. Oman has also achieved several milestones like allowing women to vote and contest in elections and providing universal suffrage. The concept of Ibadi Imamate, complications due to lack of a successor to Sultan Qaboos and dwindling oil resources can create problems for Al Busaidi rule in Oman. It is here that representative political institutions can help in smooth transfer of power after the time of Qaboos.

Bahrain had a short stint of democracy in the early seventies. After the death of Sheikh Isa in 1999, his son and the new ruler Sheikh Hamad has promulgated a National Charter, organized elections for municipal council and the Parliament, and has declared the country a constitutional monarchy. Rajiv Kumar holds the process as an initiative from above. It is the ruling family that controls the pace and direction of reform guided by a strategy of system maintenance.

Basir Ahmed and Marshal Gao examine a parallel process in Qatar, where the namesake Sheikh Hamad formed a constitution drafting committee in 1999. The political processes stirred to life in Qatar around the same time as in Bahrain. There is an ample scope within the Qatari traditions for democracy to strike roots. And the institutions and experiments that manage the social relations and organize political life are positive indications.

Syeeda Khatoon considers the US democracy-promotion a myth. She analyzes the UAE rulers' dual approach of controlling and caring and finds it to be working. She examines the US policy of entering into Free Trade Area agreements with individual countries and then linking up twenty-two Arab states, Israel and the US by the year 2013 to form a region-wide Middle East Free Trade Area (MEFTA) and refutes the theory that trade can be used as a tool to fight terrorism.

We at the Jawaharlal Nehru University considered it extremely worthwhile and very timely to undertake an exercise to explore these issues. The authors, with different perspectives and on different subjects, have coalesced to put together a volume that is a serious and well-rounded treatment of the theme.

Part 1: Democracy and Democratization

1

Democratization: Some Theoretical and Methodological Considerations

Hussein Solomon

INTRODUCTION

Too often in discussions on issues of democratization, whether in West Asia or any other region, are broader theoretical and methodological considerations ignored. It is as if one could discuss civil-military relations in Saudi Arabia or the role of the clergy in Iran without referring to broader developments in the global political economy or the changes in intellectual discourse as it pertains to, for instance, security. Increasingly however the world is an interconnected whole where developments in the periphery impact on the core and vice-versa. Moreover, technological changes, cultural transformations and economic turbulence all impact on political developments. For the researcher and academic this means that whilst focusing on the tyranny of Saddam Hussein's Iraq or the power of non-state actors like Hezbollah in Lebanon we also need to take cognizance of developments outside the country and how it impacts on internal developments as well as developments in the socio-economic sphere and how this might impact on issue of democratization in the country we are researching.

What this paper seeks to do then is to contextualize democratization in a time of great upheaval where change is the only constant. Three of the most important forces driving such change are globalization, regionalization and democratization. In seeking to understand the theoretical import of these forces, of world politics, the paper will seek to conclude with some methodological considerations for the study of democratization in the Gulf region.

GLOBALIZATION, REGIONALIZATION AND DEMOCRATIZATION: EXPLORING THE INTERFACE

The concept globalization has become ubiquitous in the languages of the world. In Italian there is talk of *globalizzazione*, in Chinese of *Quan Qui Hua*, in French of *mondialization*, in German of *Globalisierung*, and in Korean of *Gukje Hwa.*[1] Despite the ubiquitous nature of the concept, there is no clear definition of what globalization means. Whilst Scholte[2] defines globalization simply as the "*...process whereby the world is becoming a smaller place*", he does go on to note that, "*Discourses of globalization have become a prime site of struggle between, broadly speaking, conservatives who deny such a trend, liberals who celebrate its presumed fruits, and critics who decry its alleged disempowering effects*".[3] How could one concept elicit such strongly diverse perspectives? Perhaps part of the answer lay in the comment by Gillian Youngs[4] that "... *the most obvious quality of discourses of globalization is their all-encompassing intention or nature, their orientation towards descriptions, explanations or theorizations of the whole, the global*". Such totalizing discourses on the part of supporters and critics of globalization tend to ignore the nuanced complexity of processes of globalization; that globalization can be both positive and negative; empowering and disempowering; emancipatory and oppressive.

Within the developing world context, discourses on globalization invariably focus on the negative. Giles Mohan[5] for instance notes how pervasive the influence of the International Monetary Fund and the World Bank is on African countries pointing out that 38 out of 43 sub-Saharan African countries are undergoing structural adjustment programmemes. Similarly Grugel and Hout[6] argue that globalization is an uneven process and that 'weak states' have less means to hold globalization at bay. Implicit in such an argument is that globalization is essentially a negative process. Islamists on the other hand point to the gratuitous violence, foul language and nudity which often accompanies Hollywood movies being circulated in the Gulf region. However such arguments also ignore the positive in relation to Africa: globalization has resulted in the strengthening of a global democratic ethos, seen so vividly in the international human rights regime. Thus Kwame Ninsin[7] argues that globalization "... *makes African governments vulnerable to democratize because of their dependence on foreign capital*". Thus whilst dependence on foreign capital is not a good thing, it is a positive development when international actors take this dependence and use it as leverage to pressurize those authoritarian governments to democratize.

Similarly global solidarity has been mobilized in support of the Iranian electorate which has felt that the June 2009 election was stolen by the incumbent President Ahmadinejad and his hardline supporters. This global solidarity was largely organized through new age internet technologies like Facebook and Twitter. The fact that globalization is undermining the power of states, bypassing sovereignty, and creating precedents for external intervention in defence of human security is not a bad thing within the context of repressive state structures. How this has come about is briefly examined in our discussions of the historiography of the concepts of security and sovereignty below.

THE HISTORICAL EVOLUTION OF THE CONCEPT 'SECURITY'

Traditionally, security was almost exclusively understood to refer to the security of states and military security.[8] In this way, security came to mean national security and was synonymous with defence. This Clausewitzian conceptualization of security is clearly evident in the following definition of security by Bellamy: "*Security itself is relative freedom from war, coupled with a relatively high expectation that defeat will not be a consequence of any war that should occur.*"[9] Bellamy's rather narrow view of security is further echoed by another parochial perception of security by Giacomo Luciani who commented that "*[n]ational security may be defined as the ability to withstand aggression from abroad.*"[10] As such, the study of security in the post-1945 period was dominated by such concepts as 'containment', 'deterrence', 'flexible response', 'massive retaliation', 'balance of power', 'mutually assured destruction' (MAD) and an overarching concern with nuclear strategy.[11] This was clearly evident during Reagan's presidency when the world had to familiarise itself with the Strategic Defence Initiative (SDI), more commonly known 'Star Wars' programme.

This is not to say that there were no alternative voices to be heard challenging this dominant security-centred paradigm which, it could be argued, has dominated strategic discourse from the time of Sun Tzu, almost two thousand five hundred years ago! As early as 1705, the German philosopher Leibniz spoke of the need for the state to provide common security (*la securité commune*) to its citizens and the French philosopher, Montesquieu, noted that true political freedom could only occur when people are secure.[12] What is interesting is that both these philosophers were concerned with the security of individuals and not primarily concerned with the security of states.

In 1950, the political scientist, Lasswell argued for a broader conceptualization of security as:

> "... all measures which are proposed in the name of national security do not necessarily contribute to the avowed end .... Our greatest security lies in the best balance of all instruments of foreign policy, and hence in the co-ordinated handling of arms, diplomacy, information, and economics; and in the proper correlation of all measures of foreign and domestic policy."[13]

Lasswell's views were reinforced by McNamara, the former United States Secretary of State, who pleaded for a less military-political focus on security in 1968. This was later echoed by Galtung's reference to "*...four highly credible, but also totally avoidable threats to our existence on earth—war, hunger, repression and eco-disaster.*"[14]

Despite these dissident voices, the juggernaut of military-centred security studies continued to hold sway. How does one explain this effective marginalization of voices appealing for a more holistic understanding of security? One answer could possibly be that the fear of nuclear annihilation was so overwhelming that all else paled into insignificance. This is a view certainly subscribed to by United States President Eisenhower when he declared:

> "... with both sections of this divided world in possession of unbelievably destructive weapons, mankind approaches a state where mutual annihilation becomes a possibility. No other fact of today's world equals this in importance—it colours everything we say, plan and do."[15]

This dominance of the traditional paradigm was not to last, however. Changes in the strategic environment in the 1970s necessitated a rethinking of conventional understandings of security. According to Carim,[16] five factors laid the foundations for a 'devaluation of the military's currency' in the 1970s:

> the beginnings of *détente* between the superpowers in the early 1970s as exemplified by the signing of the *Strategic Arms Limitation Treaty* (SALT 1) in 1972;
> the American experience in Vietnam which exposed the limits of imposing military solutions to certain types of conflict;
> the financial costs of this campaign in conjunction with a world economic recession which fuelled a deleterious inflationary spiral;
> America's economic decline relative to Japan and the European Economic Community which were competing more successfully in international markets; and the quadrupling of oil prices by the Organization of Oil Exporting Countries (OPEC) in the 1970s that sent shock waves throughout global economies and exposed the West's external dependence on strategic resources.

These tectonic shifts in the global security landscape shook the very edifice of the dominant paradigm as Americans were forced to concede that threats to their national security also stemmed from a flagging economy. This new concern regarding the economic dimensions of security is perhaps best captured in the definition of security by Blair, Deputy Assistant Secretary of State for Public Affairs, who told the US Congress in 1972 that "[*o*]*ur national security today depends on things like balance of payments, economic affairs, foreign assistance* ..."[17] The mere acceptance of the economic dimensions of security by the establishment served to bolster those marginalized voices calling for a widening of the security agenda. Thus, the events of the 1970s effectively opened the sluice gates for further criticism of the dominant paradigm.

One of the first of those to take advantage of these changing circumstances was what has been termed the 'alternative security school'. The thrust of this approach was informed objectively by Reagan's categorization of the Soviet Union as an 'Evil Empire' and the arms race that it engendered. Proponents convincingly argued that more arms did not mean more security—more nuclear weapons did not result in a safer planet. In this, their work was inspired by the intellectual tradition of Herz who, in the early 1950s, introduced the idea of the 'security dilemma':

> "*... a structural notion in which the self-help attempts of states to look after their security needs tend, regardless of intentions, to lead to rising insecurity for others as each interprets its own measures as defensive, and the measures of others as potentially threatening.*"[18]

Herz's theoretical insights found practical expression in the work of the alternative security school that introduced the radical notion of 'security interdependence' to the strategic discourse. According to this notion, Western security was intimately related to that of the Soviet Union and vice versa; modern weaponry had created objective security interdependence. This meant that it was necessary for the West; for example, to recognize the fact that increases in Soviet weaponry did not necessarily improve Western security. The reverse was also true.[19] This rather abstract notion was given concrete expression in concepts such as 'arms control' and 'non-offensive defence'. The notion of security interdependence rapidly gained support under the banner of common security. For example, the 1982 Palme Commission provided political support for the idea of common security, arguing that "*... states can no longer obtain security at each other's expense, but only through co-operative efforts.*"[20]

The ideas of security interdependence of the 1980s were further developed in the 1990s by scholars like Kennedy, Breytenbach, Tehranian, Obi, Nathan, Cottey, Krasna, Van De Veer and Dabelko, and Lizee and Peou who argued that the emergence of transnational security threats such as drought, narco-trafficking and pollution necessitated transnational or collective responses.[21] Thus, Kennedy notes that "*[i]n this larger and more integrated sense, 'national' security becomes increasingly inseparable from 'international' security.*"[22] These notions of common or collective security, of course, built on the earlier scholarship of 'complex interdependence' scholars such as Keohane and Nye.[23]

It would be wrong to assume, however, that these debates in the security discourse were only confined to the West. Ideas of common security had already entered the discourse of the *Politburo* of the Soviet Union. This was motivated in large part by Gorbachev's understanding that the Soviet economy could not sustain a new arms race and that this meant that the superpower stand-off needed to be addressed decisively. Carim[24] puts it this way:

> "*In conjunction with his domestic policies of glasnost (openness) and perestroika (restructuring) which aimed to revive the Soviet political and*

economic system, Gorbachev galvanized the process of détente by proceeding with unilateral Soviet disarmament and by urging a series of arms control agreements."

Thus, the 1990s witnessed the rapid demilitarization of superpower relations. One aspect of this demilitarization was the knock-on effect it had on international relations scholars such as Barry Buzan and Ken Booth. Such soul-searching questions as 'what is security, whose security, and security from what threats?', were now being asked.[25]

In answering the question of whose security needs to be addressed, Booth argued that the problem with traditional security perspectives was that it equated security exclusively with state security.[26] The problem with this perspective, as Buzan rightly argued, was that state security was often purchased at the expense of human security, specifically in the dictatorships of the third world; consider here Duvalier of Haiti, Bokassa in the Central African Republic, Pol Pot in Cambodia,[27] Amin in Uganda and Saddam Hussein in Iraq. In practice, this meant that people became the primary referent of security as opposed to the state. New security thinking therefore increasingly focused on what has been termed 'human security', as opposed to traditional state-centric security. According to the *Bonn Declaration* of 1991, human security is "*... the absence of threat to human life, lifestyle and culture through the fulfillment of basic needs.*"[28] This definition, in turn, has been greatly guided by feminist contributions to new security thinking. Feminists strongly argue that there is a need for 'care' to be incorporated into any security discourse. This seeks to place the security concerns of the ordinary man and woman on the street at the very core of any security strategy.[29]

One of the practical consequences of considering human security as opposed to state security, or making people the primary referent of security, is that it becomes possible to identify threats to human security at subnational, national and transnational levels.[30] Thus, human security necessitated the broadening of the security agenda to include non-military threats. According to Buzan,[31] the security of human collectivities is affected by threats emanating from five sectors: military, political, economic, social and environmental. These insights have resulted in a radical revision of traditional definitions of security. Today, most definitions are wider and tend to complement the definition of human security given above. For instance, Ullman's[32] definition of security provides a more adequate conceptual 'fit' to contemporary reality than do most traditional ones:

> "... a threat to national security is an action or sequence of events that (1) threatens drastically and over a brief time span to degrade the quality of life for the inhabitants of a state, or (2) threatens significantly to narrow the range of policy choices available to the government of a state or to private nongovernmental entities (persons, groups, corporations)."

To be sure, the new security agenda did not go unchallenged by those who sought to retain security's traditionally narrow military and state-centric approach. These critics argued that the broader the concept of security, the fuller, and potentially unmanageable, the threat agenda would become.[33] But Booth levels several counterarguments against this criticism. It is sensible to quote his response in some detail:

> "First, it must be conceded that broadening the concept does greatly widen the agenda. So what? This is what the political process is all about: making choices between competing demands. Bureaucratically, the implementation of security does not have to be dealt with by the same ministry, just as 'defence' has a land, sea and air component and 'foreign policy' has diplomatic, strategic and commercial aspects. So, while the security agenda should be broadened, it need not become unmanageable. Second, to leave the agenda narrowly defined by military considerations will leave security advice narrowly dominated by military specialists. There will be times when this is justifiable, since there will be times when the military threat deserves special consideration and there is a particular urgency to military threats. Ever since the time of Thomas Hobbes—but in reality earlier—security has been the primary obligation of governments. To place an item on the security agenda is therefore to raise its profile. If we are serious about human rights, economic development, the lot of women and so on ... then we must simply accept the problems of an expanded agenda and of the need to settle the question of priorities in the political process. To control the agenda up to a point is to control policy. Yes, an expanded agenda is by definition potentially more unmanageable: but one needs to ask why somebody wants certain issues such as human rights off that agenda? And why do they want to privilege [military] threats?"[34]

Despite these criticisms, the proponents of the new security agenda seem to have weathered the storm and have come to dominate current security discourse. This is perhaps best illustrated by the manner in which new security thinking has revolutionised the discipline of Strategic Studies. Commenting on the relationship between security and Strategic Studies, Carim notes that "*... the concept of security is central to Strategic Studies in much the same way that power is central to Politics and wealth is central to Economics; that is, they are inextricably linked, but conceptually distinct.*"[35]

Traditionally, Strategic Studies has been dominated by a military understanding of security. Evans and Newnham[36] define classical Strategic Studies as:

> "... the field of inquiry that is concerned to examine the ways in which actors use their military capabilities to achieve political goals, in particular,

with the way in which the threat and use of force has served these ends. It is sometimes referred to as the Clausewitzian tradition after the nineteenth century Prussian strategist who did so much to advance the symbiosis between war and state policy ... Strategic studies has been primarily concerned with military power as the key attribute which has to be converted into usable instruments."

Strategic Studies' lopsided emphasis on military prowess at the expense of non-military security threats has opened it to criticism from those who have argued that its substance needs to be informed by the debates around the widening of the concept of security. Chipman, the Director of the International Institute for Strategic Studies (IISS) argued that "*Strategic Studies has been dominated by perversion and has resulted in a blinkered perspective which is unable to foresee, explain or even understand sources of threat other than those emanating from military confrontation.*"[37]

The dominance of new security thinking is also illustrated by the fact that members of the IISS were called upon to change a key text of their Constitution at an extraordinary general meeting in 1992. They had to approve the following:

> "The object for which the Institute is established is to promote on a non-party basis the study and discussion of an exchange of information upon any major security issues including without limitation those of a political, strategic, economic, social or ecological nature."

The original version read:

> "The object for which the Institute is established is to promote on a non-party basis the study and discussion of and the exchange of information upon the influence of modern and nuclear weapons of warfare upon the problems of strategy, defence disarmament and international relations."[38]

This has resulted in a radical change in the substance or 'stuff' of Strategic Studies to include small-arms proliferation, narco-trafficking and organized crime, mass migrations, economic insecurity, ethnicity, religious fundamentalism, and regional power clientelism.[39] The real difference between this and earlier approaches to Strategic Studies was the emphasis on the security of individual human beings. While aspects of Strategic Studies, for instance counter-insurgency warfare, did appreciate threats to security emanating from non-military problems, it viewed these in the light of national security considerations of the state.

The above discussion on the IISS is not meant to create the impression that the substance of Strategic Studies was to be defined and decided by them. Rather, it is used as an illustrative example of how new security thinking has moved from the margins to the very core of Strategic Studies. Similarly, in 1996 the Institute for Defence Policy changed its name to the Institute for

Security Studies. Accompanying this name change was a change in the Institute's mission statement from enhancing stability on the African continent to enhancing human security in Africa.

But the impact of new security thinking was not confined to theoretical discourse: it has had a tremendous influence on policymakers. Increasingly organizations like the Gulf Cooperation Council and the League of Arab States increasingly see the inter-relationship between the political, the economic, the social and military developments. Thus in recent years both the Arab League and the GCC have been playing key roles in issues as diverse as economic development, support for trauma counseling for Palestinian refugees and conflict mediation and resolution.

This widening of the security agenda has also impacted on the role of the armed forces in the changing global security landscape. Consider, in this regard, the various tasks the military has performed more recently. In Austria, the army is used for the construction of anti-avalanche 'breaks', the stabilizing of ski ropes and the development of alternative energy sources (solar and water). In Bulgaria and Cuba, soldiers are used to plant trees and to create national parks and nature reserves in their military localities. A similar situation exists in Finland where commanders of each military district are responsible for the environmental welfare. In South Africa, the South African National Defence Force (SANDF) is used to support police operations against crime and to curb the influx of illegal immigrants into the country. In France, the Navy is used to minimize pollution at sea. In Italy, the army has set up the Geographical Military Institute for the study of seismic cartography of the soil, tectonic (rock) modifications, movement of the earth's crust and subsidence. In Jordan, the army is used to combat locust invasions.[40]

The underlying point of the above discussion is that the concept of security has undergone a radical transformation from one meaning state security to one meaning human security. In the process, it also confirms the process of democratization—the process whereby ordinary people are empowered. These trends also find resonance in the manner in which sovereignty has developed over the years.

RECONSTRUCTING SOVEREIGNTY IN AN ERA OF HUMAN SECURITY AND INTERVENTION

Often, one hears of tyrants engaging in the internal repression of their citizens decrying any form of sanctions or intervention, arguing that this violates their state's sovereign integrity. In this, the Saddam Husseins and Slobodan Milosevics of the world are drawing upon a particular philosophical tradition which views sovereignty as "*...protection against external influence in a state's affairs.*"[41] Sovereignty, as a legal and political construct arose in Europe at a time when medieval feudal states slowly gave way to absolutist nation-states.[42] Commenting on this Deng *et al.*,[43] notes that sovereignty developed "...*as an instrument of feudal princes in the construction of territorial states. It was believed that instability and disorder; seen as obstacles to stable society would only be overcome by viable governments capable of establishing firm and effective control over territory and population*".

As the old social order decayed and crumbled, absolute monarchs were installed all over Europe; and each of these had their own praise singers and sycophants justifying the 'New World Order'. In England, this saw Hobbes' translating the social contract as people surrendering all their rights to the Ruler.[44] In this way, the Ruler was sovereign. Jean Bodin also endorsed this view and this philosophical tradition contributed to the rise of the absolutist monarchy and the nation-state in Europe.[45]

This did not mean that the philosophical tradition, which was soon transformed into an established orthodoxy, did not go unchallenged. A rich and varied alternative discourse could still be heard above the cacophony of the sycophants. Other social contract theorists such as John Locke and Jean Jacques Rousseau stridently argued against the notion that at the time of the social contract, the people transferred all rights to the Sovereign Ruler. From this emerged the idea of limited and popular sovereignty—that the Ruler had a clear but limited mandate from the people and that its violation by the Ruler could justify popular resistance to the Ruler.[46]

Of course, Locke and Rousseau's ideas were not entirely unique and drew upon the earlier works of Althusius. This German Calvinist, who drew inspiration from ancient theories of popular rights argued in 1603 for the "... *revolutionary right of active resistance to rulers who violated their contract.*"[47] This view was later endorsed by Suarez, who argued that "... *the Ruler always remained limited by positive law and the permanent rights of the People.*"[48] Similarly, the German philosopher Wolff, argued that the people were free to choose how much power to devolve upon government and how much to retain.[49]

By the 1780s the fierce debates between supporters of absolute monarchy and the proponents of popular sovereignty took a new twist with Kant arguing that the state, as opposed to an absolute monarch, was the agent and representative of popular sovereignty or as Rousseau put it, the 'general will'. As in Hobbes' sovereign, Kant's state "... *absorbed all popular rights including the right to rebel or disobey.*"[50] Fuelled by the American War of Independence, the French Revolution and the Industrial Revolution which heralded a new class structure in Europe and North America, Kant's notion of a sovereign state supreme in its domestic jurisdiction and free form external influence became the norm.

As the twentieth century draws to a close, it is increasingly clear that the myth of sovereignty denoting national governments being supreme in their territorially defined jurisdictions is cracking. The Angolas and the Afghanistans, the Somalias and the Yugoslavias clearly illustrate the inadequacy of the concept in these troubled times. It is also clear that "... *even as the traditional concept of sovereignty erodes there is no presumptive, let alone adequate replacement for the state. The locus of responsibility for promoting citizens' welfare and liberty, for organizing co-operation and managing conflict ... remains with the state.*"[51] For academics, then, the challenge is to rethink the notion of sovereignty in an era of interdependence that has witnessed profound global change. Highlighting the enormity of this challenge, former United Nations Secretary-General Boutros Boutros-Ghali stated:

> "A major intellectual requirement of our time is to rethink the question of sovereignty not to weaken its essence which is crucial to international security and co-operation, but to recognize that it may take more than one form and perform more than one function. This perception would help solve problems both within and among states".[52]

Supporting this shift in intellectual discourse has been developments that contributed to a radical change in the global strategic landscape, which enabled key policy-makers to be receptive to these new ideas.

The first of these movements is the process of democratization that has been gathering tremendous momentum from the nineteenth century. This has increasingly challenged Kant's notion of the state as the embodiment of all popular rights. In an era where a democratic ethos prevails and where violations of human rights are quickly beamed via satellite into people's homes, a popular consciousness has developed that state security (read sovereignty) is often purchased at the expense of human security. It has also led to the notion that in the final instance, the people are sovereign and that the state, as Kant had argued, acts as the agent of that popular sovereignty. Unlike Kant, however, it argued against the notion of a state that absorbs all popular rights, including the right to rebel. Moreover, it also emphasizes that for the power of the state to be recognized as legitimate, it must be exercised responsibly and within the mandate given to it. Sovereignty constructed in this way means that the state uses its resources to enhance the human condition of its citizens—at the very least providing for the basic needs of its people.[53]

Given the enormity of power the state has at its disposal *vis-à-vis* the individual citizen, it is equally clear that state power needs to be constrained. Here, new social contracts have evolved—the Constitution, a Bill of Rights, etc.—clearly limiting the power of the state. This, together with an elected Parliament and an independent judiciary are supposed to make governments accountable to the people and reinforcing the idea that the state is an agent of popular sovereignty. The existence of several tyrannical regimes however, clearly illustrates the limits of such domestic accountability. In such a situation, it is increasing becoming obvious that agents (states) who violate the trust of their people are increasingly being held accountable to the international community, effectively other states. But this raises another question: why should states pursuing their own national self-interest (in the classical realist genre) care about human rights violations/atrocities committed in other states. The answer to this question relates to the second movement taking place in the world today.

The myth of an independent sovereign state impervious to outside influence was recognized by states as problematic for centuries. Since this myth, however, was crucial for the construction of nation-states from disparate peoples, states found it useful to perpetuate the myth. States realized that just as no two people can live in total freedom without encroaching on the freedom of others and therefore need the regulatory mechanism of the state; so too states need some regulatory framework, no matter how primitive, to guide the relations between states. Thus Evan Luard[54] notes that:

> "Already during the Middle Ages, conventions had emerged about some aspects of states' conduct: for example, the treatment of heralds, declarations of war, diplomatic practice and similar matters. The rules of chivalry established a code governing the behaviour which knights should adopt towards each other in the battlefield… Canon law established rules about the conduct of war and other aspects of state conduct. In particular the doctrine of "just war" laid down for what purpose war was justifiable and rules about the ways which wars should be conducted".

From the nineteenth century onwards, there emerged the idea among some states that war was not a rational way to achieve their foreign policy objectives; that war was detrimental to both their political alliances and commercial ventures. Thus from the Congress of Vienna in 1815 after the Napoleonic wars to the Hague conferences of 1899 and 1907, states sought to create mechanisms which they hoped would prevent the occurrence of war and would regulate its conduct, should it occur. At the end of the First World War in 1918, this went a step further when states "… *accepted the discipline of compulsory conciliation of their disputes by signing the Covenant of the League of Nations*".[55] At the end of the Second World War, and with the establishment of the United Nations' Organization in 1945, states were once more willing to surrender a part of their sovereignty for the promise of international peace offered by the new organization. Under the new United Nations system, the international behaviour of states was subjected to the political authority of a Security Council that was more powerful than the Council of the League of Nations.[56]

As time wore on, it became increasingly clear to states that their relations with other states was not the only thing which needed regulation. Increasingly, it has become obvious that how states (agents) relate to their domestic constituencies can also serve to undermine international peace and security and hence endanger the national interests of other states. How does this come about? Samuel Makinda[57] notes that "...[j]*uridical sovereignty without popular sovereignty can result in human insecurity*". Indeed, social exclusion of a particular group from economic of political power; ethnic cleansing and the like has resulted in more than 20 million refugees and 30 million internally displaced people.[58] These then become a source of regional insecurity as they flee into neighbouring states. In the process, the international order is itself threatened.

The politics of exclusion pursued by some states that deliberately undermine the human security of their citizens also adversely affect international stability in other ways. In some cases those affected populations bearing the brunt of state repression choose to fight back. The Kosovar Liberation Army (KLA) is an example of this. But this only serves to intensify the domestic conflict whilst at the same time regionalizing it as the KLA needs neighbouring countries from which to stage assaults against the hostile government of Slobodan Milosevic. The example of the Democratic Republic of the Congo is currently the archetypal example of how a civil war threatens to involve an entire continent as Angola, Namibia, Zimbabwe, Rwanda, Uganda, Burundi, Chad and Sudan all have become involved in the politics of this Central African behemoth. In West Asia, the spill-over effects of Iraq and the Israeli-Palestinian conflict is clearly evident in tiny Jordan swamped as it is with a human deluge of refugees from both Palestine historically and, more recently, Iraq.

Recognizing that insecurity anywhere is a threat to security everywhere states have decided to band together for the cause of international security. For instance, acknowledging that an intrinsic relationship exists between agents (states) not acting responsibly towards their citizens and international peace, states have in various international fora begun to regulate this domestic realm to ensure that states are in the final instance accountable to the international community for their actions. This resulted in the development of a normative code by which a state's actions could be held up for scrutiny. The 1948 Universal Declaration of Human Rights, the 1966 International Covenant on Civil and Political Rights, the 1966 International Covenant on Economic, Social and Cultural Rights as well as a vast array of other human rights instruments became a part of these global norms by which state actions could be monitored.[59]

The flip side to this, of course, is that those states, which do not adhere to these global norms, open themselves up for international intervention by the global community. In this regard Kalypso Nicolaidis[60] notes that state sovereignty can be effectively bypassed when "*...a state stops fulfilling the basic responsibilities and functions that go along with sovereignty*". Sovereignty can also be transferred as was the case of when the Palestinian Liberation Organization (PLO) took up a seat in the UN General Assembly in

1974. This was a clear expression that the PLO had more legitimacy than the occupying Israeli state in representing the interests and aspirations of the Palestinian people.

Despite the development of these global norms, the truth is that during much of the Cold War dictators such as Pinochet, the Shah, Hussein, Mobutu and Suharto held sway—nurtured and assisted by superpowers who displayed scant regard for the precepts of popular sovereignty or human rights. With the demise of global bipolarity and the beginnings of a new international consensus regarding sovereignty as responsibility, the way has become clear for the further development of international law to ensure accountability—that states act as responsible agents of popular sovereignty.

One of the earliest examples of this new consensus occurred in 1991 with UN Security Council Resolution 688. This demanded an end to Iraqi aggression against the Kurds in northern Iraq and authorized a military operation to establish safe havens on Iraqi territory. In this way international humanitarian organizations were guaranteed access to the Kurds for the purposes of providing both protection and humanitarian relief. At the time, the United States' Ambassador to the United Nations remarked that "*...this was the first time a significant number of governments denied the states' right to the sovereign exercise of butchery*".[61] Since then the UN Security Council has authorized forcible intervention in Somalia in 1992, Haiti in 1994 as well as in Yugoslavia.

The advent of forcible intervention in the affairs of a state represents a watershed in our theoretical understandings of sovereignty in the current international system. Dan Smith[62] puts it this way:

> "The most familiar social science definition of the state is that it is the entity with the monopoly of the legitimate means of force within a given territory. Humanitarian intervention—especially forcible—breaks the states' monopoly of force and rejects its legitimacy. It thus contradicts our understanding of the most basic function of sovereign statehood".

In this way forcible intervention reinforces the notion of sovereignty as responsibility and that states who violate the trust of their citizens will be held accountable for their actions (or inaction) to the international community.

Of course, developments in international law are not simply confined to the question of forcible intervention but also to what John Dugard[63] refers to as the "*...internationalization of criminal law*". This is most clearly seen in the Pinochet case and Tripoli's handing over of the two Libyans to the Netherlands for trial under Scottish law for the bombing of Pan Am Flight 103 over Lockerbie in 1989. It has also resulted in the establishment of an International Criminal Tribunal for the Former Yugoslavia in The Hague.[64] The International Criminal Tribunal for Rwanda in Arusha and the 120 states that signed an agreement in Rome in July 1998 to establish an International Criminal Court also serves to consolidate the trend.[65]

These are momentous developments and support the view that international law "*...appears to be moving away from being premised on a system of sovereign states towards the development of a common law for a world community of individuals. In the past states were the sole legal persons; in the twentieth century this hard shell has been breached and international law now concerns itself not just with states but also with individuals*".[66]

What is even more revealing is that in the cases listed above, the defendants have not sought to challenge the authority or jurisdiction of the courts. For instance, Jean Kambanda, who was the Rwandan Prime Minister at the time of the genocide in 1994, pleaded guilty to all charges in the indictment against him including those of genocide, complicity in genocide and crimes against humanity. Consequently he was sentenced to life imprisonment on 4 September 1998.[67]

The case of General Augusto Pinochet, former military dictator of Chile holds special importance to our subject at hand and deserves closer scrutiny. On 16 October 1998, as the former dictator lay in a London hospital bed, recuperating from back surgery he was arrested by the British police. This followed a Spanish magistrate issuing of warrants for Pinochet's arrest and extradition in connection with 94 murders and disappearances. Following his arrest, Pinochet was found by a three-judge panel of the High Court to be immune from prosecution for any crimes he might have committed whilst he was head of state from 1973 to 1990. When the case went to the House of Lords on appeal however, three of the five Law Lords ruled against Pinochet. Whilst the High Court restricted itself to English law which has no exceptions to state immunity, the Law Lords argued that under international law, Pinochet's crimes against humanity do not enjoy immunity. In a landmark judgement, Lord Nicholls noted:

> "International law has made plain that certain types of conduct, including torture and hostage-taking are not acceptable conduct on the part of anyone. This applies as much to heads of state, or even more so, as it does to everyone else, the contrary case would make a mockery of international law".[68]

As in the case of Jean Kambanda, what is interesting of the General's defence counsel is that it did not challenge the legality or the jurisdiction of the court. Rather the defence counsel argued that Pinochet is suffering from chronic depression which has resulted in him being mentally unfit to stand trial for extradition.[69]

These developments in international law serve to emphasize the notion of sovereignty as responsibility whilst at the same time making states, as agents of popular sovereignty, accountable to the international community.

The twentieth century will certainly go down as one of the bloodiest centuries in the history of humanity. Beginning on the bloody plains of Armenia to the trench warfare of World War I, the gas chambers of Auschwitz and Daschau, the killing fields of East Timor, Cambodia and Sudan Yugoslavia and now Angola and now the DRC, the twentieth century has taken man's inhumanity to man to new heights. Altogether 160 million people lost their lives in this century as a result of war, genocide and state killings.[70] With the dawning of the twenty-first century there is a millennium feeling that such grave crimes committed by the Mengistus and Pinochets are not simply crimes against the victims but an affront to our collective humanity and dignity and as such should not go unpunished. Reconstructing sovereignty as responsibility, remodelling states as agents of popular sovereignty whose purpose it is to enhance the human condition of their citizens, and who are accountable not only to their domestic constituencies but to the international community as well, might go some way to resolve the historic tensions between state and human security in favour of the latter. In the final instance, it is in the creation of vibrant democracies that the historic tensions between state and human security can only be resolved.

REGIONALIZATION: NEW AND OLD

Having discussed the relationship between globalization and democratization whilst alluding to regionalization, it is important at this point to turn to the question of how regionalization fits into this triadic structure. Before proceeding with our discussion on regionalization, it may be useful for us to examine the concept of region first.

The primary, common sense usage of the term 'region' connotes physical contiguity, but as Evans and Newnham illustrate, proximity is a necessary, although not sufficient, condition for physical stipulation of region: "*Between state actors, contiguity as a variable in delineating regions produces mixed results. For example, there is a core area within the concept of 'Western Europe' which includes the founding six of the European Community. At the periphery, things become more confused. Iceland and Ireland presumably mark the Western fringes but where is the eastern fringe? Similarly, with the region of the Middle East. A core area can be identified but is Libya part of it, or of North Africa? Is Turkey part of Europe or part of the Middle East? ... Clearly, more is needed than proximity to confidently stipulate the meaning of region*".[71]

Obviously, other criteria are needed to define a region. One of the criteria, which Evans and Newnham[72] have defined, is homogeneity at the social, economic and political levels. Unlike old 'regionalism' efforts of the 1950s and 1960s with its overwhelming stress on functional integration driven by political and economic aspirations, regionalization efforts from the 1990s stressed the multidimensional aspects of regional integration building on a common value system.[73] Ultimately, as one cannot integrate apples and oranges, regional integration would need to be an integration of like-minded entities. This would also make the cohesion between national interests and regional collective interests that much easier. National entities subscribing to a common value system would also greatly facilitate the formation of common policies at the regional level. Thus, it may be argued that what is driving new regionalization efforts is a common value system. It would also stand to reason that those regional structures which are driven by a democratic value system, and where human security is paramount, are fundamentally different from those which subscribe to a less democratic ethos where state (read elite) security is paramount.

This is not all. Grugel and Hout[74] note that in the developing world, regionalization is often in response to fears of globalization. Among state elites in the south, there is an assumption that in banding together they could reduce the hegemony of the West, which they see as driving globalization. That the situation is more nuanced is obvious, but this view is a myth which state elites encourage as it deflects from their own failures.

METHODOLOGICAL CONSIDERATIONS FOR DEMOCRATIZATION IN THE GULF REGION

Having briefly examined the theoretical and global megatrends, what is their methodological import to the democratization debates currently taking place in the Gulf region?

First, it is clear in the discussions above that the debates on democratization have been shaped by Western intellectuals reflecting their Western experience of what democracy means to *them*. This is an important caveat to bear in mind. Arab and Iranian discourses on democratization would be different reflecting their culturally specific experiences. The cultural specific interpretation of democratic practice is clearly evident in various Pew surveys which found that Muslims in the Gulf region overwhelmingly wanted to live in a democratic polity which was sharia-based. This need not be a contradiction in terms. In my view an Islamic polity can also be liberal democratic at the same time. After all, Islamic concepts such as freedom (*al-hurriya*), equality (*al-musawat*), justice (*al-adl*), and consultation (*shura*) are all norms that can be found in a liberal, multi-party, secular polity. For the West, they need to assess the cultural specific nature of democratic practice and not its form in order to assess a specific country's path to democracy. Importantly the pace of progress may not be as fast as those in the West may want it to be. The pace of progress must be determined by citizens themselves in these countries so that the more conservative elements of society can feel comfortable with the changes being made and will not seek to sabotage such progress. In the recent elections in Kuwait this year, four women were elected to parliament. In Saudi Arabia, for the first time in its history we see the appointment of a woman as a Deputy Minister. Such progress needs to be encouraged, not derided.

Second, I agree with Gillian Youngs' assessment that we need to avoid "totalizing discourses". To put it another way, there is `no one size fits all' framework in order to assess democratic practice in every country in a particular region. This histories, cultural and religious practice, economic development, demographic composition, geographical peculiarities all impact on the form and nature of democracy in a particular country. No two countries in the Gulf have gone through the exact same experience and therefore we need to speak of broad principles of democratic practice rather than scientific certainties.

Third, the forces of globalization can either hinder or accelerate democratic practice. Economic globalization has often resulted in exacerbating stark divides between the proverbial *haves and have-nots*. These can serve to promote social unrest and political agitation which in turn is manifested in emergency powers to security forces thus undermining civil-military relations in the process. Democracy in this context is jettisoned in favour of stability. On the other hand, the development of global norms against genocide and the like prevent tyrants from engaging in mass atrocities. The fact that the International Criminal Court wants to indict Sudan's President Bashir on the basis of his complicity in the Darfur genocide is in my view quite positive since such international sanction might make national governments more responsive to the needs of their people.

At the same time, however, there cannot be one set of norms for people who agree with us and a different set of norms for those who don't. These global norms must be uniform in their application if it is to have the necessary credibility to achieve its stated purpose. More importantly, the international organizations seeking to implement these norms but are also representative of the international community if it is to retain its independence and therefore credibility. Hence issues of the reform of the UN Security Council cannot be separated from the broader agenda of democratic promotion. After all, the UN cannot talk of democracy in Syria or Saudi Arabia and not be democratic in its own make-up.

Fourth, regional organizations can either promote or impede democratic practice. Here the tendency of the GCC and the Arab League to support the status quo, essentially incumbent political elites, is bound to cause festering anger which would result in added revolutionary fervour. Moreover, given the youthful profile of much of the population in the Gulf region, this festering resentment and its concomitant danger of violent eruptions of popular anger is that much greater. Democracy needs to be pursued by all actors—state and non-state in the Gulf region if stability is to be ensured. It is only democracy (however defined) which can guarantee such stability since democracy is the only political system which offers the orderly transfer for political power from one group to another.

NOTES

1. J.A. Scholte, "Beyond the Buzzword: Towards a Critical Theory of Globalization," in E. Kofman and G. Youngs (eds.). *Globalization: Theory and Practice*. New York. Pinter. 1996, p. 45.
2. *Ibid.*, p. 43.
3. *Ibid.*, p. 43.
4. G. Youngs, "Dangers of Discouse: The Case of Globalization," E. Kofman and G. Youngs, *op. cit.*, p. 60.
5. G. Mohan, "Globalization and Governance: The Paradox of Structural Adjustment in Sub-Saharan Africa," in Kofman and Youngs, *op. cit.*, pp. 292-295.
6. J. Grugel and W. Hout, "Regions, regionalism and the South," in J. Grugel and W. Hout (eds.) *Regionalism Across the North–South Divide: State Strategies and Globalization*. Routledge, London. 1999, p. 5.
7. K. Ninsin, "The Quest for Democracy," in *Africa Insight*, Vol. 30(3). December 2000, p. 11.
8. K. Booth, A security regime in Southern Africa: Theoretical considerations, *Southern African Perspectives: A Working Paper Series,* 30, Bellville: Centre for Southern African Studies, University of the Western Cape, 1994, p. 3.
9. B. Buzan, *People, states and fear: An Agenda for International Security Studies in the Post-Cold War Era,* New York: Harvester-Wheatsheaf, (2nd ed.), 1991, p. 16.
10. *Ibid.*, p. 16.
11. J. Baylis and N.J. Rengger, Introduction: Theories, methods, and dilemmas in world politics, in J. Baylis and N.J. Rengger (eds.), *Dilemmas of World Politics: International Issues in a Changing World,* Oxford: Oxford University Press, 1992, p. 9.
12. E. Rothchild, What is security?, in M. Singh (ed.), *Redefining security in Southern Africa: Workshop Proceedings,* Common Security Forum, Centre for History and Economics, King's College, University of Cambridge, 1995, p. 16.
13. J.J. Romm, *Defining National Security: The Non-military Aspect,* New York: Council on Foreign Relations Press, 1993, p. 3.
14. M. Van Aardt, In search of a more adequate conceptualization of security for Southern Africa: Do we need a feminist touch?, *Politikon,* 20(1), 1993, p. 55.
15. Quoted in X. Carim, Strategic perspectives for Southern Africa in the 1990s: Theoretical and practical considerations, *Southern African Perspectives: A Working Paper Series,* 23, Bellville: Centre for Southern African Studies, University of the Western Cape, 1993, p. 4.
16. *Ibid.*, p. 9.
17. Romm, *op. cit.*, p. 5.
18. Buzan, *op. cit.*, p. 4.

19. N.J. Wheeler and K. Booth, The security dilemma, in J. Baylis and N.J. Rengger (eds.), *Dilemmas of World Politics: International Issues in a Changing World,* Oxford: Oxford University Press, 1992, p. 45.
20. *Ibid.*, p. 45.
21. P. Kennedy, *Preparing for the Twenty-first Century,* London: Fontana Press, 1993, pp. 129-130; F.A. Magno, Environmental security and the South China Sea, *Security Dialogue,* 28(1), 1997, pp. 97-112; E Ottone, Overcoming poverty and exclusion as causes of insecurity in Latin America, *Security Dialogue,* 28(1), 1997, pp. 7-16; W. Breytenbach, Conflict in Sub-Saharan Africa: From the frontline states to collective security, *The Arusha Papers: A Working Series on Southern African Security,* 2., Cape Town: Centre for Southern African Studies, University of the Western Cape and Dar es Salaam: Centre for Foreign Relations, 1995, p. 3; P. Lizee and S. Peou, Cooperative security and the emerging security agenda in Southeast Asia: The challenges and opportunities of peace in Cambodia, *York Centre for International and Strategic Studies (YCISS) Occasional Paper,* 21, Toronto, Canada: Centre for International and Strategic Studies, York University, 1993, p. 1; C.Y. Obi, Environmental conflict in Africa, *African Journal of Political Science,* 4(1), June 1999, pp. 40-62; L. Nathan, Good governance, security and disarmament, *African Journal of Political Science,* 3(2), December 1998, pp. 69-79; A Cottey, Central Europe transformed: Security and cooperation on NATO's new frontiers, *Contemporary Security Policy,* 20(2), August 1999, pp. 1-30; J.S. Krasna, Testing the transnational issues for international security, *Contemporary Security Policy,* 20(1), April 1999, pp. 57-64; S.D. van De Veer and G.D. Dabelko, Redefining security around the Baltic: Environmental issues in a regional context, *Global government: A review of multilateral and international organizations,* 5(2), April-June 1999, pp. 221-250; Majid Tehranian and David Chappell (eds.), *Dialogue of Civilizations: A New Peace Agenda for a New Millennium.* I.B. Tauris and Toda Institute for Global Peace and Policy Research. London, 2002; Majid Tehranian (ed.) *Bridging a Gulf: Peacebuilding in West Asia.* I.B Tauris and Toda Institute for Global Peace and Policy Research. London. 2003.
22. Kennedy, *op. cit.*, p. 130.
23. R.O. Keohane and J. S. Nye, *Power and Interdependence: World Politics in Transition,* Boston: Scott Foresman and Company, 2nd edition, 1989.
24. Carim, *op. cit.*, p. 9.
25. Booth, *op. cit.*
26. *Ibid.*, p. 5.
27. Buzan, *op. cit.*, p. 43.
28. A.H. Omari, Regional security: One view from the frontline states, *The Arusha Papers: A working Paper Series on Southern African Security,* 5. Cape Town: Centre for Southern African Studies, University of the Western Cape and Dar es Salaam: Centre for Foreign Relations, 1995, p. 4.
29. K. Krause, Critical theory and security studies, *YCISS Occasional Paper,* 33, Toronto: Centre for International and Strategic Studies, York University, 1996; Van Aardt, *op cit.*, pp. 55-59; J.B. Elshtain, Feminist themes and international relations, in J. Der Derian (ed.), *International Theory: Critical Investigations,*

London: Macmillan Press Ltd., 1995; J.A. Tickner, Hans Morgenthau's principles of political realism: A feminist reformulation, in J. Der Derian (ed.), *International theory: Critical investigations,* London: Macmillan Press Ltd., 1995.
30. Booth, *op. cit.,* pp. 3-4; Solomon and Cilliers, *op. cit.,* p. 6.
31. Buzan, *op. cit.*, p. 19.
32. Quoted in Romm, *op. cit.*, p. 4.
33. *Ibid.,* p. 6.
34. Booth, *op. cit.*, p. 6.
35. Carim, *op. cit.*, p. 7.
36. G. Evans and J. Newnham, *The Dictionary of World Politics,* London: Harvester-Wheatsheaf, 1990, p. 379.
37. J. Chipman, The future of strategic studies: beyond even grand strategy, *The Roundtable,* 322, 1992, p. 135.
38. P. Vale, Can international relations survive? *International Affairs Bulletin,* 16(3), 1992, p. 100.
39. S. Bearman (ed.), *Strategic Survey 1990-1991,* London: Brasseys for IISS, 1991, pp. 18-21.
40. M. Harbottle, New roles for the military: Humanitarian and environmental security, *Conflict Studies,* 285, London: Research Institute for the Study of Conflict and Terrorism, 1995, pp. 16-19.
41. F.M. Deng, S. Kimaro, T. Lyons, D. Rotchild, and I.W. Zartman. *Sovereignty as Responsibility: Conflict Management in Africa.* The Brookings Institution. Washington, D.C. 1996, p. vii.
42. F.H. Hinsley, *Sovereignty.* Cambridge University Press. Cambridge. 1986, p. 62.
43. Deng, *et al., op. cit.*, p. 2.
44. Hinsley, *op. cit.*, p. 145.
45. S. Makinda, "Sovereignty and Global Security," *Security Dialogue*, Vol. 29(3). 1998, p. 282.
46. Deng. *et al., op. cit.,* p. xx.
47. Hinsley, *op. cit.*, p. 132.
48. *Ibid.*, p. 135.
49. *Ibid.*, p. 152.
50. *Ibid.*, p. 156.
51. Deng, *et al., op. cit.*, p. 6.
52. B. Boutros Boutros-Ghali. "Empowering the United Nations," *Foreign Affairs* No. 71. 1993, p. 99.
53. Deng, *et al, op. cit.,* p. xvii.
54. E. Luard. *Basic Texts in International Relations.* Macmillan. London. 1992, p. 143.
55. Hinsley, *op. cit.*, p. 227.
56. *Ibid.*, p. 227.
57. Makinda, *op. cit.*, p. 286.
58. Deng, *et al, op. cit.*, p. xiii.
59. B. de Villiers, D.J. van Vuuren and M. Wiechers. *Human rights documents that paved the way.* Human Sciences Research Council. Pretoria. 1992.

60. Quoted in D. Smith. "Sovereignty in the Age of Interventions," in A. McDermott (ed.) *Sovereign Intervention.* International Peace Research Institute. Oslo, p. 16.
61. *Ibid.*, p. 15.
62. *Ibid.*, p. 14.
63. J. Dugard, "Lockerbie is a triumph of good sense over tradition," *The Sunday Times*. Johannesburg. 25 April 1999.
64. P. Ahavan, "Justice in The Hague, Peace in the Former Yugoslavia? A Critical Commentary on the United Nations War Crimes Tribunal," *Human Rights Quarterly* Vol. 20(4). 1999, pp. 737-816.
65. G. Robertson, "A Question of Sovereignty," *Newsweek International*. 7 December 1998.
66. G. Evans and J. Newnham, *The Dictionary of World Politics: A reference guide to concepts, ideas and institutions*. Harvester-Wheatsheaf. New York. 1992, p. 151.
67. United Nations General Assembly, Fifty-third session, Agenda item 50. Report of the International Criminal Tribunal of the Prosecution of Persons Responsible for Genocide and Other Serious Violations of International Humanitarian Law Committed in the Territory of Rwanda and Rwandan Citizens Responsible for Genocide and Other such Violations Committed in the Territory of Neighbouring States between 1 January 1994 and 31 December 1994 A/53/429–S/1998/857. United Nations. New York. 1998, p. 3.
68. Robertson, *op. cit.*
69. *Ibid.*
70. *Ibid.*
71. Evans and Newnham, *op. cit.*, p. 281.
72. *Ibid.*, p. 281.
73. S.K.B. Asante, Regionalism and Africa's Development: Expectations, Reality and Challenges. St. Martin's Press. New York. 1997, p. 7.
74. Grugel and Hout, *op. cit.*, p. 4.

2

"Modern States or Family Enterprises?" Some Theoretical Reflections on Democratization and State Formation in the Gulf Region

Dietrich Jung

In assessing the challenges for democratization in the Gulf region, we are confronted with the very same phenomenon as in other parts of the Middle East: the remarkable resilience of authoritarianism.[1] Contrary to Asia, Latin America and Easter Europe, subsequent waves of democratization seemingly have bypassed the Arab world. Arab countries as a whole have not liberalized politically over the past decades and the Middle East in general remains to be the "world's most unfree region" (Schlumberger 2006: 35). That distinguishes the Arab parts of the Gulf from the rest of the Middle East, however, is that political and economic power is "all in the family" (Herb 1999). In the Arab Gulf monarchies, social power is not in the hands of specific cartels of elites or particular state classes, may they be of military, bureaucratic or clerical origins. Rather, government institutions and economic resources are under the control of dynastic monarchies, extended ruling families which have monopolized the highest state offices (Herb 1999: 2-4). With reference to the family-and clan-based nature of political authority in the Arab Gulf, the political systems of the Gulf principalities and Saudi Arabia are often labeled as traditional forms of rule. To a certain extent, these systems of rule remind us of pre-modern polities based on personal ties to which Max Weber referred with the concept of patrimonialism. From this perspective, the Gulf states are perceived as remnants of a pre-modern past, despite their highly sophisticated technological infrastructures. Yet to what extent is this judgment true? Are the Gulf states traditional political systems disguised by a smoke-screen of superficial modernity? What are the prospects for modernization and democratization in the Arab Gulf?

This chapter intends to give a tentative answer to these questions from the theoretical perspective of historical sociology. It will argue that the current debate about democratization in the Gulf is predicated on normative standards about modern democratic statehood which have travelled from the analytical text books of historical sociology into the common knowledge of scholars, journalists and policy makers. The sociological concepts themselves are based on abstractions from some particular experiences of European state formation and its very late result: the democratic national state based on the rule of law. Given this Eurocentric background of historical sociology, it has been asserted that its conceptual tools are ill-equipped for analyzing post-colonial states. Contrary to this wide-spread assumption, I will defend the analytical applicability of these concepts as ideal types. The conceptual apparatus of historical sociology can still serve as our core tool-kit for the analysis of contemporary state formation and for an assessment of the prospects of democracy in the Gulf. Yet turning it rather uncritically into normative blueprints for on-going state-building processes is flawed. While scholarly analyzes can be informed by the generalizations of sociology, these generalizations can neither predict the future paths of democratization nor serve as a norm for the rather unique and path-dependent ways in which states historically evolve.

In order to underpin this thesis, I will first discuss the legacy of historical sociology and briefly present the conceptual apparatus with which it has furnished our knowledge about the modern state. Then I will move to an explication of the different meanings of statehood based on the analytical distinction of the state as an institution, an image and a social practice. Against this background, then, this chapter concludes with some ideas regarding contemporary processes of state and democracy building in the Gulf region.

STATE, LEGAL AUTHORITY AND DEMOCRATIZATION: THE LEGACY OF HISTORICAL SOCIOLOGY

The understanding of the state in international politics has its roots in Max Weber's classical definition of modern statehood. With reference to the violent history of European state-building, Weber defined the central feature of modern statehood as "the monopoly of the legitimate use of physical force within a given territory" (Weber, 1991: 78). In Weber's words, the war-prone formation of state monopolies of physical force was a long-lasting process of "political expropriation" in which all political communities other than the state gradually had been deprived of the means of coercion (Weber, 1991:83). However, the establishment of state monopolies of physical force should not be conceptualized in mere power relations through which power holders carry out their will despite any resistance from the subordinated. In order to establish consolidated states, the factual monopoly of the use of physical force has to be considered legitimate by both rulers and ruled. Stable systems of political authority do not only rest on a monopoly of coercion alone, but this state monopoly also has to be anchored in the cultural order of society. A political order needs legitimacy.

Long-lasting political institutions require a stable set of rules that in normative and cognitive ways regulate the social conduct of rulers and ruled. In referring to the inner justification of systems of domination, Weber precisely distinguished political authority from mere power relations by the category of legitimacy. His concept of legitimacy is intended to give an answer to the question of when and why people obey (Weber, 1991:78). According to Weber, modern statehood rests on legal or rational authority, i.e. the belief "in the legality of enacted rules and the right of those elevated to authority under such rule to issue commands". This modern authority based on formal legal procedures he distinguished sharply from pre-modern or traditional forms of authority, which rest on personal ties and the "established belief in the sanctity of immemorial traditions and the legitimacy of those exercising authority under them" (Weber 1968a: 215).

In the 1930s, Norbert Elias critically took up Weber's core definition and conceptualized European state formation as a "civilizing process." In doing so, he applied a double perspective:

The civilizing process, seen from the aspects of standards of conduct and drive control, is the same trend which, when seen from the point of view of human relationships, appears as the process of advancing integration, increased differentiation of social functions and interdependence, and the formation of ever-larger units of integration on whose fortunes and movements the individual depends, whether he knows it or not (Elias 1994:332).

In his theory of the civilizing process, Norbert Elias put together the macro-sociological aspects of state formation and the micro-sociological consequences of this process: the ways in which the evolution of the modern state has shaped social practices. Combining Weber with Freud, he defined the immanent link between the macro-and micro-levels as the conversion of outer constraints into self-restraints, and concluded that the formation of modern states has been reflected in increasingly differentiated patterns of self-control on the side of the individual (Elias, 1994: 443-56). The pacifying institutional setting of modern statehood was accomplished by a particular normative restriction of the public behaviour of individuals. In this sense state structures and social practices are inseparably knitted together and the maintenance of public order relies on both functioning state institutions and forms of social action that are able to transform legal authority into daily practices.

In historical terms, however, this civilizing process has not been "civilized" at all. On the contrary, Elias traced the origin of both the internal pacification of society and the autonomy of the modern individual back to an unrestricted and violent elimination contest in which any individual or small group struggled among many others for resources not yet monopolized (Elias, 1994: 351). In mainly abstracting from the history of France, Elias differentiated between two distinct phases in the emergence of the modern state monopoly of physical force: In the first phase, a factual monopoly of physical force is established. An increasing number of people lose direct access to the means of force, which progressively become centralized in the hands of a few and thus placed outside open competition. In the second phase, this relatively private control over the monopoly of physical force tends to become public, i.e. it moves from the hands of state-makers into a political setting of legal institutions and appointed rulers under the control of the public. (Elias, 1994: 345-55).

While the first phase of the monopoly process is associated with absolutist and authoritarian forms of rule, the second phase gradually deposes coercive state-makers and establishes structures of legal political authority. The two phases conceptualize the transition from traditional to rational authority in the emergence of the modern state. Consequently, state formation comprises not only the establishment of the monopoly of physical force, but also the transition of the normative and institutional order on which this monopoly rests from personal rule toward democratic governance.

From the perspective of "state-builders", however, this transition of forms of authority was never intended. On the contrary, sociology conceptualized the formation of the modern democratic state as the non-intended outcome of the intended actions of European state builders. In his article *War Making and State Making as Organized Crime,* Charles Tilly compared the early European state-builders with "criminal" racketeers (Tilly 1985). Their interest was not to build states, but to acquire material resources through coercive action. Accordingly, Elias' first phase of the monopoly mechanism could be understood as a system of protection and extraction, leading to the accumulation and monopolization of the means of physical force in the hand of state-makers. The second phase, Tilly described as a long-lasting negotiation process between state-makers and the emerging capitalist bourgeoisie in which "the pursuit of war and military capacity, after having created national states as a sort of by-product, led to a civilianization of government and domestic politics" (Tilly 1990: 206).

In terms of global state formation, this long-lasting negotiation process can be traced in a legalization of state-society relations which were accompanied by a gradual increase of state capacities. The modern state and democratic social practices developed in the expansion and growing density of written formal law, framing the specific societal space in which civil society could emerge. Thereby, Jürgen Habermas identified four particular steps of juridification:

The establishment and consolidation of the monopolies of physical force and of taxation in the absolutist state.

They break with the personal power monopoly of the absolutist state in constitutional monarchies by legally anchoring state power in political institutions and civil law.

The bourgeois revolutions initiated the nationalization of the state monopolies, eventually bringing about the democratic nation-state with its separation of juridical, legislative and executive powers.

The formation of the welfare state tamed the autonomous dynamics that spring from the accumulative logic of the economic system and incorporated a variety of social functions into the domain of modern statehood (Habermas 1986: 356-63).

In light of this ideal type of four steps of juridification, processes of state formation in the Gulf region seem to be stuck on the second step. Political economists try to explain this stagnation regarding the legalization of state-society relations with the help of the concept of the rentier state. At least implicitly based on Tilly's logic of protection and extraction, this concept analyzes the resilience of authoritarian rule in Middle Eastern politics through the ways in which regional states were integrated into the international system. Applying the lenses of political economy, this concept refers in particular to the oil-rich monarchies in the Gulf. The main argument runs as follows: By achieving huge economic rents at the international level the rulers of oil-producing states did not need to establish effective representative institutions. The political economy of the region rendered the crucial relation between taxation and representation irrelevant. In short, a circularity of the competencies of territorial control and economic extraction simply does not exist. Consequently, the regional oil-producing states have gained their material foundation and political legitimacy primarily from the international system. So far, this separation between ruler and ruled, between state and society, has prevented the above-mentioned processes of monopoly nationalization and of the legalization of state-society relations. Thus, the Arab Gulf states have been able to build up an enormously high level of regime security while holding societal demands for more participation at bay.

THE MODERN STATE AS INSTITUTION, IMAGE AND SOCIAL PRACTICE

Political scientists summarized the conceptual legacy of historical sociology and European state formation in an analytical ideal type of the modern state. In institutional terms, statehood is defined as a centralized form of representative government, based on electoral procedures and a set of administrative, policing and military organizations. The modern state claims the legitimate monopoly of physical force which state agencies exert over a certain territory and relatively cohesive population, forming a community of citizens with political, social and economic rights (cf. Sørensen 2004:14).

In the academic field, this ideal type of the state is primarily an analytical instrument to measure empirical statehood. It does not directly portray the "real world" but represents an instrument of academic research. The definition, therefore, disregards the historical length as well as the social and developmental steps which eventually resulted in this form of a modern social contract between state-builders and society. Yet this image of the state has travelled from the social sciences into the conceptual world of political actors and societies at large. It attained a normative quality, telling us what a state ought to be. It is a globally relevant ideal of political order according to which we imagine the modern state as a transcendental and neutral power, as a democratically controlled arbitrator above societal conflicts. With this image of the state in mind we judge political action along distinctions such as legal/illegal, formal/ informal or public/private in order to measure and judge social action. Yet already Max Weber was well aware that the three dimensions of the state as an institution, an image and a social practice do not necessarily match:

> "When we inquire as to what corresponds to the idea of the 'state' in empirical reality, we find an infinity of diffuse and discrete human actions, both active and passive, factually and legally regulated relationships, partly unique and partly recurrent in character, all bound together by an idea, namely, the belief in the actual or normative validity of rules and of the authority-relationships of some human beings towards others. This belief is in part consciously, in part dimly felt, and in part passively accepted by persons who, should they think about the 'idea' in a really clearly defined manner, would not first need a 'general theory of the state' which aims to articulate the idea" (Weber 1904:99).

In reality the modern state is both an abstract and coercive macro-structure and a network of interdependent social actions of every-day life. Modern statehood consists of two dimensions: historically developed and relatively stable institutional structures and culturally defined social processes. The institutional structure gives societies politically isomorphic forms. In this sense the sociological definition of the national state developed into a formal blueprint for the political organization of societies. Modern statehood is a central feature of world culture and its ideal image has been formalized in most state constitutions (cf. Meyer *et al.* 1997). Yet the second perspective, the state as social practice, characterizes the actual social content of statehood as forms of permanent interaction and ephemeral social groupings. On this level, we can observe a complex and often amorphous tangle of social actions of which we make sense in reference to the ideal image of the state. Apparently, the rules of statehood as an organizational pattern and the logic of social practices do not necessarily correspond. In particular the post-colonial state is characterized by competing and conflicting organizing principles and social practices. This contradicting interface between the state as institution, image and social practice becomes particularly transparent when zooming in on individual political leaders.

Francois Médar, for instance, analyzed African statesmen as "political entrepreneurs," referring to both the symbolic and material sides of legitimate rule (Médar 1992). In accumulating economic, political and social resources, the political "big men" act in a system of personalized power in the name of the abstract institution of the state. In this way, these statesmen represent both the patriarchal chief of an extended network of personal ties (traditional authority) and the head of a formally institutionalized system of rule (legal authority). The contradiction of their position is apparent in three strategies of social action that are necessary for their political survival. In order to extract resources from international and transnational donors, they have to pretend that they are acting according to the standards of modern statehood, that's to say following the rules of good governance which emanate from the normative image of the state. As political entrepreneurs, however, they apply strategies of personal enrichment in accumulating external and internal resources within their networks of personal ties. Finally, they do have to meet the normative expectations of "traditional" African societies for a redistribution of their resources within a system of clients. Caught in this pattern of often contradicting organizational and social constraints, the "big man entrepreneur" must act according to a hybrid normative setting, containing elements of both the universal image of the state and the particularistic values of local social practices.

In sharp contrast to African leaders, the rulers of Arab Gulf monarchies are not subject to pressures by the international donor community. They have abundant economic resources at their disposal in order to fulfill the reciprocal demands of wealth distribution and re-distribution. However, this does not mean that these Arab monarchs are free from political and economic pressures of international actors. In particular the Second Gulf War clearly showed their dire need for military protection. Consequently, they have faced similar international demands with respect to international norms of state behaviour and good governance as their poor African counterparts. To a large extent, also the patriarchal rulers in the Arab Gulf must act within these hybrid patterns of norms and social practices which result from a complex mesh of international, regional and local expectations.

In perceiving the Arab Gulf states as representatives of traditional forms of statehood, we apply the sociological definition of the modern state in a normative way. Moreover, political and scholarly observers label social practices which are based on the reciprocal rules of family and kinship relations as forms of corruption and nepotism, the informal distribution of social resources appears as an illegal mode of behaviour. The political elite of Arab monarchies, however, have to take into consideration both the formal norms associated with the legal foundations of modern statehood and the social norms of their local constituencies. The answers to questions about state-and democracy building in the region have to be found in these structural contradictions in whose framework the incumbent rulers of Kuwait, the United Arab Emirates or Saudi Arabia act.

STATE-FORMATION AND DEMOCRATIZATION IN THE GULF REGION: SOME TENTATIVE REFLECTIONS

In a recent article, Francis Fukuyama argued for 'Stateness' First" (Fukuyama 2005). He discerned in contemporary interventionist policies by Western states a contradiction between state-building and democracy promotion, between, on the one hand, the monopolization of physical force in the hand of the state and, on the other hand, the building of public and legal institutions which can constrain the power monopoly of the state. Indeed applying the categories of historical sociology, some cases of contemporary state formation are characterized by a confusion of the (chrono-) logic of the two phases of Elias' monopoly mechanism. In cases such as Afghanistan and Iraq, institutional features of the second phase—constitutions, elections, representative bodies—have been attempted to be implemented before the first phase, the establishment of a legitimate state monopoly of physical force, has successfully been completed. Informed by the normative image of the modern state, these cases of interventionist state-building processes tend to turn up-side-down the social logic of European state formation in which the coercive formation of state monopolies preceded both the formal legalization of political authority and the enhancement of state capacities.

Looking at the Gulf region, with the clear exception of Iraq where the monopoly of physical force was eroded by successive international interventions, the first phase of the monopoly mechanism has largely been completed. The modern political map of the region began to take shape in the eighteenth century. The demise of the Safavid dynasty in 1722 and the withdrawal of foreign powers from the northern shores of the Gulf enabled local tribal groups to extend their realms of power. The local rulers could later consolidate their relative independence under British colonial supremacy. Beginning with a treaty between the Sultan of Muscat and the English East India Company in 1789, a series of treaties between Great Britain and the coastal principalities of the Arab Peninsula emerged. Thereby, British domination over the Gulf had a double face: it was confined to foreign affairs and security issues whereas local political and cultural institutions, as well as the related social practices, remained untouched (Ramazani 1997: 28). Thanks to British protection, the principalities were able to ward back the political aspirations of regional powers such as the Ottoman Empire, Iran and the emerging Saudi Kingdom. In accepting British hegemony in the Persian Gulf and, subsequently, the existence of the neighboring principalities, Abd al-Aziz

Ibn Saud, the founder of modern Saudi Arabia, also could secure his rule over the Arab Peninsula with British support. In the course of the nineteenth and the twentieth century, the consolidation of monopolies of physical force in the region eventually took place as a complex interplay between the ruling families, tribal confederations and Great Britain.

Similar to many post-colonial states, in this historical process the Arab Gulf states achieved a form of "negative sovereignty": a formal legal entitlement which actually hides the lack of empirical statehood, that's to say the social and institutional content related to the previously mentioned definition of the modern state (Jackson 1990). The decolonization process established statehood first and foremost as a form of external representation, as a formal territorial and legal framework of international politics guaranteed by the world state system and by international law. The local rulers were able to establish monopolies of physical force, however, these state monopolies have remained precarious and, as the Second Gulf War clearly showed, still rely on the support of external powers. Moreover, behind the facade of modern state institutions social practices of a quite different nature have continued. The synchronization of the state as institution and as daily social practices as in Elias model of the civilizing process is still under way. From this perspective, democratization in the Gulf region does not only mean the building of representative institutions, but also the transformation of social practices which guarantee the daily functioning of democratic rule. How to achieve this long-term goal?

Certainly not through forms of foreign intervention such as in the current coercive state-and democracy-building attempts in Afghanistan or Iraq. There, a multiplicity of actors are involved, taking over a broad range of tasks from combating and disarming militias to the building of political, social and economic institutions. Although oriented toward the image of the state, these "new protectorates" only vaguely remind us of forms of legal political authority which we can call a state. Rather, we are confronted with a kind of "controlled anarchy" (Schlichte 2003), with fragmented political arrangements in which various international, transnational, regional, national and local interests and competences overlap. For all these actors the image of the state serves as a central normative reference, whereas they are following their own goals on the ground. Whether these complex social arrangements will ever lead to viable states—nobody knows.

For the Gulf States the point of departure is certainly by far better than in the cases of Afghanistan and Iraq. Although rather in its infancy, processes of the legalization of state-society relations are observable in all Gulf principalities and in Saudi Arabia, yet in different degrees. The oil monarchies have been able to achieve a "fair amount of social compliance" and lack prolonged periods of social and political frictions. The ruling families have incorporated tribes, clerics and increasingly the business class into the political establishment, thus enhancing the legitimacy of the state; forms of legitimacy that are based on hybrid mixtures of both patterns of traditional and legal authority, however, with a visible tendency to increase its legal components (cf. Kamrava 2005: 340). To perceive these states as traditional remnants of the past is simply wrong. This judgment is the result of both superficial analyzes and the confusion of normative ideal types with historical reality.

A case in point is the situation of women in Saudi Arabia, a very popular topic in the global public debate. Looking at gender segregation in Saudi Arabia, the rigid separation of male and female spaces has been a constant social feature. There is hardly any country in the world that knows a more rigid exclusion of women from the public space. In the light of our own normative standards, this continuing public exclusion of women might be interpreted as an anti-modern kind of social stagnation. Yet by closer inspection we can detect rapid social change within the female realm. Amélie Le Renard's work shows, for instance, in which ways the lives of Saudi Arabian women have changed dramatically in terms of education, work, leisure activities and the intermingling of people from different kin. It is not wrong to argue that the implementation of religiously justified gender segregation by the Saudi state has been instrumental in the erosion of the customary roles which women played in Arabian society. At first glance rigid gender segregation appears as a remnant from pre-modern times. Yet in its institutionalization by the Saudi state, it turned into an opportunity structure for Saudi women, opening a social space for modern change (Renard 2008).

The lesson we can learn from historical sociology is to understand state formation as an ongoing process with an open end. State formation is characterized by both successful state-building and state-decay, also in European history possibly more states disappeared than became established according to our modern image of the democratic state. Both phases of the monopoly mechanism are extremely fragile and war-prone periods of institution-building and social transformation. What decides about success or failure is contextual and cannot be derived from the abstract concepts of sociology.[2] Given the general contingency of historical contexts, contemporary state-builders are facing the same general uncertainty as their European predecessors, namely that also their intended actions will shape un-intended outcomes. The political rational and public justification of democratic governance cannot be found in sociological reasoning or scholarly guided long-term state-building strategies. The decision-makers in both state agencies and non-governmental organizations are not driven by sociological grand schemes, but by their own organizational interests and the dominant issues of every-day politics. From this perspective, a gradual legalization and therewith a process of democratization of the Arab Gulf states seems under way. The fact that these states are still ruled by families must not be an obstacle to further democratic developments. Michael Herb has convincingly argued that these dynastic monarchies have a potential for social compromise which might enable them to evolve in constitutional directions as this happened in Europe (Herb 1999). Indeed, the four steps of juridification in Europe, often have been accompanied by the gradual transformation of monarchs from autocratic rulers to representative heads of state.

NOTES

1. The author has no particular specialization in the Gulf region. Therefore, the focus of this essay is on theoretical and conceptual reflections, only contextualized with respect to the Arab Gulf. For publications about the resilience of authoritarianism in the Middle East by the same author, see: Jung 2006, 2007a and 2007b.
2. Regarding state-society relations in the Arab Gulf States, one of the most important contextual feature is connected to labor migration. The high percentage of foreigners working in these states is a clear peculiarity of the region. The prospects for democratization will be contingent on the ways in which the Gulf States will handle the social and legal situation – exclusion versus inclusion – of their immigrant population. Moreover, their different political loyalties and citizenship relations to other state make internal political developments in the Gulf State prone to foreign intervention.

REFERENCES

Elias, Norbert (1994). *The Civilizing Process. The History of Manners and State Formation and Civilization*, Oxford: Blackwell.

Fukuyama, Francis (2005). Building Democracy After Conflict. "Stateness" First, *Journal of Democracy,* 16 (1): 84-88.

Habermas, Jürgen (1986). *The Theory of Communicative Action: Lifeworld and System: A Critique of Functionalist Reason*. London: Polity Press.

Herb, Michael (1999). *All in the Family. Absolutism, Revolution, and Democracy in the Middle Eastern Monarchies,* New York: State University of New York Press.

Jackson, Robert H. (1990). *Quasi States: Sovereignty, International Relations, and the Third World,* Cambridge: Cambridge University Press.

Jung, Dietrich (ed.) (2006). *Democratization and Development. New Political Strategies for the Middle East,* New York: Palgrave MacMillan.

——(2007a). "Islam and Politics: A Fixed Relationship?" *Critique: Critical Middle Eastern Studies,* 16 (1): 19-3.

——(2007b). Democratizing the Middle East. Democracy Promotion as a Means of Achieving International Security? in: Sisodia N.S. and Ashok K. Behuria (eds.): *West Asia in Turmoil: Implications for Global Security,* New Delhi: Academic Foundation.

Kamrava, Mehran (2005). *The Modern Middle East. A Political History since the First World War,* Berkeley: University of California Press.

Médar, Jean-Francois (1992). Le 'Big Men' en Afrique: esquisse d'analyze du politicien entrepreneur, *L'Année Sociologique* 42: 167-92.

Meyer, John W., John Boli, George Thomas and Francisco Ramirez (1997). World Society and the Nation State, *American Journal of Sociology* 103 (1): 144-81.

Ramazani, Rouhollah K. (1979). *The Persian Gulf and the Strait of Hormuz,* Alphen aan den Rijn: Sijthoff and Noordhoff.

Renard, Améli Le (2008). Only for Women: Women, the State, and Reform in Saudi Arabia, *The Middle East Journal* 62 (4). 610-29.

Schlichte, Klaus (2003). State Formation and the Economy of Intra-State Wars, in: Dietrich Jung (ed.): *Shadow Globalization, Ethnic Conflicts and New Wars: A Political Economy of Intra-State War,* London and New York: Routledge.

Schlumberger, Oliver (2006). Dancing with Wolves: Dilemmas of Democracy Promotion in Authoritarian Contexts, in: Dietrich Jung (ed.): *Democracy and Development. New Political Strategies for the Middle East,* New York: Palgrave Macmillan.

Sørensen, Georg (2004). *The Transfromation of the State: Beyond the Myth of Retreat,* New York: Palgrave MacMillan.

Tilly, Charles (1985). War Making and State Making as Organized Crime, in P. Evans, D. Rueschemeyer and T. Skocpol (eds.). *Bringing the State Back In,* Cambridge: Cambridge University Press.

——(1990). *Coercion, Capital, and European States, AD 990-1990,* Oxford: Basil Blackwell.

Weber, Max (1904). 'Objectivity' in Social Science and Social Policy, in: *Methodology of the Social Sciences,* translated and edited by Edward A. Shils and Henry A. Finch, New York: Free Press (1949).

——(1968a). *Economy and Society: An Outline of Interpretive Sociology*, edited by Guenther Roth and Claus Wittich, Volume I, New York: Bedminister Press.

——(1968b). *Economy and Society: An Outline of Interpretive Sociology*, edited by Guenther Roth and Claus Wittich, Volume II, New York: Bedminister Press.

——(1991). *From Max Weber: Essays in Sociology*, edited, with an introduction by H.H. Gerth and C. Wright Mills, with a new preface by Bryan S. Turner, London: Routledge.

3

Democratization in the Greater/Broader Middle East and the Gulf

Gulshan Dietl

> [in the Arab world] The dominant image of the US is not the Statue of Liberty but the photographs of prisoner abuse at Abu Ghreib; pro-Western liberal reformers feel they have to distance themselves from the US and are targeted for accepting grants from organizations like the National Endowment for Democracy. ...a strong push for political change coming from Washington at this juncture would be counterproductive.[1]

> ...there is virtually no chance that this area will be stable during the next decade. Threats arise from the domestic fragility of many of the regimes; the endemic instability in Egypt and Algeria; the challenge of political Islam; rivalries among moderate and radical Arab nations; an enduring threat from Iran and perhaps from a revived Iraq; the continuing struggle between Israel and the Palestinians; the vast oil wealth of the Persian Gulf and Caspian basin; the persisting large-scale arms transfers into the region; any further acquisition of WMD by one or more states in the area; and the uncertain future foreign policy orientation of Russia. All these factors, plus events and variables we cannot foresee, will make the Greater Middle East the most precarious region in the world.[2]

Today, the US sermons on democracy have been suspended; the banner of democracy is folded and shelved; and the old trusted unelected leaders continue to operate according to US preferences. It is difficult to recollect in the present circumstances that it was a major issue—not just discursively but also on the ground—only a few years back. The paper seeks to recapitulate the broad strands of the "democratization debate" and relate it to the Gulf region.

GREATER MIDDLE EAST INITIATIVE

The US-Middle East Partnership Initiative (MEPI) predates the Greater Middle East Initiative (GMEI). MEPI was introduced by the then Secretary of State

Colin Powell at a talk to the Heritage Foundation in December 2002. It envisaged an Entrepreneurship Training Programme to bring businessmen to the US for management training; running Campaign Schools for aspiring politicians; bringing women politicians to the US to witness elections in progress; and so on. It was interpreted by many as providing ideological cover of democracy building to the US Administration's grand ambitions for changing commercial law throughout the Middle East[3] leading to a Free Trade Area. A few hastily signed bilateral trade agreements followed the Initiative.[4]

The war on Iraq, ostensibly, was also to usher in democracy—in addition to all the rest of the blatant lies that the Bush administration trotted out. Even as the rest of the lies were exposed to be such, the pretext of "democratization" continued to serve as a legitimizing prop. A few months after the "Mission Accomplished" pronouncement, democratization was elevated to the primary rationale even as terrorism and the weapons of mass destruction were relegated to the background. At a major speech before the National Endowment for Democracy (NED) and again in London, Bush resorted to democracy as his main defence of the Iraq war. "Iraqi democracy will succeed—and that success will send forth the news, from Damascus to Tehran—that freedom can be the future of every nation," Bush said. "The establishment of a free Iraq at the heart of the Middle East will be a watershed event in the global democratic revolution." The statement was also aimed at stopping the slipping support for the US occupation of Iraq at home and abroad.[5] The State of the Union address on 24 January 2004 called for expansion of the NED's budget for 2005 by $40 million to be exclusively channelled to the Middle East. Also in January, the US Office of Management and Budget which assists the president in overseeing the financial spending of federal government programme announced the allocation of $450 million to be spent on democracy promotion in Iraq in the first six months of 2004.[6]

As a multilateral initiative with the European Allies, the idea was first mooted by the Vice President Dick Cheney at the World Economic Forum in Davos. "Our forward strategy for freedom commits us to support those who work and sacrifice for reform across the Greater Middle East," he said. "We call upon our democratic friends and allies everywhere, and in Europe in particular, to join us in this effort."[7]

The London-based *al-Hayat daily* attained a major scoop, when it published the classified text of the Working Paper on the GMEI, that the US proposed to table at the G-8 Summit at Sea Island, Georgia, in the coming June.[8] The Working Paper had already been distributed to the G-8 countries and was expected to be endorsed by them. None of the GME countries was taken into confidence. The Paper claimed that together with the Euro-Mediterranean Partnership, the US Middle East Partnership Initiative and the multilateral reconstruction efforts in Afghanistan and Iraq; the Working Paper would demonstrate the G-8 commitment to reform in the region. The Greater Middle East was defined to include the Arab states, Afghanistan, Iran, Israel, Pakistan and Turkey.

It was a comprehensive plan; thought through to the last detail. The ingredients, methodology and the expected result—all made it look like a laboratory-ready controlled experiment. It urged the G-8 countries to get their "classics" translated and donate them to the schools, universities and local libraries in the GME; provide computer access to the people in post offices; help modernize the banking services; sponsor training programmes for journalists and exchange programmes for parliamentarians; provide in-country advisors on WTO accession to guide them toward identifying and removing non-tariff barriers to trade, and once the accession is complete, provide assistance to implement the WTO commitments.

The most interesting resolve of the G-8 was spelled out as: "Working with those countries that demonstrate a serious willingness to hold free and fair elections", the G-8 could actively provide pre-election assistance like voter registration, monitoring groups to ensure free and fair elections and to look into complaints regarding the process.

The reactions to the Working Paper went all the way from suggestions on improvement to an outright indignation. The European reactions were predictable; they would prefer partnership to imposition, would insist on a sustained long term commitment that involved Palestine-Israel Peace Process, would adopt a country-by-country rather than the region-wide approach, emphasize modernization over democracy and so on. They also objected to the inclusion of Afghanistan and Pakistan as it reflected ignorance and anti-Muslim bias. France called the original draft condescending and likely to backfire.[9] The French Foreign Minister Dominique de Villepin summarized this concern in an interview with *Le Figaro*: "If we want to be credible, we can't ignore the Israeli-Palestinian conflict. Re-creating a dynamic for peace is an indispensable condition for any initiative in the region."[10] The German Foreign Minister Joschka Fischer, addressing the same conference, noted: "The key regional conflict, namely the Middle East conflict, should neither be set aside nor allowed to block this initiative from the outset." Some European countries prepared their own drafts providing agency to the states themselves.

Tony Blair was virtually the only European leader who wholeheartedly proclaimed his support for the idea. Addressing a joint session of the US Congress amidst thundering applause, he said: The spread of freedom is the best security for the free. It is our last line of defence and our first line of attack. And just as the terrorist seeks to divide humanity in hate, so we have to unify it around an idea. And that idea is liberty....We must find the strength to fight for this idea and the compassion to make it universal.[11]

The US itself was totally committed to it and totally confident of its utility. In June 2004, it planned to table the proposal at three summits: the G-8, the

US-EU and NATO. Thereafter, a review process would be built into the annual summits of all the three alliances. To give traction to the process, Secretary of State Colin Powell discussed the initiative with the NATO chief as well as the French and Turkish foreign ministers. Assistant Secretary of State Beth Jones held talks with European Union envoys in Dublin, where the US-European Union summit was be held in June, and national security adviser Condoleezza Rice briefed other European officials.

There were influential voices within the US who contributed additional prescriptions. Senator Richard Lugar, Chairman of the Foreign Relations Committee, called on the NATO to train the Middle East militaries in peacekeeping, counterterrorism, military reform and civilian overview. Senator John Edwards explicitly called for a Helsinki-type organization that would assist civil society and political parties to monitor elections and manage crises.

On the other hand, Zbigniew Brzezinski, who was the National Security Advisor to President Jimmy Carter, cautioned that the democracy push is like "trimming the sails on a sinking ship unless you address the Arab-Israeli issue." Democracy right now is a slogan, he said. "Probably worse than that, it is a deceptive device to justify postponement in the peace process. And that will have damaging consequences to our position in Iraq and with the Arab world." There were concerns expressed by others about the defective assumptions on which the initiative was based and recommended incentives rather than punitive policies to spur progress in the region.[12]

Others saw it as a mad plan that Bush tried to boost the morale of his neocons with.[13] The neocons' seemingly disinterested global quest for democracy, for good against evil, for reinforcing good Iraqis against bad, and for good Muslims against bad was dubbed an "imperial endeavour" and likened to Reagan's repudiation of détente so as to roll back the evil empire, heralding a democratic revolution.[14]

And then, there were questions on the very compatibility of stability in Iraq and democracy in its neighbourhood. "If stabilizing Iraq is the US's most immediate priority, and if the support of neighbouring governments is necessary, then these broader efforts at democratization need to be subordinated to the more immediate goal of stabilization."[15]

BROADER MIDDLE EAST PARTNERSHIP

It was the US Undersecretary of State for Economic, Business and Agricultural Affairs Alan P. Larson, who introduced the revised version of the GMEI; now rechristened the Broader Middle East Partnership. His tone was conciliatory and his rationale less offensive. In short, the proposal was in marked difference to the earlier initiative. He maintained that the proposal was in "response" to Arab calls for change and reform. He cited as evidence the Arab League summit declaration, the calls issued by the Arab Human Development Report, the Alexandria Library statement and the declarations at Sanaa, Yemen, and Aqaba, Jordan.

He went further: the proposal was to establish a forum where it would be possible for ministerial level representatives, including foreign and economic ministers, from the Middle East and the G-8 member states, "to discuss how to learn from each other's experiences."[16] He named Algeria, Bahrain, Jordan, Yemen, Afghanistan and Turkey as the countries attending the G-8 Summit and explained that since the venue was small, it was not possible to accommodate a larger group. The countries from outside the region could also be of assistance, he added.

In a damage control gesture for the leak of the GMEI in *al-Hayat*, he said that it was only a working paper and its leak had caused a great deal of unhappiness in the US administration. The new revised draft, in contrast, was the "greatest, the most widespread example of sharing internal G8 working documents with non-G8 countries that has ever taken place." The Middle Easterners contributed lots of constructive advice and feedback to its final version, he said.

The G-8 Summit was held in Sea Island, Georgia, from 8 to 10 June 2004. It approved two documents; 1, Partnership for Progress and a Common Future with the Region of Broader Middle East and North Africa and 2. G-8 Plan of Support for Reform. "Support for reform in the region will go hand in hand with support for a just, comprehensive and lasting settlement to the Arab-Israel conflict", the statement said. More conciliatory statements followed: "Change should not, and cannot be imposed from outside...Each country is unique and their diversity should be respected. Our engagement must respond to local conditions and be based on local ownership...each society will reach its own conclusions about pace and scope of change." The Summit laid the groundwork for future meetings by securing commitments from G-8 countries and regional governments to jointly create development and education programmes.[17]

The website of the Secretary of State put out a rather concise account of the Summit achievement:

> From an idea of partnership to a growing reality, the Broader Middle East and North Africa (BMENA) Initiative represents genuine co-operation between the G8 and European nations and the governments, business and civil society of the region, in order to strengthen freedom, democracy and prosperity for all. The leaders of the G8 industrialized nations and countries of the BMENA launched the Partnership for Progress and a Common Future—a blueprint for how G8 and Middle Eastern countries could best work together to support indigenous calls for reform—at the G8 Sea Island, Georgia, summit in June 2004.[18]

There was a general sense of disappointment among the pro-democracy champions. The neocons dubbed it "appeasement" to the Europeans and to the Arabs and expected little to come out of the watered-down draft that was approved.

THE GULF: EMERGENCE OF STATES AND EVOLUTION OF DEMOCRACY

The states in the Gulf have a commonality running through their historical experiences. The state borders in the entire Middle East are of relatively recent origin and, at times, arbitrary. According to Simon Bromley, the victorious European allies in the First World War—the British and the French—stumbled into creating a state system in the Middle East for want of a better alternative, not out of belief or design. And once the state—building strategy had been fixed upon, it was prosecuted with indecent haste and with little or no attention to the realities on the ground.[19] Thus, it was the British High Commissioner in Baghdad, Sir Percy Cox, who drew the borders of Iraq, Saudi Arabia and Kuwait in a desert camp in Uqair one night in late November 1922. Iraq itself was put together out of the three Ottoman provinces of Baghdad, Basra and Mosul. The seven small sheikhdoms were motivated to merge together to form the United Arab Emirates (UAE). The British arrogated upon themselves the tasks of "drawing lines on the map, appointing rulers, elaborating structures of bureaucratic administration and taxation, even training and equipping armies."[20]

The process of state-formation began, according to Bromley, only after the British ceased to exercise control and conferred formal independence on these entities. Ilia Harik contests the thesis and asserts that "colonialism affected the boundaries of the Arab states, but it did not, with the exception of the Fertile Crescent case, create those states."[21] He does concede that the colonial powers affected the structures of many governments, especially by creating a modern civil service and sometimes the nucleus of a modern standing army, and by leaving a major mark on the local political elites.

The non-participatory nature of the political systems in the Middle East has meant that the rulers′ legitimacy rests on a blend of ethnic, sectarian and temporal props. The Alawis in Syria, the Takritis in Iraq, the Maronites in Lebanon and so on. The temporal legitimacy is exclusively that of performance rather than that of representation. In the Gulf region, in addition, it is also hereditory. With the exceptions of Brunei and Bhutan, the ruling monarchies of the world today are located in the Arab world, and apart from Morocco and Jordan, all of them are situated on the Western shore of the Gulf. There are twelve of them in all: al-Khalifah in Bahrain, al-Sabah in Kuwait, Qaboos in Oman, al-Thani in Qatar, al-Saud in Saudi Arabia, al-Nayhan in Abu Dhabi, al-Maktoum in Dubai, al-Qasimi in Sharjah, al-Naimi in Ajman, al-Mualla in

Umm al-Qaiwan, al-Qasimi in Ras al-Khaima, and as-Sharqi in Fujaira. The Kingdom of Saudi Arabia or al-Mamalik al-Arabiyya as-Saudiyya has the dubious distinction of being named after its ruling dynasty.

In the early nineties, the political processes were slowly stirring to life. With the Gulf War over, Kuwait liberated, and foreign forces packing up to leave, the whispers of democratic expression grew louder across the Gulf region. The battle of the ballot was won in Kuwait with the successful completion of a free election in October 1992. The other states made tentative moves in that direction, but stopped short of a decisive action. The Saudis issued two major laws: The Basic Law of Government and the Consultative Council Law.[22] The formation of a sixty-member consultative council was announced to mark the tenth anniversary of Fahd's rule. It was to be a body representing business, professional, academic and religious elite. Appointed by the King for a period of four years, it would have the right to put questions to the Council of Ministers, make suggestions on the laws-in-the-making and submit them to the King, and consider the international agreements. Neither in the mode of is formation nor in the scope of its authority was it a great leap forward.

The royal decree establishing it said that "it would operate in compliance with the existing system of government and in adherence to Sharia". The government has made it abundantly clear that it is not a pale version of Western-style parliament. Instead, it is projected as an organic development of consultative process that goes back to the Prophet. Since its formation, it has been expanded in number if not in the sphere of activities; thus, in 1997 it went upto 90, in 2001 to 120 and in 2005 to 150. Various ministers have appeared before it to appraise it of their ministries' working. The Sauds did not promise democracy and did not permit elections. But they did confer a Bill of Rights on the Saudi citizens—however limited and incomplete.[23]

Even Iraq went through the motions of presidential referendum and parliamentary elections. By the end of the decade, there was a general optimism regarding the direction of civil and political life. People at the grass-roots level were organizing themselves into human rights movements, environment groups, professional associations, women's organizations and so on. In the Arab world, the civil societal formations were becoming active enough to make "the coersive impulses of ruling Arab elite increasingly difficult to act out", according to Saad Eddin Ibrahim.[24]

THE US–GULF INTERACTIONS ON DEMOCRATIZATION

The regional regimes detected elements of Helsinki Accord into the Working Paper on GMEI. The Accords were signed by thirty-five countries including the US, the Soviet Union and almost all the European states. They were fairly broad-based, but the human rights and fundamental freedoms became the key issues. The dissident groups in the Soviet Union and East Europe cited the Accords as legitimating their demands. The US, in the circumstances, took it upon itself to protect them. The Arab rulers feared the same fate as befell the governments in communist states. At the same time they were also confident that their benefactors would prefer autocrats to Islamists who might replace them in electoral contests, and stability to political unrest that might produce a flight of refugees to Europe.

The US encouragement for democracy did enthuse educated, urban middle classes. The Arab Human Development Reports had identified three deficits in the Arab world, namely, of freedom, education and women's empowerment. The US pronouncements came as an acknowledgement of their grievances and assessments. The reaction in the Gulf was comparatively muted.

In general, the Arab masses knew it to be a lot of rhetoric with no follow-on action. Not many considered Bush to be the suitable candidate for the role of a liberator. And side—tracking the Palestine issue made it a dishonest and empty gesture. The belated incorporation of the issue at the G-8 Summit did not rectify the perceptions. There was a general belief in the GME that the democracy rhetoric was only a cover to hide its policy on the Palestine issue; and that policy was believed to be a nod to Sharon's plan to unilaterally disengage from the areas it chose to and build a dividing wall to define and secure its own borders. The people did not trust or welcome outside interference into their domestic situation; in fact, it made them more loyal and more patriotic.

Saudi Arabia

In Saudi Arabia, there were instances of the reformers, who saw the time opportune to make their voices heard—sometimes winning small concessions, sometimes yielding ground. At least once, the politics of dissent manifested itself overground, when hundreds demonstrated in Riyadh and Jeddah demanding economic and political reforms in October 2003. More than 150 of them were arrested. In quick succession, Hussein Shobokshi, a popular columnist, was banned from writing after he published an article that fantasized his daughter driving him to a polling booth. The piece ruffled a few feathers as the Saudi women cannot drive and the men had not voted till then. In March 2004, Matrouk Faleh, Ali Demaini and Abdullah Hamid were arrested for "issuing statements and collecting signatures on petitions" calling for adopting a "constitutional monarchy and using Western terminology in demanding political reform". They were handed down long prison sentences after a closed-door trial.

Thus, the US calls for democracy had worked both ways. It did encourage the democracy advocates; but it also hurt their case. It was easy for the rulers to brand them as American agents. The Saudi Minister of Interior Prince Nayef was reported to have told them: "The government is not weak and the United States will not protect you."[25]

Iran

In the case of Iran, there were no exhortations to democracy. In the immediate aftermath of the war on Iraq, the US pronouncements on terrorism, pre-emptive strikes, regime change and remaking the geopolitical landscape of the region had ominous implications for Iran. More specifically, the country was called a member of the "Axis of Evil", was identified as the next target, was threatened with surgical strikes at its nuclear installations, its exiled opposition leader was projected and promoted as an alternative to its regime and its opposition-in-exile the Mujahideen-e-Khalque was encouraged to mobilize to destabilize Iran. The overwhelming American presence on both its flanks put Iran into a pincer and opened up its territory for monitoring at close quarters.

There was a stream of resolutions in American Congress seeking foreign aid appropriations for regime change in Iran. The CIA received a "non-lethal presidential finding that put into motion a CIA plan that included a coordinated campaign of propaganda, disinformation and manipulation of Iran's currency and international financial transactions.[26] In normal circumstances, the CIA is permitted to collect information; only a presidential finding can authorize covert action. In this case, the operations were to remain short of deadly force.

The Iranian response was two-fold in the circumstances. First, it rejected the "pre-packaged recipes form afar" and sought support for the governments that drew their legitimacy from the people.[27] Second, it reached out to the Gulf rulers, particularly Saudi Arabia. The Iranian foreign minister attended the Arab League summit in Riyadh in March 2007. In May, Ahmadinejad made an official visit to the United Arab Emirates, a country with which Iran has a long-standing territorial dispute. Within a few months thereafter, he visited Bahrain and participated in the Organization of Petroleum Exporting Countries (OPEC) summit. Towards the end of the year, he was invited to perform Hajj by the Saudis and to participate in the Gulf Co-operation Council (GCC) summit in Doha. He was the first Iranian president to have performed the Hajj while in office, and the first Iranian president to have been invited to the GCC Summit. Predictably, he proposed security and economic pacts for the "Persian Gulf" in his address there.[28]

Iraq

Iraq was the epicenter of American exercise in democratizing the region. A host of influential authors prescribed a new order to be the "primary task of a pax Americana",[29] urged that as the West's last military state and its last remaining empire, the US take up the responsibility for "imperial restructuring and ordering"[30] Niall Ferguson, the celebrated historian of Imperialism, called Iraq only the frontline of an American imperium that aspired to be much more than military dominance along a vast and variegated strategic frontier and also meant economic, cultural and political predominance within and without that frontier.[31]

The most fundamental dichotomy of the "democratic Iraq" project was this: The goal of a freely elected government in which the people were sovereign was to be implemented under an imperial domination by undemocratic means. How was that circle to be squared?[32] Anyway, the measures like constitution drafting, referendum and elections were undertaken in the country under the watchful eyes of the US authorities.

Gulf Co-operation Council (GCC)

The internal dynamics in the GCC came to a surface on the issue of democratization. By then, Qatar had a Constitution, duly ratified by a referendum. It created a forty-five-member parliament; thirty of whom were to be elected. It was authorized to monitor the executive branch of the government and approve the state budget. Women were given the right to vote. A woman won a seat on the Municipal Council. And a woman was appointed the minister of education. Article fifty of the Constitution assured freedom to worship to all religions. Article forty-eight granted freedom of the press. And the Qatar-based *Al-Jazeera* was quietly revolutionizing the Arab society and its world-view.

The reactions from the Gulf rulers were as divergent; as a result. While the King of Saudi Arabia shunned the event at the Sea Island, the ruler of Qatar lent enthusiastic support to it. In a signed article in the *Daily Star*, he cited Caliph Bakr al-Siddiq, who insisted, "Reform yourself and the people will follow suit." He rejected the argument that the conflict with Israel should serve as an excuse to oppose reform, discounted the claim that the reforms could threaten stability and security in the region and pronounced that "a number of the Arab nation's sufferings are attributed to self-imposed heavy restrictions, and an arsenal of home-made pretexts and excuses to oppose reform."[33]

LINGERING DISCOURSE AND CONTINUING EVOLUTION

The democracy proponents adopted three distinct postures: they claimed it was genuine, they found fault at the margins for its short lifespan, and they gave naïve suggestions for improvement. "An ambitious strategy of democracy promotion is poised to be a major pillar of US foreign policy for many years after 9/11, just as Cold War containment, trade liberalization, and development assistance were pillars of American policy in the decades after 1945", was an expression of faith.[34] "Democracy in the Middle East during the Bush administration suffered from inadequate strategic thought and uneven implementation due partly to the newness of the policy, but also to the fact that few US officials really understood or accepted it", was almost a sigh of regret.[35] And then, there were five specific suggestions for a likely future experiment:

(1) consistent commitment to democratic procedures; (2) modest goals; (3) targeted means; (4) long-term investments in civil society, and perhaps more importantly, (5) strong partnerships established with local and regional groups, who bring to the table tested expertise, long-term horizons, and vested interest in success.[36]

And then, there was a debate at the theoretical level. "...in the future, policymakers should focus less on democratic peace theory to design their pro-democracy strategy, and pay greater attention to the literature on democratic transition, such as sectarian conflict, local human rights abuse, dislocated populations, territorial disputes, and transnational terrorism."[37] The suggestion did not endorse or reject the "democratic peace" theory; it only found it less relevant than the theories dealing with democratic transition.

A second theoretical debate concerned the linkage between democracy and terrorism. The democratization project was undertaken—or at least justified—as a means to diminish terrorism and secure the Western world. If the GME would become democratic, the citizens there would be less prone to terrorism; that was the basic premise of the justification. What then would explain the terrorist groups like Brigante Rosse in Italy, the Bader-Meinhof and the Red Army Faction in Germany, the Red Army in Japan, the IRA in England, the ETA in Spain and scores of others that emerged and operated in the mature democracies of Europe and Japan?

Was the call for democratization sincere? There is no doubt that it represented an ideological conviction for many who advocated it for its own sake. There were others who preached it as a precondition for resolving the Palestine issue. The Bush administration found it a convenient argument to wage a war on Iraq. And dropped it when it was not needed anymore. Even during the short time that it was paraded around; its application was on a case-by-case basis. The presidential finding on Iran did not seek to promote democracy but destabilize it. The Syria Accountability and Lebanon Sovereignty Restoration Act of 2003 required the President to selectively impose some of the specified sanctions: reducing diplomatic contacts; banning US exports to Syria; prohibiting US businesses from investing or operating in Syria; restricting travel of Syrian diplomats to Washington and the UN; banning Syrian aircraft from taking off, landing in or flying over the US; and freezing the Syrian assets in the US. The elections of Hamas in the Palestinian territory and the Hizbollah in Lebanon were greeted with unconcealed hostility.[38] Finally, the democracy-resister rulers in the GME found it easy to scare away the democracy-promoters by a simple question: what if the Islamists were to win the elections? That was not a hypothetical question; it had nearly happened and had to be scuttled in Algeria.

Was the call for democratization in the national interest of the United States? Not in the short and the medium term; may be not even in distant future if the state system survives. The US national interests would be best served by dealing with a few despots not accountable to the public opinion at home. In a democracy, people would demand to scrutinize relations with the US. They would ask for control over their natural resources like oil, justice for the Palestinians, closure of American bases, rejection of democratic sermons and eventually replacement of the time-tested American friends at the helm of affairs.

The ideological pretensions to civilize the natives is an indispensable ingredient of the colonial discourse. Restructuring, reordering, civilizing, democratizing have always been the goals announced, or justifications invented, to deodorize the bloody and brutal situation on the ground. It is that which sets it apart from the imperial aloofness. "Oderint dum metuant", that is, "let them hate us as long as they fear us", the Empire would thunder.

> "Take up the White Man's Burden
> And reap its old reward:
> The blame of those ye better,
> The hate of those ye guard", the Colonizer would mourn.

Neither the Greater Middle East Initiative nor the Broader Middle East Partnership was devoid of colonial agenda. And neither of them was the first exercise nor will it be the last one.

Like everything else, however, there was some positive fallout of the attempt; intended or otherwise. The Gulf political weather stirred a little, like the rest of the GME. An oft-quoted story bears repetition once more. After staging a successful referendum to approve/disapprove his leadership, the ruler announces the results". Ninety-nine point nine percent have voted in favour." Applause. "There are, however, sixty-six negative votes cast." A palpapable sense of fear runs through the crowd as someone asks, "Who are they?" "Well, the sixty were cast in our embassies abroad." "And the rest?" "We are looking for them," assures the ruler. The scene could have been enacted in most of the Middle Eastern states. The leader could have been a former army officer, a religious guide or a pretentious prince.

The result is the politics of manoeuvring rather than the politics of the masses. An individual seeks his own linkage to the source of power and masters a nimble footwork to chalk out his own route to it through the ever-shifting alliance of power-brokers. The democracy promotion project did create some movement in the placid water of the Gulf. Some people felt empowered enough to send petitions to the rulers requesting certain freedoms; some more went further to voice their expectations on their own; the rest knew better and waited. The rulers, on their part, conferred some rights and granted some freedoms. Mostly, the voices asking democratic reforms were silenced through imprisonment, co-optation, favours to selected elites and some steps towards representative/responsive systems.

The ruler of Qatar scored points over others and used them in the intra-GCC interactions. Iraq went through motions of democratic practices under the American Liberation/Occupation. Iran was singled out for the harshest treatment.

The Gulf has been moving at its own pace in the meanwhile. There are no triumphant democracies nor are the nightmare scenarios visualized by Blackwill and Sturmer come true.

Finally, a serious academic debate around democracy ensued. Its main contribution, probably, was to put democracy at the centre of the Political Science/ International Relations disciplines. Even if it happened only because democracy was linked to issues of security, terrorism, imperialism and so on. The issues that have always preoccupied the best and the brightest minds.

NOTES

1. Francis Fukuyama, America at the Crossroads: *Democracy, Power and the Neoconservative Legacy* (Yale University Press, New Haven, 2006), p. 187.
2. Robert D. Blackwill and Michael Sturmer, "Conclusions" in Robert D. Blackwill and Michael Sturmer, eds., Allies Divided: *Transatlantic Policies for the Greater Middle East* (MIT Press, Cambridge, 1997) p. 304.
3. The correct geographic nomenclature for Middle East and the accepted usage in India is "West Asia". Since the paper deals with terms like the Greater and Broader Middle East, I propose to use it for the sake of consistency.
4. Christopher Candland, "The US Greater Middle East Initiative: Implications for Persian Gulf Economies and Polities", *The Iranian Journal of International Affairs* (Tehran), Vol. 19, number 2, Spring 2007, pp. 81-94.
5. *Washington Post*, 7 November 2003.
6. The NED uses the US tax payers' money to promote favoured politicians, political parties and inject money and influence into domestic elections of foreign countries. Interestingly, its operation inside the US is illegal.
7. Robin Wright and Glenn Kessler, "Bush Aims for "Greater Middle East Plan: Democracy Initiative to be Aired at G-8 Talks" *Washington Post*, 9 February 2004.
8. *Al-Hayat* (London) 13 February 2004.
9. Steven R. Weisman, "Powell tries to Reassure Kuwaitis and Saudis", *New York Times*, 21 March 2004.
10. Glenn Kessler and Robin Wright, "Arabs and Europeans Question 'Greater Middle East' Plan", *Washington Post*, 22 February 2004.
11. Transcript of Blair's speech in http://edition.cnn.com/2003/US/07/17/ blair.transcript/ Accessed on 3 November 2009
12. Steven A Cook, "The Right Way to Promote Arab Reform", *Foreign Affairs*, 84(2), March-April 2005, pp. 91-102.
13. Simon Jenkins, "The Coalition Bids Goodbye and Good Riddance to Iraq", *Daily Star* (Beirut), 11 June 2004.

14. Mahmood Mamdani, *Good Muslim, Bad Muslim: America, the Cold War, and the Roots of Terror* (Pantheon Books, New York, 2004), pp. 231-259.
15. James Dobbins, "US Policy and Diplomacy", in Markus E. Bouillon, David M. Malone and Ben Rowswell, eds., *Iraq: Preventing a New Generation of Conflict* Lynne Rienner Publishers, Boulder, 2007) pp. 203-212.
16. "US-led 'Broader' Middle East Initiative Changes Focus as G8 Summit nears: Washington claims it's only responding to Arab Calls for Change", George S. Hishmeh, *The Daily Star*, 4 June 2004
17. Jeremy Sharp, *The Broader Middle East and North Africa Initiative: An Overview* (CRS Report for Congress) http://italy.usembassy.gov/pdf/other/RS22053.pdf. Accessed on 3 November 2009. The last meeting of the G-8 and regional states' foreign ministers met in Marrakesh, Morocco on 23 November 2009. Secretary of State Hillary Clinton represented the US; signifying the Obama administration's continuing support for the democracy promotion.
18. http://bmena.state.gov
19. Simon Bromley, *Rethinking Middle East Politics: State Formation and Development* (Cambridge, 1994) p. 47.
20. *Ibid.*, p. 84.
21. Ilia Harik, "The Origins of the Arab State System", in Giacomo Luciani, ed., *The Arab State* (Routledge, London, 1990) pp. 1-28.
22. For a legal analysis of the Saudi Basic Laws, see A. Michael Tarazi, "Saudi Arabia's New Basic Laws: The Struggle for Participatory Islamic Government", *Harvard International Law Journal* (Cambridge), vol.34, Winter 1993, pp. 258-275.
23. Rashed Aba-Namay, "The Recent Constitutional Reforms in Saudi Arabia", *International and Comparative Law Quaterly,* (London), Vol.42, No. 2, April 1993, pp. 295-331.
24. Saad Eddin Ibrahim, "Arab Elites and Societies After the Gulf Crisis", in Dan Tschirgi, ed., *The Arab World Today* (Lynne Rienner, Boulder, 1994) pp. 85-89.
25. David B. Ottaway, "U.S.-Saudi Relations Show Signs of Stress: Reformers Labelled 'Agents of America'", *Washington Post*, 21 April 2004
26. Brian Ross and Richard Esposito, "Bush Authorizes New Covert Action against Iran", http://blogs.abcnews.com/theblotter/2007/05/bush_authorizes.html Accessed on 3 November 2009
27. Mohammad Ali Eskandari, Your History of Folly in Our Region", *The Guardian,* 14 April 2004.
28. There is a bitter controversy over the nomenclature; the Iranians insisting on retaining the original term the "Persian Gulf", the Arabs seeking to make it the "Arab Gulf" or at least just the "Gulf".
29. Deepak Lal, "In Defense of Empires", in Andrew Bacevich, ed., *The Imperial Tense* (Ivan R. Dee, Chicago, 2003) pp. 29-46.
30. Michael Ignatieff, "The challenges of American Imperial Power: Critical Essay", *Naval War College Review* (Newport), Spring 2003, pp. 1-9.
31. Niall Ferguson, *Colossus: The Rise and Fall of the American Empire* (Penguin Books, London, 2005)

32. Larry Diamond, *Squandered Victory: The American Occupation and the Bungled Effort to bring Democracy to Iraq* (Henry Holt and Company, New York, 2005) p. 312.
33. Emir Hamad Bin Khalifa Al-Thani, "Out of Fog through Arab Reform", *Daily Star*, 21 June 2004.
34. Gerard Alexander, "Making Democracy Stick", *Policy Review* (Stanford), number 134, December 2005-January 2006, p. 45.
35. Michele Dunn, "The Baby, the Bathwater, and the Freedom Agenda in the Middle East", *The Washington Quarterly*, volume 32, number 1, p. 140.
36. Valerie Bunce, "The Tasks of Democratic Transition and Tranferability", *Orbis* (Philadelphia), volume 52, number 1, Winter 2008, p. 40.
37. Arthur A Goldsmith, "Making the World Safe for Partial Democracy? Questioning the Premises of Democracy Promotion", *International Security* (Harvard), volume 33, number 2, Fall 2008, p. 145.
38. "The day Hamas won the Palestinian democratic elections the world's leading democracies failed the test of democracy. Rather than recognize the legitimacy of Hamas as a freely elected representative of the Palestinian people, seize the opportunity created by the result to support the development of good governance in Palestine, and search for a means of ending the bloodshed, the US and the EU threatened the Palestinian people with collective punishment for exercising their right to choose their parliamentary representatives." Bush failed the democracy test, according to the Hamas. Khalid Mishal, "Hamas Ready for a Just Peace" *The Hindu*, 1 February 2006. Reprinted from the *Guardian.*

4

The Dynamics of Change in the Arab Gulf

Rushda Siddiqui

Till the 1960s, when technology permitted for the oil of the Arab Gulf states to be the world's cheapest and most accessible source of energy, and the windfall profit from its global sale changed the economic status of its citizens, the Arab Gulf was largely 'pre-modern', 'patriarchal feudal', 'nomadic tribal or Bedouin'. Ethnically, the Arabs of the Persian Gulf assert strong affinity with the Arabs in the rest of West Asia and North Africa. They share more than a racial affinity to include social, religious, cultural, economic and historical similarities. The increase in the global demand for oil as a source of energy transformed the economic character of the region in the 1950s and 60s. By the 70s, it was in a position to give the region significant global political and economic clout. With the discovery of the use of oil as an economic resource, the Gulf States were confronted with the challenge of developing economically while preserving social integrity, and balancing quasi-traditional political systems with greatly enhanced regional and international responsibilities.

With the profits from the oil, the Gulf states got a break from poverty and socio-political marginalization. Simultaneously, it increased the dimensions of the variables of change for the region to include religion, political-economic-military involvement of external powers in fostering socio-political change in the region, and the shifts within the domestic socio-economic dynamics. It fomented the asymmetries within the polities of the region to create an imbalance in the regional social, political and economic equations. While other post-colonial states were changing to either imitate socialist governments or experiment with liberal ideologies, the Arab Gulf was strengthening its feudal structures, as the perpetuation of the feudal polity suited the global market economies. It suited the market forces to negotiate with one central command, rather than with democratic systems that could turn protectionist, or could seek a deal that would cut the profits of the oil players in the long run. The oil wealth converted their economies to rentier economies, which re-shaped the balance of power between the ruling elites and their societies.

THE CHANGING DYNAMICS OF POWER IN THE GULF

There are two levels at which the oil wealth changed the dynamics of socio-political and economic equations in the Arab Gulf.

Firstly, with the first flush of the power of the petro-dollar in the 1973 Arab-Israeli conflict the Arab-Arab, and Muslim-Muslim equations in the region got re-defined. The regional strategic power dynamics shifted from Egypt, Lebanon, Syria and Turkey to the Arab Gulf. The oil money was now the new financer of the Arab Israeli conflict, as well as the local aid giver to the underprivileged Muslim populations across the world. For the West too, the third Arab-Israeli conflict was an indicator of the changed power balance in the region. It made them shift their focus from securing the Suez to securing the Hormuz, and working to ensure that they did not suffer an oil blockade again. As a result, the focus of the Western powers shifted to increasing their military bases in the region and formulating a policy whereby a large scale confrontation between the Arabs and Israel would not recur. This was achieved by active intervention in the socio-political dynamics of each nation state in the region. Even if there was to be a confrontation, the new elite and the social dynamics within each nation state would not allow it to turn into a full-fledged war.

The second level of change in the Arab Gulf lay in the domestic socio-political dynamics of change. The rentier economy re-molded state society equations. As the state stopped taxing its' citizens and maintaining them from its own coffers, it became easy for the ruling elite to remold the society. It could now buy the society into conforming to its ideals, expectations and ethos. The result was the closer bonding between the Western political elites and the elites of the Arab Gulf. This helped the Gulf elites retain the feudal political and social hierarchy with an external support that was not coercive. The governments in the region could easily buy its opposition rather than crush it.

At a regional level, the new found strength of the petro-dollar re-aligned the social dynamics of religion based movements that saw a shift from the Ikhwan-ul-Muslimeen of North Africa to the Wahhabis of Saudi Arabia. As a result of their symbiotic relation with the House of Saud, the Wahhabis grew to becoming the most influential school of sunni thought from North Africa to South East Asia. The state governments of the Gulf encompassed it within their policy to channelise funds to assist in the expansion of the religious movements outside the region. As a result, while on the one hand the Muslim Brotherhood was being suppressed and was under pressure to be more pliant, the Wahhabis were getting a free hand to expand and grow. Rentierism had allowed for a symbiotic relationship to grow between the state and the largest social movement.

However, despite their ability to provide economic security to their own people, the governments of the Arab Gulf kept repeatedly getting drawn into the Arab-Palestinian quagmire. The creation of Israel and the subsequent regional conflicts changed the dynamics of socio-political equations within their countries. Till date, it is the Israel-Palestinian relation that remains the key element in defining the dynamics of change in the region. For the ruling elite of the Arab Gulf, at one level they needed to take on the leadership role and lead their societies into the conflict. At another level, they needed to keep power equations between the Islamists from the rest of the region (particularly the Ikhwan ul-muslimin) and themselves, tilted in their favour.

STATE FORMATION IN THE ARAB GULF

To study the dynamics of change that the Arab Gulf faces today, one would need to go back in history, particularly of collapse of the Ottoman Empire and the advent of European colonialism in the region that impacted society at different levels. It changed the constituents of middle classes, the poor and the elites. Economically, colonization monopolized foreign trade as well as the supply and management of public utilities and tied the local currencies and foreign trade earnings to the mother country's central banking system. In brief, the old socio-political and economic systems were destroyed, and those that survived, fell into the trap of marginalization and neglect.[1]

The Arab Gulf did not undergo colonialism in the same manner as did the other states in West Asia and North Africa. As it lay on the strategic route to India, the British decided to make it into a protectorate, under which the British maintained control in external relations of the Gulf States, and deliberately kept out of internal administration. In other words, local elites were given a level of autonomy to manage the equations between themselves, the British and the population. With the increase in the usage of oil as an energy source, it became imperative for Britain to keep a socio-political and economic hold on the states in the Gulf, even if they decided not to directly colonize it.

Insofar as the individual rulers' relations with his subjects were concerned, there was no attempt to impose western-style institutions such as parliament or assemblies. The platforms for interface between the feudal elites and their populace remained untouched. While there was a structure of English law and British administration, the economic, political and social relations between the rulers and their people remained unaffected. The British consciously did not try to alter social, criminal, civil laws or methods by which the rulers controlled their subjects, though these entailed procedures and punishments repugnant to Western thinking.[2]

Halim Barakat argues that with the passage of time, western intervention in domestic socio-political dynamics has become the single most dominant variable for change in the region. The process of intervention started by the British in the 1800s. He argues that the subsequent period saw further attempts to establish fragmented pieces of Arab world as separate states based on the Western Orientalist 'mosaic' perception, whereby they define as 'national' constituents a few subgroups in Arab society. Western scholarship till date support and propagate the concept of mosaic states and mosaic societies, which is understood by analysts as a tool to politically and socially fragment the region. Conflicts within society are understood as in-built and inherent to the populations. As a result, the policy makers from the West seek solutions to the political and social problems in the region, in the tools of management.[3]

The need to intervene in the domestic dynamics of the Arab Gulf is seen as necessity by the Western powers, over time. From the military intervention under the era of European colonization to the democracy campaigns under the Bush administration, the West has been seeking to be part of the socio-economic and political dynamics of the Arab Gulf. As the economic and political dynamics of Europe and the US underwent change, so did the strategic importance of the Arab Gulf for them. The announcement made by Britain on 16 January 1968, to withdraw troops from the Gulf by the end of 1971, heralded the end of an era. Economically, oil was the only factor involved in determining a Western policy as it was gaining strategic importance for the US, NATO and its allies. With the emergence of the Cold War the security of oil supplies from the Gulf became a matter of global strategic importance. In the Western power dynamics too, the US became the largest economic and military player in the region.[4]

The onset of the Cold War set into motion the first stage of transformation in the dynamics of US-British and Arab polities. Though prior to the 2003 war for occupation of Iraq, the United States was repeatedly drawn into conflicts in the Gulf, whether it was to support Saddam Hussein to counter the Iranian Revolution, or to topple the Saddam regime to stop him from developing nuclear weapons, it was dictated by the strategic interests of its allies in the region. From 1973, the scale of US intervention in West Asian politics through the Arab Gulf had only witnessed an increase.

CHALLENGES TO THE ARAB GULF GOVERNMENTS

The challenge of change for the Arab Gulf states can be broadly classified into two distinct sections of regional and domestic, though neither can be studied in isolation. There are various overlapping areas where the regional has affected local change at the nation-state level, and the local change has been trans-national in character.

US Policy Towards the Arab Gulf

The first catalyst of change that has affected the region has been the fluctuating religional policy of the Western superpower of the time. Prior to WWII it was the policy of the British and French, while after the creation of Israel and the onset of the Cold War, it was the 'US Middle East Policy'. The hallmark of a presidency in the US, from Nixon to Obama, has been its policy in West Asia and North Africa. The US interests in the Gulf have been two pronged. The first interest has been purely economic, i.e., to ensure access by the industrialized world to the region's vast resources. The second was to deny the Soviets political and military control over those resources.

President Nixon developed an initial US Gulf policy by establishing Iran and Saudi Arabia as the 'twin pillars' of US interests in the region. For President Carter, the Soviet occupation of Afghanistan shifted the theater of Cold War to the Arab Gulf. Later, Ronald Reagan re-affirmed the Carter administrations' classification of the Gulf as being of 'vital interest' to America, though his stance was tougher, and more interventionist than his predecessors.

For history, 1979 will remain a land mark year when the world underwent major political and economic changes. The larger changes had a ripple effect that changed the dynamics of countries that were not even remotely present or associated with the change. The Iranian Revolution and the overthrow of the Shah and taking of US hostages by Khomeini's forces, the Soviet move into Afghanistan and the creation of a Mujhahideen to counter Soviet move were just two events that started the re-structuring process of the US policy towards West and South Asia. The Iranian revolution had made the US re-work its policy towards the region. Their focus now shifted to the domestic instability in the Gulf, which they understood was providing fodder to the Soviets. The efforts till then were to alternately balance military and political power balance between Iran and Iraq, to counter Islamists and the growing Soviet influence in the region.

With the end of the Iran-Iraq war and the collapse of the Soviet Union, the US again needed to change its priorities and policies in the region. Aware of their being the sole superpower in the world, from 1993-1997, the Clinton Administration articulated a policy of 'dual containment', in an effort to keep both Iran and Iraq weak rather than preserve a power balance between them. They had to weigh the concerns of the Gulf countries whose interests they were protecting. During this period, Saudi Arabia and Kuwait were primarily concerned about the conventional threat from Iraq and wanted Iran as a counterweight to Saddam. The military options that had been repeatedly used by Saddam Hussein, had made Arab Gulf states sharing geographic borders with Iraq, apprehensive of its next move.

For the governments of the lower Gulf that were geographically further from Iraq, Iran posed a greater threat than Iraq. This pulled the US into active intervention in the regional political and military dynamics of the Arab Gulf. Whether it was the governments of states like Bahrain that accused Iran of fomenting Shiite inspired unrest in their country in 1981 and again in 1996, or the government of UAE suspecting Iranian intentions in asserting complete control over the largely uninhabited Gulf island of Abu Musa, the US as the dominant military power in the region was forced to mediate and negotiate. The aim of the dual containment policy was to weaken both Iran and Iraq so that they do not pose a threat to the Arab Gulf. With the end of the Cold War, the US now had a free hand in following a more discriminate policy in the region. Iraq could be contained economically through sanctions, and militarily by strengthening US bases in the region. Most importantly, by economically and militarily containing both regional powers, the US could now chart out a fresh approach to the Israel-Palestinian conflict.

The next phase of US intervention in the domestic politics in West Asia and North Africa, particularly in the Arab Gulf, came with 9/11 and the subsequent declaration of a Global War on Terror. 9/11 gave the US an excuse to pursue a more vigorous and assertive policy in the region. The priorities of the Bush administration had grown to include religion, the safety and security of its ally Israel and the possibility of potential Weapons of Mass Destruction in the region.

The challenge of September 11, 2001, led to the moral crusade that guided Washington's numerous strategies towards the region. Nestled in a difficult crucible of 'pre-emptive strikes', that for all practical purposes threatened to remove regimes in the name of 'liberation', the democratization agenda was disputable.[5] Under the post 9/11 campaign for promotion of democracy, western and international organizations funded numerous projects intended to help democratize Arab Gulf politics, applying a strategy conceived largely to influence post-communist transitions and political liberalization around the globe. Democracy promotion projects—broadly, those designed to enhance legislative, judicial, and civic responsibility—differed from most traditional services-delivery aid programmes in their high grant component, the channeling of funds around the executive branch of government, and the output of ideas and information.[6]

The extent of US intervention on domestic social and political structures of the Arab Gulf has been studied through the education programmes and civil society movements supported by them. Works by John Anderson[7], among others, document the mechanism of US functioning in the field of socio-political change in the Arab Gulf. They point out that the US partially funds programmes under the democratization campaign, but use the leverage to control the Arab educational system. This has been marked, particularly since the occupation of Iraq after 2001. George Bush Jr. made the Kantian logic that democracies won't fight wars with each other as the bedrock of the US foreign policy in the Arab Gulf.

A Council for Foreign Policy study on Arab democracy pointed out that with the assistance of Arab partners such as Egypt, Saudi Arabia, Jordan,

Bahrain, Kuwait, and Morocco, the United States built a remarkably good record of achieving its objectives—notably, protecting the free flow of oil from the Gulf, ensuring Israel's security, confronting rogue states, battling terrorism, and during the Cold War, containing Soviet influence in the region. Yet the terrorist attacks on New York and Washington, DC, on September 11, 2001, challenged the underlying assumption of U.S. Middle East policy that more interaction with the West would make the Arabs friendlier as a society. The Bush administration believed the best way to 'drain the swamp' that produces terrorists was to promote democracy and reform more broadly in the region.[8] The US follows a policy that contradicts itself. It has led to a situation where the US supports democracy and governments it calls 'authoritarian regimes'. It opposes radical Shiite and Sunni religio-political movements, while supporting Wahhabis and counter Islamist movements at the same time.[9]

The governments in the region are struggling to balance their power with their own societies and the socio-political aspirations of their Western allies. The challenge of democracy, till date, remains the single largest challenge to the society and polity of the Arab Gulf.

Regional Challenges

Apart from oil and the external military presence in the region, the most significant challenge that the Arab Gulf has had to face has been the challenge of religion based states in the region. The states of Pakistan, Iran and Israel use religion as a notion to give themselves an identity. Though they are not theocratic states in the classical sense of the term, they represent three important challenges to all states where Muslims are a significant part of the population.

Pakistan

The occupation of Afghanistan drew the Pakistan into the strategic balance of power in the region. Since its creation, the Pakistani Islamists variant of understanding of Islam, their idea of an Islamic state, their philosophy and political activeness have always been a challenge to the Wahhabi leadership, particularly in the global context. Also, unlike other ideological states, Pakistan had little opportunity to develop as a mere nation state, based on territory, institutions and citizenship: it always stuck to its ideological and transnational claim of being the vanguard for all Muslims, across the globe.

Since its creation, the clash of leadership for guiding Sunni Muslims has been a challenge that both state actors and non-state actors between Pakistan and the rest of the Muslim governments, particularly those of the Arab Gulf. The clash between the fundamentalists of who preached and practised the purer form of Islam came to the forefront with the Wahhabis, while the expansionist idea of Muslims being a single identity was used by the state to disparage the Islamic credentials of the governments of West Asia and North Africa. As a result, the Arab Gulf governments had to deal with the influence of the fundamentalist ideology of the Pakistani state in forums like the Organization of Islamic countries, while the Wahhabis and the Sufis have had to work towards containment of the fundamentalist ideas of the Brelvis.

As Pakistan integrated the US foreign policy into its own foreign policy, the challenge for the Arab Gulf states became a quagmire. The US and British use of the petro-dollars to fund the exercise of using the ISI to create a force of non-traditional soldiers, spreading the concept of jihad through madarsas, created a force that after successfully containing the Soviets became a loose cannon that threatens to destabilize the existing political regimes and structures across West Asia. If the creation of the non-traditional forces and movements was the first challenge that the Arab Gulf governments had to address, the second challenge that they had to address was the containment of the movements within their own territories. The contingent of Arab Gulf volunteers who joined the mujhahideen and later the Taliban or Usama's network, work on the goal of removing the US troops from the Holy Land and their own homelands.[10]

With time Pakistan posed a challenge when the US decided to use it to implement a policy of spreading Islam through madarsas, particularly the concept of violence and jihad, creating the Mujhahideen in Afghanistan to resist Soviet expansion, in the 1970s and 1980s. The role of the United States in interpreting the term jihad, teaching it through the system of madarsas across the globe[11], propagating the idea of holy warfare, grooming and arming the populations to wage the holy war and free the land of the defiling communists, has been responsible for creating a legacy of fanatics that is at war with the West today.[12]

Iran

The challenge thrown up by the successful revolution of the Iranians has only increased with time. The first challenge that the revolution threw up was in the form of having an organized Islamist movement. Ayatollah Khomeini's success lay in the organization using his formulation of an ideal Islamic State, organizing the followers in a manner that could overthrow the existing government, along with all its structures of governance, and replace it with their own. The similarities between the pre-revolutionary government under the Shah and the monarchies/ emirates of the Arab Gulf were strong. The rentier economic structures and the feudal political systems were toppled by a group of fundamentalists. Traditionally, a fundamentalist movement creates a yardstick by which it measures the performance of the other states and societies. States, societies and individuals who fall short of the ideals are seen as the 'Other', who need to be either reformed or liquidated.

Today, though the teachings and ideology of Ayatollah Khomeini remain a central point of reference for Iran, it is challenged by national, regional and international hostility and problems that require pragmatic solutions that are not always in accordance with these teachings. The world's second largest exporter of oil, with one of the largest populations in the region Iran remains a regional and international challenge. Iran's geopolitical position at the crossroads of the West Asia, the Gulf, Caucasus and Central Asia has made the country a key strategic actor. It has the region's strongest military and naval competence.

Since the Revolution of 1979 the Western world has associated Iran with irrational religious fundamentalism. The Arab Gulf governments contained the spill-over of the socio-political movements within their own borders, by buying out the Islamist leaders within their countries. The Arab Gulf states have extensively taken the assistance of external military forces for containing the fundamentalism from spreading. Stationing of the US troops is one such measure, as are the measures of creating Islamists and using international intelligence agencies to monitor the movements of trans-national Islamists. These moves have ensured that opponents of the government are identified, tracked and controlled before they could become a threat to the stability of the government.

Israel

The most important regional challenge to the Arab Gulf states comes in the form of Israel. The creation of a Jewish state, in the middle of the Muslim Arab world with no clear mandate for the same from both the sides, was enough to have put Israel on an offensive. From the struggle for Jewish statehood in the 1940s to the wars of 1967 and 1973, Israel's existence has hinged on its military strength. As a result for Israel today, security dominates the domestic political agenda above all other issues. And though Israel is seen as a militarily aggressive country, it has not relented in militarily defending what it considers morally, historically and legally its. The Israeli occupation of Palestinian territory and its attacks on Lebanon in 2006 and Gaza in 2008 did little or nothing to improve Israeli security, led to high of civilian casualties, serious accusations of war crimes, and a socio-political gulf between the region and Israel.

After its creation, with time, Israeli rhetoric became staunchly anticommunist, skillfully mobilizing friends in Washington by presenting Israel as a bulwark against communism and a strategic asset. When this appeal became anachronistic, some Israelis developed a new rhetorical basis for strategic cooperation with the United States on the basis of cooperation against fundamentalist Islam. The normalization of Israel's relations with the rest of the world, however has made it increasingly imperative over time for Israel to constantly modify its foreign policy doctrine.[13]

There has been hostility between Israel and the region, from the time of its creation. Till date, the Arab-Israeli conflict remains one of the principal drivers of insecurity in the West Asia and North Africa. The Islamists in the region focus on the Zionist rhetoric that has harboured the ambition of establishing a 'Greater Israel'. Greater Israel is an irredentist term that denotes historical and Biblical boundaries for the Land of Israel. It is an interpretation of the term of the Promised Land that led to the displacement of the Palestinians, an expansionist ambition to establish a the whole kingdom which would bring ruin to the region, according to the Islamists. Though the borders of Greater Israel are not clearly defined, it would tentatively comprise of modern-day Israel, Jordan, Lebanon, much of Egypt, Syria, Iraq, Saudi Arabia, as well as parts of Turkey and Kuwait, though the exact definition of Greater Israel is open to interpretation. The expansionist ambitions of the Israel are a challenge to the Arab Gulf. On the one hand, a hypothetical success of Greater Israel would make it a neighbour. On the other hand, it would come at the cost colonization and displacement of millions of Muslims, who look to the Arab Gulf for economic, military and religious leadership and refuge.

The issue of survival and security is a question that besieges all three states of Pakistan, Iran and Israel. The need to protect their identity in a hostile world, safeguard their uniqueness and to ensure that they are not swallowed up in the new secular world, has shaped the focus of the primary role of the state in these states. The basic insecurity of their existence has led to the states being dependent on the armed forces to be the biggest state and social player in these states. Their leaders are aware of the responsibility of making and projecting a strong religion[14], both in terms of religious discourse, and in terms of being the ideal state. The ideal state would be able to militarily and ideologically counter enemies that are perceived as strong and potentially overwhelming.

The acquisition of nuclear weapons and technology has therefore been a top priority for the three states. Though only Pakistan has till date declared its nuclear arms stockpile, the other two states have been working towards acquiring nuclear weapons. The conspiracy theory schools have declared Israel to be the most heavily nuclear armed state in Asia, after China, the claims can never be validated. However, Israel does have an access to the US weapons and technology, in case of a crisis. Also, though Iran does not have known or proven nuclear weapons it has managed to acquire the capability to assemble the technology. Being surrounded by nuclear capable states, who could turn hostile at any time, has been a challenge for the Arab Gulf governments, both in terms of diplomacy as well as military capability.

RELIGION AS A DYNAMIC FOR CHANGE

Another framework within which the events and the state and social formations of the region is analyzed uses the dynamics of religion. Islam being the dominant religion, and since the time of European colonization the only vent for socio-political and economic grievances in the region, it is understood as a fission causing variable. The role of religion in the process of state or social formation cannot be undermined. The development of a specific state and social system cannot, however, be studied in isolation. With the passage of time, as the world has shrunk due to more economic, social, cultural, political interactions, so has the development of the two systems.

With the built-in fundamentalism within Wahhabism and the rise of Usama bin Laden, the focus has been on the built in violence in the preachings of Wahhabism, and by extension, Sunni Islam. Though Wahabbism is not a sect, but as a variant of Sunni Islam, it remains one of the richest forms of Sunni Islam that the world sees today. Sunnism, does not have sects. However, there is a tradition for a re-interpretation of the Quran and the ideals of the religion in Sunnism, and Wahabbism represents one such strain of re-interpretation. Conspiracy theory credits the British with having made Wahabbism into a political, socially intolerant and illiberal movement. Abd-al-Wahhab, advocated a return to the practices of the first three generations of Islamic history, and his preaching found favour with the House of Saud. As the House of Saud gained control over the holy cities of Mecca and Medina, the outreach of Wahhabism grew across the world. With time, Wahhabism has grown to be the dominant form of Sunni Islam in Saudi Arabia. The British support to the Wahhabis and later the American support to the House of Saud has had long term implications for the socio-political developments both in the Arab Gulf and the region of West and South Asia.

THE ECONOMIC DYNAMIC

Though the region is known to be oil rich, it was only after the shift of the European industries to oil as a fuel, that the economic dynamics of the region changed. The global shift in technology to oil, the dynamics of political equations between the ruling elites and the societies within the boundaries of a nation state underwent major transformation, as did the equations between the states and societies in the region of West Asia and North Africa.

With the growing strength of oil as a source for revenue, the concept of rentier states began to be applied to the entire region. The theory was originally developed in relation to Iran's mid-20th century economy, when the Shah of Iran was able to amass major income from the nationalization of the oil revenue. Hussein Mahdavy, the economist who first popularized rentier state theory, believed that the 1951-1956 period represents a landmark in the economic history of the region. It began an era when radical nationalizations transformed ex-colonial models of petroleum exploitation into what he termed 'fortuitous etatism'. Massive amounts of foreign currency and credit generated by petroleum development, flooded the state coffers which Mahdavy argued, turned some oil-producing countries into rentier states. Kuwait and Qatar are extreme examples of the phenomenon, with limited capabilities for industrialization and few alternatives to rentierism. The case of Iran was important to Mahdavy because, given its size and potential, it had alternatives that the extreme cases lacked.[15]

Once the economy of oil became the primary economy, the governments became free of any social obligations towards their citizens. The concept of surrendering political rights by citizens in return for social services and goods provided by the government came to a naught. The accountability from the state now needed new parameters. Since the state is not dependent on taxation, the only way its society can seek accountability from its government is by seeking an accountability of its process of expenditure, particularly on the manner in which it spent it on the welfare of its citizens.

The unearned aspect of the rentier income of the Arab Gulf states has been a major cause for the Western scholarship's disdain for the Arab Gulf. The manner in which the revenue has been spent, has been a subject of debate for the last three decades. The external variable as a factor in determining the manner of expenditure is unique in the case of the Arab Gulf. Most advocates of the 'Resource curse theory' contend that after the discovery of oil, many Arab Gulf States failed to diversify and expand their economies beyond the oil sector.

There are two aspects to the debate about rentierism in the Arab Gulf. The income of the Gulf comes not from a simple sale of its oil, but from the sale of the developed products. The state needed and still needs to invest in technology for extraction of oil, refining it, and selling it in the global market. None of these technologies are present in the region. For this it needs to depend heavily on the global capitalist forces to invest and develop in the technologies of exploring oil basins, digging and refining the oil as well as marketing it in the global market.

Since the West had a stake in the rent accruing from the national resources, they were never ready to allow the country to own its own resources. The economies therefore could not be called rentier economies, as they did not own the rent totally. Through the oil conglomerates, the Western governments have been controlling the economic structures of the rentier economies. Economists like John Waterbury have classified the post-WWII economies of West Asia and North Africa as ISI (Import-Substituting-Industrialization) economies. These economies are characterized by investing capital in the industrial development projects and importing other goods that would fill the lacunae in the other sectors like agriculture or consumer products.[16]

Domestically the oil wealth brought an abundance to the region that had been witnessing chronic poverty. The 1970s saw massive infrastructural development in the region. The external intervention in the region grew, but not as a military intervention that would seek direct occupation or indirect colonization. A large part of the income of the region once again went to consultants, advisors and developers from the West. The most important part of the external investments in the Arab Gulf, till date, lies in the investments made in the military sector.

With the emphasis increasing on the social welfare sector, the Arab Gulf governments, over a period of time, have outsourced a major part of their defence duties. For example, Saudi Arabia pays over 18 billion dollars to the United States to protect Saudi sovereignty. It has allowed the US to develop a naval base within its boundaries. In return the US formally enlists Saudi Arabia as an ally, which has immense political and economic connotations in the changing political, military and economic dynamics of the region.

CONCLUSION

Since the end of the Second World War, and the discovery of the use of oil as an economic resource, the Gulf states have been confronted with the enormous challenge of developing economically while preserving social integrity, and with balancing quasi-traditional political systems with greatly enhanced regional and international responsibilities. The oil blockade by the Arabs during the 1973 Arab-Israeli conflict, brought home the economic strength of the region. It was to counter the blackmailing power of the oil economies of the region, that the United States in particular, and the Western world in general re-designed their foreign policies. Regimes were cultivated as political allies and an external legitimacy was given to governments so that they could crush any opposition they would face within their populations.

There are two aspects to the dynamics of change in the Arab Gulf. The first is regarding the role of religion in shaping the challenges of change and the state responses to it, and the second is the changing political power equations in the strategic environment of the region. Though the two are inter-related changes, a distinction needs to be made with regard to the role of the state and the role of the external forces in the situation.

The external variables that have been responsible for change, though most powerful and important, cannot be studied in isolation. The inter-linked internal movements of change also need to be evaluated within the larger context. Most of what is dubbed as a reaction to the West, like the religio-political movements of the fundamentalist Muslims, or the Shia-Sunni strife that threatens to overthrow the existing socio-political equilibrium, or the movement of establishing and funding madarsas across the globe, are changes that have implications not only within each country, but in the regional and global political scenario as well.

The biggest challenge of change that the region faces, that is largely a carryover of its history, is the challenge of the changing West. Western scholarship and understanding of the region has been in terms of grouping various aspects of society, history, geography, and polity of the region, and being selective in the understanding of the subject. The broader prism within which the region is evaluated is economic, whereby the Arab Gulf, becomes a rentier economy. Rentierism is supposed to be the primary reason why the region has failed to develop foundations for democracy, or reasonable civil society institutions.

The period from the 1950s to the 1970s was marked by a wave of nationalization of economy. The governments from Egypt to Kuwait wanted a control over the revenue that was accruing from their economies. Nationalization, as a concept ran counter to the European logic of free trade, and a process of integration of the global economy. Historically, the year 1979 was a landmark in the history of the state society relations between states and Muslims across the globe. It was the year of the Soviet invasion of Afghanistan and the ensuing mobilization of Muslims from across the globe for a jihad against the communists, it was also the year when Ayatollah Khomeini returned from exile and overthrew the established monarchy of Iran, and with the signing of the peace treaty between Israel and Egypt the regional balance of power shifted to the Arab Gulf from Egypt.

The rhetoric of the dynamics of change in the Arab Gulf would vary from countering Islamists, to containing rogue states and states that plan to acquire or build weapons of mass destruction. They would go on to include the inherent flaws in the social and economic structures of the Gulf States, if not of the states surrounding the region. The solutions too would vary from political democratization with the exclusion of the Islamists from the political processes to the promotion of reform movements within Islam. However, behind the rhetoric, the variables that shape the dynamics of change within the Arab Gulf would remain purely economic, social and political. The role of the Western world to ensure that the existing state and social formations do not undergo any significant change till it is economically beneficial and provides a strategic base for an outreach to the rest of Asia, is the biggest stabilizing factor in the dynamics of change in the region.

NOTES

1. El-Ghonemy, Riad, *Affluence and Poverty in the Middle East*, Routledge, London and New York, 1998, p. 30.
2. See Uzi Rabi, Britain's 'Special Position' in the Gulf: Its Origins, Dynamics and Legacy, in *Middle Eastern Studies*, Vol. 42, No. 3, 351-364, May 2006, p. 354.

3. Barakat, Halim, *The Arab World: Society, Culture, and State*, University of California Press, 1993, p. 6.
4. For the post Second world war politics in the Persian Gulf see, Rabi, N. 3, pp. 355-6.
5. See http://www.mepc.org/journal_vol11/0412_kechichian.asp (accessed 16 April, 2009).
6. Sheila Carapico, "Foreign Aid for Promoting Democracy in the Arab World", *Middle East Journal*, Volume 56, No. 3, Summer 2002, p. 379.
7. See *Religion, democracy and democratization*, Ed. by John Anderson, Routledge, 2006.
8. http://www.cfr.org/content/publications/attachments/Arab_Democracy_TF.pdf also see (http://news.bbc.co.uk/2/shared/bsp/hi/pdfs 04_02_08_world_bank_arab_education2.pdf accessed on 24 January, 2009).
9. http://www.saudi-us-relations.org/articles/2008/ioi/080228-khouri-respect.html (accessed on 24 January, 2009).
10. A comprehensive reading on the rise of the mujahideen, the Taliban and bin Laden is John Cooley's *Unholy Wars: Afghanistan, America and International Terrorism*, Pluto Press, 2002. It discusses the role of the combined secret service agencies from Europe to the US, Saudi and Pakistani in creating forces have in the long term contributed to creating a force that is destabilizing South Asia and is posing a serious challenge to the security of Asia and the United States. Also see, 'Afghanistan Crisis Of Impunity: The Role of Pakistan, Russia, and Iran in Fueling the Civil War', *Human Rights Watch Report*, July 2001 Vol. 13, No. 3 (C), http://www.hrw.org/reports/2001/afghan2/index.htm#TopOfPage (accessed on November 22, 2008), and "The Afghan quagmire" by M.B. Naqvi, *The News International*, http://www.thenews.com.pk/print1.asp?id=33642 (accessed November 22, 2009).
11. The idea was incorporated in the school syllabi and taught through schools and *madarsas* across Afghanistan. Today the Education Ministry of Afghanistan is attempting to reverse the literature taught in schools. It is working to erase the imageries of violence and interpretation of the terms of jihad in textbooks. The literature that was used to create the forces of *mujahideen* in Afghanistan in the 1980s, is the literature that is used by the non-state forces today to mobilize forces against the US and its allies. This literature is at the root of the teachings that are used by movements like the Taliban and also by network leaders like Osama Bin Laden or Abu Sayyaf. See "The ABC'S of Jihad in Afghanistan* Courtesy, USA", By Joe Stephens and David B. Ottaway, *Washington Post*, 23 March 2002, Posted online on 3 April 2002, http://emperors-clothes.com/news/abc.htm; and also see the news report at: http://www.cbc.ca/news/background/afghanistan/schools.html
12. The Pakistani Inter-Services Intelligence (ISI) was the inter-agent used in the majority of these activities to disguise the sources of support for the resistance. Under Reagan, U.S. support for the mujahideen evolved into an official U.S. foreign policy, known as the Reagan Doctrine, which included U.S. support for anti-Soviet resistance movements in Afghanistan, Angola, Nicaragua, and elsewhere. See http://www.freedomfiles.org/war/isi.htm (accessed 22 December 2008).

13. See Cohen, Raymond, "Israel's Starry-Eyed Foreign Policy", *Middle East Quarterly*, vol.1, no. 2, June 1994.
14. I am borrowing the term from the book, Strong Religion: The Rise of Fundamentalisms Around the World, Gabriel Almond, et.al, eds., The University of Chicago Press, Chicago, 2003.
15. What is a Rentier State?, *Biot Report #227*, June 23, 2005, http://www.semp.us/publications/biot_reader.php?BiotID=227 (accessed on 20 December 2008).
16. See the works of John Waterbury, Tim Niblock and Rodney Wilson in this regard. The *World Economic Outlook: Globalization and Inequality*, October 2007, is also a good indicator of the assessment of the Arab economy from the perspective of the financial institutions.

PART 2: MEDIA AND THE MARKET

5

Media and Democratization in the Gulf Cooperation Council Countries

Omair Anas

The information revolution that has swept the Western world over the last two decades is now transforming the Arab world. New radio stations, websites and text messaging services are just a few of the mediums breaking down cultural barriers and challenging the hardened old order.[1]

Globalization as a journey and as a destination, and as a medium and an objective involves plenty of regional and national tensions most often in the form of culture, religion and political considerations to which the Arab world is not an exception. The last century has observed great transformations in the economic makeup of the world which has also brought about major changes in the political, social and cultural domains of modern societies of nation states. Technological and scientific developments which emerged in Europe to fulfil the new and urgent requirements of its industrializing societies also empowered the people and groups which became part of democratization and the democratic process later. It is still argued that the ongoing process of globalization per se is a European Phenomenon[2] given its historical roots to Europe's transition from a 'cottage age' to a 'post-industrial society'. The people and leaders of the Arab societies and particularly of the Gulf Cooperation Council (GCC) countries have encountered the process amid global power struggles, regional conflicts and ideological and cultural clashes. The Arab world's response to the political changes of the world is determined, to a great extent, by these tensions and conflicts. Democratization and political reform projects have been influenced by these determinants. Media can facilitate the social and cultural changes as well as political reforms; however, media in liberal democratic systems and media in non-liberal democratic systems are driven by different imperatives. Market and ideology are points of divergence for media in either system. The democratization process tries to bring the market as the centre of society and defines societies in context of market dynamics. In this paper we will try to identify how far media can facilitate the democratization process in the GCC region.

CONTEXTUALIZING GCC MEDIA

State is meant to be a sovereign authority, sovereignty based both on consent and coercion, with clear territory and legitimacy to rationalize its authority. Tribes in the Arab Gulf region constitute a different solidarity based on kinship, unlike western states, where 'mechanical solidarity'[3] is the only basis of state citizen relation. The modern nation state had posed serious challenges to existing quasi-tribal quasi state structures in the Arab world. The post world war political settlements and the discovery of oil further necessitated re-arrangement of the state, making new alliances of tribes, religious groups and urban ruling elites in the Gulf countries. Religion became the only source of legitimacy for the newly developed state mechanism in the region. The tribal chieftainship and state authority often clash with each other in modern Gulf States. The 'Identity of Arabness' continued as the major identity beyond the modern and newly formed nation states in the Arab world. In their search for their own national identities, media provided (newly emerged states with the) the best tool to create a sense of national identity through controlling and regulating media content.[4]

Circulation of tribes in the ruling system was a salient feature of the 'Natural State' which existed till its collapse in mid nineteenth century mainly due to the entrenched sea power of Britain and loss of control over the Ottomans. Following the collapse of the 'Natural State', from being commercial ports to the tribal interior, Arab Gulf States gradually lost their political gravity in favour of urban ruling elites. Interest groups were reconstituted and reformed which led to the emergence of the state in which tribes rather than sea traders played dominant roles. Emergence of dynastic rule was the direct outcome of the end of a circulation system which existed during the period of the 'Natural State.' The changing political economy of the Gulf States further allowed border disputes in the Gulf region which had never seemed important during the Ottoman period. The period between the treaties of 'Perpetual Truce' in 1853 to Uqair Conference in 1922, marked by appearances of new boundaries in the Arab Gulf, led to the birth of concepts of territory based sovereignty and nationality. Before the emergence of new boundaries, these tribes knew no borders or territories. The introduction of borders was strange for them and they resisted such new political identities. Being the land of the Prophet and subsequently the Prophet's companions' propagation of Islamic values, the tribal social structures remained closely attached with religion and religious authorities. Tribal values co-opted religion easily and Islam did not dismantle the tribal structure at once, rather the neo-patriarchal structure prevailed and religion and tribalism helped each other. Hosting pilgrimages like Hajj and Umrah were not only the source of their annual income, but also source of legitimacy. France and Britain facilitated the emergence of Arab states on the global map without Ottoman control. Since Religion became an important source of legitimacy, the Ottomans were blamed with violating Islamic rules and thereby causing the decline of Islam.[5]

Direct foreign control by the French or British authorities in the Gulf region often met with strong indigenous resistance by religious leaders, unlike in Egypt and Levant where Arab nationalism had played a vital role. The Zaidi Movement in Yemen from 1676, the Ibadi Movement in Muscat from 1718 and the Wahabi-Saudi Movement in Najd from 1744 dominate the political landscape of the Gulf region till today. Religious sensitivities played a vital role in the impending cultural face of the region, mainly in the domain of freedom of expression in which media constituted key position. Oil, religion and security issues have had lasting effects on the media regime in the GCC region.

Amongst the important political developments which have affected the GCC media are the Civil War in Oman, the Dhofar Rebellion in 1962-1975, the Iranian Revolution in 1979, the Iran-Iraq War from 1980 to 1988, the Iraqi aggression on Kuwait, and the subsequent Operation Desert Storm led by U.S. against Iraq in January 1991. These events have also exposed the vulnerability of the GCC states as opposed to the European states and thereby forced them to define press laws.

In a region where political systems developed on patriarchal relationship, media's ideal role would also be appropriated in that framework. Media's role to promote political accountability, freedom of expression and democratic political culture has evolved in a European context where democracy and other political discourses have emerged during industrialization process. Nationalism as an imaginative practice had also come out as part of 'Print Capitalism' and 'Print Nationalism.' Media have been considered as the fourth estate in democratic countries and Information Communication Technology (ICT) has become benchmark for the democratization process. The question arises in the context of Arab and GCC region where do these societies stand in these paradigms? Theoretically, do Arab and GCC societies fulfil the criterion of being an 'Information Society' or 'Network Society'? With the fact that the GCC region stands highest in the Arab index of ICT, their potential to transform into a democratic system is still debatable. (See Tables 5.1) Two of the 'Third Waves,' namely, Agriculture and Industrial Waves have not occurred in the GCC states. Their direct encounter with the third wave (oil industry) may not produce similar socio-political situations as the industrialization did in Network Societies of the western world.

Industrialization was the main force behind the Western media which expanded its economic gains in the market economy whilst Arab media like other third world media emerged as an idealist media to protect national identities and support national movements. Here, journalists considered themselves as the vanguards of freedom, self-determination and religious

Table 5.1: Aspects of Political Leadership to Promote Use of ICT

	ICT Strategy Clearly spelled out	*ICT Implementation Plan Clearly articulated***	*Operational ICT-Dedicated Research Facilities*	*Plan of ICT-Dedicated Research Facilities*	*Operational Technopole Initiative*	*Plan of Technopole Initiative*	*Existence of Technology Incubator*	*Planed Technology Incubator*
Gulf								
Kuwait	✓	✗	✓	✓	✗	✓	✓	✓
Saudi Arabia	✓	✓	✓	✓	✓	✓	✓	✓
Bahrain	✓	✓	✓	✗	✗	✓	✓	✓
Qatar	✓	✗	✗	✗	✗	✗	✓	✓
U.A.E.	✓	✓	✓	✓	✓	✓	✓	✓
Oman	✗	✗	✗	✓	✗	✓	✓	✓
Levant								
Lebanon	✓	✓	✓	✓	✗	✓	✓	✓
Syrian AR	✗	✗	✗	✓	✗	✓	✓	✓
Jordan	✓	✓	✓	✓	✓	✓	✓	✓
Egypt	✗	✓	✓	✓	✓	✓	✓	✓
Maghreb								
Tunisia	✓	✓	✓	✓	✗	✓	✓	✓
Algeria	✗	✓	✓	✓		✓	✓	✓
Morocco	✓	✓	✓	✓	✓	✓	✓	✓

Key. ✓ = Yes, ✗ = No.

* Our definition is that an ICT strategy is clear when individual countries publish a set of strategic in the held, enter through a national plan or some other medium or mark measurable and quantifiable accomplishments up to milestone path.

** Our definition is that an ICT plan is clear and operational when budgets have been dedicated to the ICT strategy, a task force, whatever the format, is operationally in place and when clearly published implementation process is underway.

Source : http://www.weforum.org/pdf/Global_Competitiveness_Reports/Reports/GITR_2002_2003/content.pdf revival. In idealist role, Arab media was closely attached with all the ideological groups struggling for freedom or revival of Islam. Kai Hafez argues that in the West, identification of mass media with or as 'political parties' easily discredits their objectivity claims. The media in authoritarian countries have to face a double challenge. The extraterritorial situation of satellite television enables them to take over a number of the functions of political parties and political movements. The idea of Arab broadcasting being able to articulate and mobilize civil society, and encourage democratic transformation is surely a part of the fascination with these media.[6]

Capacity of media to facilitate or create situation for changes is well recognized by media scholars, however, they underscore that the direction of change in each country and society can't be identical. With two different contexts, expectation that *Al-Jazeera* and *Al-Arabiya* should act like *Cable News Network (CNN)* or *British Broadcasting Corporation (BBC)* will be a naïve expectation. Nonetheless, there are internal and external pressures which further allow media proliferation in the region and subsequently, the proliferation of information networks and ICT penetration, which is one of the standards of democratization set by the United Nations Educational, Scientific and Cultural Organization (UNESCO). Of some pressures, demographic pressures in the form of youth bulge, diversification of economic bases and lessening dependency over oil and petroleum products, countering religious extremism and defending national identities can be figured as important internal pressures. Externally, security concerns stemmed from the conflict situations in Iraq, US—Iran-Israel tensions, and terrorism pose serious pressures.

Demographic Limitations

Gulf countries have had a huge deficit of human resources both in terms of quality and quantity. With the lowest expenses in Research and Development added to a limited local population, GCC states are completely dependent on an expatriate work force, keeping their traditionally educated workforce in the public sector regardless of their work product. Extensive developmental projects, mainly of construction sector, have been planned and initiated after the first and second oil boom. Building huge infrastructure and service networks requires enormous amounts of human resources which is not possible without allowing foreign workers from across the world to enter the GCC states.

Local population growth rate is among the highest levels in the world and it is projected that Arab countries have to create 100 million jobs up to 2025. The youth population in the GCC region is more advanced and used to experience global consumerism, unlike earlier generations. With visible knowledge deficit, GCC leaders have to fulfil economic, social and political aspirations of their youth population.

Diversification of economy has been recognized as the principal way to face the challenge. The dominance of oil revenues in their national economy, characterized as rentier economy, has kept away their local population from participating in productive activities. Engaging local people in non-oil sectors is identified as a way to participate in globalized economic interaction.

In recent years, Gulf States have allowed the entry of the private sector which has led to the emergence of the middle class, though somewhat dependent. Though the reversed principle of 'No Taxation without Representation'[7] is main characteristic of newly emerging middle and entrepreneur class, the people engaged in private sectors tend to seek for more participation in state affairs. Educated women are emerging in the workforce, especially in Bahrain, Qatar, and the United Arab Emirates (UAE). Kuwait has pioneered amongst the GCC states in granting more political rights to women. In recent years all GCC states have introduced gradual political reforms. The way GCC states respond to the political aspirations of local people will decide the nature of political transition in the region. The pattern of reform initiatives in recent years suggest that the GCC countries are heading towards 'Oasis' or 'Fertile Gulf' rather than 'Sandstorm' scenario. The Oasis scenario according to World Economic Forum (WEF) describes a scenario in which the GCC states are nevertheless able to achieve substantial institutional reforms. The Fertile Gulf scenario describes the rise of the GCC countries as innovation hubs in a global environment characterized by robust demand for energy and increasing globalization.[8] To make this transition smooth, based on economy and development concerns, they are forced to employ accommodative strategies rather than suppressing the opposing voices as media proliferation, ICT and information technologies (IT) have reduced the choices of states.

In these contexts, Arab GCC states have adopted cautious strategies to respond to external and internal challenges, prevent political fallouts of media proliferation as well as ensure economic gains. GCC countries along with other Arab states have been forced to respond to the media proliferation industry facilitated by globalization. GCC countries have allowed media in four different strategies as Mohammad I. Ayish has hypothesized[9]:

Re-inventing state broadcasting into more independent structure
Emulating private broadcasters' practices, especially in entertainment
Launching alternative "state affiliate" broadcasting services with private character
Allowing "non state affiliated" broadcasters to operate

An overview of GCC media would reveal the fact that most of the media outlets in late 1990s were initiated within aforesaid strategies. For example in Saudi Arabia impact of *Cable News Network (CNN)* during Operation Desert Storm was so pervasive on Arab audiences that it created an immediate call for their own media networks to substitute CNN. Members of the ruling Saudi family came forward and invested in the installation of satellite Arabic television channels in Europe. Other countries followed suit by launching their own channels. *Middle East Broadcast Corporation (MBC)* was first Saudi media venture initiated privately by Prince Walid Ibrahim in London in 1991 followed by *Arab Radio and Television* jointly by Prince Saleh Kamel and Prince Alwalid bin Talal and *Orbit* by Khalid bin Abdulla in late nineties. MBC owner Prince Walid Ibrahim was close to the King Fahad. Al-Jazeera's main rival TV network Dubai based *Al-Arabiya* is also offshoot of MBC. Saudi Research and Marketing Group, (SRMG) is umbrella media company run by Saudi government. The leading pan *Arab news* paper *Al-Sharq al Awsat* started in 1978, Arab news (English Daily) started in 1975 are run by Saudi Research and Publishing Company (SRPC), a SRMG firm. In Qatar after dismantling ministry of information in 1996 Qatari government introduced *Al-Jazeera* as a private satellite TV with huge financial assistance. The assistance still continues as *Al-Jazeera* failed to make itself a profitable venture largely due to economic boycott by American and Saudi companies. UAE left behind of Saudi and Qatari media experiment in 1990s, UAE adopted multipronged strategies. Dubai Media City (DMC) is a completely new where media are regulated by Technology and Media Free Zone Authority. Outside of media city there are limited media outlets and are mostly controlled by the state like Abu Dhabi TV and other news papers.

Given the nature of ownership, the procedures for appointing editors and the legal framework for media regulations are all carved out according to the aforesaid strategies. Arab media outlets can be seen closely attached with ruling families in various ways. It can be argued that media networks in the GCC regions, to some extent, have been started as political projects of states rather than independent units of the media market driven by profit gains. Economic imperatives behind media proliferation, especially in news media, are still unclear. Economic aspects of the media industry involve a wide range of factors which include audience surveys, expansion of the advertisement market, competition to control broadcast market and competition for other profit making media industry. The region has shown some progress in all of these standards which is not enough to prove that the broadcast industry is mainly for economic and commercial purposes. Frequent bans on Al-Jazeera in a variety of Arab states, launching counter Al-Jazeera TV channels, economic boycott of Al-Jazeera by Saudi companies in the region provides ample of proof that a lot of politics is involved in the current media proliferation in the region. Lack of transparency in media auditing, absence of independent unions for media professionals, media regulation authorities and independent media watchdogs are the common features of GCC media. Some media experts have called news channels as 'political pornography' or 'soft porn,'[10] given their obsession with politics. In an absence of direct linkages between commercial output and growth of media, channels are turning to governments or individuals allied with governments to cover their losses. This continued dependency on the government is bound to dilute media's role in social change. This further supports the suggestion that privatization of satellite TV in the region and the democratization process is unlikely to be facilitated by these media.[11]

RECENT MEDIA REFORMS AND DEMOCRATIZATION

A brief appraisal of current media reforms as part of the democratization and political reform process in the region will be useful to further discussion. Here, country wise media reforms are being discussed: (See Table 5.2).

Bahrain[12]

The 1965 Press Law continued till the country underwent major reforms facilitated by the Emir and the 2002 Press Law was introduced. According to the 2002 Press Law, offences "against the Islamic faith, the unity of the people, and the person of the king," "inciting division or sectarianism," undermining the country's security and libel are punishable by prison sentences of six months to five years. An alternative law was drafted in 2005 by a group of Members of Parliament and submitted to the Parliament. In August 2005, the government announced that it would replace the Information Ministry with the Bahrain Radio and Television Commission, the new regulatory commission for the media. Though private print media is allowed, broadcast media outlets are still run by the government. A special draft law regulating the licensing of private television and radio channels was endorsed by the Shura Council in 2004 and submitted to the Parliament for consideration.

There are 17 categories under which journalists are accountable to their editors, media owners, and to the government, and can be penalized. The Upper House of the Parliament passed a revised draft of the press law that would decriminalize press offences, protect the confidentiality of sources, ensure access to official information, and end criminal responsibility for publishers. Nevertheless, the draft law still needs to be passed by the Lower House, an elected body heavily influenced by conservative religious perspectives, which rejected a similar bill three years prior. The government in May 2008 proposed amendments to decree-Law Number 47 of 2002 to the Parliament. According to these proposals, all prison sentences for media workers will be abolished along with other offences. An independent monitor will be appointed, rather than a government official, who would look after media businesses.

Among key articles amended in recent media reforms are Article 16 and Article 86, according to which prison sentences are abolished for distributing

Table 5.2: GCC Media Laws

Bahrain	2003	1979	Ministry of Information (MOI)	Bahrain Journalist Association	Print/TV	Yes	Yes	No
Kuwait	2006	1961	MOI	Kuwait Journalist Association	Print/ TV (2004)	Yes	No	No
Oman	2004 Private Radio and Television Companies Law	1984	MOI	Omani Journalist Association (2005	Print only	Yes	No	No
Qatar	Ministry of Information is abolished	1979	MOI	Pending	Print only	No	No	No
Saudi Arabia	1963 Publishing and Printing Law	1963 Publishing and Printing Law	Ministry of Culture and Information	Saudi Journalist Association (2003)	Print only	Yes	Yes	No
UAE	New Media Law is approved in Aoril 2009	UAE Federal Law No. 15 of 1980 for Printed Matter and Publications	MOI	UAE Journalist Association	Print only/ TV in Media Cities	Yes	Yes	No

Source: Adapted from 'Report on Arab Journalists 2005, Arab Federation of Journalists' (http://www.faj.org.eg/reportinfo.asp?which=37) and 'Media Sustainability Index, Middle East 2005 IREX'.

publications without a licence, before they are granted or after being banned or cancelled (Articles 16 and 86). Abolition of Article 21 under which foreign publications could be seized and even though distribution of these publications still has to be authorized, a refusal can in future be appealed (Article 17). Likewise, under Article 4 paragraph 5, a reason must be given for any refusal to grant a licence to a printer. Opening up printing, publishing and press activities for foreigners has been allowed with some preconditions in Article 7.

Kuwait[13]

The Press and Publishing Law of 1961 provided sanctions for fines and imprisonment. The 1976 amendments further empowered authorities to suspend the licenses but later these restrictions were softened. Now Kuwait is in the process of revising its 1961 Press Law of which the first package of amendments has been introduced in 2006.

The 2006 Press Law includes a prohibition list in which the publication of material that insults God, the Prophets, the companions of the Prophet, the family of the Prophet, Islamic beliefs, criticism of the King, disclosing secret or private information, or calling for the regime's overthrow are prohibited and subject to criminal charges. Citizens can also point out such charges and demand legal action against press persons and authors. The Ministry of Information controls and regulates the media, and approves license to media outlets. However, the new law makes clear that licenses should be issued within 90 days of application, and if other wise an explanation for the delay or refusal should be provided. The new law also restricts the ministry's right to cancel the license without approval of a court order.

Article 36 and 37 of the Kuwaiti Constitution protects the freedom of speech and the freedom of the press; "Freedom of opinion and scientific research shall be guaranteed. Every person shall have the right to express and propagate his opinion verbally, in writing or otherwise, in accordance with the conditions and procedures specified by law." However, the conditions of "in accordance with the conditions and in the circumstances defined by law" restrict the freedom (UNHCR). Nowadays, Kuwait seems to be the most tolerant country for media where private newspapers were already allowed and private broadcasting has been allowed since 2006.

Oman[14]

In a major breakthrough for media reforms, the 2004 Private Radio and Television Companies Law allowed the licensing of private broadcast media for the first time in the last 35 years. As a result of Private Radio and Television Companies Law of 2004, one private television broadcasting station began in 2005 and three private radio stations, besides two state-owned television stations. Most of the newspapers are owned by private owners with close links to the royal family. Among prohibited practices in media, libel, voicing criticisms of the Sultan, or printing material that leads to "public discord, violation of the security of the state, or abusing a person's dignity or rights" are treated as criminal offences. The Ministry of Information (MOI) is empowered to regulate and monitor media and may censor any material regarded as politically, culturally, or sexually offensive. MOI may also issue licenses to journalists for their profession which discourages freelance journalism. Revocation of journalists' licenses is decided by the ministry.

Qatar[15]

Qatar is known for its forthright pan-Arab satellite network *Al-Jazeera* and many political reforms carried out by the Emir Khalifa after his accession to power in 1995. The 2003 Constitution includes freedom of expression as a constitutional right. Amongst the most striking features of the Qatari media regime is the revocation of Ministry of Information. Qatar became the first Arab country without a Ministry of Information since 1995.

Criticizing the government, the ruling family, or Islam are subject to prosecution under the penal code. By law, all publications are subject to licensing by the government.

Before revocation of the Ministry of Information, Law No. 8, 1979 was enforced, which included 102 articles with similar features as that of other GCC countries. In the absence of any formal press law, the old press law is still being practiced which allows the Qatar Radio and Television Corporation, and customs officers to censor both domestic and foreign publications, and broadcast media, for religious, political, and sexual content prior to distribution. However, Qatar gave a strong message to other Arab countries by abstaining from a meeting of Ministers of Information of the Arab League, which approved a new charter to control and censor satellite channels and transmissions.

Saudi Arabia[16]

Print and Publishing Regulation passed in 1963 regulates both print and electronic media. The Press Law elaborates three main areas: establishment of any media outlet, rights and responsibilities of journalists, and penalties. Ministry of Culture and Information is empowered to issue licenses, regulate media activities, revoke licenses and control the Saudi Journalists Association's governing board by allowing only approved candidates to run in its elections. The ministry also appoints the Editor-in-Chief and the Chairman of the Board in all companies from among candidates chosen by each board. It also has the power to dismiss them.

The press is also closely checked by the Director-General of Broadcasting, Press and Publications. A 1982 Royal Decree also requires journalists to adhere to stringent self-censorship specifically dealing with foreign or national Heads of State. The press is basically considered as a tool to educate people, inform government views, and promote national unity. Criticism of the royal family and the religious authorities is forbidden, and press offences are punishable by fines and imprisonment.

United Arab Emirates (UAE)[17]

UAE is engaged in reshaping its media regime profile to make it more media friendly. A redrafting exercise of the existing press law, i.e. the UAE Federal Law No. 15 of 1980 for Printed Matter and Publications has concluded in April 2009 after the approval of the new draft law by the President. The new law has cancelled penalizing journalists. The UAE law like other GCC press laws prohibits criticism of government, rulers and ruling families, and friendly governments. All publications are required to have licenses from the state.

The UAE, in its effort to reshape media, has undertaken a unique experiment which has resulted in the creation of Media Cities. The experiment of Media Cities proved to be economically vibrant and profitable. Dubai Media City started working in 2004 and is now the home of nearly 550 media companies including *CNN*, Sony Broadcast and Professional, McGraw Hill publication, and *Al Arabia*. The London-based Saudi company *Middle East Broadcasting Centre (MBC)* has also shifted to the Dubai Media City. The Dubai Media City media companies are not under jurisdiction of local laws and enjoy greater freedom to function. For example, 100 per cent foreign ownership is allowed, unlike outside of free zones which has a limit of 49 per cent. Creativity City, under Fujairah Culture and Media Authority (FCMA), and the Abu Dhabi government are also working out similar projects in competition with Dubai. The Ministry of Information and the government run newspapers and television stations, etc. The closure of the Ministry of Information and Culture in 2006 was followed by the establishment of a National Media Council (NMC) and the creation of a separate ministry for Culture, Youth and Community Development. The National Media Council's role is to supervise all media developments in UAE. All jurisdiction of the earlier Ministry of Information came to NMC. Private media is closely linked with ruling families.

NEW MEDIA LAW 2009

The UAE Federal National Council (legislature) had passed a new Media Law in January 2009 whose draft has been approved by the Supreme Council and the President in April 2009 after a cross section debate amongst UAE's civil society, right groups and government officials. The new UAE Press Law, a revision of the Press and Publications Federal Law of 1980, states that there shall not be prior censorship of any media outlets in the country.

The new law has also attracted sharp criticism from rights groups[18], because the new law fails to enhance the freedom of media. The legislation threatens to fine anyone who publishes information that damages the UAE.'s reputation or harms its economy. Potential fines range from 50,000 U.A.E. Dirhams ($13,600) for minor violations to as much as 1 million Dirhams for criticizing the ruling family. The only relief given to journalists is to protect them from imprisonment in the course of their professional duties.

MEDIA AND DEMOCRATIZATION: A CRITIQUE

Media's capacity to bring political change is always seen with scepticism by social scientists. Big media like TV channels are not considered fit for initiating changes for two reasons: domination of organizational goals—politics or market forces hinder media from engaging in changing the status quo of the state, rather its own survival requires state support in some form or the other; Secondly, the media was never considered as a primary social actor, but rather was determined by actors such as the government, lobbies, or political parties.

However, this perspective seems to work only for terrestrial TV which developed only by the state's direct help. Emergence of transnational satellite channels and new media like internet and digital media products require a regulation beyond the nation state regulators. In the age of globalization, geo-linguistic unity and regionalism has come to use it in the early democratization process. (Hafez: 2004) Arab televisions have shown a great deal of interest in the reforms debate and the democratization process. Especially in a region where other political and social institutions and the civil society are so weak, media tends to fill the vacuum. In the absence of political parties, media's emphasis on political change assumes extra responsibilities which contradicts media's ideally prescribed role as "informers" and "educators".

Extending Alterman's argument that 'the technological changes seem likely to a restructuring of power relationship in the Arab world", it can be proposed that GCC states are bound to share power more and more both domestically and regionally. GCC is the region where most of the print media outlets are privately owned, though by members of ruling families. Differences of opinion within different newspapers over internal issues, religious extremism, moderate Islamic values, etc. (for example, differences between *Al-Jazeera* daily and *Al-Watan* of Saudi Arabia) show that media's role is still important. Clashes of opinion are discernable in different media outlets. Each group is propagating its own opinion beyond immediate commercial calculations.[19] Surveys support that most of the media professionals from 14 Arab countries are in favour of democratic change and identify themselves as democrats however Islamists and nationalists distance themselves from it.

ARAB JOURNALISTS' POLITICAL PHILOSOPHY

Muneera Fakhroo, a Bahraini journalist and social activist, counts three taboos of GCC media: Religion, Sex and Politics.[20] Media is prohibited to deal with these taboos freely obstructing the evolution of GCC media into a freer media. Added by ownership pattern, these taboos and other political and cultural considerations invite stringent media laws, self-censorship and secret media regulations. In case of Saudi Arabia, for example, dismissal of editors and journalists is very common. In 2003 Jamal Kashoggi, a leading intellectual and editor of liberal newspaper *Al-Watan*, was relieved and reinstated after four years in 2007. The much hyped success story of *Al-Jazeera* is also somehow similar, which only made better use of self-censorship in favour of its channel, for example *Al-Jazeera's* excessive coverage of international news and least attention to local news. *Al-Jazeera's* typical coverage policies manifest the realization that criticizing the local government would cost the channel without any substantial results in popularity. Even the very debate of democratization and reform is packaged in the format of international politics and as part of an American project though it is not the only aspect. The "red lines" have been outlined by all media outlets as not to be crossed by their journalists. Issues such as the ruling family, Islam, and national unity are treated with great sensitivity and fall under "red lines." Criticizing friendly nations or presenting

Table 5.3: "Politically, which philosophy best describes you?"

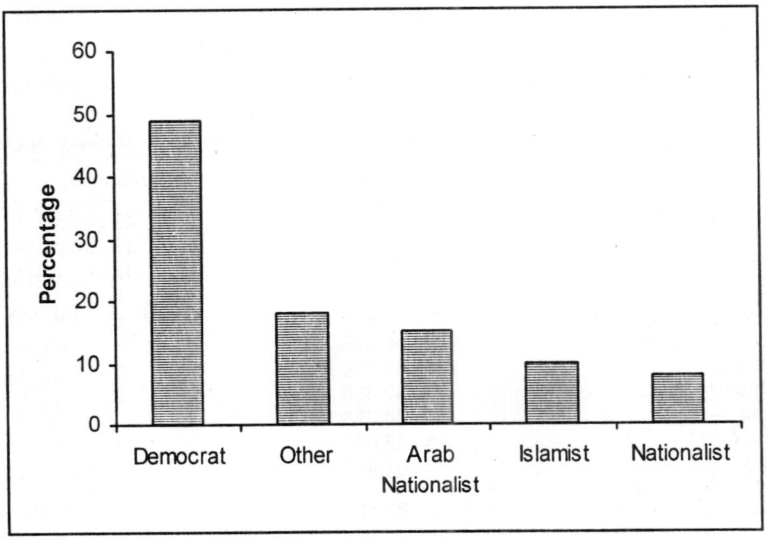

Source: Pintak, Lawrence (2008) *The role of the media as watch dogs, agenda setters and gatekeepers in Arab states*, Harvard World Bank Workshop 29, 31st May, 2008.

views that challenge the state's position on particularly sensitive national issues is also discouraged.[21]

In the middle of these contexts, there are positive developments visible which ultimately normalize the reform process by developing public opinion. For example, expanding the service sector is something agreed upon by most of the GCC leaders in order to diversify their economies. Media, and especially the broadcast media industry, is potentially the most profitable sector which is still untapped in the region. A few experiments in UAE and Bahrain have supported the idea. For example, the GCC region is now hosting nearly half a dozen satellites to cater to media services in the Arab and GCC regions.[22] Among the present satellites in GCC, Bahrain based *NoorSat* has been launched in December 2004, Al Yah Satellite Communications Company PJSC (*Yahsat*) is also a private joint stock company fully owned by Mubadala (an investment arm of the Government of Abu Dhabi), Kuwait based *GulfSat* established in partnership with the Ministry of Communications, Kuwait and global industry leader Hughes Network Systems USA, Abu Dhabi based telecommunication satellite Thuraya, and the very recently announced first private satellite in broadcast industry '*SmartSat*' which will be started from Dubai with a $500 million investment from Kuwaiti and Jordanian TV companies.[23]

Like the satellite industry, the advertisement industry is also expanding in the GCC region. Data shows that the GCC region is spending 41 per cent on advertisement expenses. Advertisement industry trends show that media outlets are in competition with each other to have a larger slice in the advertisement cake. This further requires restructuring media (See Table 5.4).

Table 5.4 : Statex-Multi Country: Cumulative Quantitative Monitoring from January to December 2007

Amount in USD

Country	*Amount*	*Amount %*
Pan Arab	3,675,703,670	43
UAE	1,470,032,979	17
KSA	1,081,974,526	13
Lebanon	571,343,957	7
Kuwat	500,692,915	6
Egypt	427,455,293	5
Jordan	275,033,900	3
Bahrain	198,537,428	2
Qatar	188,324,325	2
Oman	95,882,640	1
Syria	18,001,492	0
Total	8,502,983,126	100

IPSOS-STAT/Statex © Printed 13-2-2008

Source: Ipsos State 2007 accessed http://mediame/sites/default/files/Ipsos2007 Bycountry.pdf

In a more positive outlook, media's potential role in reform discourses is supported by the view that the media industry in GCC is gradually transforming into a more professional media. In its report about Arab media IREX Washington has surveyed in 2005 Arab media in five areas, namely, Free Speech, Professional Journalism, Plurality of News Resources, Business Management, and Supporting Institutions. Despite all odds GCC states have topped the Arab region and have shown greater interest in promotion of media although appropriated in their own strategy to minimize negative political fallouts. (See Table 5.5)

CONCLUSION

In the Arab world where democracy and political freedom are still long awaited goals, media can facilitate the democratization process. Notions such as 'Satellite Democracy' and 'Television Democracy' have been frequently used to indicate the rapid change in the media landscape of GCC region especially after the arrival of *Al-Jazeera* in Qatar. Arab public sphere involvement in political re-imagination has now become a regular practice of GCC media outlets which have initiated many political discussions. Although media's capacity to convert mediated political debates into full fledged systematic political pluralism is limited, its capacity to facilitate the process and force the trio of owners, regulators and audiences to respond to global changes positively has significantly increased. Arab audiences are not equivalent to voter citizens nor do the satellite channels seem identical to the political groupings, yet their capacity to create a new political imagination will determine the direction of the democratization process. Creating a Pan-Arab political imagination such as the one by *Al-Jazeera*, New Arabism i.e. *Al-Arabiya*, strengthening national identities or reassertion of global Islamic identity as part of a global 'Ummah' are a few political debates which have been facilitating the political process. The way to democracy has become complex and confused and some times poses contradictory to Islam and 'Arabness.' In this context, that 'democracy' should be the only result of awaited political reforms can be a naïve supposition. GCC media represent the scepticism towards the West-driven campaign for democratization under various programmes like Greater Middle East Initiative and others. This further requires exploring the constituents of popular world views of Arab and GCC media which has been discussed earlier in contextualizing the GCC media discussion. Media in the Arab world is operating in an evident political vacuum which could have created mobilization for political activities. This is where Arab civil society shows a certain degree of ambivalence about democracy. Democratization as a process of transition from an 'undemocratic' form of governance to a 'democratic' form requires supporting institutions or political parties lacking in the region. Media nowhere

Table 5.5: Index of All Objectives in Arab Media—Average Scoring for All objectives, 2005

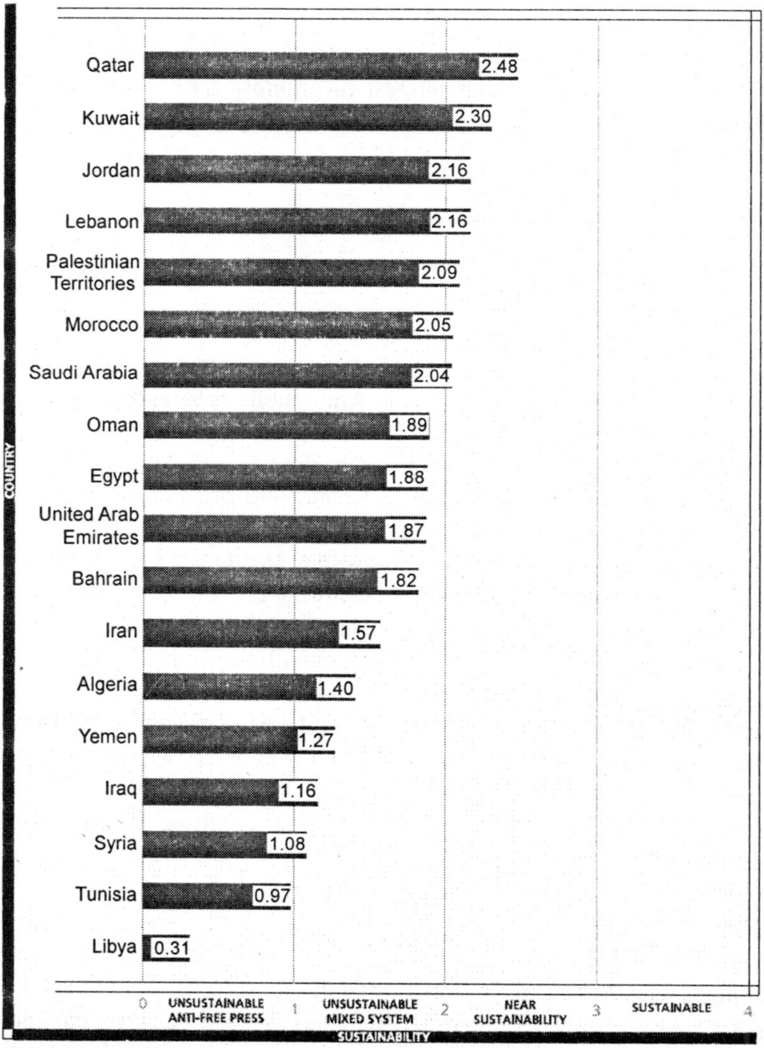

Source: IREX, Media Sustainability Index Middle East and North Africa 2005.

can play a dual role of a political party as well as an 'informer or educator'. The failure of American sponsored Arabic TV channel Al-Hurra presents a good example which started political discourses which had no local receivers and was regarded as a tool for American propaganda. In conclusion, media's main function lies with its capability to create a political imagination closer to democratic reforms. Such a process is neither a switch on-off process nor an impossible task. Media in the absence of political institutions or parties and civil society have to deal with existing institutions like religion, tribes and ruling elites. In this complex situation media's role in the GCC states becomes very crucial but with sufficient potential to influence the debate of democratization even though they are controlled and financed by the undemocratic ruling class.

NOTES

1. MeHugh, Kristin (2006), 24/7: *The rise and Influence of Arab Media*, Stanley Foundation
2. Ferguson, Marjorie (1992), The Mythology about Globalization, *European Journal of Communication*, Vol. 7, No. 1, pp. 69-93.
3. Khouri, (Koshener: 1991), *Tribes and State formation in the Middle East*, pp. 93, California: University of California Press.
4. Alterman, Jon B. (1999), Shrinking the World and Changing the Rules, *Middle East Insight* March-April 1999 (30-32).
5. Naqeeb, al Khaldun Hasan, (1990), *Society and state in the Gulf and Arab Peninsula: a different perspective* London: Taylor & Francis. pp. 50-75.
6. Hafez, Kai, (2004), *Arab Satellite Broadcasting: An Alternative to Political Parties*?, Cambridge Arab Media Project: The Media and Political Change in the Arab World, 29-30 September 2004
7. Sakr, Naomi (2003) Freedom of expression, accountability and development in the Arab region, *Journal of HumanDevelopment*, 4 (1). pp. 29-46, March 2003, accessed online 15 Januray 2009 URL: http://westminsterresearch.wmin.ac.uk/1282/1/Sakr_2003_final.pdf.
8. World Economic Forum (2007) Gulf State Scenarios: GCC Countries and the World: Scenarios to 2025 accessed 20 March 2009 URL: http://www.weforum.org/pdf/scenarios/GCC_report.pdf
9. Dynamics of Development in Arab Broadcasting accessed 24.02.2009 URL: http://www.iue.it/RSCAS/Research/Mediterranean/mrm2008/pdf/13_WS-Description.pdf
10. Fandy, Mamoun (2008) The Al-Qaeda/Israel Riddle, *Al-Sharq al Awsat* 3rd February 2008, accessed 20.03.09 URL: http://www.aawsat.com/english/news.asp?section=2&id=11661
11. Sakr, Naomi (2004), Privatization Alone Will Not Loosen Arab Governments' Grip on Broadcasting, *Arab Reform Bulletin*, December 2004, Volume 2, Issue 11.

12. IREX MENA Media Laws in the Gulf, Accessed 20 March 2009 URL: http://www.irex-mena.org/programs/medialaws.asp
    Reporters without Borders (2008) Bahrain: Press law amendments hailed but journalists still face jail and websites risk closure, released on 4th July. Accessed 20th March 2009 URL: http://www.hrea.org/lists2/display.php?language_id=1&id=9011)
    Freedom House, *Freedom of the Press 2008-Bahrain*, 29 April 2008. accessed 11 April 2009 URL: http://www.unhcr.org/refworld/docid/4871f5ed28.html
    IREX MENA (2005) Media Sustainability Index, Washington, PP 133-147
13. Freedom House, (2008) Freedom of the Press Kuwait, Accessed 11 April 2009. URL: http://www.unhcr.org/refworld/docid/4871f612c.html
    IREX MENA Media Laws in the Gulf, Accessed 20 March 2009 URL: http://www.irex-mena.org/programs/medialaws.asp
    IREX MENA (2005) Media Sustainability Index, Washington PP 182-193.
14. Freedom House, (2008) Freedom of the Press Oman, Accessed 11 April 2009. URL: www.unhcr.org/refworld/publisher,FREEHOU,OMN, 4871f6242,0.html
    IREX MENA Media Laws in the Gulf, Accessed 20 March 2009 URL: http://www.irex-mena.org/programs/medialaws.asp
    IREX MENA (2005) Media Sustainability Index, Washington PP 195-208
15. Freedom House, (2008) Freedom of the Press Qatar, Accessed 11 April 2009. URL: http://www.unhcr.org/refworld/docid/4871f62828.html
    IREX MENA Media Laws in the Gulf, Accessed 20 March 2009 URL: http://www.irex-mena.org/programs/medialaws.asp
    IREX MENA (2005) Media Sustainability Index, Washington PP 209-222
16. Freedom House, (2008) Freedom of the Press Saudi Arabia, Accessed 28th April 2009. URL: http://www.unhcr.org/refworld/docid/4871f62dc.html
    IREX MENA Media Laws in the Gulf, Accessed 20 March 2009 URL: http://www.irex-mena.org/programs/medialaws.asp
    IREX MENA (2005) Media Sustainability Index, Washington PP 223-236
17. Freedom House, (2008) Freedom of the Press United Arab Emirates, Accessed 28th April 2009. URL: http://www.unhcr.org/refworld/docid/478cd5545.html
    IREX MENA Media Laws in the Gulf, Accessed 20 March 2009 URL: http://www.irex-mena.org/programs/medialaws.asp
    IREX MENA (2005) Media Sustainability Index, Washington PP 237-250
18. Human Rights Watch (2009) UAE: Media Law Undermines Free Expression, accessed 20 May 2009 URL: http://www.hrw.org/en/news/2009/04/13/uae-media-law-undermines-free-expression
    Committee to Protect Journalists letter sent to Sheikh Khalifa bin Zayed bin Sultan Al Nahyan
    President of the United Arab Emirates accessed 11 April 2009 URL: http://cpj.org/2009/03/cpj-concerned-about-uae-draft-media-law.php
19. Study of Media Laws and Policies for the Middle East and Maghreb, The Stanhope Centre for Communications Policy Research, Stanhope House pp. 19 accessed 15 March 2009 URL: http://www.internews.org/regions/mena/amr/execsummary_english.pdf
20. Muneera Fakhroo, 12th February, 2007, *Al-Ilam al hukoomi wa altijaree wal farq bainahuma,* State media and Commercial Media and Difference between

them, *Al-Waqt* (Arabic), accessed 8th April 2009 URL: http://www.alwaqt.com/blog_art.php?baid=2416

21. Study of Media Laws and Policies for the Middle East and Maghreb, The Stanhope Centre for Communications Policy Research, Stanhope House pp. 19 accessed 15 March 2009 URL: http://www.internews.org/regions/mena/amr/execsummary_english.pdf
22. (http://www.noorsat.com/), (http://www.yahsat.ae/home.htm, (http://www.gulfsat.com/).
23. SmartSat joins Dubai rush 17.02.09 accessed on 25.02.09 URL: http://www.rapidtvnews.com/index.php/200902173167/smartsat-joins-dubai-rush.html

6

New Market Spaces and Challenges to the State Sovereignty in the Arab Gulf Region

M.H. Ilias

INTRODUCTION

There are several tendencies offering fundamental component for an alternative mode of politico-spatial discourse to emerge in the contemporary Arab Gulf region. For more than two decades, the region has witnessed a series of diverse yet shared movements that brought profound changes to the socio-political landscape. These radical changes have largely been a result of the petroleum boom-bust cycle, which culminated in a thorough social and economic transformation, with massive infrastructure development, proliferation of new means of communication, exposure to international economy and the emergence of new social spaces etc. New market spaces like special Economic Zones, Free trade zones, Shopping Malls are some of the new social spaces which set in motion interesting novel political practices. These new social spaces have successfully replaced the old ones such as mosques, souks, majlis and streets in the region.

Among them, the establishment of Special Economic Zones (SEZ) has been the most significant one that produced a radical re-imagining of conventional notions associated with the geography and politics. The special stature of new market spaces generally involves two major considerations. Firstly, they are meant mainly for display; not for common use or the consumption of the ordinary people. Secondly, being removed from the use of ordinary people, such spaces have acquired immunity from the rules of the land. With less value, high exhibitory value and greater political immunity, they become the sacred spaces of capitalism.

This paper seeks to analyze the politico-spatial practices that collectively characterize the new market spaces in the GCC states. However, its major concern revolves around two questions; how such spaces pose a challenge to the people's participation in the political process, procedural democracy and the state sovereignty and how do they replace the traditional 'unprofanable' or sacred spaces' of religion. And this paper limits itself to dealing only with Special Economic Zones (SEZs).

However, to fully comprehend these developments, it would be appropriate to define what a sacred space is. The sacred spaces are conventionally the spaces that in some way belonged to the religion and ultimately to God. As such they are removed from the free use of human being and having only exhibitory value no real use value.[1] Lefebvre in his work *The Production of Space* has identified sacred space as a graduated state of absolute space with asymmetrical social relationships and the presence high-handed administrative apparatus of religion. The emergence of sacred space in history, according to him, was marked by the construction of city-states, when absolute space of the primitive villages and nomadic tribes transformed into the sacred cities.[2]

A sacred space, however, is not merely discovered, or founded; it is claimed, owned, and operated by people for advancing specific interests.[3] 'Sacredness' as a property intrinsic to space is, therefore, constructed, not 'given' and necessarily inscribed by people. Foucault focuses on this aspect of sacred geographies. For him sacred site is an instrument of power, that is, the area controlled by certain kind of juridico-political or cultural powers.[4] As contested spaces, they are tied up with, and draws meaning from a hegemonic and hierarchical social and political practices. Bordieu also has used the term 'sacred space' with similar connotation in order to mean the peculiar 'spatial order', which legitimates the systematic social inequality, by means of special spatial practices, religious symbols, signs and codes.[5]

The most significant aspects of sacred spaces are their 'hierarchical power relations of domination and subordination, inclusion and exclusion, appropriation and dispossession.[6] Van der Leeuw has identified four kinds of politics in the construction of sacred space. He outlined a politics of pocession whereby every establishment of "a sacred place is a conquest of space; a politics of property whereby a sacred place is 'appropriated, possessed and owned."[7] Its sacredness is maintained through claims and counterclaims on its ownership. There is "a politics of exclusion also, whereby the sanctity of sacred place is preserved by maintaining boundaries."[8] The other significant issue to be discussed along with sacredness is of desire. The desire for space inevitably leads to the monopolizing of geography where the space can best be manipulated and the spaces of others are rendered invisible. The desire for the space is reflected through the spatial behaviour of the group that represented the space.[9]

Sacred spaces may be, therefore, read, not only as divine or religious, but also as the reflections and reproductions of social, political or economic desires. The formation of sacred sites, thus, can take many forms.[10] Agamben exposes this aspect of sacredness and opens up the possibilities of extending the site of analysis beyond conventional sacred spaces.[11] For him, every object, which is placed in a separate sphere and kept far from popular use, is 'sacred'. Removing commodities largely from the popular use, capitalism also shows the salience of sacredness. It is therefore important to analyze the 'entrepreneurial, social, political and other 'profane forces' that constitute the construction of sacred space.

With less use value and high exhibitory value, the economic zones become the sacred spaces of capitalism. As a commodity, they are separated from themselves and showcased for spectacular exhibition not essentially for real consumption. The spectacular exhibition makes them 'museumized' objects with less possible common use.[12] This analogy between sacred spaces of religion and capitalism becomes very apparent while analyzing the nature of organization and the kind of political immunity being enjoyed by both the conventional sacred spaces of religion and the new ones of capitalism in a sovereign state. Both are allowed to be operated freely within the state and are seldom liable to the political and legal constrains and spatial determination of the nation-state.

The Special Economic Zones (SEZs) in the Gulf region are specific geographical regions that have special laws and nature of governance different from and more liberal than a country's typical ones. This paper scrutinizes a facet of 'sacred spaces' that has spawned with new economic zones across the Arabian Gulf region. It is an attempt aimed at examining the nature of sacredness and seeing how symbols, narratives and experiences of the sacred space are produced and operated within the realm of economic zones.

SACRILIZATION AND DE-SACRILIZATION OF SPACES IN THE MUSLIM MIDDLE EAST

Levi-Strauss has noted that the sacred is 'a value of indeterminate signification. Sacred in itself, is empty of meaning and therefore susceptible to reception of any meaning whatsoever.[13] The sacred space, indeed, represents a location for 'formalized symbolic performances'[14], and a place, where meanings are at constant change with changing symbolic practices. All religions, thus, construct sacred spaces through their own specific symbols, narratives and meaning system. People identify, find a meaning and establish their attachment to the sacred spaces through these distinctive narratives. Conflict arises, however, when the narratives of one group seeks to silence or displace those of others, and when one group seeks to impose hegemony over others. So, in order to understand the nature of religious landscapes, representations and practices, these spaces must be examined within a contextualized spatial framework that is cognizant of such symbols and narratives. Even when these things are put within a specifically religious frame of reference, it is important to analyze the 'social, political and other sacred forces' that constitute the construction of sacred space. These forces may include some non-religious entities which often entail specific rituals, historical linkages, memories[15] and desire to control a place.[16] Loosely put, sacred spaces comprise a variety of traditions or a set of discourses and practices often not necessarily adhered to spiritual worlds. Chidester and Linenthal argue that the sacred is situational because it is 'at the nexus of human practices and social projects.'[17] Hence, 'nothing is inherently sacred'.

This observation is unambiguously relevant, when we talk about sacred spaces in the Middle East, since they are the object of many competing interpretations and cannot be separated from secular social, economic and political practices. Since religious significance is scarcely isolated from more general political factors in Islam, any discussion of 'sacredness' in the Middle East ought to be carried out in the wider context of politics.

Moreover, the complexity of behaviour obscures any clear-cut distinction between profane and sacred spaces within Islam. The history of the evolution of Medina as a sacred city illustrates this situation very well. Medina has been a divine site in religious reference with the presence of one of the three holiest shrines in Islam. Speaking politically, Medina enjoyed a distinctive position as the capital of the Muslim state at the time of Mohammed and the first four caliphs and was later considered the norm of Islamic society. This 'sacred organization' of Medina was, thus, retained, despite the great political, economic and ethnographic developments, which resulted from the later conquests.[18] But all the factors that went into making Medina a holy place, were not necessarily adhered to the spiritual world. To be more specific, physical attributes like trade and commerce were also accounted and the 'physicality' of place also had significance in its making.

Forces, such as commerce in the Islamic world, cuts both the ways. They may work towards sacralization and de-sacralization at the same time. Trade, which is otherwise considered to be an organ of profanation,[19] and often gathers meaning in opposition to the sacred can also be defined here as something that removes things and places from common use and transfers them to a separate sphere of emporiums. As the main expression of pious behaviour, pilgrimage always sanctions this passage from profane to the sacred. It eventually becomes an independent activity sometimes may be an activity independent of religious affiliation, but demanding a religious allegiance. Likewise, sacred spaces, themselves may be lying on any major trade route, may be with proximity to some resources or suitable for large-scale agricultural development. Physical geography (strategic importance as well) is always taken into consideration in creation of sacred spaces. So, in the process of de-profanation, religious and theological factors find their place within a matrix of wider political, social or economic factors. The separation between sacred and secular at the material, symbolic and ideological levels, in this sense, is more fluid than rigid.

Though the emergence of sacred places in the Middle East was marked by the construction of city-sates, when natural space of the primitive villages and nomadic tribes transformed into the sacred cities, the first Muslim transformation of the sacred places came into being only from seventh century onwards.[20] The religion (Islam) was instrumental in legitimating such spaces. Early Islamic dynasties made them the places, where ultimate source of authority was vested in God, not in the nation or the state and rulers were only custodians.

Nevertheless, the development was not just limited to the construction of sacred spaces only. Almost parallel to it, Middle East also witnessed the emergence of Islamic cities.[21] Unlike the early cities of religious importance, the newly emerged 'Islamic' cities assumed the primacy of civilization, culture and economy (additionally with that of religion).[22] They were at the disposal and the free movement of ordinary people, despite the holiness most of them were having with the presence of holy shrines or pilgrim centres. Apart from being holy cities, centres of worship, pilgrimage or religious learning, they contained many functions. Though featured mostly by 'Islamic' components, like congregational mosques, religious schools, Sahria courts, residential quarters with their ethnic or religious solidarity, cemeteries and shrines of saints, they were the hubs of secular and commercial activities as well.[23] The three Islamic elements that characterized Islamic cities, according to Janet Abu-Lughod, were: a distinction between the members of the Umma and the outsiders, which led to juridical and spatial distinction by neighborhoods; the segregation of the sexes which gave rise to a particular solution to the question of spatial organization; and a legal system which, rather than imposing general regulations over land uses of various types in various places, left the litigation of the neighbours the detailed adjudication of mutual rights over space and use.[24]

CAPITALISM AND RELIGIOSITY OF SPACE

As discussed earlier, the practice of making 'sacred spaces' is not entitled exclusively to religion. In relation to the issues of sacredness of space, religion and capitalism may find a common ground of understanding and a mutual interest in protecting it. Both serve an indispensable role in demarcating and consolidating spaces and legitimating the exclusionary 'sacred' practices within them. Capitalism, in its liberal version ends up, most of the times, either with redefining the place set by religion or with invoking religion to demarcate it. It is quite interesting then to understand, how capitalism in its advanced stage becomes instrumental in the formation of sacred spaces.

The major avenues, where the interests of religion and capitalism merge together is 'museumization' which refers to a process of transformation of meanings and consequent separation and removal of things, places or people from common use and transfer them to a separate sphere. This means that both make the things impossible to profane. The term 'profane', in contrary, denotes to something that was once sacred or religious, is returned to the use and property of human being as removed from the sphere of the 'sacred'.[25] The capitalist religion in extreme phase aims at creating such spaces something absolutely unprofanable with high exhibitory or exchange value than the use value and realizes in such pure form of separation.

At the deepest levels, capitalism incorporates religion without its metaphysics. It could not fully depart from religious norms, though it could successfully be a vehicle for secularization of faiths.[26] Walter Benjamin analyzes that the western capitalism, for instance, is bound up with more generic characteristics of Christianity than most of its proponents are willing to acknowledge. "It (capitalism) is a cult religion, perhaps the most extreme and absolute one that has ever existed. In it, everything has meaning only in reference to the fulfillment of a particular cult, not in relation to an idea."[27] Similarly, as what happens in religion, despite its apparent 'all-inclusive' attitude, capitalism in its liberal version becomes radically limited in its capacity for tolerance, its ability to acknowledge a spectrum of views and its ability to create a pluralist society. Hence, to ground a firm nonreligious, nonmetaphysical morality is difficult for Capitalism. In this regard, at the material, symbolic and ideological levels, the distinction between religion and capitalism becomes a tricky issue.

As discussed earlier, in both the cases (of religion and capitalism), everything is exhibited in its separation from itself and impossibility of human use becomes apparent. Agamben, in his work *Profanations* draws parallels between these two. To quote him: "not only there is no religion without separation, but every separation also contains or preserves within itself a genuinely religious core."[28] Like religion, capitalism also generalizes the structure of separation that defines its own things of 'sacred' (not for the use of ordinary people) and 'human' (for free use). In the commodity, capitalist separation inheres in the very form of the object, which splits into valuable and worthless.

This resemblance becomes more noticeable, when it comes to Special Economic Zones, where spaces are divided from themselves and placed in separate spheres based on exhibitory value and they expose the strong affinities between the religious and liberal capitalist discourse. Such sacred spaces of capitalism are far from human use and kept 'religiously' for display. What cannot be used by ordinary population, as such, given over to consumption or to spectacular exhibition. The 'divine spaces' of economic zones often appear to be multivalent, and require an acknowledgement of simultaneous, fluctuating and conflicting investment of sacred and secular capitalist meanings on one site. The only thing, which makes the new sacred spaces of special economic zones different, is the shift in form and content of narratives. Sacred spaces in the normal case are made through oral histories and popular narratives, but the mass media has taken its role now and acts as visual analogue to both.

DIVINE SPACES OF ECONOMIC ZONES IN THE GULF

The regime of the Special Economic Zone (SEZ) indeed appears to be an apparently revolutionary economic (legal as well) concept which evolved very quickly in the region. Generally, it is argued that the concept becomes attractive because it is much easier to resolve the problems of infrastructure and governance on a limited geographical area than it is to resolve them countrywide. Such economic zones can be insulated from the broader juridical and economic context of the country and be treated as a separate 'system' within the system. In many of the Middle Eastern countries, these exclusive rights (which were given earlier to divine territories of religion) given to such zones pose challenges to state sovereignty. This part discusses some general points on the nature of the 'religiosity' in treating SEZs and how do they challenge the sovereign rights of states in the Gulf region. It also underlines the political significance of examining sacred geography, at least in terms of the intersection of sacred and secular forces in the making of such spaces or places.

The category 'SEZ' in the region covers a broad range of more specific zone types, including Economic Cities (EC), Free Trade Zones (FTZ), Export Processing Zones (EPZ), Free Zones (FZ), Industrial Estates (IE), Free Ports and others. Rather than having a common meaning and purpose, SEZs mean many things to many states. Generally, they are the result of diversification of the national economies beyond dependency on the oil sector. For some states, they act like advance economic tools or vehicles to support greater competition and advancement in liberalizing markets. For others SEZ offers a better avenue to invest more sensibly in the future to solve several challenges, like booming population and unemployment. The goal, for some states, which depends less on oil income, is usually an increase in foreign direct investment (FDI) in the country.[29] Critics, however, focus on the real estate component, at a time when the land becomes the major resource, replacing oil in the rentier economies in non-oil rich economies like Dubai. Anyway, there may be a clear understanding that a well-implemented and designed SEZ can bring about many desired benefits for a host-country: increase in employment, FDI attraction, general economic growth, foreign exchange earnings, international exposure, and the transfer of new technologies and skills. Active use of the economic zones as a policy instrument for achieving an overall system transition, at the same time, has far-reaching social, economic and legal implications as well.

As elsewhere in the world, special economic zones (SEZs) in the Arabian Gulf region have special laws that are more liberal than a country's typical laws. In countries like Saudi Arabia, such zones represent a politico-legal compromise apart from enjoying some exclusive rights for the purpose of exploring and exploiting, conserving and managing the natural resources. Such zones have developed over the past two decades into self-contained mini-economies along the line of 'one country, two systems'. They enjoy a special political as well fiscal regime, which is much milder than that of the rest of the area. This is not just in terms of tax exemptions, incentives on customs duties or something like that, but this 'immunity' is extended to politics and system of governance. As a specially administered area, Aramco in Saudi Arabia is enjoying similar immunity from the typical laws of the land. Laws are more liberal here to accommodate a sort of pluralism by pressure. In contrast to the general condition, Aramco has room for endorsing religious views of 'others' (of non-Muslims) and allows them to have respective places of worship.

The economic zones in the region in general have a different structure of governance and political accountability and participation. In other words, they can be defined as something which is maintained separately with greater amount of immunity from the country's juridical domain. As a sphere transferred to the exclusive use of 'economic elites', economic zones attain high 'display value' rather than the real 'use value'. Given over to spectacular exhibition, 'use of all' and popular participation become impossible. 'Religiosity' emanates, by and large, from these immunities. Global finance sanctions 'the sacredness' of such spaces further and facilitates a passage from the 'use of all' to the use of 'miniscule few', from 'the profane to the sacred', or from 'human sphere to the divine'.

Issues of specific rights and exclusive claims over the SEZs illuminate the affinities between religious and capitalist discourses over the 'divine spaces'. One way to examine this affinity is to compare the legal autonomy being enjoyed by the sacred spaces of both; religion and capitalism. This autonomous stature involves a consideration of two manifestations of internal sovereignty, namely political and legal sovereignty. Internal political sovereignty refers to the ability of state to conduct political business independent of pressures or compulsions from within. Internal legal sovereignty denotes to the ability of state to make its own laws without limitations imposed by an outside agency.

State sovereignty in the Middle East, in general, encounters massive threat from various sources. The processes and phenomenon, like economic liberalization, integration of state politically and economically into regional forums (the GCC) and rise of political Islam have contributes much to the erosion of state sovereignty. When post-colonial states surrender much of their political and monetary sovereignty to the neo-liberal forces, Islam has seized the popular imagination by capturing the mantle of anti-imperialist, populist ideology in most Muslim majority states. But the developments in the Arab Gulf speak particularly of a shift of focus from tribal/religious structure to the economic zones as the major force to challenge the state sovereignty. With a wide range of manifestations, they promise a new equation to the relationship between the 'sacred' and 'sovereign'. With the similar sort of independence and autonomy being possessed by holy spaces of religion, these spaces are more or less free from constrains of the local political units and their spatial determinations.

As the old holy places are being replaced by the new ones of capitalism, the realm of 'sacred' is extraordinarily ambivalent now. As Ahmed and Donnan put it appropriately, mosques are being replaced by the malls as the cultural (religious as well) centres.[30] It is true to a great extent in the Gulf as the malls are not just the major source of entertainment. When you are in Dubai, the place to where people take you first will be malls than any historically important places or cultural monuments. As Marchal notes, "the way the society seems to function at the grassroots level indicates that it is organized as an archipelago of communities whose contacts and interactiosn are clearly limited to the market."[31]

At a moment when the GCC States have lost innumerable sovereign powers to neo-liberal global restructuring, market serves an indispensable role in consolidating and demarcating 'sacred' geographies. When landscapes are sometimes created to replicate 'sacred worlds' as understood by particular groups, physical factors contribute to the 'sacredness' of spaces. One of the most noticeable illustrations of this shift is a plan championed by Saudi to build six new economic cities throughout the country. Especially striking feature of this plan is the choice of location for establishing such zones. And no wonder, the proposed site for Knowledge Economic City is nowhere other than Medina, which is supposed to be one among the two 'holiest' cities for Muslims.

DUBAI: THE CITY AND SACREDNESS

Among the Gulf States, the United Arab Emirates was an early adopter of economic zones. It has established, or is in the process of building, at least 31 economic zones. In terms of diversity also SEZs in UAE stand apart; they are ranging from media and entertainment, industrial to IT, to research and development. Jabal Ali Free Zone the most prominent one among the SEZs illustrates the situation better. It has been given special powers and legal incentives regarding some of the otherwise sensitive matters like immigration. Aiming to attract global commerce, Jabal Ali boasts minimal restrictions only and thus subscribes global 'difference' socially. To achieve this objective, the local authority has command over a wide range of affairs including financial regulations in the region, labour issues, environmental protection, and project licensing as well as municipal affairs. Jabal Ali allows business to operate without having a local partner, *kafil,* which is otherwise unimaginable all around the GCC and possess more liberal immigration regime and visa laws.

To realize a similar future, Qatar has established economic zones within the capital city of Doha to encourage foreign investments with a business-friendly atmosphere. The zones-heralded as 'New Dubai'-will have sustainable buildings, a shipping port, an international airport, a light rail transit system, and complete urban infrastructures. Bahrain is developing the Bahrain Investment Wharf (BIW), in addition to its current two ports and industrial zones (Mina Sulman and North Sitra Industrial Estate). Though the form of economic zones may differ in various places, the content remains same everywhere. In developing these cities, the government will play the role of regulator, facilitator, and promoter with the private sector providing the capital, the landowners and the developers.

The developments in Dubai, the commercial capital of UAE, speak eloquently of a radical re-imaging of space and politics. It is interesting to discuss about the nature of 'religiosity' in treating the city. Dubai itself is such a big space where the parallel between capitalism and religion becomes very pertinent. The City occupies exactly the space, function and exclusiveness once reserved for 'sacred spaces' of religion. Interestingly, the City's recent fame comes from its projection as a 'politically neutral' city in the Gulf region.[32] This adjective may be to make a new strategic asset out of it and thereby to attract business minded people and multinational corporations and give the city an added edge over other cities in the region who are trying to emulate its success. However, this projection also helps rewriting the spatial history of the land and disengaging old 'politico-religious' narratives that the land possessed in the past. The policies of depoliticization and depopulation are better served among the other things.

Interestingly, Dubai has become a point of reference for all the Middle Eastern states-a model that everyone wants to replicate. Countries of the region, no matter whether they are politically on the opposite side, are not indifferent to the success of Dubai.[33] Political neutrality of the city is the major attraction. Dubai can hardly be seen as a major player in regional or international politics. Should this apparent lack of political aura be seen as a weakness? No, one might, instead, be tempted to view this weakness as more of an asset than a liability.[34] This lack of political prominence allows a form of strategic opportunism by which politics and economics could be handled with a loose constituency and without too much interference.[35] Political neutrality is undoubtly a strategic asset of profound value.[36] The relatively weak political status of Dubai is, thus, an advantage that a politically powerful Dubai would lack. The other strategic asset of Dubai is its neutral stand in many of the sensitive issues. Dubai actually benefits out of political instability in the region and attracts even warring groups to sit and negotiate over a table. As Abdulkhaleq Abdullah puts it; "it is only in Dubai where Americans and Iranians can meet amicably, talk to each other decently and spy on each other's intentions with relative ease."

The other catchphrase, 'uniquely apolitical' facilitates deconstructing Dubai's old map and the City becomes the site of an active replacement of old landmarks with the new ones. The basic idea of political locatability has disappeared as a reference point in an effort to remap the old geography. The cartographic representation of Palm Islands (the largest reclamation projects in the world and will result in the world's largest artificial islands with a cosmopolitan city) offers a textbook example to this new practice.[37] Relying on sketches, the map of Palm Island enmeshes us in diverse levels of reality. Apart from serving the purpose of 'exhibition of its property', the diagrammatic representation of Palm Island helps achieving and maintaining the cartographic balance in favour of the new identity of the city. The images as seemingly benign and apolitical, thus, become highly contested symbols used to assert this new identity. So the new map in addition to their theoretical usefulness, has a high degree of practical applicability to depoliticize the landscape. It is through the production of new map that the political embellishment is achieved. Map serves here as a tool to re-write the spatial history of the land and as a significant function of deployment of power and the legitimization of it.

In Dubai's case the new map is not merely a cartographic practice that marks the land, but a political sign system constructing distinct modes of spatial arrangements. The question of new spatial formation in UAE is also raised and illustrated by various examples of its absence or presence. New market spaces have established their own set of hierarchies that produce the codes of inclusion and exclusion. Although it does constitute only a part of this work's concern, it seems appropriate to give a gist of current cleavages in the GCC societies, since this must perhaps be the major source of spatial exclusion. Historically, the line of division was demarcated between citizen *watini* and foreigner *wafid.* Class and ethnic/national stratification systems are overlapping in a more confused state here. The division between citizens and foreigners still runs deep in the Gulf but taking new turns. In addition, the societies are now stratified in terms of class and what matters more now is the different forms of separation and control in tune with the new mode of social stratification.[38]

Gavrielides sketches out the situation in a lucid manner: "Christians from Goa work exclusively as maids and governesses for urban Kuwaiti families...Baluchis are employed as door keepers by Kuwaiti families."[39] Nepalese and Tamils form Sri Lanka generally fill up the slots of security personnel and office boys respectively, while America and Western European countries contribute many well paid managers. The middle stratum is comprised mainly of South and East Asian clerks and middle level government employees. Nationals, in addition to their national and ethnic consciousness, have a clear perception of their status in this new vertical/class hierarchy.

What strike as more significant are the different forms of separation and control. Tantamount almost to a sort of *ghettoization*, there has been a distinctive spatial segregation. There are specially designated areas or exclusive enclaves for locals and each category of expatriates. In Dubai for instance, there are "areas labelled frankly on bus route maps as 'labour camps.'[40] The only expatriate community, which is immune to this selective spatial control, is of highly-paid Americans or Western Europeans.

CONCLUSION

What makes an object sacred is its unavailability for ordinary use. To maintain the sacredness, religion removes or separates things, places and people from common use and transfers them to a separate sphere. Religion fulfils it through a series of divine practices like rituals or sacrifices, which collectively help sanctify the passage of something from common use to the sacred. From this perspective, the practice of separation and transferring of things to exclusive use does not seem unique with religion. The same is true with capitalism as well. What draws a parallel between these two is the removal of things from popular use. Capitalism possesses similar apparatus that effect and regulate the separation and make the commodities for limited use.

As discussed earlier, capitalist religion categorizes the things in accordance with their exhibitory value or exchange value not essentially matching with their use value. The commodities with higher exhibitory value are kept in separate spheres, where the use of all becomes impossible. The 'sacred' as opposed to the profane world of use of many is, therefore, given over to the use of few.

In this sense, the obstinate denial for the popular use and spectacular exhibition of the space make the economic zones in the Gulf, where display dominates the use or consumption, sacred ones. The theological canon of 'sacred' as the impossibility of ordinary use finds almost similar expression here. Hence the realm of the 'sacred' has now been transferred from the divine geographies of religion to a wide range of commercial spaces (such as economic zones and shopping malls and commercial complexes) carrying an element of 'religiosity'.

Similarly, when we talk about the sacredness of such spaces, we need to understand the considerable political and juridical freedom and liberty that the new economic zones enjoy under the present economic regimes. With greater amount of immunity and political neutrality, the economic zones in the region, therefore, occupy the space and function once meant for the holy places of religion. Like the earlier ones, the new sacred spaces are also seldom concerned about the political consequences that their existence and maintenance make. The 'sacredness' is revisited with the new economic zones have potentialities to pose serious threats to the internal political as well as legal sovereignty of the state, where they are located.

NOTES

1. Georgio Agamben, 2007, *Profanations,* (New York), p. 73.
2. The sacred space, according to Lefebvre, represents city-states, despots and divine seats, holy cities and divine dynasties. See Henri Lefebvre, 1991, Lefebvre, H. 1991. *The Production of Space*, (Oxford).
3. See David Chidester and Edward T. Linenthal, 1995, 1995, "Introduction", in D. Chidester, and E.T.Linenthal, (eds.), *American sacred space* (Bloomington), pp. 1, 42.
4. Due to the unequal access to the space and representative nature of some groups, the spaces become the site for certain groups to exert their power. Michael Foucault, 1980, "Geography and Power", in Colin Gordon (ed.), *Power/ Knowledge: Selected Interviews and Other Writings 1972-1977*, (New York), pp. 69-70.
5. Pierre Bordieu, 1994, *Outline of a Theory of Practice*, (Cambridge), pp. 5-14.
6. See Chidester and Linenthal, n. 3, p. 17.
7. Gerardus Van der Leeuw, 1986, *Religion in essence and manifestation.* (Princeton, NJ), pp. 10-31.
8. *Ibid.*
9. Spatial behaviour refers to the way through which the social forces act towards the conception of space and the manner in which they produce the spatial structures and power hierarchies.
10. Noga Collins-Kreiner, Religion and Politics: New Religious sites and Spatial Transgression in Israel, *The Geographical Review*, vol.98, no.2, April 2008, pp. 197-213, p. 199
11. Agamben, n.1.
12. Museumization refers to a process in which objects or ideas are withdrawn from popular use, and kept in separate spheres. With mere exhibition and next to impossible common use of objects, museum occupies the space and function once reserved for the Temple, where the processes, like sacrifice makes possible the passage of 'ordinary' things to 'sacred'. For further details Agamben, n.1.
13. As quoted in Chidester and Linenthal, n.3., p. 9.
14. *Ibid.*, 9
15. Memories and narratives include those of some seminal events through which the society has passed into or those associated with sacred figures or heroes. In the Middle East's case cutting across the religious lines, prophets and saints were the agents of memory. See Oleg Grabar, 2001, "Space and Holiness in Medieval Jerusalem", *Islamic Studies,* vol. 40, no. 3-4, pp. 681-695, p. 685.
16. Smith, 1978: 88) Jonathan Z. Smith, 1978, "The wobbling pivot", in Smith, J.Z., (ed.), *Map is not territory: studies in the history of religions*, (Leiden), pp. 88–103.
17. Chidester and Linenthal, n.3., p. 6.
18. El-Ali, 1970, "The foundation of Baghdad", in A.H.Hourani (ed.), *The Islamic City: A Colloquium*, (Oxford), p. 89.
19. Profanation is the process of returning the sacred things to the use of human being, by freeing them from the religious norms.

20. Albert H. Hourani, 1970, "Islamic City in the Light of Recent Research, in A.H. Hourani (ed.), *The Islamic City: A Colloquium*, (Oxford).
21. The expansion of the Muslim Arabs during the 7th and 8th centuries has already been credited with significantly increasing the degree of urbanization in the Middle East with the introduction of a new urban form the 'Islamic city'.
22. It is debatable, how far are such features as we have described in the city as human community and as a physical entity, peculiar to the Muslim world and how far are they to be explained in terms of Islam? Hourani argues that they can be explained very little in terms of Islam. "We must look for other types of explanation." See Hourani, n.20, for further details of the debate.
23. Wagstaff argues, except in the case of the new foundations, the Arabs did not introduce a model Islamic town. Many of the features were either inherited from pre-existing towns or emerged gradually over time, through a process of convergence. Proliferation of the mosques and other Muslim religious buildings became so noticeable in the matured Islamic towns only from 12th century onwards. See J.M. Wagstaff, 1980,"The Origin and Evolution of Towns: 400 BC to AD 1900", in J.M. Wagstaff (ed.), *The Changing Middle Eastern City,* (London), pp. 20-22.
24. Janet Abu-Lughod, 1985. "Book Review (What Drives Third World City Growth? A Dynamic General Equilibrium Approach by Allen C. Kelley; Jeffrey G. Williamson)", *Contemporary Sociology*, Vol. 14, No. 4, pp. 528-530.
25. Agamben, n. 1, pp. 73-5.
26. Europe is a textbook example, where capitalism became the prime agent for secularization of the protestant faith.
27. Cited in Agamben, n.1,73.
28. *Ibid*., 74
29. For instance in the UAE, wherein having only a tiny percent of the oil reserves, SEZ has become adept at conjuring up ventures for others to finance.
30. Akbar S. Ahmad, 1994, and Hastings Donnan. 1994, "Islam in the Age of Postmodernity" in Akbar S. Ahmad and Hastings Donnan (eds.), *Islam, Globalization and Postmodernity,* (London).
31. See Roland Marchal,2005, " Dubai : Global City and Transnational Hub", Madawi Al-Rasheed, *Transnational Conncetions and the Arab Gulf,* (Oxford).
32. Abdulkhaleq Abdulla, 2008, "A Politically Neutral City", *Gulf News*, 13, February.
33. This is very evident from Iran's attempt to replicate Dubai model in many places including Kish Island.
34. Roland Marchal, n. 31.
35. The apparent weakness of Dubai reflects in backing up its sovereignty claims over its own territory. Dubai does not want to allow spoiling the party with Iran by raising the issue of disputed islands, though there are concerns from GCC.
36. Abdulkhaleq Abdulla, n.32.
37. The Palm Islands are artificial islands in Dubai, United Arab Emirates on which major commercial and residential infrastructure will be constructed.
38. For details see Paul Dresch, 2006, 'Foreign Matter: The Place of strangers in Gulf Society', Globalization and the Gulf, in John W. Fox et al (ed.),

Globalization and the Gulf, (London), pp. 200-219, and Ann Nga Longva, 1997, *Wells Built on Sand: Migration, Exclusion and Society in Kuwait*, (Boulder).

39. G. Gavrielides, 'The Anatomy of Parliamentary Elections in Kuwait' in L.Layne (ed.), *Elections in the Middle East: Implications of Recent Trends* (London), p. 162.
40. Spatial segregation is very pertinent and accommodations are arranged in relation to status, which we can analyze in class terms or ethnic-national terms. See Paul Dresch, n. 38.

REFERENCES

Abdulla, Abdulkhaleq. "A Politically Neutral City", *Gulf News*, 13, February 2008.

Abu-Lughod, J. 1985. "Book Review (What Drives Third World City Growth? A Dynamic General Equilibrium Approach by Allen C. Kelley; Jeffrey G. Williamson)", *Contemporary Sociology*, Vol. 14, No. 4 (Jul., 1985), pp. 528-530.

Agamben, G. 2007. *Profanations,* New York: Zone Books.

Ahmad, Akber S. and Hastings Donnan. 1994. "Islam in the Age of Postmodernity" in Akbar S. Ahmad and Hastings Donnan (eds.), *Islam, Globalization and Postmodernity,* London: Routeledge.

Barker, Chris. *Cultural Studies: Theory and Practice*, London: Sage Publications.

Bordieu, P. 1977. *Outline of a Theory of Practice*, Cambridge: Cambridge University Press.

Chidester, D. and Linenthal, E.T. 1995. "Introduction", in Chidester, D. and Linenthal, E.T., (ed.), *American sacred space*, Bloomington, IN: Indiana University Press, 1-42.

Collins-Kreiner, Noga, "Religion and Politics: New Religious sites and Spatial Transgression in Israel", *The Geographical Review*, vol. 98, no. 2, April 2008, pp. 197-213.

Dresch, Paul. 2006. "Foreign Matter: The Place of strangers in Gulf Society", Globalization and the Gulf, in John W. Fox et. al (ed.), *Globalization and the Gulf,* London: Routeledge.

El-Ali. 1970. "The foundation of Baghdad", in A.H. Hourani (ed.), *The Islamic City: A Colloquium*, Oxford: Bruno Cassirer.

Foucault, Michel. 1980. "Geography and Power", in Colin Gordon (ed.), *Power/ Knowledge: Selected Interviews and Other Writings 1972-1977*, New York: Pantheon, pp. 69-70.

Grabar, Oleg. 2001. "Space and Holiness in Medieval Jerusalem", *Islamic Studies,* vol. 40, no. 3-4, pp. 681-695.

Hourani, A.H. 1970. "Islamic City in the Light of Recent Research, in A.H. Hourani (ed.), *The Islamic City: A Colloquium*, Oxford: Bruno Cassirer.

Ilias, M.H. 2007. *Space, Memory and Jewish National Identity*, New Delhi: New Century Publications.

Lefebvre, H. 1991. *The Production of Space*, (Oxford), Blackwell.

Longva, Ann Nga, 1997, *Wells Built on Sand: Migration, Exclusion and Society in Kuwait*. Boulder: West View Press.

Machal, Roland, " Dubai: Global City and Transnational Hub", Madawi Al-Rasheed, *Transnational Conncetions and the Arab Gulf,* Oxford: Routledge, 2005.

Smith, J.Z. 1978. The wobbling pivot. In Smith, J.Z., editor, *Map is not territory: studies in the history of religions*, Leiden: E.J. Brill, 88-103.

Van der Leeuw, G. 1986. *Religion in essence and manifestation.* Princeton, NJ: Princeton University Press.

Wagstaff, J.M. 1980. "The Origin and Evolution of Towns: 400 BC to AD 1900", in J.M. Wagstaff (ed.), *The Changing Middle Eastern City,* London: Croom Helm.

PART 3: SAUDI ARABIA: OPPOSITION AND HUMAN RIGHTS IN A LIBERALIZING AUTOCRACY

7

Democratization in Saudi Arabia

Jajati K. Pattnaik

The democratization in Saudi Arabia that is ingrained in the philosophy of popular political participation and an elected legislature in lieu of a clan based structural one has propelled the academia, activists and the policy makers for an in depth as well as theoretical study of the subject. The resilience of the Islamic as well as liberal opposition in the kingdom has ordained the ruling clique for political openness. As a consequence to this, al-Saud regime has introduced a set of reforms in the form of Majlis al-Shura, partially elected municipal council, professional syndicates and national dialogues towards the consolidation of the process of democratization. But here it raises important propositions. These are: (i) whether democratization is to be mirrored in the structural prism of western matrix or its institutional apparatus is to be rooted in cultural moorings; (ii) whether the stability of the ruling class is under threat from the Islamic as well as liberal spectrums or the regime would subside them through politics of fragmentation or repression; (iii) whether the civil society is autonomous in nature or banks upon the state; (iv) whether the reforms made under al-Saud legitimacy indicate any trend towards electoral democracy in near future or participatory democracy in future. While discussing this subject on the basis of these propositions, this paper would analyze different facets of Saudi politics and draw conclusions on the basis of its findings.

STATE FORMATION IN SAUDI ARABIA

As an Islamic state, the political culture of Saudi Arabia with overwhelming Islamic denominations shapes major aspects of social interaction. Islam's influence on political culture is traditionally interpreted in two general categories: religious and temporal. These categories seek to define the theological beliefs and transcendentally ordained ethical duties on the one hand and the interests of the ruling dynasties, military and financial affairs on the other.[1] Saudi politics, in fact, has never unyoked itself from religion, as religious loyalties remain the primary base of political legitimacy. Al-Saud family in tandem with the Ulama (Religious Scholars) has claimed legitimacy of the people, and this politico—religious symbiosis is witnessed since the reign of first house of al-Saud in 1744.[2] Abd al-Aziz al-Saud, who consolidated the Saudi Kingdom in 1932, managed to combine the principles of both with pragmatic ambitions of statehood. Thus, he created an ideology which helped him to strike out the religious and political differences of the provinces by rejuvenating the unambiguous teachings of Islam. The basic structure of authority was retained. In keeping with the patriarchal traditions, the ruler remained the sole arbiter of power and justice. The concept of 'consensus' was introduced to tide over the mutual rivalries that characterized the Saudi society in its formative phase. From that time onwards, the pattern of political organization in Saudi Arabia has toed the line set by its founder. Ibn Khaldun's concepts of "Royal Authority" and "Assabiyah" (Group Solidarity) were employed, to justify the strong leadership of the King to rule the people.[3]

THE ROYAL FAMILY AND HEGEMONY

The Royal family not only consists of Abd al-Saud's sons, but also it includes their grandsons and descendants of the extended clan. The Sudairi, the Shammar and the Bani-Faisal are the major factions.[4] Sudairi is the most powerful group in the Kingdom. The Crown Prince Sultan Ibn Abd al-Aziz al-Saud belongs to this group and his full brothers are installed in different important positions of the Saudi Government. Shammar faction is the second powerful group in the Kingdom. The present King Abdullah Ibn Abd al-Saud belongs to Shammar tribe of the northern Najd and he holds a strong position among the Najd tribes.[5] Bani-Faisal is the third major powerful group in the Kingdom and it consists of eight sons of the late King Faisal Ibn Abd al-Saud. The present Foreign Minister Prince Saud al-Faisal al-Saud belongs to this group. Besides him, his full brothers also occupy important positions in the Saudi Governmental set-up.[6]

The Royal council is formed out of the Royal family with exclusive membership, enormous powers and a secret modus operandi. This council is contemplated more to be an inner group that operates with key members of the royal coterie. This inner group functions as the sole channel of communication between the Members of Royal family and the Council of Ministers.[7] This group helps in reaching a broad consensus on key political issues and takes a fairly large number of Royal members into confidence on policy measures. This further plays a role in sorting out internal strife within the family and, thus, maintains the image of unity. This is the most powerful political institution in the country, notwithstanding the fact that inner group remains anonymous and unacknowledged in the Kingdom. The study of the Royal family shows that it is a conglomerate of extended clan. Within the Royal family, the Sudairi faction operates as the predominant group in the kingdom. All important portfolios of the government are handled by the Sudairi brothers. While the Shammar and Bani Faisal factions operate as the other influential groups.

The hegemony of the Saudi state is based on Islam and the rentier state model. The Council of Higher Ulama as an institution was created in 1971 through a Royal decree. It accords legitimacy to the regime by issuing fatwas and sermons. The Ulama are "to express opinions on Shariah regarding matters submitted to them by Wali al-Amir (The King)."[8] The Council of Higher Ulama observed "It is necessary in a situation like this that Ulama clarify the Islamic ruling on the matter so that the people of this country and elsewhere may be aware of the correct standpoint on it. The Council of the Senior Ulama approves therefore, of the steps taken by the ruler, may Allah lead him to success, in inviting some forces equipped with arms that frighten away anyone who thinks of invading this land."[9] They legitimize the actions of the state disseminating the hegemonic discourse in media. Al-Saud legitimacy is also partly drawn from the rentier state mechanism which is based on the premise that "state-society relations seem predicted on the principle of no taxation, no representation."[10] The authority of the state is founded on the welfare system as well as bureaucratic structure thronged on state patronage. Rentierism concedes legitimacy to the regime affording services to the citizens without expecting any proceeds from them. Afterward, it consolidates state power and approves of supremacy of the regime over social distribution.[11]

It is evident that the hegemony of the al-Saud regime is based on the twin principle of Islamic discourse and rentier paradigm. The Ulama having an alliance with the Royal family provides legitimacy to the authority. On the other, the rentier state model helps the regime in guaranteeing its stability through distributive capability.

POLITICS OF MEMORANDUM

The Free Princes Movements led by Prince Talal ibn Abd al-Aziz in the sixties and the Islamist opposition followed by the seizure of the Grand Mosque of Mecca in 1979 did not prove to be a catalyst for political change in the past. The successors of the founder of the kingdom during this period viz. Saud (1953-1982), Faisal (1964-1975) and Khalid (1975-1982) did not initiate any political reform towards the democratization of the system. However, during the Gulf crisis of 1990-1991, Saudi Arabia began to open up to the outside world by allowing the US—led coalition forces to the kingdom. This decision of the regime had tremendous effect upon the Saudi society and their religious beliefs paving the way for re-beginning of opposition. Subsequently, a beleaguered resistance of liberal and conservative Islamic groups launched its tirade against the al-Saud dynasty.[12] They unveiled a memorandum of reforms to put the political system in a proper order. The petition for change enunciated by forty three liberal conservatives called for consultative Council, restoration of municipal council, independence of judiciary, freedom of the press, reorganization of religious police, reform of educational system, ensuring equality of all citizens and opening space for public participation of women in various fields.[13]

The political climate prevailing in the Kingdom dragged the Ulama out into the mainstream thereby boosting the morale of the fundamentalist struggle. The Ulama traditionally resistant to change started interpreting the American presence as a veritable satanic act mediated by the King, a deliberate design to subvert the Islamic character of the Saudi society. They launched a campaign for the restoration of the Islamic order, by whipping up popular sentiments against the monarch.[14] The movement though initially disorganized found focus and a leadership in the Ulama led by Fahd Bin Awa and Safar al-Hawali. They along with the other Islamists submitted a letter of demands to the king in May 1991 demanding necessary reforms in the political, social and economic sectors.

These are: Establishment of an Islamic Consultative Council (Majlis-al-Shura) comprising of specialized persons from different fields to conduct the domestic affairs of the country as well as the external policies of the nation; Removal of all laws and regulations that violate Shariah; Reflection of honesty, sincerity, and good behaviour by all officials inside and outside the country to protect the interests of the nation and its image abroad; Promotion of justice and equality among all the members of the society to realize one's rights and duties; Supervision and accountability of all officials and setting up of a transparent state; Prevalence of justice in the reward of national wealth among all classes of society; Creation of an Islamic economy through abolition of all types of monopoly and illegal wealth; Getting rid of restriction on Islamic Banks and purification of public and private institutions from usury; Setting up of a strong army matched with potential weapons to protect the country and it's Holy Places; Reorganization of mass media in conformity with Islam and to relegate the non-conformist agenda; Formulation of foreign policy to secure the interest of the Muslim Community (Ummah) manifesting the Islamic credentials of the country; Development of the religious machineries of the state with human and material resources to fulfill their objectives; Amalgamation of all judicial institutions investing them with complete independence; Protection of the rights of the individuals and removal of all kinds of oppressions that violate human freedom.[15]

The letter of demands submitted by the Islamist opposition was quite radical in nature. It put strong impact upon the kingdom and pressed the Saud monarch for introducing political reforms. Subsequently, King Fahd declared Basic System of Rules in March 1992 for beginning the process of democratization in Saudi Arabia.

POLITICS OF ORGANIZED OPPOSITION

Politics of organized opposition had significant impact upon the stability of the regime. CDLR (Committee for Defence of Legitimate Rights) was formed in 1993 as an organized Islamic group to unfetter the Saudi state from corruption and mismanagement.[16] The programme of the organization, as outlined by Muhammed al-Masari, the spokesperson, dealt with the 'Saudi legitimacy and its external actions.'[17] It focused upon the Royal family, gross violation of human rights and Country's special relations with the United States. The group launched an electronic revolution using cassettes, faxes and internet to make a popular dent in the kingdom. The message of the CDLR is quite discerned in its news letter Huquq (Rights):

> Honest and responsible media are a very important alternative to the distorted view given to our people by the official media. This alternative media will be received by a nation thirsty for sincere words and real news. Although we do not have the money that the government media has, our followers will do their best to distribute our message and this message will reach the hearts and minds of millions.[18]

In order to quell the movement, Saudi authority immediately arrested Muhammad al-Masari. Subsequently, Masari fled from the kingdom and setup the Headquarter of the organization in London. CDLR faxes newsletters to six hundred centres through CompuServe every week. The same information is also transmitted through email and its web home page. It also receives information regarding the affairs of the Royal family through disgruntled Saudi business persons, military officers, intelligence Officials and clerics.[19] Alarmed by the amplifying nature of challenges, kingdom made a tactical alliance with the British Government for deportation of al-Masari to the Caribbean island of Dominica. But al-Masari does not seem to be in a mood to relent.[20]

MIRA (Movement for Islamic Reforms in Arabia) spearheaded by Sad al-Faqih came out of a split in CDLR (Committee for the Defence Legitimate Rights) in March 1996 over differences on policy and methodology of the latter. Faqih craved for a discourse confined to Saudi Arabia whereas al-Masari thought of a broader discourse having alliances with the other Islamic movements in the region.[21] The movement got sustenance from the Letter of Demands and sought to implement Shariah in Saudi Arabia. Emphasizing upon transformation of the system Faqih says "True political reform will inevitably entail a restructuring of the Saudi regime itself. All the problems of the regime are linked to the Royal family and its monopoly on power. This is a fundamental problem that every Saudi opposition seeks to eradicate."[22] He disapproves of the current regime on various grounds such as (i) monopolization of the power by the al-Saud family; (ii) dependence of Saudi Arabia upon the United States for security; (iii) stress on ascriptive factor or patrimonialism in the recruitment of political elites or bureaucracy rather than achievement consideration or meritocracy; (iv) nexus between ulama and the royal family, and the role of the former in according legitimacy to the regime.[23]

The Committee Against Corruption in Saudi Arabia (CASA) that suddenly got into oblivion towards the end of nineties reappeared in 2002 focusing against Al-Saud regime through Internet. It pursues liberal political and social agenda based on Islam. Article 1 of the organization says: "CASA is a peaceful organization whose sole purpose is to change the Saudi Arabian status quo using Internet as a worldwide campaign tool. CASA is not associated or affiliated with any political or religious group. CASA condemns violence, fundamentalism, and extremism and supports the interests of both the United States and Saudi Arabia."[24] Article II says: "CASA is committed to identifying alternative leadership in Saudi Arabia that will govern the country without corruption and malice. This alternative leadership needs to include independently—minded businessmen, intellectuals, and other Saudis who wish to bring Saudi Arabia into the Twenty-first century without disrupting either Saudi societal mores or its Islamic roots."[25] The text of CASA indicates that the organization seeks change in political system within an Islamic structure.

The above organized groups, that is, CDLR, MIRA and CASA call for restructuring of the system largely using electronic means for expressing their dissent against the Royal family. No doubt, after the bifurcation of CDLR, the nature of opposition became divided, but their techniques and content continue to pose challenge to the al-Saud authority.

CONTEXTUALIZING DEMOCRATIZATION IN POST 9/11 PERIOD: ISLAMIST-LIBERAL PERSPECTIVE

In the aftermath of the 9/11 incident, Saudi ideology and its institutions became the prime source of criticism which created ample scope for a new political culture in the country. The United States called for political reforms focusing upon freedom, democracy and human rights.[26] The 'Islamist liberals' taking advantage of this tried to generate a broader consensus over political reforms and resurfaced with pragmatic ideological connotations for democratization of the system. The key figures among them are Abd al-Aziz al-Qasim, Abdallah al-Hamid, Mansural-Nuqaydan and Muhammad Said Tayyib.[27] Their ideological underpinnings are to be understood for analyzing the nature of consensus for political reforms in Saudi Arabia.

Shaykh Abd al-Aziz al-Qasim criticizes the contemporary Islamist movements for their aversion towards the western political systems. Although he casts doubt over the efficacy of those systems, still he considers them source of inspiration for the Muslims. He believes that Islam needs a political system through which justice can be secured and its norms be defined in the true spirit of *ijtihad* (application of reasoning). Democracy is experimented as the best form of government and the Muslims can emulate it to build a just society. No doubt, the operational mechanism would vary in conformity with the value system or the cultural norms of a society. He also suggests the setting up of a genuine civil society to buttress the cause of Islamic democracy.[28]

Keeping a common position with al-Qasim, Abdallah al-Hamid perceives dynamism in Islam citing the example of medieval jurist Ibn Hanbal who had tremendous influence on wahhabism in Saudi Arabia. Al-Hamid says: "He (Hanbal) completed important tasks, such as compiling the Prophet's traditions, but he also expressed views. Among them are some that are open to *ijtihad*, and wherever there is *ijtihad*, there is some right and some wrong...It is essential to borrow from our ancestors, for they have played an important role, but what I criticize is the behaviour of these traditionalists who refuse to go beyond them...who regard them as saints, as if they were the incarnation of the Book and the Sunna."[29] Al-Hamid observes that salafism in conservative form is closer to the religious set-up of Saudi Arabia. On the other, salafism in innovative form is conspicuous by its absence. Hamid says "Ibn Taymiyya has fashioned a discourse capable of dealing with the problems of his era, and in this sense, he is an innovator. However, those of his disciples who have today made him an absolute reference and hope to solve our contemporary problems with his ideas are imitators and conservative salafis."[30] He adds "what we need are people who base themselves on the Book and the Sunna to find solutions to the particular problems we face: globalization, human rights, civil society, United Nations, etc... Can one find in Ibn Taymiyya's medicine chest remedies to these problems?" What al-Hamid suggests in this context is the revival of innovative salafism to address the problems of contemporary society or "return to the pious ancestors and not simply to their productions, with a clear vision of what the *maqasid* (objectives) of the Shariah ought to be."[31] It is on this basis that the Shura could be evolved and be ingrained in its own cultural milieu without imbibing the model from the west.

Muhammad Said Tayyib in his book on "Intellectuals and a Prince...Shura (Consultation) and the Policy of Open Door" called for freedom of speech, democracy, and protection of human rights in a liberal perspective. However, since nineties he has reformed his ideas within Islamic paradigm. He says "Religion is a red line I do not want to cross—and which I do not want to get close to; this is true particularly for all the questions to which there is a clear answer in the Quran and the Sunnah."[32] It is derived that Tayyib seeks to define his liberal philosophy inside an Islamic framework.

"Strategic Vision for the Present and the Future" based on the ideological undercurrents of Islamic-liberals was signed by one hundred four persons having background from academics, bureaucracy, media, business, medicine and engineering. The document was sent to the then Crown Prince Abdullah in January 2003.[33] It included policies to augment the relations between the citizens and the state, achieving social justice and equity, amnesty to political prisoners, provision of basic human rights to all with protection of women rights under Shariah and ceasing discrimination on religious, sectarian and social lines.[34] It entailed that the Shura is possible through reforms in the Basic Law of Governance. Their demands incorporated: Legislative, executive and judicial wings of government are to be operated within the structural matrix of separation of powers; Consultative Council (Majlis Al-Shura) is to be directly elected by the citizens with similar provisions of direct elections for representative Councils at the provincial level; An independent and impartial judicial structure is to be created in consonance with the principles of Quran. Its pillars are to be solidified providing immunity to the judges and increasing the powers of the appeals court; Human rights provisions viz. freedom of speech, assembly, elections and participation are to be guaranteed through a Royal proclamation; Civil society institutions are to be permitted in order to accelerate the pace of political participation and peaceful dialogue.[35]

It is observed that the Islamist liberals are not antithetical to the concept of democratization in Saudi Arabia. They advocate the establishment of a directly elected legislature (Majlis al-Shura), civil society institutions and human rights conditions for the emergence of a participatory democracy. What they prescribed was that the modus operandi of the system would be based on Islam with recourse to *ijtihad*.

POLITICAL REFORMS TOWARDS DEMOCRATIZATION

The reform process begun by the late King Fahd was consolidated by the present King Abdullah for ensuring people's participation in the decision making system. Here, the question is how far those reforms accentuate the process of democratization in Saudi Arabia? So, in this background, the nature of political reforms pertaining to the Majlis al-Shura, (Consultative Council), Municipal Council, Civil Society, Civil Liberty and National Dialogue are analyzed for an in-depth understanding of the process of democratization in Saudi Arabia.

Majlis al-Shura (Consultative Council) established on December 29, 1993 as a sixty member nominated body became 150 in 2005.[36] Article 67 of the Basic System of Rules outlines the functions of this legislative body. It says; "The regulatory authority (Consultative Council) lays down regulations and motions to meet the interests of the state or remove what is bad in its affairs, in accordance with the Shariah. This authority exercises its functions in accordance with this law (the Basic System of Rules) and the laws pertaining to the council of ministers and the law pertaining to the Consultative Council".[37]

The constitution entrusts the Council the responsibility to debate the policies of the government and propose draft regulations to the King. The Consultative Council performs the following functions. It (I) expresses opinions on the general policy of the state. '(Article 15); (ii) 'proposes amendment in an executive law' (Article 23), (iii) 'studies international laws, charter treaties, agreements and make appropriate suggestions regarding them' (Article 15); (iv) 'interprets regulations'(Article 15); (v) 'discusses the annual reports submitted by the ministry and other government bodies and make appropriate suggestions regarding them' (Article 15); (vi) 'questions the ministers and other government officials' (Article 22).[38]

The above functions, which were earlier enjoyed by the Council of Ministry, are at present, entrusted to the Consultative Council. The actions of the Government are to be approved by the Consultative Council. Otherwise, they are to be referred back to the King. Normally, the Consultative Council does not by pass the Council of Ministers without the consent of the King. Even then, its power to judge the work of the Council of Ministers is an important development in the Saudi Political System.

All said and done, the present Consultative Council does not perform role of legislature as has been the case in democratic political systems. The views of Islamic scholars regarding the legislature are at complete variance when it is conceptualized in the context of Saudi Consultative Council. Here, the Consultative Council remains merely a regulatory body rather than a purely legislative organ. So, the concept of Consultative Council in the real sense is yet to take its shape in the politics of Saudi Arabia. Similarly, Regional Councils institutionalized in all the thirteen provinces of the kingdom also fail to provide popular access to the citizens at the provincial level.

At present, the Council is perceived as major institutional mechanism in Saudi Arabia for redressing the grievances of the people. There are also debates that the Majlis al-Shura may be a directly elected body in place of a nominated one in future. However, in order to qualify for an electoral democracy, the system should have universal adult suffrage, competitive politics with multi-party system, periodic election through secret ballot system, connectivity with the electorate through media and political campaigning.[39] But it is noticed that none of the parameters are present in Saudi Arabia so far the Majlis is concerned.

The historic statement made four decades ago by the prince Salman bin Abdulaziz became a reality when the country organized its first ever partially elected 178 member Municipal Council in 2005 for ushering grass root democracy.[40] It said "It is clear that members of the Municipality Council will be elected by the general public through balloting paper which is the crucible where the good public elements will fuse and select a leader who will be a connecting link between the government and the people, that leader should be a qualified and intelligent person who could speak on behalf people and demand what his people in his area particularly needed and what Riyadh in general needed. Since elections generally depend on voter turn out, therefore the success or failure of the idea of the Municipal Council depended largely on the citizens themselves. There is no doubt that we took this step because we are sure that our citizens in Riyadh are very enlightened and have the spirit of participation and co-operation that would make the Municipal election a reality, by will of Allah."[41] The Saudis elect half of the Municipal members directly and the Minister of Rural and Municipal affairs nominates the other half from among the distinguished citizens. The powers of the Municipality are vested with the Municipal Council for monitoring and decision making. The Head of the Municipality acts as the executive authority aided by the Municipal departments. The Municipal Council selects its Chairman and the Deputy Chairman for a period of two years. The Minister of Rural and Municipal Affairs is vested with the power to decide the number of members for Municipalities.[42]

The Saudi authority deemed that the Municipal Councils would ensure empowerment of the people at the urban grass root level. It anticipated that the Councils would manage major part of the governmental work and decrease the burden of the departments. It also held that the elections would increase public participation in decision making system and provide better services to the people. Dwelling upon the Municipal Council Abdulrahman al-Zamil, a member of Majlis said: "This will have a tremendous impact on the municipality work, with the public being able to oversee the distribution of land and usage of land, as well as overseeing social programmes and the allocation of funds for services. But more importantly, it is a psychological break."[43]

No doubt, the formation of Saudi Municipal Council is a stepping stone towards the process of further democratization in future, but one should be realistic in the assessment of the degree of democratization of the Municipality system. Neither the Municipal Councils are fully elective nor are they fully gender representative. The nomination character may impede the autonomy as well as the delivery capacity of the Council. The representative nature of the Council also makes it a limited institution which is confined only to the male members of Saudi society.

Civil society is the sphere of public life which is 'open voluntary, self generating and autonomous from the state.' It consists of a number of organizations which may be economic, cultural, developmental, issue oriented, informational and educational in nature.[44] The Saudi authorities are gradually allowing the civil society institutions for expanding the scope in public life. Professional organizations or syndicates such as Saudi Dental society; Saudi

Pediatric Association; Saudi Ophthalmologic Society; Saudi Pharmaceutical Society; Saudi Engineering Association; Saudi Management Organization; Saudi Society for Technology, Development and Transfer; Arab Network for Environment and Development; Al-Nahda Women Association in Riyadh; King Abdullah Foundation; King Faisal Foundation; King Khalid Foundation; National Society for Human Rights; Saudi Environment society; Saudi Computer Society; Council of Saudi Chambers of Commerce and Industry; Jeddah Chamber of Commerce and Industry; Mecca Chamber of Commerce and Industry; Riyadh Chamber of Commerce and Industry; Independent Journalist Association etc. are operating in different spheres for articulating the interest of the society.[45] In the absence of political parties, the role of these organizations becomes highly important to negotiate between the state and the society. But here the question arises how far the civil society institutions are autonomous from control of the state? Since the Saudi authority closely monitors the society, it would be difficult on the part of the professional associations to articulate anything against the interest of the Saudi regime.

Civil liberty envisages freedom of speech, assembly, freedom from arrest, detention and right to fair trial. Its objective is to limit the arbitrary power of the state providing basic human rights to all.[46] Coming to Saudi Arabia it is observed that the country is participant to the Genocide Convention, Slavery Convention and the Supplementary Convention on Slavery.[47] However, it is not a signatory to the Universal Declaration of Human Rights since it objects Article 18 of the document which spells out "Every one has the right to freedom of thought, conscience and religion; this right includes the freedom to change his religion or belief; and freedom alone or in community with others, and in public in private, to manifest his religion or belief in teaching, practice, worship and observance."[48] Rather, Saudi Arabia ratified Cairo Declaration of Human Rights as it regards it as 'Binding Divine Commands'.[49] Article 10 says "Islam is the religion of unspoiled nature. It is prohibited to exercise any form of pressure on man or to exploit his poverty or ignorance in order to force him to change his religion to another religion or to atheism."[50] Besides the Cairo Declaration, Saudi Arabia also promulgated Basic Law of 1992 to safeguard the human rights in Kingdom.[51]

The following constitutional provisions are important in the context of promoting civil liberty conditions in Saudi Arabia. These are: The state protects human rights in accordance with the Shariah:" (Article. 23); "The state provides security for all citizens and residents on its territories. No one may be confined, arrested or imprisoned without reference to law" (Article 36). "Mass media and other vehicles of expression should employ civil and polite language, contribute towards education of the nation and strengthen unity. It is prohibited to commit acts leading to disorder and division, affecting the security of the state and its public relations, or undermining human dignity and rights" (Article 39). "Councils held by the King and the Crown Prince are open for all citizens and anyone else who may have a complaint or a grievance. A citizen is entitled to address public authorities and discuss any matters of concern to him." (Article 43)[52]

At the institutional level, National Society for human Rights was established in 2004 to deal with the matters pertained to domestic violence, prisoners, bureaucracy, employment and naturalization among others. Later, the Saudi Government set up an eighteen member Human Rights Commission to find out human rights violations by the government and the private institutions; bring remedial measures for the infringement of rights, look into the execution of international agreements and inspect the prisons and detention centres. It was also empowered to present their findings to the king.[53]

The discussion shows that Saudi Arabia is poised to promote the civil liberty through constitutional as well as institutional devices. From the statutory perspective, the document protects human rights and prevents illegal arrest and detention. However, the practice does not match with the theory. The Amnesty International and Human Rights Watch report prolonged detention, ill-treatment, unfair trials, prisoner of conscience, application of flogging and extensive practice of capital and corporeal punishment in Saudi Arabia.[54] Besides this, the text of the law does not mention freedom of speech and expression which is an essential ingredient of civil liberty.

National Dialogue is a novel mechanism adopted by the Saudi regime to engage civil society in reform process of the kingdom. In order to begin the process, the First National Dialogue was convened in Riyadh from 15-18 July 2003 to discuss "National Unity, Role of Ulama, International Relations and Their Effect on National Unity"[55] Taking a nod from this, King AbdulAziz Centre for National Dialogue was set up to protect the interest of the people and pave the way for reforms in eliciting public opinion through dialogue. Subsequently, the Second National Dialogue was held from 27 December 2003-1 January 2004 attended by clergy, intellectuals and academics on the theme "Excess and Moderation: A Thorough Review".[56] It dwelt upon the legal, political, social, economic, psychological and media issues "with a view to formulating suggestions to help confront the symptoms of excess".[57] The Dialogue sessions concluded with the following suggestions: (i) Awakening the religious institutions for a consensus over terrorism, Jammat al-Muslimin, Dar al-Harb, Dar al-Kufr, Dar al-Islam, al-Taifa al-Mansura; (ii) Making a comprehensive study of the religious 'excess'and its impact upon the Saudi society; (iii) Accelerating the pace of political reforms for public participation through directly elected Shura and regional councils; iv) Facilitating the civil society by setting up of trade union and voluntary agencies; (v) Promoting better contact between the regime and the ruled; (vi) Effective management of public funds for attaining transparency and accountability in the system; (vii) Rationalizing the religious message in an open manner in consonance with the present developments; (viii) Repudiating individual fatwa which involve the interest of the state and its future and augmenting the machineries through qualified persons on the subject; (ix) Creating dialogue in Saudi society and making it viable through educational institutions for upholding public interest; (x) Introducing innovative educational curricula for inculcating values of tolerance and moderation; (xi) Buttressing the position of women in different aspects of Saudi society; (xii) Promising fair trial of the accused persons involved in violence and terrorism; (xiii) bringing in an inclusive policy for engaging youth in the right perspective and to get rid of extremism.[58]

The third and the fourth National Dialogue covered issues on Women's Rights and Young People's Expectations respectively in 2004. The Fifth National Dialogue was conducted in December 2005 on the theme "We and the Other: A National Vision for Dealing with World Cultures" represented by a cross section of personalities.[59]

The sessions ended with a National Vision based on the following important points: (i) Bringing in Islamic social system and justice for humanity; (ii) Developing civil society institutions for protecting public interest and increasing interface with the others; (iii) Stressing on human values for safeguarding human rights, dignity and freedom; (iv) Assisting with the international organizations and commissions for the protection of women rights; (v) Promoting tolerance and dialogue across the nations and the societies; (vi) Considering Basic Law of Ruling as the common guiding principle in relationship with the others; (vii) Positive attitude towards the expatriates and implementation of national laws for securing their rights.[60]

National Dialogue sessions viz. sixth on "Education and Ways of Improvement", Seventh on "Work and Employment: Dialogue between Society and Work Related Institutions" and Eighth on "Health Services: A Dialogue between the Society and Health Institutions" were held successively in 2007, 2008 and 2009 to tone up the reform process in kingdom.[61] The outcome of all the dialogue sessions, if properly carried out, would gradually ensure a participatory political culture. However, its success hinges upon the Saudi leadership and capacity of the civil society for political bargaining in future.

CONCLUSIONS

While observing the process of democratization in Saudi Arabia, the following inputs may be considered:

Democratization is to be interpreted not necessarily in the structural matrix of westernism. The universal principles of democracy like popular participation, justice, equity, transparency and accountability may be contextualized in the cultural milieu with recourse to *ijtihad* for bringing necessary transformation in the polity. The only difference is that the operational mechanism would vary vis-à-vis the other paradigms. The ideological legitimacy sustained by the Saudi regime in a symbiotic relationship with the religious establishment is to be redefined in the true spirit of Islam. The al-Saud regime maintains stability either through co-optation of moderate elements or through a policy of repression of the radical groups. The opposition at present seems divided either on ideological or personal considerations. The emergence of MIRA out of a split in CDLR clearly illustrates the politics of fragmentation. A common approach and coherent policy adopted by the different Saudi constituencies could be a successful factor in Saudi politics.

Civil society which operates in the form of professional syndicates is not completely immune from the government control. An autonomous civil society can only augment the functioning of the system from the perspective of developmental democracy. Neither the civil society is autonomous in Saudi Arabia nor is it truly democratic. If any change is to be ushered in the system, then the civil society is to become vibrant and all-embracing. Besides this, the civil liberty conditions are also to be strengthened through new promulgations bridging the gap between the statutory provisions and the realistic circumstances paving the way for democratic culture in the system.

The reforms introduced by the Saudi establishment are only nominal in nature. Majlis al-Shura is yet to be a directly elected legislative body. The partially elected municipal councils do not fully qualify for an electoral democracy. A democratic invention in kingdom requires the variables of electoral democracy; civil society and the cultural moorings. The invention is explicated in following formula.

Let us assume

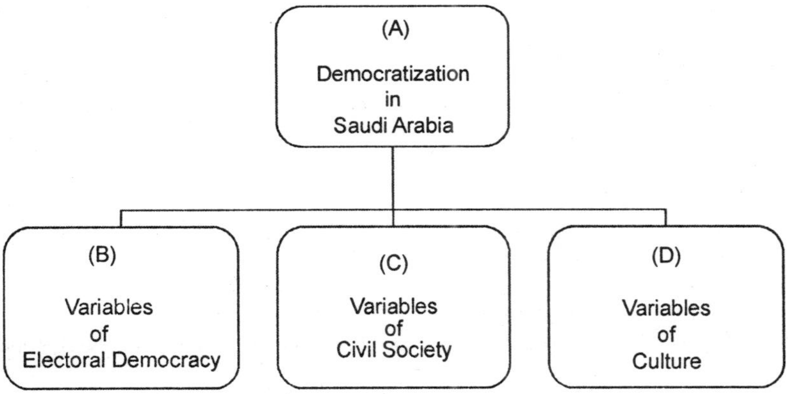

A- B + C + D

(a) Democratization in Saudi Arabia;
(b) Variables of Electoral Democracy (Universal Adult Suffrage; Free and Fair Election; Secret Ballot System; Bi Party or Multi Party System and Free Media);
(c) Variables of Civil Society (Autonomous Professional organization; Civil Liberty and Protest or Peaceful Demonstration) and;
(d) Variables of Culture (Cultural foundations of the society with recourse to *ijtihad*);

It is derived that the reforms carried out by the al-Saud regime indicate the trends of electoral democracy in limited perspective at the urban grass root level. The reform initiatives spearheaded by the King Abdulaziz Centre for National Dialogue may prompt the Saudi authorities to introduce a partially elected legislature in future. However, one should not be pessimistic in approach. The reforms that look piecemeal today may be instrumental in the growth of participatory democracy in future.

NOTES

1. Akbar S Ahmad, "Mullah, Mahdi and Mosque: Emergent Trends in Muslim Society", *Arab Studies Quarterly,* vol. 4,1982.p. 127.
2. Joseph A. Kechichian, "Ulama –Saud Politics", *International Journal of Middle Eastern Studies,* vol.18, 1986, p. 53.
3. Summer Scott Huyette, *Political Adaptation in Saudi Arabia*, (Boulder, London:Westview Press,1985), pp. 129.
4. Gulshan Dietl, *Through Two wars and Beyond: A Study of Gulf Co-operation Council*, (New Delhi: Lancer Publications,1991), pp. 26-29. Jajati K. Pattnaik, *Strategic Bulletin*, vol.ii, no. i, January-February, 1997, p. 33.
5. *Ibid.*
6. Dietl, no.4, pp. 28-29.
7. *Ibid.*
8. Mamoun Fandy, *Saudi Arabia and the Politics of Dissent,* (London: MacMillan Press Ltd. 1999), no. 8, p. 37.
9. *Ibid.*
10. *Ibid.* p. 26.
11. Girijesh Pant, *The Arab Gulf Economies: From Crisis to Reform,* (Delhi: Har Anand publications, 1996), pp. 93-95.
12. Jajati K. Pattnaik, "Saudi Regime at the Crossroads", *The Observer of Business and Politics,* 6 June, 1996.
13. Gulshan Dietl, *Saudi Arabia, People, Politics, Policies*, (New Delhi: NBT, 2006) p. 50.

14. Jajati K. Pattnaik, "Islamic Fever Grips Saudi Arabia," *Asian Recorder*, August-11 August, 1996.
15. R. Hrair Dekmejian, "The Rise of Political Islamism in Saudi Arabia," *MiddleEastJournal*, Vol.48, No.4, 1994, pp. 630-631.
16. Fandy, no. 8, p. 116.
17. *Ibid*, p.135.
18. Mamoun Fandy, "Cyber Resistance: Saudi Opposition between Globalization", *Comparative Studies in Society and History*, Vol. 41, No., 1, January 1999, p. 135.
19. Fandy, No. 8 pp. 128-129.
20. Pattnaik, No. 12.
21. Fandy, No. 8, p. 150.
22. *Ibid*, p. 167.
23. *Ibid.*
24. Daryl Champion, *The Paradoxical Kingdom: Saudi Arabia and the Momentum of Reform*, (London:Hurst and Company,2003), p. 253.
25. *Ibid.*
26. Talmiz Ahmad, *Reform in the Arab World*, (New Delhi, India Research Press), 2005, p. 3.
27. Stephane Lacroix, "Between Islamists and Liberals: Saudi Arabia's New Islamo-Liberal Reformists", *Middle East Journal*, Vol. 58, No.3, 2004, pp. 346-355.
28. *Ibid*, pp. 347-348.
29. *Ibid*, p. 349 .
30. *Ibid.*
31. *Ibid*, pp. 349-350.
32. *Ibid*, 355.
33. Richard Dekmejian, "The Liberal Impulse in Saudi Arabia", *Middle East Journal*, Vol. 57, No. 3,2003, pp. 404.
34. *Ibid*. p. 405-406.
35. *Ibid.*
36. Anthony H. Cordesman, *Saudi Arabia Enters the Twenty-First Century*, (Washington, D.C., Centre for Strategic and International Studies, 2003), p. 361.
37. Rashed Aba –Namay, "The Recent Constitutional Reforms in Saudi Arabia," *International and Comparative Law Quarterly*, Vol. 42,1993, p. 310-311.
38. *Ibid.*
39. www.freedomhouse.org/template.cfm Accessed on 8 May 2009.
40. Cordesman, No 36, p. 363.
41. http://www.mofa.gov.sa Accessed on 30 May 2007.
42. *Ibid.*
43. Digby Lidstone, "Grassroot Reforms", *MEED*, 17-23 October, 2003, 2007.
44. Larry Diamond, *Developing Democracy:Towards Consolidation*, (Baltimore: The John Hopkins Press 1999), pp. 221-234, See Jajati k. Pattnaik, "Revisiting Political development; A Theoretical construct," *Journal of Peace Studies*, Vol. 13, No. 3 July-September 2006, pp. 76-81.
45. www.arabdecision.org/coun-se-3-11.htm Accessed on 11 May 2009.

46. Iain McLean and Alistair McMillan, *Concise Dictionary of Politics*, (New York, Oxford University Press, 2007) p. 78.
47. Dietl, No. 13, p. 55.
48. http://www.un.org/en/documents/udhr / Accessed on 16 May 2009
49. Dietl, No. 13, p. 55.
50. http://www.religlaw.org/interdocs/docs/cairohrislam1990.htm Accessed on 16 May 2009.
51. http://www.mofa.gov.sa/detail.asp Accessed on 23 May 2009 .
52. *Ibid.*
53. http://www.amnesty.org/en/region/Saudi-arabia Accessed on 22May 2009. See http://www.amnestyusa.org/all-countries/Saudi-arabia/page.do Accessed on 22 May 2009, see Dietl, No.13, p. 59.
54. *Ibid*, p. 57.
55. http://www.kacnd.org/eng/ Accessed on 22 May, 2009.
56. *Ibid.*
57. *Ibid.*
58. *Ibid.*
59. *Ibid.*
60. *Ibid.*
61. *Ibid.*

8

Saudi Arabia: Transition to a Liberalized Autocracy?

Ajish Joy

Studying democratization in Saudi Arabia can often feel like an exercise in futility. In all available global rankings of democratic governance Saudi Arabia normally finds itself in the bottom. No definition of democracy or democratization-even when stretched to the limits—can account for the Saudi system. Democracy of course is one of the most widely defined, interpreted and debated concepts in modern political science. Classical theories of democracy recognize three main types—direct democracy, representative/ liberal democracy and plural democracy.[1] Apart from these classical theories, Collier and Levitsky have identified over 550 subtypes of democracy such as 'authoritarian democracy,' 'neopatrimonial democracy,' 'military-dominated democracy,' and 'protodemocracy.[2] However, on an elemental level democracy involves fair, free, and frequent elections, rule of law, an independent judiciary, a network of institutional regulation including a constitution and accountability towards the governed. If popular representation is the raison d'être of democracy and independent judicial oversight its lifeblood, then Saudi Arabia is nowhere near democratization.

In the past two decades however, the Kingdom has witnessed several events including the setting up of a Consultative Council, promulgation of Basic Laws, a round of municipal elections and most importantly the coronation of a new King who has professed the need of opening up the political space in the Kingdom. None of these events though can be considered as steps towards democratization. At best, they can be called delicate, incremental moves towards political and social reform but not really sufficient for democracy. These reform measures are steps in the direction of self-perpetuation and preservation from the House of Saud than anything else.

In the following sections this paper will look into the major reform initiatives, reformist pressures, institutions, events and regime-strategies in Saudi Arabia and will argue that the political system in the Kingdom is moving in the direction of a liberal autocracy.

HISTORICAL OVERVIEW

The history of the Kingdom of Saudi Arabia begins in 1744 with the establishment of Saud rule in Diriya, located in Nejd. The Kingdom was established and flourished under an alliance between Mohammed ibn Saud and Sheikh Muhammad ibn Abdul Wahhab. The latter provided religious legitimacy to the political ambitions of Saud while the Kingdom helped in spreading the puritan version of Islam taught by Sheikh Wahhab. The earlier Saudi Kingdoms faced ruin under Ottoman attacks as well as tribal skirmishes. The present Kingdom was established by Abdul-Aziz ibn Saud, a descendant of Mohammed ibn Saud who recovered lost territories like Riyadh in 1902 and captured most of Nejd by 1906. With help from the religious zealots (Ikhwan) he annexed most of Arabia. Al-Hasa region was conquered before the First World War and Hejaz in 1924 by defeating Husayn ibn Ali—the Sharif of Mecca. In 1932, Nejd and Hejaz was combined as the Kingdom of Saudi Arabia.

Hejaz had a history of representative institutions like the National Council for Mecca, which was established in December 1924. This was further expanded as a National Consultative Council, in 1925 with powers including national security. Abdul-Aziz had to incorporate the representative nature of Hejazi politics or face rebellion there and to this end he made some concessions to the region. He promulgated a constitution for Hejaz on September 3, 1926, after appointing his son Faisal as the viceroy to the region. In 1927 he set up a body of eight men to advise Faisal. Of these four men were to be appointed after consultation with 'men of integrity and experience' while the remaining four could be appointed at the government's discretion.[3] The King also set up the "Commission on Inspection and Reform," to review the administrative system and according to its recommendation established a Council of Deputies (*Majlis al-Wukala*) on December 30, 1932, after the establishment of the Kingdom of Saudi Arabia. It had representatives from the ministry of Internal Security, Foreign Affairs, and Finance.[4] The *Majlis al-Wukala* was expanded to 25 members in the early 1950s but when Saud became the King after the death of Abdul Aziz its functions were transferred to the Council of Ministers as Saud came under political pressure from the other members of the royal family.[5]

After Prince Faisal became the Prime Minister in 1958, the Council of Ministers was developed into a formal decision-making body, with legislative, executive and administrative functions. A Basic Law of Governance was also prepared by Faisal. Faisal's Basic Law dealt with the system of government and creating institutions such as the Office of the Attorney General, and the National Council (*al-Majlis al-Watani*).[6] After Faisal became the King followed by a palace coup however, the pace of the reforms deteriorated mainly due to the economic windfall which was the result of the oil crisis of 1973. Reforms were promised on a regular basis during the reign of Khalid as well. When Fahd took over as the King he appointed Interior Minister Nayef as the head of a committee to look into the possibilities of reviving the Basic Law package of Faisal.

It was in the backdrop of these events that the Iraqi invasion of Kuwait took place. The petition fever which originated in Kuwait soon spread to Saudi Arabia. The first petition was submitted by a group of 43 prominent liberal activists calling for political reforms. They wanted that Sharia shall remain as the sole source of law but they demanded to limit the unfettered discretionary power of the ulema in interpreting the laws. Other demands were the modernization of the judicial system, enhanced rights for the media, and expanding the scope of representation. The clerics under the leadership of Sheikh Abd-al Aziz bin Baz soon came up with their petition to the king. The clerics wanted to set up an institution for them to examine the laws passed by the government to ensure that they are not in conflict with the sharia. They also demanded reduction of taxes, permitting the establishment of Islamic financial institutions, bureaucratic accountability, and elimination of corruption.

THE BASIC LAWS

Faced with an increasing turmoil and understanding the gravity of the situation, in February 1992 King Fahd issued a set of laws, *al nizam al asasi lil hukm*, the Saudi Basic Law, the Law of the Shura Council code, and a Law for regional governance. The Basic Law opens with the declaration that Quran and Sunnah are the constitution of Saudi Arabia, essentially foreclosing any questions regarding "constitutional reforms". Moreover, according to the Basic Law, the legitimacy of the rulers is not derived from consensus or popular support. Legitimacy and sovereignty flow from Quran and Sunnah. This provides a major leeway to the rulers as Quran, sunnah and sharia do not specifically address the conduct of most administrative and governmental matters in this age.[7] The basic laws also institutionalized the rule of the House of Saud by declaring the rules of succession—that the throne will remain with the male descendants of Abdul Aziz Ibn Saud. In a way, the Basic Laws served an important purpose for the Saudi establishment by formalizing and codifying the unbridled powers enjoyed by the king and reinforced his role as the absolute monarch. He is in charge of the general and judicial administration and remains the referral point between all the branches of the government. According to article 44 of the Basic Law, the King is the ultimate source of judicial, executive and legislative powers. He is also the supreme commander of the armed forces.

The King holds the power to appoint the Crown Prince—the heir apparent, the second most important job in Saudi Arabia. He can dismiss the Crown Prince and name someone else at any time. He heads the Council of Ministers which serves at his pleasure. The King also serves as his own Prime Minister. He also holds the power to dismiss the Consultative Council.

Article 26 of the Basic Law says that the state protects human rights in accordance with the Sharia, echoing the Cairo Declaration on Human Rights in Islam.[8] Subjecting human rights to sharia means that fundamental rights like protection from "torture or cruel, inhuman or degrading treatment or punishment" are not supported by the Saudi Basic Law. It also puts in jeopardy the rights of non-Muslims. The law is silent on right of free speech, association, assembly, seriously undermining the rights of individuals. Interestingly, as the Human Rights Watch has pointed out, the Saudi basic Law was prepared by a Committee headed by Prince Nayef, heading the Interior Ministry the principal government agency identified with most violations of human rights in Saudi Arabia.[9]

The Basic Law addressed the issue of the royal succession and declared that the right to the Saudi throne will be with the sons and grandsons of the founder King Abdul Aziz, making nearly 500 princes eligible to be considered for succession.

THE ALLEGIANCE COMMISSION

King Abdullah further institutionalized the procedure of succession by setting up an Allegiance Commission. He amended Section "C" of Article 5 of the Basic Law which now reads, "The invitation to pledge allegiance to the King and select the Crown Prince would take place according to the provisions of the Allegiance (Bay'a) Commission's Law". The Allegiance Commission Law[10] was passed on October 20, 2006, thereby putting in place an institutional framework through which the House of Saud would appoint its successors. "A relevant set of bylaws was passed in October of 2007, immediately followed by the formation of the Allegiance Commission in December".[11] The new institution is comprised of the sons of founding King Abdul Aziz. The grandsons would represent those who are deceased, incapacitated or unwilling to assume the throne. The King and Crown Prince can nominate a son each to the council. According to Article 6 of the Allegiance Commission Law, "if the King passes away, the Allegiance Commission will pledge allegiance to the Crown Prince. Once the new King takes over, he can nominate one, two or three candidates as the new Crown Prince before the Allegiance Commission. The Commission can accept or reject those candidates and if all three are rejected, the Commission can nominate a suitable candidate. If the King disagrees, he can put up another candidate and the Commission will vote to decide between them. The entire process however, is to be completed within 30 days. The Allegiance Commission Law, under article 11 deals with the situation in which the King is incapacitated. It can ask for a medical report and if the report finds that the King is temporarily incapable of discharging his duties, the Commission will ask the Crown Prince to stand in till the King recovers. If the inability is permanent, the Crown Prince will be invited to take over as the new king. This will ensure that the Kingdom will not face embarrassing situations like the one in which an incapacitated King Fahd remained in office for ten years after suffering a debilitating stroke. The Allegiance Commission Law will take effect after the current Crown Prince Sultan accedes to the throne.

THE CONSULTATIVE COUNCIL

The Saudi Consultative Council, the Majlis al-Shura was constituted under the Shura Council Law, issued by Royal Decree No. A/91. It is a nominated body which is supposed to be the equivalent of legislative assembly. However, in a state where Quran and Sunna forms the constitution and sharia the legal code, the concept of legislation, or *tashri'a*, can be complicated. Human beings can only interpret God's law, not make their own. This view has been followed in Saudi Arabia. Throughout its existence, the government has never claimed the right to legislate, only to "regulate" in order to supplement, though not contradict, the Sharia".[12] Even this regulation is generally the sole preserve of the cabinet. When the Majlis was introduced its function was purely advisory and was limited to discuss and express opinion on socio-economic development plans, international laws, charters, treaties, agreements, annual reports submitted by ministries and other government bodies.

After being a nominated deliberative body for nearly a decade, the Majlis got its scope widened in November 2003 when King Fahd amended articles 17 and 23 of the Shura Council law. Earlier, the Majlis resolutions were to be submitted to the Cabinet first. If the cabinet agrees with it, the king proclaims it and in case of a disagreement the King makes the final decision. The amended article says that the "resolutions shall be submitted to the king who decides what resolutions to be referred to Cabinet. If views of both Shura Council and Cabinet agree, the resolutions are issued after the king's approval. If views of both councils vary the issue shall be returned back to Shura Council to decide whatever it deems appropriate, and send the new resolution to the king who takes the final decisions".[13] The amendment thus enhanced the power of the Majlis vis-a-vis the cabinet. However, the law provides the ultimate power of decision to the King who is the Prime Minister and the head of the cabinet. Article 23 initially held that a new bill or amendment shall be proposed by at least 10 members. The amendment removed this stipulation.

The members of the Majlis are drawn from a vast pool with diverse backgrounds. Normally influential princes, the heads of tribes, universities, business houses and trade bodies suggest the names of potential candidates to the Saudi Cabinet. The cabinet, led by the King makes the final appointments (not exclusively from the list submitted). "Members, who tend to be highly educated and experts in their respective fields, are viewed as performing the function of consultation. While the rulers generally take account of the Council's views, its influence, rather than being grounded in law, has been a function of its members' prominence and diversity."[14] As Ammoun points out, the Majlis has come to exhibit a representative nature but not just of the Saudi society. More than that, it "represents the royal family's different clans, their political and economic interests, their ideological and political tendencies…their social bases, meaning their clientele". As a result those who do not constitute the clientele of any prince-like the recently urbanized and debedouinized population" is not represented adequately.[15] The strength of the Majlis has been expanded periodically. It started with sixty members, which was raised to ninety in the second term in 1997. The 2001-2005 Council got its strength expanded to 120. In April 2005, at the beginning of the new four-year term the membership was further increased by thirty up to 150.

Under King Abdullah, the Majlis has also witnessed the introduction of more 'politically oriented' members making it look different from the apolitical technocratic conclave which it used to be. This has led to more lively debates, especially on controversial subjects. The discussion on the new traffic law in the summer session of 2005 was an example. A liberal reformist member "Muhammad al-Zulfa, proposed to include the legalization of driver licenses for women on the agenda. The proposal ignited a major controversy and the Majlis had to address this highly explosive matter in public for the first time."[16] However, it never made it to the final agenda. The Council has also invited women to participate in open discussions to obtain their inputs.

Camille Ammoun argues that the events that followed the 1991 Gulf war, like the promulgation of Basic Laws and the setting up of the Consultative Council shall be seen as "institutional openings" rather than political reform or a democratic opening.[17] These were attempts by the Saudi establishment to prolong their rule by opening up the administration and integrating the Saudi society into it, thereby giving the people a sense of empowerment while keeping the prevailing power-structure intact.

ISLAMIST GROUPS AND THE REFORM TRENDS

In the immediate aftermath of the Gulf war, several groups of Islamists came to the forefront of the reform process in Saudi Arabia. The fact that the Kingdom had to bring in 'infidel' troops to defend itself raised a lot of uncomfortable questions and the Islamists used this opportunity to advance their agenda. None of the Islamists groups were calling for democratic reforms, what they wanted was a change in the existing structure. One such prominent group was the *Sahwa* (*Al-Sahwa al-Islamiyya*—The Islamic Awakening). The *Sahwists* were "neither lower class nor tribally identified. Instead, the common denominator was membership in the new middle class: graduates of higher education working as professionals or administrators".[18] Led by clerics like Salman al-Awda, and Safar al-Hawali, the *Sahwists* were influenced by the Muslim Brotherhood in their political ideology though they stuck to Wahhabism on social issues. In 1992, the sahwists submitted a memorandum to the head of clergy Sheikh Bin Baz in which they deplored the "total chaos in the economy and society, widespread bribery, favouritism, and the extreme feebleness of the courts and criticized virtually every aspect of domestic and foreign policy, and demanded a more rigorous application of Islamic law.[19] They also demanded a reorientation of the Saudi foreign policy by breaking off the ties with countries perceived to be antagonistic towards Islam. Saudi government responded by cracking down severely on the sahwist leadership.

The period also witnessed the rise of a neo-salafi group, inspired by a Syrian cleric Nasr al-Din al-Albani. This group rejected all schools of Islamic jurisprudence including Wahhabism and hence they were known as rejectionists. For them the source of all rules and governance shall be the strict literal reading of Quran and the *hadith* without any human interpretation. They were only concerned about the moral and religious aspects of life and were critical of any political activity. They argued that the present order in Saudi Arabia has become corrupted and it needed to be put back on track strictly and literally following Quranic principles. Jihadists like Osama bin Laden were another Islamist group who demanded reforms and called for a violent overthrow of the House of Saud alleging that it has deviated from the fundamental wahhabi tenets. Laden who was "at heart a *sahwist*, whose views were shaped by Al-Hawali[20] and his call to overthrow the Saudi regime came after the decision to bring the coalition forces. Laden was in favour of opposing Saddam Hussain but he wanted it to be done by the *mujahidin* not the 'infidel' forces.

Another group of Islamist reformers who rose into prominence especially after the 9/11 attacks were the Liberal-Islamists. Incidentally, they were tolerated by the rulers and some even got some discrete encouragement. They were much less dogmatic than the *sahwists* and the neo-salafists and their main focus was on political issues. They were more nationalistic in outlook, did not care much about pan-Islamism, supported the House of Saud and were critical of the Wahhabi ulema. Mansur al-Nuqaydan, Muhammad Sa'id Tayyib, Abdullah al-Hamid, Abd al-'Aziz al-Qasim, and Hasan al-Maliki were some of the prominent members of this group. They criticized the Hanbali School of jurisprudence followed by the Wahhabis and Mansur al-Nuqaydan had questioned the credibility of Hanbal himself. He has also argued that Quran is open for interpretation as required. According to him, "it is the interests and objectives that ought to determine the way we read Quran not the other way around. The Quran is an open book: with it everything is possible".[21] The

Liberal-Islamists have demanded a revision of school curriculum and the text books which portray non-wahhabis and non-Muslims as apostates and infidels withdrawn. Abd al-'Aziz al-Qasim, put forth the argument that Islamism and nationalism can coexist. According to him, the concept of homeland-*watan* is present in Quran making it legitimate and he refers to Prophet Mohammed's attachment to Mecca as a justification for his argument.

The Shia in Saudi Arabia have faced decades of discrimination from the Saudi rulers, ulema and the majority Sunni population. Their demand for reforms increased in the wake of the Iranian revolution. They were led by Sheikh Hassan al Saffar and his group—Organization for the Islamic Revolution in the Arabian Peninsula (OIR, *Munathamat al-Thawra al-Islamiyya fil-Jazira al-Arabiyya*). The rulers were ruthless in suppressing the Shia movement and gradually the Saudi Shia realized that fighting the establishment was not an option. During the petition fever after the Gulf war, the Shia leadership declared itself as a movement for Saudi Shia and changed its name to the Reform Movement.[22]

The Saudi government as a response declared that anti-Shia references will be removed from text books.[23] It also released some prisoners who were arrested after the 1979 Ashura revolt and permitted some of the exiled Shia to return. The government also promised to end discrimination against the community in government recruitments.[24]

AFTER 9/11

The 9/11 events decidedly enhanced the influence of external factors into Saudi political reform, especially as 15 out of the 19 hijackers who crashed planes on 9/11 were Saudi nationals. The American public opinion against Saudi Arabia was vehement and so were some official reactions. Laurent Murawiec, a Rand Corporation analyst who briefed the Defense Policy Board argued that Saudis are active at every level of the terror chain, from planners to financiers, from cadre to foot-soldier, from ideologist to cheerleader," and labelled Saudi Arabia as "the kernel of evil, the prime mover, the most dangerous opponent" in the Middle East.[25] Sentiments hardened in Saudi Arabia as well especially among the Saudi public. The government though irritated by the negative press received by the Kingdom, took measures to alleviate American concerns. The al-Haramain Islamic Foundation, with alleged links with Al Qaeda was shut down and the Kingdom enacted legislations to make money-laundering much more difficult.[26]

THE NATIONAL DIALOGUE

The year 2003 witnessed another wave of petitions calling for political reforms in Saudi Arabia. In January, a petition 'Vision on the Present and Future of the Nation' was submitted by liberal academics and intellectuals. This was followed by a Shia petition 'Partners in the Nation'. Another one was "In Defense of the Nation" and a fourth one titled 'A National Call to the Leadership and People Together Constitutional Reform First' was submitted in December. All the petitions were more or less similar in content like enhancing political participation, independence for the judicial branch, a permanent constitution based on the Shari'a, fair redistribution of wealth, and improvements to the status of women. Crown Prince Abdullah responded to the petitions by opening the King Abdul-Aziz Centre for National Dialogue. The first National Dialogue session held in June 2003, discussed the causes of Islamist violence and concluded that the lack of political reforms is the major factor contributing to terrorism. The second session took place in December 2003 based on the topic 'Extremism and Moderation: A Comprehensive Methodological View'. By initiating a dialogue between different religious and ideological strains in Saudi Arabia through these two sessions, there was an acknowledgement of the Kingdom's religious and intellectual diversity which had hitherto been denied because of the Wahhabi dogma.[27] The discussions were criticized by the conservative leaders while Prince Abdullah declared that reforms will move forward while avoiding "darkness and reckless adventure."[28] The third round was held on the topic 'Women: Their Rights, Duties and the Relation of Education to Them' in June 2004. The fourth session in 2004 discussed the topic 'Youth Issues: Current Conditions and Future Prospects' while the fifth session held in December 2005 was on the subject "We and the Other: A National Vision for Dealing with World Cultures". The other topics debated at the National Dialogues were Education: Reality and Ways of Improvement (2007), and 'Work and Employment; Dialogue between Society and Work Related Institutions' (2008). The 2009 session will explore the relation between Society and Health Services.[29]

While the National Dialogue started off as a noble initiative for the purpose of reform, its effectiveness is considerably less. It does not have an institutional function and the membership is limited to individual sessions for which a participant is invited. Moreover, the recommendations made by the National Dialogue carries only an academic interest as there is no institution to ensure its implementation.

Saudi Arabia also faced violent terrorist attacks during this period. From 2003 to 2005, the Kingdom suffered a number of attacks by terrorists, leading to a crackdown. The US invasion of Iraq made things all the more difficult for Saudi Arabia. However, by the end of 2005 the Kingdom managed to prevent further attacks and was also successful in eliminating or incarcerating most of the notorious terrorists.

MUNICIPAL ELECTIONS

Saudi Arabia held municipal elections in 2005. It was to fill half the municipal council seats while the other half was to be filled by government nomination. Women were not permitted to vote which government attributed to administrative and logistical reasons. The elections were held in three phases starting on February 10, 2005 and concluding on April 21, 2005. For the 178 councils, 608 candidates were permitted to contest. "Many Saudi citizens took a sceptical or apathetic view of the elections. The candidates belonged basically to the Islamist groups, tribals, businessmen and liberal intellectuals.[30] The election was tightly monitored by the government and resulted in the victory of moderate Islamist candidates.

RESHUFFLE IN 2009

After the reforms brought about in the matters of succession by finalizing the bylaws of the Allegiance Commission, King Abdullah introduced another set of new appointments and reshuffles in February 2009. An American-educated former teacher, Nora bint Abdullah al-Fayez, was appointed as deputy education minister in charge of a new department for female students. She has thus become the first woman in Saudi Arabia to hold such a position. Prince Faisal bin Abdullah, the king's son-in-law and a former intelligence official was appointed as the new Minister of Education. He will be assisted by Faisal bin Muammar, who headed a body set up in 2003 to promote social and economic reforms.[31] The ousted minister, Abdullah al-Obaid, was earlier secretary general of the Muslim World League.[32]

The King also removed two major figures in Saudi Arabia who were considered to be vehemently opposed to any sort of reform. Sheikh Saleh Luhaydan, head of the supreme judicial council, (who once gave a ruling that owners of TV channels broadcasting immorality can be killed) was replaced by Saleh bin Humaid, head of the Majlis al-Shura. Similarly, hardliner Sheikh Ibrahim Al-Ghaith, the head of the Commission for the Promotion of Virtue and the Prevention of Vice (Muttawa—the notorious Saudi religious police) was replaced by a more moderate Abdul Aziz bin Humain. Sheikh Mohammed Al-Issa was appointed as the new justice minister while the outgoing Justice Minister Abdullah Al-Sheikh was appointed as the head of Majlis al-Shura.

King Abdullah re-established the 21 member Grand Ulema Commission, the board of senior clerics which issues official religious rulings, and appointed representatives of all four schools of Sunni Islam, so breaking the monopoly, of the arch-traditionalist Hanbali School associated with Wahhabism.[33] Ambassador to Lebanon Abdulaziz Al-Khoja was appointed as the new minister of information and culture. Another change took place in Saudi Human Rights

Commission where Bandar Al-Aiban replaced Turki bin Khalid Al-Sudeiri. As a part of the reshuffle, Abdullah Al-Rabia was appointed health minister and Muhammad Al-Jasser became the Governor of the Saudi Arabian Monetary Agency (SAMA), the Kingdom's central bank.

APPOINTMENT OF THE SECOND DEPUTY PRIME MINISTER

Another interesting event occurred on March 27 2009 when Interior Minister Prince Nayef was appointed as the second deputy Prime Minister. In Saudi Arabia, the King holds the post of the Prime Minister while the Crown Prince is the first deputy Prime Minister. The post of the second deputy prime minister was created by King Faisal when he appointed Prince Fahd to the post. From then onwards the second deputy prime minister was considered as the crown prince-in-waiting. But when Abdullah took over as the King, he chose not to appoint anyone to the post and the Allegiance Commission was set up to decide the matter of succession. Therefore the sudden appointment of Nayef as the second deputy Prime Minister created ripples within the royal family. The move assumed more significance because of the reports that the current crown prince Sultan has been abroad since November, recuperating from an operation for cancer in New York.[34] There were however other reports that Nayef's appointment was purely a technical one as King Abdullah was leaving Saudi for a few days to participate in the Arab League and the G20 Summits. The appointment however evoked a response from Prince Talal who demanded that Allegiance Commission's authority should not be undermined by assuming that Nayef will also be the crown prince-in-waiting. ""I am appealing to King Abdullah to have the royal court declare what is meant by this nomination and that it does not mean that he will be the crown prince," Talal said in a press release.[35]

Prince Nayef is seen as a part of the conservative faction of the House of Saud. Within a month of King Abdullah's reformist reshuffle including the appointment of the first female deputy minister, Nayef publicly stated that he saw no need for either elections or women members of parliament.[36] Nayef's appointment has raised apprehensions among the reformist camp already. "If he became king, our feeble hopes for reforms are finished," declares a commentary on an opposition website popular among the kingdom's Shia minority. There was also the counter argument which says that "given the deep religious conservatism of Saudi Arabia's Sunni majority, Prince Nayef's reputation for toughness may actually allow him to push more strongly for reform than the current, mild-mannered king."[37] Another interesting though possibly unrelated event was the publication of Saudi National Society for Human Rights' Report just a week before Nayef's elevation. It was highly critical of the Interior Ministry under Nayef "and is unlikely to have been released without the express say-so of another powerful member of the royal family."[38]

STRATEGIES OF REGIME SURVIVAL

Saudi rulers are adept in handling dissent through a variety of means. Blessed with the oil wealth, the Kingdom is capable of buying out potential dissidents. This rentier nature of the economy ensures that the rulers are not dependent on the subjects for survival and as a result there is no real accountability. The Kingdom can always argue that since the taxation is limited, so shall be the representation. The Saudi government attempts to co-opt the dissidents as well. As a result, many reformist leaders have taken up attractive positions with high salaries in academic or religious institutions ensuring their silence. Apart from individual dissidents, the government also provides patronage for pro-government media outlets, NGOs and other private agencies making them tied and bound to the regimes. The government also has the Majlis al Shura as a potential bait for the rebellious. The Majlis was set up at a time when several technocrats and academicians were in the forefront of reformist movements. King Fahd filled the 60 seats of the first Majlis with those technocrats and academicians, thereby ensuring their loyalty. Thus "reforms have helped consolidate the power of the al-Saud family in political life".[39]

The oil revenue has helped the Kingdom to invest more in security systems, other coercive apparatuses and bureaucratic networks. When co-option and buying out do not work, the Saudi government can put into use their coercive tactics. The Saudi General Intelligence Directorate—*Al Mukhabarat Al A'amah*, presently headed by Prince Muqrin has been efficient in this regard. All the political, religious and other such movements are strictly under the watch of the security agencies and the Kingdom closely monitors people who travel and study abroad and maintain links with foreign groups. The coercive tactics are normally not the first choice of action as the Kingdom adopts the "carrots first" policy. Another effective method employed by Saudi Arabia in managing dissidence is by taking control of the intellectual environment in the country and defining its context. All intellectual content and discourse in the Kingdom, from school curricula to newspaper articles is provided by the state.

The House of Saud employs a masterful use of religion to perpetuate its reign. Almost all socio-political decisions made by the Kingdom are legitimized by the Wahhabi clergy. Since the Kingdom came into existence as a result of an alliance between politics and religion, religious legitimacy is the most important factor sustaining the reign of Saud. Consequently, the Kingdom defines its "people as subjects (*ra'ya*) following a shepherd (*ra'y*) who cares for them and to whom they are loyal (*wala'*)."[40] This makes the King the vice regent of Allah and obeying him is a religious duty. The Saudi rulers have effectively used religion to counter the Pan-Arabist movement which threatened all the Gulf monarchies. In response to Nasser's Arab solidarity, King Faisal took the lead in forming the Organization of Islamic Conference in 1969. King Fahd also took the same route in 1982 when faced with strident criticism from Iranian leader Ayatollah Khomeini that the Saudi Kings are corrupt and un-Islamic. He changed the way of addressing Saudi Kings from "His Majesty" to the "Custodian of the Two Holy Mosques". Similarly, when faced a difficult situation after the Mecca Mosque take over incident in 1979, the Kingdom sent several hundreds of its young population to fight against the Soviet Union in Afghanistan. This diverted the fanaticism and energy of the restive and ideologically motivated which spared the Kingdom from their activism.

TOWARDS A LIBERALIZED AUTOCRACY

Liberalized autocracy is a term popularized by Daniel Brumberg to define a system of government that "allows for a measure of political openness and competition in the electoral, party, and press arenas, while ultimately ensuring that power rests in the hands of ruling regimes".[41] It protects the incumbent regime and ensures that no real change in the ultimate power structure is permitted. The unfettered economic openness is also a hallmark of this regime.[42] Egypt, Morocco and Kuwait are examples of such countries in the region.

In this sense, one can argue that Saudi Arabia is moving in the direction of fellow GCC states like Kuwait (considered to be partly fee by Freedom House), Bahrain and Qatar. From being an absolute autocracy; Saudi Arabia has permitted controlled elections, created institutions like the National Dialogue, attempted some reform in the education sector, institutionalized succession, enhanced some functions of the Majlis, and has started talking to non-wahhabi groups like sufis and shia. It has also been tolerant to the activism of groups like the Islamic-liberals-some of who even wrote about challenging the Hanbali School. If the repeated attempts to tame the ultraconservative clergy become successful, it will provide further opportunity to the rulers to move in the direction of liberalized autocracy. As Brumberg puts it, liberalized autocracies tolerate "a range of ethnic, social, and religious groups, thus creating a level of incipient, if unruly, pluralism. Paradoxically, it is precisely this level of pluralism that abets the regime "survival strategies" of liberalized autocracies. By playing one group against the other, they divide their opponents, thus enhancing the regime's room for manoeuvre and autonomy from any one group."[43] Moreover, such limited openings provide a safety valve to release the pressure created by the demands for real reforms. Even as it provides some openings, the government has put in place clear "red lines", ensuring that the prerogatives of the executive are not circumscribed by legislation and judicial oversight.[44]

The sequentialist theorists of democratization like Samuel Huntington, Adam Przeworski and Fernando Limongo and lately Fareed Zakaria support the concept of liberalized autocracy and argue that it shall continue till conditions are ripe for total democracy. They support an indefinite postponement of democracy-in the form of competitive elections until the prerequisites like liberal institutions are established and a favourable environment is attained. This point is supported by Kaplan who says that "democracy and multiparty systems are best suited to nations that already have efficient bureaucracies and a middle class that pays income tax, and where primary issues such as borders and power-sharing have already been resolved, leaving politicians free to bicker about the budget and other secondary matters."[45] Saudi Arabia is way behind reaching such a stage and therefore in prevailing circumstances liberalized autocracy is the best political reform the country can hope for. Critics of liberal autocracy like Thomas Carothers, Daniel Brumberg, Jason Brownlee and Marc Plattner argue that liberal autocracies liberalize precisely to maintain their autocratic nature by offsetting the accumulated political pressure in their countries. Comfortably ensconced in power the liberal autocrats will never prefer to move in the direction of democratic reforms beyond a point. With all the actors, including the rulers and the opposition having identified tangible benefits, the "trap of liberalized autocracy" will set in. When the rulers feel that the reforms are progressing too far for their comfort, they immediately switch in the opposite direction, and when the danger blows over reverses the direction again. Such an "unstable cycle of opening and closing-liberalization and de-liberalization is the biggest problem liberalized autocracy creates: It snares regimes in an "endless transition".[46]

While this argument holds merit, for a country like Saudi Arabia which has never experienced any sense of liberal measures before, liberal autocracy sure seems the best option for now and under King Abdullah, the Kingdom is progressing in that direction.

CONCLUSION

A study of the Saudi political system reveals the fact that the Kingdom has surely embarked upon a process of reforms. It was kick-started by the events after the 1991 Gulf war and has continued though the pace has been painfully slow. The institution of the Consultative Assembly, promulgation of the Basic Laws, the setting up of the Allegiance Institution, the Municipal elections, the initiation of the National Dialogue and some key changes in the cabinet and other important bodies were steps in this direction. The events of 9/11, the rise of Islamist groups in Saudi Arabia, the terrorist attacks within the Kingdom and most importantly the taking over by King Abdullah have aided the process. Undoubtedly, Saudi Arabia is relatively more liberal now than it was a couple of years ago (it has even improved its scores in the Freedom House ratings). However, the steps taken cannot be considered as steps towards democratization. The House of Saud will never permit democratization because it will mean the end of *Saudi Arabia-Arabia of the Sauds*. So what we are witnessing is House of Saud's attempts to perpetuate their reign. They have decided that permitting limited and tightly controlled political and social openings are the best means to go about it. The Saudi royal family does not face a crisis of legitimacy, it is sitting on top of billions of petrodollars, the tribal affinities and loyalties are quite entrenched. Therefore the best way forward for them is to rule like benevolent despots in a liberalized autocracy. For now, superficial measures like a nominated national council with advisory function, elections to municipal councils with no real power serves the purpose of the rulers and the ruled to a certain extent. For the average Saudi subject on the street, any reform is real progress because the Kingdom has been prohibitively authoritarian for so long.

NOTE

1. "Defining Democracy: Concepts and Measures", see http://ksghome.harvard.edu/~pnorris/Acrobat/Democracy1.pdf
2. David Collier and Steven Levitsky, *Democracy 'With Adjectives': Conceptual Innovation in Comparative Research,* Working Paper #230-August 1996, Kellogg Institute for International Studies, University of Notre Dame, http://kellogg.nd.edu/publications/workingpapers/WPS/230.pdf
3. Peter W. Wilson, and Douglas F. Graham, *Saudi Arabia: The Coming Storm*, M.E. Sharpe (June 1994) NY, p. 43.
4. Joseph Kostiner, *The Making of Saudi Arabia, 1916-1936: from Chieftaincy to Monarchical State*, Oxford University Press, 1993, p. 150.
5. Rahshed Aba-Namay "Constitutional Reforms: A Systemization of Saudi Politics," *Journal of South Asian and Middle Eastern Studies*, Vol. 16, No. 3, Spring, 1998, pp. 44-48.
6. Prince Turki al-Faisal, "Evolution of the Constitution of Saudi Arabia", Excerpts from a lecture, at the University of Oxford, UK, available on http://www.mofa.gov.sa/Detail.asp?InSectionID=4357&InNewsItemID=91348
7. Gianluca Paolo Parolin, "Generations of Gulf Constitutions: Paths and Perspectives in Khalaf, Abdulhadi and Giacomo Luciani (eds), *Constitutional Reform and Political Participation in the Gulf,* Gulf research Centre, Dubai 2006:62
8. Cairo Declaration on Human Rights in Islam, Aug. 5, 1990, U.N. GAOR, World Conf. on Hum. Rts., 4th Sess., Agenda Item 5, U.N. Doc. A/CONF.157/PC/62/Add.18 (1993) [English translation]. University of Minnesota, Human Rights Library, http://www1.umn.edu/humanrts/instree/cairodeclaration.html
9. Human Rights Watch Country Report, Saudi Arabia: 1992, http://www.hrw.org/

reports/1992/saudi/INTROTHR.htm#TopOfPage (Human Rights Watch Report 1992)

10. The Allegiance Institution Law, cited from http://www.saudiembassy.net/2006News/Statements/TransDetail.asp?cIndex=651
11. Awadh Al-Badi, "Institutionalizing Hereditary Succession in Saudi Arabia's Political Governance System: The Allegiance Commission", *Arab Reform Brief*, 20 February 2008, http://www.arab-reform.net/IMG/pdf/ARB_20_A.Saoudite_A.AL_Badi_ENG.pdf
12. Rashed Aba-Namay, "The Recent Constitutional Reforms in Saudi Arabia", *International Comparative Law Quarterly*, Vol 42, Number 2, April 1993, (p 309)
13. Official website of the Consultative Council, http://www.shura.gov.sa
14. "Can Saudi Arabia Reform Itself?" International Crisis Group, Middle East Report, No 28, 14 July 2004
15. Camille Ammoun, "The Institutionalization of the Saudi Political System and the Birth of political Personnel", in Khalaf, Abdulhadi and Giacomo Luciani (eds), Constitutional Reform and Political Participation in the Gulf, Gulf Research Centre, Dubai 2006, p 227
16. Hamzawy, Amr, "The Saudi Labyrinth: Evaluating the Current Political Opening", *Democracy and Rule of Law*, Number 68, April 2006, Carnegie Endowment for International Peace p. 11.
17. Ammoun, No. 15, p. 217.
18. Joseph Kostiner, "State, Islam and Opposition in Saudi Arabia: The Post Desert-storm Phase". MERIA Journal Volume 1, No. 2-July 1997
19. Gwenn Okruhlik, "Networks of Dissent: Islamism and Reform in Saudi Arabia", *Current History*, January 2002, p 25
20. *op cit*. No. 14, pp. 5-6.
21. Stéphane Lacroix, "Between Islamists and Liberals: Saudi Arabia's New 'Islamo-Liberal' Reformists", *Middle East Journal*, Volume 58, Number. 3, Summer 2004, pp. 353-54).
22. Doaa Hussein Alam, "Political Trends in Saudi Arabia", *Al Ahram Democracy Review*, Issue No. 27, July 1, 2007.
23. Graham E. Fuller, and Rend Rahim Francke, *The Arab Shi'a: The Forgotten Muslims* (New York, Saint Martin's Press, 1999, p. 190).
24. *The Shiite Question in Saudi Arabia*, International Crisis Group, Middle East Report Number. 45, 19 September 2005, p. 4. http://www.crisisgroup.org/library/documents/middle_east___north_africa/iraq_iran_gulf/45_the_shiite_question_in_saudi_arabia.pdf
25. Thomas E. Ricks, "Briefing Depicted Saudis as Enemies", *The Washington Post*, August 6, 2002; http://www.washingtonpost.com/ac2/wp-dyn/A47913-2002Aug5
26. Rachel Bronson. Rethinking Religion: The Legacy of the U.S.-Saudi Relationship. *The Washington Quarterly* 28, pp. 121-137, 2005.
27. Ammoun, No. 15, p. 236.
28. John E. Peterson, *The Arab Gulf States: Further Steps towards Political Participation*, Gulf research Centre, Dubai 2006, p. 43)

29. Official website of the King Abdul-Aziz Centre for National Dialogue, http://www.kacnd.org/eng/
30. Pascal Ménoret, "The Municipal Elections in Saudi Arabia 2005", *Arab Reform Initiative*, 27 December 2005, http://www.arab-reform.net/spip.php?article1
31. Asmaa Alsharif, "Saudi Speeds up Education Reform, Clerics Resist" April 15, 2009 www.reuters.com/article/latestCrisis/idUSL9588418
32. Nina Shea, "New Hope for Reform in Saudi Arabia"? *National Review Online*, February 16, 2009, http://www.hudson.org/index.cfm?fuseaction=publication_details&id=6021
33. "Saudi Arabia: Tiptoeing towards Reform", *The Economist*, February 19 2009, http://www.economist.com/displaystory.cfm?story_id=13145049
34. Ian Black, "Saudi Arabia's Succession Remains a Delicate Matter", *The Guardian*, 6 April 2009 http://www.guardian.co.uk/world/2009/apr/06/saudi-arabia-succession-monarchy
35. Donna Abu-Nasr, "Saudi King Clarifies Succession", *The Washington Times*, March 28, 2009http://www.washingtontimes.com/news/2009/mar/28/king-names-half-brother-to-key-succession-post/
36. Simon Henderson, "Desert Schism: Prince Nayef Bids for Saudi Throne", Policy Watch #1501, March 31, 2009, The Washington Institute for Near East Policy, http://www.washingtoninstitute.org/print.php?template=C05 &CID=3038
37. "Saudi Arabia's Prince Nayef: A Rising but Enigmatic Prince, *The Economist*, April 2 2009, http://www.economist.com/world/mideast-africa/displaystory.cfm?story_id=13414090
38. Hugh Miles, "Keys to the Kingdom: Inside Saudi Arabia's Royal Family", *The Independent*, London, 29 March 2009, http://www.independent.co.uk/news/world/middle-east/keys-to-the—kingdom-inside-saudi-arabias-royal-family-1656644.html
39. Gwenn Okruhlik, "The Irony of Islah (Reform)", *The Washington Quarterly* 28:4 pp. Autumn 2005, p. 155.
40. *Ibid.*, p. 153.
41. Daniel Brumberg, "Democratization Versus Liberalization in the Arab World: Dilemmas and Challenges for US Foreign Policy", July 2005, Strategic Studies Institute, U.S. Army War College, Carlisle, PA, http://www.strategicstudiesinstitute.army.mil/pdffiles/pub620.pdfhttp:// www.strategicstudiesinstitute.army.mil/pdffiles/pub620.pdf
42. Khalil Al-Anani, "Liberal Autocracy in Egypt", Saban Center for Middle East Policy, Brookings Institution, June 24 2008http://www.brookings.edu/opinions/2008/0624_egypt_alanani.aspx
43. Brumberg, No. 41.
44. Ray Takeyh, "Democratization in the Arab World: Ways Ahead?" *National Interest* February 02, 2005, Cited from the Belgravia Dispatch http://www.belgraviadispatch.com/2005/02/democratization_in_the_arab_ wo.html
45. Robert Kaplan, "Was Democracy Just a Moment?" Atlantic Monthly, December 1997, www.theatlantic.com/issues/97dec/democ.htm
46. Daniel Brumberg, "Liberalization versus Democracy, Understanding Arab Political Reform" *Democracy and Rule of Law Project*, Number 37, Carnegie Endowment for International Peace, May 2003 (Brumberg 2003:13)

BIBLIOGRAPHY

Aba-Namay, Rashed "Constitutional Reforms: A Systemization of Saudi Politics," *Journal of South Asian and Middle Eastern Studies*, Vol. 16, No. 3, Spring, 1998, pp. 44-48.

Aba-Namay, Rashed, "The Recent Constitutional Reforms in Saudi Arabia", *International Comparative Law Quarterly,* Vol. 42, Number 2, April 1993, (p. 309)

Abu-Nasr, Donna "Saudi King Clarifies Succession", *The Washington Times*, March 28, 2009 http://www.washingtontimes.com/news/2009/mar/28/king-names-half-brother-to-key-succession-post/

Alam, Doaa Hussein, "Political Trends in Saudi Arabia", *Al Ahram Democracy Review*, Issue No. 27, July 1, 2007.

Al-Anani, Khalil "Liberal Autocracy in Egypt", Saban Centre for Middle East Policy, Brookings Institution, June 24 2008, cited from http://www.brookings.edu/opinions/2008/0624_egypt_alanani.aspx

Al-Badi, Awadh, "Institutionalizing Hereditary Succession in Saudi Arabia's Political Governance System: The Allegiance Commission", Arab Reform Brief, 20 February 2008, available on http://www.arab-reform.net/IMG/pdf/ARB_20_A.Saoudite_A.AL_Badi_ENG.pdf

Al-Faisal, Turki, "Evolution of the Constitution of Saudi Arabia", Excerpts from a lecture, at the University of Oxford, UK, Available on http://www.mofa.gov.sa/Detail.asp?InSectionID=4357&InNewsItemID=91348)

Alsharif, Asmaa, "Saudi Speeds up Education Reform, Clerics Resist", Reuters, April 15, 2009, www.reuters.com/article/latestCrisis/idUSL9588418

Ammoun, Camille "The Institutionalization of the Saudi Political System and the Birth of political Personnel", in Khalaf, Abdulhadi and Giacomo Luciani (eds), *Constitutional Reform and Political Participation in the Gulf*, Gulf Research Centre, Dubai, 2006.

Black, Ian "Saudi Arabia's Succession Remains a Delicate Matter", *The Guardian,* 6 April 2009, http://www.guardian.co.uk/world/2009/apr/06/saudi-arabia-succession-monarchy

Bronson, Rachel. "Rethinking Religion: The Legacy of the U.S.—Saudi Relationship". *The Washington Quarterly* 28, 2005, pp. 121-137.

Brumberg, Daniel "Democratization Versus Liberalization in the Arab World: Dilemmas and Challenges for US Foreign Policy", July 2005, Strategic Studies Institute, U.S. Army War College, Carlisle, PA, http://www.strategicstudiesinstitute.army.mil/pdffiles/pub620.pdf

Brumberg, Daniel "Liberalization versus Democracy, Understanding Arab Political Reform" Democracy and Rule of Law Project, Number 37, Carnegie Endowment for International Peace, May 2003.

Cairo Declaration on Human Rights in Islam, Aug. 5, 1990, University of Minnesota, Human Rights Library, http://www1.umn.edu/humanrts/instree/cairodeclaration.html

"Can Saudi Arabia Reform Itself?" International Crisis Group, Middle East Report, http://www.crisisgroup.org/home/index.cfm?id=2864&l=1, July 2004.

Collier, David and Steven Levitsky, "Democracy With Adjectives: Conceptual Innovation in Comparative Research", Working Paper #230—August 1996, Kellogg Institute for International Studies, University of Notre Dame, http://kellogg.nd.edu/publications/workingpapers/WPS/230.pdf

"Defining Democracy: Concepts and Measures", see http://ksghome.harvard.edu/~pnorris/Acrobat/Democracy1.pdf

Fuller, Graham E. and Rend Rahim Francke, *The Arab Shi'a: The Forgotten Muslims*, New York, Saint Martin's Press, 1999.

Hamzawy, Amr, "The Saudi Labyrinth: Evaluating the Current Political Opening", Democracy and Rule of Law, Number 68, April 2006, Carnegie Endowment for International Peace.

Henderson, Simon "Desert Schism: Prince Nayef Bids for Saudi Throne", Policy Watch #1501, March 31, 2009, The Washington Institute for Near East Policy, http://www.washingtoninstitute.org/print.php?template=C05 &CID=3038

Hudson, Michael C., "The Political Culture Approach to Arab Democratization: The Case for Bringing It Back In, Carefully." in *Political Liberalization and Democratization in the Arab World, vol. 1, Theoretical Perspectives*. Ed. Rex Brynen, Bahgat Korany, and Paul Noble. Boulder, CO: Lynne Rienner Publishers, 1995. pp. 61-76.

Human Rights Watch Country Report, Saudi Arabia: 1992, http://www.hrw.org/reports/1992/saudi/INTROTHR.htm#TopOfPage (Human Rights Watch Report 1992)

Kaplan, Robert, "Was Democracy Just a Moment?" *Atlantic Monthly*, December 1997, www.theatlantic.com/issues/97dec/democ.htm

Kostiner, Joseph, "State, Islam and Opposition in Saudi Arabia: The Post Desert-storm Phase". *MERIA Journal* Volume 1, No. 2, July 1997.

Kostiner, Joseph, *The Making of Saudi Arabia, 1916-1936: From Chieftaincy to Monarchical State*, Oxford University Press, 1993.

Lacroix, Stéphane, "Between Islamists and Liberals: Saudi Arabia's New 'Islamo-Liberal' Reformists", *Middle East Journal*, Volume 58, Number. 3, Summer 2004.

Ménoret, Pascal, "The Municipal Elections in Saudi Arabia 2005", *Arab Reform Initiative*, 27 December 2005, http://www.arab-reform.net/spip.php?article1

Miles, Hugh, "Keys to the Kingdom: Inside Saudi Arabia's Royal Family", *The Independent*, London, 29 March 2009, http://www.independent.co.uk/news/world/middle-east/keys-to-the—kingdom-inside-saudi-arabias-royal-family-1656644.html

Mordechai Abir, *Saudi Arabia in the Oil Era: Regime and Elites; Conflict and Collaboration,* London: Croom Helm, 1988.

Official website of the Consultative Council, http://www.shura.gov.sa

Official website of the King Abdul-Aziz Centre for National Dialogue, http://www.kacnd.org/eng/

Okruhlik, Gwenn, "Networks of Dissent: Islamism and Reform in Saudi Arabia", *Current History*, January 2002.

Okruhlik, Gwenn, "The Irony of Islah (Reform)", *The Washington Quarterly,* 28:·4 pp. Autumn 2005.

Parolin, Gianluca Paolo, "Generations of Gulf Constitutions: Paths and Perspectives in Khalaf, Abdulhadi and Giacomo Luciani (eds), *Constitutional Reform and Political Participation in the Gulf,* Gulf research Centre, Dubai 2006.

Peterson, John E, *The Arab Gulf States: Further Steps towards Political Participation,* Gulf research Centre, Dubai 2006.

Ricks, Thomas E, "Briefing Depicted Saudis as Enemies", *The Washington Post,* August 6, 2002; http://www.washingtonpost.com/ac2/wp-dyn/A47913-2002Aug5?

Salame, Ghassan (ed), *Democracy without Democrats? The Renewal of Politics in the Muslim World,* London: IB Tauris, 1994.

"Saudi Arabia's Prince Nayef: "A Rising but Enigmatic Prince", *The Economist,* April 2 2009, http://www.economist.com/world/mideast-africa/displaystory.cfm?story_id =13414090

"Saudi Arabia: Tiptoeing towards Reform", *The Economist,* February 19 2009, http:/ /www.economist.com/displaystory.cfm?story_id=13145049

Shea, Nina, "New Hope for Reform in Saudi Arabia"? *National Review Online,* http:/ /www.hudson.org/index.cfm?fuseaction=publication_details&id=602, February 16 2009.

Takeyh, Ray "Democratization in the Arab World: Ways Ahead?" *National Interest,* February 02, 2005, cited from the Belgravia Dispatch http://www.belgravia dispatch.com/2005/02/democratization_in_the_arab_wo.html

The Allegiance Institution Law, cited from http://www.saudiembassy.net/2006News/ Statements/TransDetail.asp?cIndex=651

"The Shiite Question in Saudi Arabia", International Crisis Group, Middle East Report, September 2005.

Wilson, Peter W., and Douglas F. Graham, *Saudi Arabia: The Coming Storm,* M.E. Sharpe, New York, 1994.

9

Gradualism in Saudi Arabian Reforms and the Role of Opposition

Stanly Johny

In any of the Arab Gulf countries, we can't see a consolidated liberal democracy. Even in the larger West Asia, most of the political systems, though some of them have parliaments and elections, are authoritarian in nature which do not respect the liberal political rights of citizens. Saudi Arabia is not an exception. The Saudi political system, legitimized by the strident version of Wahhabi Islam, has, however, withstood several domestic and regional challenges in the past. The country, named after the ruling al-Saud family, has seen the rise of violent Islamism, reformist movements, sectarian clashes, economic breakdown etc. over the last eight-and-a-half decades. The regime has given in to both to the Islamists and the reformists several times whenever its interests were at stake. But it was not easy for the liberal ideas to take root in a country where the traditional Wahhabi ideology and practices were deep-rooted and institutionalized by the state mechanisms. Therefore, the evolution of the liberal voice in Saudi Arabia, which played a major role in the reform, was a very complicated process in the Kingdom. The liberals' first challenge was to develop a public sphere, where they can engage in debates that were not sponsored by the state. This public sphere has to play a major role in the shaping of political system and social order in any liberal society. In Saudi Arabia, this is still in a nascent stage.

LEGITIMACY FROM WAHHABISM

Though the Kingdom of Saudi Arabia was founded only in 1932, the al-Saud family has a long history of military and political activity in the region. From their base in Najd, the family made many efforts to expand its hegemony over the Arabian Peninsula. Even as the puritanical Wahhabi movement could capture many power centres in West Asia in 19th century, the al-Saud continued to enjoy power in Riyadh till the rival Rashidi family seized control with the Turkish backing. However, the al-Saud, under the leadership of Abd al-Aziz bin Abd al-

Rahman al-Saud defeated the Rashidis and regained the lost control of Riyadh in 1902. The 1902-1932 period saw Abd al-Aziz, who was later known as Ibn Saud, expanding his authority over adjacent provinces like al-Hasa in the East, Asir in the South and Hijaz in the west. On 23 September 1932, both Riyadh and Hijaz were merged together and the Kingdom of Saudi Arabia was formed.

Ever since the formation of the Kingdom, the al-Saud family's monopoly over power has not faced potential challenges, though there were plenty of dissident voices. Initially, Kind Abd al-Aziz used military power to silence the local leaders who challenged his authority. The King embraced the Wahhabi brand of Islam and the same became the foundations of the country. The relationship between the Wahhabi Islam and the Saudi state has been close and supportive. As the al-Saud family drew legitimacy from Wahhabism to rule the Kingdom and silence its opposition, the puritanical ideology gained prominence across the peninsula as the royal family built a state based on its principles. Ever since, the ideas of the 18th century religious cleric Ibn Abdal-Wahhab exerted a powerful hold over the Saudi population and the Wahhabi clergy enjoyed huge influence over the public affairs in the Kingdom. The religious leaders have had a strong say in the shaping of the society and they can directly involve in the educational system, social conduct and several other issues. The regime used several strategies like coercion, pressure and inducement to dampen the internal challenges and win over tribal leaders. The end result was a political system founded on a narrowly defined social base that institutionalized the Wahhabi ideology.

From 1932, the state had been ruled without a written constitution, without an electoral system, and without any political party, labour unions, parliament or any other agencies that constitute the public sphere in liberal societies. Any organization outside the government control was prohibited. This absolute monopoly over power in effect did not let any dissident voice come out into the public for over a long period. Though the founder King had promised a Constitution and a Consultative Council in the initial days of the unification of the country, that had never materialized. Later the ruling class listed ideological and religious reasons to legitimize the political system. The government maintained that only *Quran* could be seen as the Constitution. Similarly the absence of any legislative body was explained by the argument that in Islam, *Sharia* was the supreme law. In that context, the *Ulama* and the King issued *fatwas* and Royal Decrees respectively from time to time, supplementing the *Sharia*, to guide the government.[1]

THE RISE OF LIBERAL VOICES

The 1940s was a crucial period in the history of the Kingdom as major oil recoveries shot up the revenue of the state, a development that helped the royal family centralise power and amass wealth.[2] The foundations of a welfare state had also been laid during the same period, though the unequal distribution of wealth at the initial stage and huge shares kept aside for the royal family had increased the social inequalities. Till the late 1950s, a major part of the oil revenues was at the direct disposal of the King.[3] As the royal family amassed huge wealth, the majority of the population continued in poverty. This unequal distribution of wealth, coupled with other socio-economic tensions, created the conditions for an unsettled polity. Underground movements like he National Reform Front and the Free Saudis and the Free Officers came out in the public during this period demanding reforms in the political system.[4]

The 1950s saw a major crisis evolving within the ruling family with a power struggle between the second King, Saud, and his younger brother Prince Feisel threatening the political stability in the Kingdom. As Feisel grew as a potential threat to his powers, King Saud aligned with the liberal princes in the family and revived the talk of democratic reforms. The regional developments like establishment of the state of Israel, emergence of pan-Arabism, calls for modernization also had influence on the royal family. The liberal lobby, known as 'Free Princes', publicly demanded political reforms. Developments like the formation of the United Arab Republic in 1958, the overthrow of Hashimite Monarchy in Iraq in 1958 and the toppling of Imam Yahya's conservative regime in Yemen in 1962 sparked debates that Saudi Arabia could not withstand the sweeping changes taking place across the region. In 1960, there were rumours that the King would introduce a nominated parliament.[5] In the same year, the Free Princes, led by Prince Talal bin Abd-al Aziz, whose support the King enjoyed, submitted a demand for a partially-elected body to Prime Minister Feisel. However, their demand was turned down. This triggered one of the worst power struggles within the family that saw the Crown Prince resigning his prime ministerial position, but only to return with more influence later. Feisel's resignation, however, did not help the liberal lobby. After regaining powers, King Saud lost interest to initiate reforms.

When Feisel resumed prime ministerial responsibilities in 1962, he announced a 10-point agenda, rekindling hopes among the liberals. The Crown Prince said the government would promulgate a "fundamental law" that will "set down the basic principles of the government" and also provide the "basic rights of the citizens, including that of freedom of expression within the limits of Islamic faith and public policy".[6] Soon after he became the King in 1964, Feisel constituted a committee comprising of several members of the Council of Ministers to draft a constitution. But, there were no major initiatives thereafter to take the pledges ahead from the King's side, thanks to the return of regime stability and economic prosperity. The oil boom in late 1960s and 1970s helped the government build a welfare state that caters to the material needs of the population. The King also strengthened the ruling family's ties with the conservative *Ulama* and the tribal leaders.

THE RISE OF ISLAMIST OPPOSITION

According to many analysts, Islam remains a double-edged sword for the al-Saudi family. Even as it legitimized the rule, the puritanical Wahhabi ideology left ample space for the hardliners to turn against the regime any time if they think the rulers are drifting away from the ideological commitments. If the founder King Abd-al Aziz exploited extremism against the Turks, expanded his influence to other provinces with the help of the religiously-inspired *Ikhwan* force and enjoyed huge influence over the *Ulama*, his successors had to struggle to counter the challenges from the extremist quarters. The decline of pan-Arabism and other Arab modernization movements in West Asia in the 1970s and the emergence of extremism and Islamic revolutionizm had an extremely unnerving effect on the Gulf monarchies. Following the 1979 Iranian Revolution, there was a dramatic seizure of the Makkah Mosque and uprisings among the Shiites in the eastern region of Saudi Arabia. The November 1979 seizure of the Mosque that cost 177 rebel and 127 government lives posed a fundamental, though symbolic, challenge to the monarchy. The rebels, most of them from the Wahhabi sect, believed that the royal family had become corrupt, the state was promoting heresy and religious scholars were collaborating with the royal family in spreading immoral practices. This in effect challenged the monopoly of the state over religious affairs.[7]

The Saudi government responded cautiously to these challenges. The government gave more power to the Islamists on the one hand and revived the talk of a *Majlis al-Shura* or Consultative Council on the other. The government let the Islamists continue their influence in the curriculum and the teaching practices and allotted more money to the religious authorities and there was greater religious surveillance over the population.[8] At the same time, King Khalid appointed an eight-man committee in 1980 under the chairmanship of Interior Minister Prince Nayef to draft a new constitution. Khalid's successor Fahd also promised to enact a constitution and set up a national assembly soon after his accession to the throne in 1982, but no headway was made in 1980s, a period that also saw Islamist ideology gaining ground in the region. The return of Arab Afghan mujahideens from anti-Soviet guerrilla war in Afghanistan gave impetus to the Islamist groups in the country. Around 12, 000 Saudi men had gone to Afghanistan to fight the Soviet troops in 1980s.[9] By supporting the cause of the Afghan mujahideens, the Saudi regime tried to underpin its domestic Islamic legitimacy as well as strengthen its claim to global Islamic leadership.

CONSTITUTIONAL REFORMS

King Fahd's Afghan policy also brought the US and Saudi Arabia ever closer. This alliance had far reaching implications at the domestic level, particularly after the Gulf war. King Fahd, who had supported Iraq throughout the Iran-Iraq war, first urged for negotiations to encourage Saddam Hussein to retreat from Kuwait. But following US Defence Secretary Richard Cheney's visit to the Kingdom, the Saudi Arabian government officially requested assistance from the US government on 7 August 1990 to solve the Gulf crisis.[10] As expected, the King's decision invited the wrath of the Islamists, who were already engaged in secret campaigns against the ruling family. On the other side, the liberals found it as an opportunity to air their views on necessary political reforms. In October 1990, the Kuwaiti ruler held the Kuwaiti People's Conference in Jeddah, a two-day mega event in which around 1,200 Kuwaiti citizens participated to chalk out strategies to liberate their country and initiate parliamentary democracy after the liberation. Drawing inspiration from this, 43 Saudi intellectuals submitted a petition to the King in December, asking him to issue a codification of Islamic law that would provide for fundamental reforms.[11] When the Islamists, who were pampered throughout 1980s voiced protests against the King's decision to allow non-Muslim troops to enter and operate in the Arabian territory to attack a fellow Muslim state, the liberals rallied to the King's defence.[12]

Like his predecessor, King Fahd also responded cautiously to the separate demands for reforms and more strident laws. The changing regional and domestic politics and the closer alliance with the US left the government with not many options but to initiate reforms. After an extra ordinary session of the Council of Ministers on 1 March 1992, the King announced a reform package that comprised three constitutional documents—the Basic Law, establishment of a Consultative Council within six months and administrative reforms at the provincial levels. The Basic Law was the de facto Constitution of the country. Since calling anything but the Holy *Quran* Constitution is sacrilege in the Saudi context, the first article of the Basic Law says *Quran* is the Constitution of the Kingdom.[13] The 60 member *Majlis al-Shura* was set up early March 1993. All members of the Council were to be appointed by the King and they were to have rights to question the Council of Ministers, make suggestions on law-making and submit them to the King. The council chairman could submit a request to the King for relevant government documents. The provincial councils, also promised in the reform package, have more powers than the Consultative Council. The provincial council members were to be appointed by the Prime Minister in consultation with governors. The council could determine the needs of the province, prioritise them and propose them to include in the state development plans.[14]

Though the Basic Law and creation of the *Majlis* were welcomed as steps in the right direction, they were not a great leap forward. The Basic Law underscores the ultimate authority of the King and there is a continuing stress throughout the document on the Islamic values underpinning social and economic organization. In a month after the promulgation of the Basic Law, the King ruled out further Democratizing steps, saying: "Our people's character and way of life are different from the ways and traditions of the democratic world... Free elections are not suitable for our country." During the inauguration of the *Majlis*, he made it further clear: "Elections are found in various places in the world and nobody objects to them, but we follow the path shown by the Book of Allah the Almighty, His Apostle, and his wise caliphs."[15]

The regime's reluctance to carry forward reforms made the reformers upset. In 1993, a group of six prominent academics and legal personalities set up an organization, Committee for the Defence of Legitimate Rights (CDLR). Seeking to eliminate injustice and support the oppressed, the committee called on people to provide it with information about injustices that had been occurring. The committee members, who were highly respected religious scholars, did not pose any threat to the Islamic system, but urged for a more accountable government and increased awareness among the people about their basic rights.[16] Still, the CDLR was banned, its members were dismissed from their jobs and its office was closed. The increasing opposition to the regime in the 1990s, both from Islamo-liberals and Islamists, indicated the eroding legitimacy of the government.[17] The economy slipped into a crisis as oil revenues fell and the welfare state was rapidly deteriorating. When the liberals withdrew from the public space in the second half of the 1990s, the Islamist critics grew in popularity.

POST-SEPTEMBER 11: LIBERALS GAINING GROUND

If the first Gulf war and the subsequent changes in the regional politics gave a big boost to the reform process in Saudi Arabia, the 11th September terrorist attack on the US opened new avenues of change in the country's history. The terrorist attack brought the Saudi leadership and the people to face many grave realities that were given less attention over a period of time. The reports that 15 of the 19 suicide plane hijackers were Saudi citizens threatened the stability of the US-Saudi relationship. Several US officials went public to criticise the policies of the Kingdom.[18] Troubles in the US-Saudi relationship increased after President George W. Bush's policy to press for democratic reforms in the region.[19] Making his administration's stand clear, President Bush, in his National Endowment for Democracy speech on 6 November 2003 said: "By giving the Saudi people a greater role in their own society, the Saudi government can demonstrate true leadership in the region".[20]

The increasing pressure from the US, coupled with domestic tensions, forced the Saudi leadership to ease the government control over public discourse. The idea of permitting public dialogue was a policy of Crown Prince Abdullah, who had been the de facto ruler since King Fahd fell ill in 1995.

Though Abdullah's reformist agenda faced major challenges from within the royal family, the domestic and regional situation stood in favour of him.[21] Finding the rise of extremist violence a more potential threat, Abdullah believed that giving more space to the Islamo-liberals would help the regime ensure stability. The increasing bombing incidents and other sort of violence by the extremists sparked a larger debate on the root cause of terrorism in the country.[22] The reformists argued that extremism grew in the country because of the closed nature of Islam and called for change. In January 2003, Crown Prince Abdullah received a document entitled, "Strategic Vision for the Present and the Future" signed by 104 professors, intellectuals, and former officials. The petitioners raised five major demand in the document: Separation of powers between executive, judicial and legislative branches, a representative Consultative Council to be elected by citizens, an independent judiciary based on *Qaran* and *Sunna*, guarantee human rights, including freedom of speech, assembly, elections and participation and establishment of civil society by permitting the formation of economic, professional and cultural associations.[23] This was followed by another petition entitled "Partners in One Nation", signed by 450 Shiites and submitted to Abdullah in April 2003. Describing the discrimination they face in the country, the Shiites called for an announcement of the country's respect for all religions and also the appointment of a national committee with the participation of the Shiites to deal with the sectarian discrimination. The Crown Prince got another petition in September, signed by 51 women. Titled as "Petition in Defence of the Nation," the petition urged the authorities to implement the suggestions made by the National Reform Documents, submitted in January.

Unlike the past, the regime took relatively open-mined approach towards the liberals. The first concrete step taken by the King in this regard was the organization of the national dialogue conference in June 2003 in Jeddah. Thirty clerics, representing all religious sects—Salafi, non-Salafi Sunnis, Sufis and Shiites—participated in the deliberations, known as "National Gathering for Intellectual Dialogue".[24] The dialogue led to the adoption of a political charter that emphasized the importance of political reforms. The subsequent announcement that partial municipal elections will be held in 2004 was a major achievement for the liberal movement in the country.[25] The October announcement was followed by the second dialogue, held in Makkah under the theme of "Extremism and Moderation: A Comprehensive Approach". So far the country had seven national dialogue sessions, with the last being held in Qassem on 22-23 April, 2008 under the theme of "Work and Employment: Dialogue Between Society and Work Related Institutions".[26] The country has now started preparations for the eighth dialogue entitled, "Health Services—Dialogue Between Society and Health Institutions".[27]

As announced earlier, the regime held Municipal elections in February-April, 2005 to 178 councils, opening a new chapter in the history of the Kingdom. When the election was a blow to the hardliners and also U-turn from King Fahd's earlier position, the liberals welcomed it as a major step in the right direction. However, Saudi women, who make up more than 50 percent of the population, were barred from voting.[28] The officials cited logistical reasons behind the exclusion, saying most women did not carry ID card and therefore they could not vote. They, however, said women would be allowed to participate in the next elections.

REFORMS UNDER KING ABDULLAH

The ascent of Abdullah as the King after Fahd's death on 1 August 2005 was welcomed with great vigour by the liberal lobby in the Kingdom. It was not a secret that the new King had a reform agenda though he reportedly enjoyed less support within the family for that. Making his plans clear, while appearing before the *Majlis al-Shura* for the first time as the King on 4 April 2006, Abdullah said: "We cannot stand still while the world around us is changing; we will continue the process of development, the national dialogue, the economic liberalization, the fight against corruption, reducing government's bureaucracy, increasing governmental work efficiency, and employing the efforts of all sincere working men and women".[29] However, the regime did not go for any radical reforms. Abdullah accepted a dual strategy: deal with the militants with a high hand and the liberals with a soft hand. The continuing national dialogues opened new avenues for limited policy level criticisms, while increased security measures have successfully countered the Islamist violence.[30]

The King's announcement of judicial reforms and his decision to set up an Allegiance Council to facilitate smooth transfer of power indicated that he was serious about initiating reforms in the Kingdom. In October 2006, the King approved the new Judiciary and Court of Grievances Laws that envisage setting up of a Supreme Court and labour tribunals.[31] The Allegiance Council, on the other hand, was a crucial step given the pattern of succession in Saudi Arabia. The Council, made up of senior sons and grandsons of the founder of the Kingdom Abd-al Aziz, was set up aimed at quelling internal power struggles between the younger generation of princess who are in line of succession. If King dies, the Council will officially name the Crown Prince as the King. Within 10 days, the new King must send the name of the person, whom he chose as the next Crown Prince. The Commission has to nominate the name within 10 days it got the King's letter.[32] The council will meet only after Abdullah's brother Crown Prince Sultan succeeded. But Sultan is in his 80s and is very ill. This keeps the hope of many reformists alive that a relatively younger prince may come to the top level in the country, who could steer the country towards modernity, tolerance and equality at a greater pace.[33]

Although the judicial and educational reforms were struck with several challenges, King Abdullah sent out a tough message to the conservative religious establishment by decreeing changes in the government 14 February, 2009. He brought new faces in the top ministries, courts, the armed forces, the central bank, religious police and the royally-appointed 150 member *Majlis al-Shura*. The sweeping change, that raised the eyebrows of many, was the King's decision to induct a woman into the Council of Ministers for the first time in the history of the country. Nora al-Fayez, an American educated school administrator, was made the minister for female education.[34] Abdullah also sacked the head of the feared religious police and the conservative minister of justice. According to reports, the first female minister could work with the King's favoured son-in-law, the new Minister for Education Prince Faisal bin Abdullah bin Mohammad, to speed up educational reforms and equalize the education of women and men. Though the striking changes were welcomed in the liberal quarters, many are still upset with the snarl's pace of reforms even after Abdullah's ascendancy to the throne.

CONCLUSION

Given the history of reforms in Saudi Arabia, one can assume that the political system in the country should evolve if it has to preserve the internal stability. Whenever there was a crisis, the rulers have responded to the people with rhetoric and limited actions. The strategy of the al-Saud family was simple at the beginning. Draw legitimacy from the *Ulama* for their rule and in turn ensure the supremacy of conservative, less tolerant Wahhabi Islam. However, the regime's over-dependence on the conservative Islam was a double-edged sword. The first major threats the regime faced were not from the so-called liberal lobby, but from the pan-Islamist groups. Unlike the Iranian brand, the Islamists in Saudi Arabia were not revolutionary in nature, who wanted to bring about radical changes at home. Rather, they stood for Islamic Puritanism and raised their voices against the Saudi rulers, accusing them of not standing up for the Islamic values. In 1980s and 1990s we can see the government giving in to the Islamists many times. Following the Makkah uprising of 1980s, the regime had actually given more powers to the religious establishment and let Saudis go abroad and fight for the cause of Islam. Though King Fahd had initiated limited constitutional reforms, the regime was extra cautious about the liberal dissident voices. The government was ready to accommodate, to certain level, the Islamist *Sahwa* critics, while it outrightly banned the Committee for the Defence of Legitimate Rights (CDLR) and arrested a few of its members.

However, the 11 September terrorist attack and the subsequent sweeping changes in the regional politics have influenced the domestic debate on conservative Islam, which gave more space for the Islamo-liberals. The liberals did not pose any radical challenge, but only demanded that the regime initiate steps to relax the strident laws, ensure equitable distribution of wealth and set up a civil society. On the other hand, the regime faced serious challenge from the Islamists and also its global reputation was at stake following the US allegation that 15 of the 19 terrorists were Saudi nationals. The monarch had to make a choice between the liberals and the Islamists. Realizing that stability could not be ensured unless reforms were initiated, Crown Prince Abdullah turned against the Islamists with a heavy hand while taking steps to cheer the reformers.

Many of his reform measures were greeted both at home and at international level. But did he stand up to the expectations of those who thought the monarch, who had a reputation for probity, tolerance and humility would have steered reforms at a greater pace? Saudi women are still awaiting the permission to drive. Many of Abdullah's educational and judicial reforms have been stalled due to opposition by the conservative establishment. Though King Abdullah made history by meeting with the Pope, the regime is still less tolerant to faiths other than Islam. However, the pace of reforms in the post-9/11 period is faster than that in 1980s an 1990s. The public sphere is now stronger than ever in the country which can stand for faster and qualitative reforms in the future. The country is changing. But given the hold of the conservative values and the religious establishment, it is illogical to expect sudden changes or democratization of the polity. Like their rulers, the Saudi population also seem to believe in gradualism.

NOTES

1. Rashed Aba-Namay (1998), "The New Saudi Representative Assembly", *Islamic Law and Society*, 5 (2), p. 235.
2. Between 1938 and 1946, the annual government revenue had averaged $14-16 million. In 1948, it crossed $53 million. By 1950, it had passed $100 billion. See Harry St. John Bridger (1955), *Saudi Arabia*, London: Benn, p. 355.
3. The state budget for 1952-03 allocated almost one quarter of the total expenditure to an item called 'Riyadh Affairs'. This was kept aside for the King's personal treasury. See David Holden and Richard Jonhs (1981), *The House of Saud*, London: Sidwick and Jackson, p:163
4. Alexander Bligh (1984), *From Prince to King: Royal Succession in the House of Saud*, New York: New York University Press, p. 62.
5. *Ibid*, p. 66.
6. Quoted in Aba-Namay, no. 1, p. 238.

7. Ziauddin Sardar (1 November, 2008), "The Battle at Islam's Heart", *Newstatesman*. For detailed information of the uprising, see Yaroslav Trofimov (2007), *The Siege of Mecca: The Forgotten Uprising in Islam's Holiest Shrine and the Birth of al-Qaeda*, New York: Doubleday
8. Gwenn Okruhlik, "Networks of Dissent: Islamism and Reform in Saudi Arabia," *Social Council Research Council*, URL: http://www.ssrc.org/sept11/essays/okruhlik.htm, Accessed on 15 March, 2009.
9. *Ibid.*,
10. Dauglas Martin (1 August, 2005), "Saudi Arabia's King Fahd Dies; Abdullah Named New Leader", *The New York Times*, Also see, Said K. Alburish (1994) *The Rise, Corruption and Coming Fall of the House of Saud*, London: Bloomsbury, pp:175-178.
11. Judith Caesar (5 July 1991), "Liberals and Conservative Press Riyadh, *The New York Times*.
12. Richard Dekmejian (Summer 2003), "The Liberal Impulse in Saudi Arabia", *The Middle East Journal*, pp-402-403.
13. Article 1 says: The Kingdom of Saudi Arabia is a sovereign Arab Islamic state with Islam as its religion; God's Book and the Sunnah of His Prophet, God's prayers and peace be upon him, are its constitution, Arabic is its language and Riyadh is its capital. The Basic Law is available on government website URL:http://www.the-saudi.net/saudi-arabia/saudi-constitution.htm, Accessed on March 20.
14. Tim Niblock (2006), *Saudi Arabia: Power, Legitimacy and Survival*, London: Routledge
15. Quotes in R. Raba Namay, p. 244
16. Ibrahim Al-Rasheed (2002), *A History of Saudi Arabia*, Cambridge: Cambridge Univesity Press, pp. 176-177.
17. Madawi al-Rasheed (Summer, 1996), "God the King and the Nation: Political Rhetoric in Saudi Arabia in the 1990s", *The Middle East Journal*, 50(3), p. 371.
18. In October 2001, Senator Joseph Lieberman said the Saudis were trying to "ride the back of al-Qaeda". Another Senator Joseph Biden accused the Saudis of "funding a significant portion of what we are dealing with now—Islam gone awry". Senator John Kerry, also Democratic Presidential candidate, said "we cannot support" Saudi Arabia's continuing support for terror groups like al-Qaeda. See, "Can Saudi Arabia Reform Itself?" *ICG Middle East Report*, 14 July, 2004.
19. For a detailed analysis of the changing currents in the in the US-Saudi relationship in the immediate aftermath of the September 11 attack, see Taufiq Subhan (September 13-19, 2003), "US-Saudi Arabia Relations: Coming of Age", *Economic and Political Weekly*, 38(37) pp. 3885-3887
20. "The Broader Middle East and North Africa Initiative: Imperilled at Birth", *ICG Middle East Briefing*, 7 June 2004.
21. The relations between Crown Prince Abdullah and his half-brother Prince Nayef were always tense. Nayef reportedly opposed Abdullah's reform-oriented domestic and pro-western foreign policies. See Michael Scott Doran (January-February 2004), The Saudi Paradox, *Foreign Affairs*, 83(1), pp. 35-51.

22. The 2003-04 period saw an unprecedented rise in Islamic violence in Saudi Arabia. The 12 May 2003 attack killed 35 people, while 17 were killed in November bombing. The interior ministry building in Riyadh was targeted by a car bomb on 21 April 2004, while the al-Kgobar siege on 29 May left 22 people, most non-Saudis, dead. See Thomas Hegghammer, "Islamist Violence and Regime Stability in Saudi Arabia", *International Affairs*, 84(4), pp. 701-715. For a detailed analysis of the Islamist opposition in Saudi Arabia and extremist violence, see Anthony H. Cordesman (2003), *Saudi Arabia Enters the 21st Century: The Political, Foreign Policy, Economic and Energy Dimensions*, London: Praeger.
23. Dekmejian, no. 12, p. 406.
24. Stephane Lacroix (Summer, 2004), "Between Islamists and Liberals: Saudi Arabia's New 'Islamo-Liberal' Reformists", *The Middle East Journal*, 58(3), pp:363-364
25. "Saudis Announces First Elections", BBC, 13 October, 2003.
26. For detailed information on the seven national dialogues, visit the website of King Abdul Aziz Centre for National Dialogue, URL: http://www.kacnd.org/eng/all_national_meetings.asp, Accessed on March 18.
27. Abdullah Al-Qarni (19 March 2009), National Dialogue Participants Slam Health Services, *Saudi Gazette*, Available on URL: http://www.saudigazette.com.sa/index.cfm?method=home.regcon&contentID=2009031932588&archiveissuedate=19/03/2009, Accessed on 20 March 2009).
28. See Kim Ghattas, Saudis' first exercise with democracy", BBC News, 10 February, 2005, URL:http://news.bbc.co.uk/2/hi/middle_east/4252305.stm, Accessed 15 March, 2009.
29. The King is quoted in, Ali Alyami (25 April 2006) "Abdullah's Reforms Must Begin in the Palace", *The Henry Jackson Society*: *Project for Democratic Geopolitics*, URL: http://www.henryjacksonsociety.org/stories.asp?id=339, Accessed on 18 March, 2009.
30. Praising the Saudi government's security policies, former CIA director Michael Hayden said in 2008: "Aggressive efforts by the Saudi security forces between 2003 and 2006 led to the death or capture of most al-Qaeda leaders and operatives within the Kingdom." See Christopher Dickey (March 30, 2009), "The Monarch Who Declared His Own Revolution", *Newsweek*.
31. "Saudi Arabia approves long overdue judicial reforms", *The Associated Press*, 5 October 2007.
32. "Saudi king names members to a commission entrusted with picking future kings", *The Associated Press*, 10 December, 2007.
33. Simon Henderson (21 January 2009), "Saudi Leadership Crisis Looms: Health of Crown Prince falters", *The Washington Institute for Near East Policy*, URL:http://www.washingtoninstitute.org/templateC05.php? CID=2994, Accessed on 6 March, 2009.
34. Abdullah Al-Asmari (17 February 2009), "Hopes Renewed from the reshuffle of Saudi Cabinet, *Saudi Gazatte,* URL: http://www.saudigazette.com.sa/index.cfm?method=home.regcon&contentID=2009021729534&archiveissuedate=17/02/2009, Accessed on 20 Mach, 2009.

10

Human Rights Reforms in Saudi Arabia: Recent Developments

Prasanta Kumar Pradhan

In recent times Saudi Arabia has taken some important steps in the direction of safeguarding the human rights of its citizens. For the first time since the establishment of the kingdom, a bill of rights was introduced for the citizens in the year 1992—as a part of the Basic Law that was promulgated by King Fahd. This was a landmark development in the history of Saudi Arabia as it was an attempt to codify the human rights law where the laws of Sharia rules supreme in the matters pertaining to protection and promotion of human rights. But this attempt is also a half-hearted one and the document remains incomplete in many aspects. Since then, no significant legislation has come up in the country; but the ruling authorities have granted some rights to the people on some issues through royal decrees and orders. In this regard, this paper attempts to highlight some of the important moves that have been undertaken by the ruling family in recent times over the issue of human rights.

In his address to the Consultative Council on 17 May 2003, the then King Fahd pledged to expand the breadth and pace of reform in the country. In his speech the King stressed the need for all internal affairs to remain open to self-revision. He emphasized the importance of civil and criminal judicial procedures and promised new laws and regulations that would provide equal access to justice for all citizens and prevent power abuse by official authorities. The King proposed to place a premium on involving women in the economy with due respect for religious precepts and teachings. He also promised to boost political and economic reform, improving the system of governance and monitoring the performance of the public sector, along with broadening popular participation in the political process.[1]

WOMEN

The issue of rights of women in Saudi Arabia has drawn much attention and has become a subject of many debates and discussions.[2] The question of rights of Saudi women, their position in the society, and their responsibilities towards the political and economic development of the country has remained controversial. Traditionally, women are kept marginalized in the kingdom in respect of their rights due to the strict interpretation of the Islamic law in the country. Issues like their education, employment and political participation etc. have drawn attention in recent times.

Women are restricted in the field of education and till 1974 women were mainly confined to commerce, humanities and education. Women were allowed to study medicine in 1975, followed by dentistry in 1980. In January 2007, the Saudi government permitted women students to pursue bachelor's degree in banking and finance. In 2002, King Khalid University in Abha admitted women to computer sciences, biology and English. Some of these university campuses have residential accommodations for female students who do not live within traveling distances. But these campuses must submit to the same rigid rules as all other women's institutions and workplaces in that they are all guarded by men or security police.

In recent years, the government has adopted some policy initiatives aiming towards improving rights of women in the kingdom. The National Dialogue Conference, held in Medina in 2004 discussed at length the issue of women's employment and its recommendations were submitted to the Majlis which outlined a comprehensive strategy for dealing with the problem. Later, government passed 'Resolution 120' which intended to expand employment opportunities of women in the kingdom. Resolution 120 included the following decisions:[3]

- Government institutions would issue licenses for women who wish to engage in economic activity, and would form special departments for women;
- The Saudi Council of Commerce and Industry Bureaus would form a women's committee to identify various professional fields in which women can train and find employment;
- The Saudi Federation of Human Resources Development would train women in various fields; areas would be prepared for special industrial projects that would employ women;
- The Ministry of Labour would develop options for distance working as one of the new modes of employment suitable for women, and would formulate a comprehensive national programme for women's development.

In January 2006, the Majlis created a women's committee as a "consultative body" and nominated the women who could be called to offer their opinion on women-related issues. But this committee fell short of what women have been asking for—full membership and equal role in the council as men. Still this move is considered as a step forward toward reaching the goal.[4] Similarly in February 2005, Saudi Foreign Minister Saud Al-Faisal announced that women would be employed in Saudi Arabia's Foreign Ministry for the first time. In 2004 then Crown Prince Abdullah told government departments to put plans in place for employing women.[5] In the same year, the authorities approved the establishment of an all-women industrial city that will host training centres and employ approximately 10,000 women at more than 80 factories.[6]

Although the government is encouraging Saudi women to participate in the labour force, women as an active force still lag behind in the development process. Though women form more than half of all university students in the kingdom, they constitute less than five per cent of the workforce.

Though women face restrictions in the employment sector, they are relatively free to own and manage their own property. They are free to inherit and manage property and women's banks play a growing role in handling assets. At present, there are around 20,000 firms owned by Saudi women; these range from ordinary retail business to various types of industry. The number of women registered in local chambers of commerce and industry is on the rise. The Jeddah Chamber, for example, has more than 2000 women members out of a total membership of 50,000. In Riyadh, the figure is over 2,400 out of total of 35,000 members. Businesswomen registered with the Eastern Province Chamber number more than 1,000 out of a total 14,000. The Jeddah Chamber of Commerce has recently established the "Khadija bint Khwailid Centre" to provide services for businesswomen, facilitate business opportunities and provide guidance to encourage women to run their own business.[7]

Women were not allowed to vote in the 2005 municipal elections in the country. They have been promised to participate in the 2009 municipal elections. But the 2009 municipal elections have been postponed at least for two years discouraging women in Saudi Arabia. In the direction of political participation of women, the recent cabinet reshuffles by King Abdullah and the induction of a women member in the new cabinet, Noura al-Fayez as the Deputy Education Minister in charge of women's affairs is a big boost for the hopes of women in the country towards greater participation in the future.

SHIAS

Throughout the history, Shias have been discriminated against in Saudi Arabia by the ruling authorities. They have bee discriminated politically, culturally and economically in their own country. Their long isolation and neglect by the state led them to take a dissident stance which was later manifested in a violent manner. The Shia reform movement started in the kingdom in 1975; and in the initial years of the movement it openly criticised the discriminatory policies of the government and adopted a violent approach towards the government. Their dissatisfaction with the government was so deep that they even refused to negotiate with the government.

But Shia political opposition to the government changed significantly in the 1990s and they entered into negotiations with the government to secure improved rights for their community. As Madawi al-Rasheed argues, in the 1990s, Shias' confrontation with the State moved away from overt riots, demonstrations and violence to one which is fought at a cultural level. Shia opposition publications and intellectual activities demonstrate that dealing with Shias' socio-economic problem cannot alone fully pacify the community. While development projects may bring about tangible amelioration in life conditions, a serious change in attitudes towards this minority remains a precondition for their integration into Saudi society as citizens with equal rights.[8]

During the initial period of Shiite protests, the Saudi regime employed a very repressive strategy and adopted coercive methods to deal with the Shiite opposition movement. The authorities arrested, jailed the protesting Shias and their leaders were forced in to exile. But with the change in the attitude of the Shias towards the problem, the government has also adopted a moderate stance towards the Shias.

On 29 April 2003, a delegation of Saudi Shias met Crown Prince Abdullah and presented him with a petition asking for a national policy of tolerance, acknowledgement of sectarian diversity, and respect for citizens' human rights, dignity and religious and intellectual freedom. The petitioners further asked that the government recognize the right of all citizens without regard to sectarian or regional background, which would entitle all to the right to worship according to their respective interpretations of Islam. Notably, the Shia appeal signed by academics, clerics, businessmen, writers, and women is based on the modern liberal notion of citizenship, without invoking divine texts and traditions, which would trigger theological controversies with Sunni religious establishment.[9] More importantly, the Shia petition was entitled "Partners in One Nation" and urged reforms emphasizing Islamic and national unity and expressed their support to the royal family.[10]

The petition called for an unequivocal announcement of the kingdom's respect for all religious sects, appointment of a national committee with the participation of Shias to deal with the question of sectarian discrimination, treating sectarian hatred as a crime, creation of an official body of Shia Islamic scholars under the guidance of the Ministry of Endowments and Islamic Affairs to arrange their religious and cultural affairs, removal of restrictions on Shia religious ceremonies, printing and importing of Shia publications, and referral of royal decrees to the Shia Sharia courts.[11]

Soon after Abdullah's accession to throne in August 2005, Shia delegations from Eastern Province and Najran separately visited King Abdullah.

Representatives from Najran's smaller Ismaili Shia community also handed Abdullah a list of requests in September 2005 when they met him to pledge allegiance. Their requests included the release of prisoners, a bigger role in the affairs of the state and the return of Shias they said were forcibly moved from Najran after a fierce government crackdown five years ago, in 2000. They also asked that they be given a chance to serve in the cabinet, consultative council and other state bodies.[12]

In the year 2003, Hasan al-Safar was invited by the King to participate in the National Dialogue. Subsequently, the municipal council elections in 2005 allowed the Saudi Shias to elect representatives for the first time to help manage their cities. Perhaps most important from a symbolic standpoint is that the Saudi Shias for the past few years have been able to commemorate their festival of Ashura, which had been banned for decades, and are particularly offensive to hard-line Salafis from the Wahhabi tradition.[13]

But even today the relationship between the Sunnis and the Shia minorities has not been cordial. There have been incidents of clashes between the Shias and the security forces and the Shia leaders have frequently expressed their anger and frustrations with the government. The Ismaili Shias of the Najran province have been raising their voices against discriminatory policies of the government against them including the plan of the Ministry of Interior to shut down Ismaili mosques in the region. They also complain that under Prince Mishal, the Governor of the province, their identity as Ismailis came under threat and that they suffered increased discrimination and interference in their affairs. Those include officials disparaging the Shia faith, and the Ismaili faith in particular, increased missionary and discriminatory charitable activity by Sunnis from outside, increased restrictions on Ismaili religious practices, and of a perceived plan to reduce the demographic weight of Ismailis by naturalizing Sunni Yemenis.[14] But with public sentiments raising high against Prince Mishal, King Abdullah dismissed him from the job. Recently, in February 2009, a clash erupted between the Shias and the state police at Medina. Two persons were killed and several other were arrested by the police. This incident witnessed several protests in the Shia dominated areas against the police action. One prominent Shiite religious leader from Al-Awamiya Sheikh Nimr Baqir Al-Nimr declared that, "Our dignity is more valuable than the unity of this land…If we don't get our dignity, then we will have to consider seceding from this country."[15] This kind of behaviour of the state and the response of the Shias shows the existence of severe misunderstandings between the government and the Shiite community.

LABOUR REFORMS

Saudi authorities have now conceded the right to the workers to form committees to defend their interests. An International Labour Organization (ILO) press release of April 2002 says that workers in Saudi Arabia are now able to defend their rights through committees at the work places. After a visit to Saudi Arabia in early 2002 by a team of ILO experts, the Saudi Minister of Labour, Ali Al-Namlah, signed the new labour rules that allow workers in Saudi Arabia—both national and foreign—to establish committees to guard their interests at workplaces where 100 or more are employed.[16]

The labour committees are to consist of three to nine members, who would serve three-year terms. The government has no role in selecting the committee members. Both management and workers will be represented in the committee. The committee may make recommendations to company management to improve work conditions, increase productivity, improve health and safety, and recommend training programmes. The Ministry of Labour and Social Affairs may send a representative to attend committee meetings. A committee must provide a written report of its meetings to company management, which will also be transmitted to the ministry.[17] Saudi Arabia has not signed the International Convention on the Protection of the Rights of Migrant Workers and members of their families. In this regard, it seems to be a major development in Saudi labour laws where millions of foreign workers are employed in different sectors.

JUDICIARY

Saudi Arabia has recently passed several important regulations to ensure a fair and balanced justice system. In September 2001, Saudi Arabia passed the Law of Procedure for the Sharia Courts to regulate the rights of defendants and legal procedures. In addition to granting defendants the right to legal representation, the law outlines the processes by which pleas, evidence and experts are accepted by the court. In January 2002, the Code of Law Practice went into effect in Saudi Arabia. The law outlines the specific requirements necessary to become an attorney, including education, registration and admission to the courts as well as licensing. The law also defines the duties and rights of lawyers, including the right of attorney-client privilege. More importantly, the Code of Law Practice does not explicitly refer to a gender requirement to become a lawyer. Thus, there is no restriction on women becoming lawyers in the courts. Also, the Code allows non-Muslim lawyers to appear before the courts when the client belongs to the same religion.[18] Earlier, the lawyers were given licenses by the Ministry of Commerce to practise law and were restricted to handle labour and commercial cases only. But now they are empowered to take up all cases and are required to obtain permits from the Ministry of Justice.[19]

Similarly, in May 2002, the Criminal Procedure Law, a 225-article Bill, was passed to regulate the rights of defendants and suspects before the courts and police. The law protects a defendant's rights with regard to interrogation, investigation, and incarceration and also grants the defendant access to the Bureau of Investigation. Prosecution are to ensure, through visits, that the rights of the defendants and persons in custody are being protected. The law also outlines a series of regulations that justice and law enforcement authorities must follow during all stages of the judicial process, from arrest and interrogation, to trial and the execution of verdicts, ensuring that the judicial process remains fair and balanced.[20]

PRESS FREEDOM

It must be mentioned at the outset that in Saudi Arabia the press is owned and controlled by the state. The Ministry of Information is the regulatory authority of the press in the kingdom. The Saudi Press Agency expresses the official government views and the government also monitors other sources of information like television and radio. The 1982 Royal Decree on Press Publications guarantees freedom of expression within the framework of Islamic and national objectives and values. All criticisms of the royal family and the authorities are forbidden. Article 39 of the Basic System of Rules states that, "mass media, publication facilities and other means of expression shall function in a manner that is courteous and fair and shall abide by state laws. They shall play their part in educating the masses and boosting national unity. All that may give rise to mischief and discord, or may defend against man's dignity and rights shall be banned."

In 2000 the government approved a wide-ranging press law that permits the creation of professional journalism societies and permits the publication of foreign newspapers in the country. The law states that local publications will be subject to censorship only in emergencies and pledges to protect free expression of opinion, however, the law obliges the authorities to censor foreign publications that defame Islam and harm the interests of the state or the "ethics of the people." But implementation of the law has not changed the current practices regarding freedom of expression.[21] In July 2001, the Council of Ministers approved a new press law establishing a journalist association to address wages, benefits and relations with management. It will issue membership cards permitting journalists to work in the country and oversee introduction of a minimum wage, job security and other benefits for journalists.[22]

GIVING SPACE TO HUMAN RIGHTS BODIES

The year 2004 witnessed the establishment of the first independent non-government human rights organization the National Human Rights Association (NHRA) to uphold the basic rights guaranteed to its citizens. The NHRA consists of 41 members who will work with the international human rights organizations and issue periodic reports on the progress of human rights in Saudi Arabia.[23] The NHRA was formed after the kingdom hosted the first ever human rights conference in Riyadh—The Human Rights in Peace and War Conference—in October 2003. The conference concluded with the issuance of the 'Riyadh Declaration', which states that respect for human life, and dignity is the foundation of human rights, and a human being deserves respect regardless of race, colour and sex. The conference also stated that violation of human rights is a crime deserving severe punishment and that to hold a person in custody without any legal basis is forbidden by Islamic laws. The conference also emphasized that disregard for privacy and property rights is a violation of human rights, and that tolerance of faith is required by Islam, which also prohibits coercing people to follow a certain religion.[24] Amnesty International and other international human rights bodies attended the meeting.

A delegation of New York based human rights watchdog Human Rights Watch arrived in Saudi Arabia in December 2006, on the first extensive fact-finding mission in the kingdom. The Saudi government allowed them access to interact with the leaders and government officials on the issue of human rights in the kingdom. The delegation focused on the criminal justice system, political rights, the status of women and foreign workers' rights. During the visit, Human Rights Watch complained that they were prohibited access to some important jails in the kingdom where they wished to visit. But the delegation was happy to learn that the kingdom expressed its seriousness to ratify the International Covenant on Civil and Political rights and the International Covenant on Economic, Social and Cultural Rights.

In October 2005, an eighteen-member Human Rights Commission was formally set up in the country. It is entrusted to ensure strict implementation of rules pertaining to human rights by all concerned government departments and private bodies, detect violations and take corrective measures; to follow up the implementation of international agreements on human rights; to summon representatives of government and private bodies as part of its investigation; to visit prisons and detention centres without prior permission; and to submit reports to the King.[25] This body, importantly, reports directly to the King; and it is also empowered to create awareness among the people and oversee the implementation of human rights according to the Sharia law in the kingdom. In September 2008, the Commission opened its women's branch which is dedicated to look into cases of human rights violations against women and children in the country.

SAUDI ARABIA AND INTERNATIONAL TREATIES

The second half of the 1990s witnessed the kingdom ratifying some international conventions related to human rights. Saudi Arabia ratified the International

Convention for the Elimination of All forms of Racial Discrimination in September 1997, the Convention on the Elimination of All forms of Discrimination Against Women in October 2000, the Convention Against Torture and other Cruel, Inhuman or Degrading Treatment or Punishment in September 1997 and the Convention on the Rights of the Child in January 1996. But it has ratified the above treaties with some reservations on some major clauses.

The government has reservations on the article 20 of the Convention against Torture and other Cruel, Inhuman or Degrading Treatment or Punishment as it does not recognize the jurisdiction of the Committee to investigate allegations of systematic torture. Saudi Arabia also has its reservations on the article 22 of the International Convention for the Elimination of All forms of Racial Discrimination which says that, "any dispute between two or more state parties with respect to the interpretation or application of this Convention, which is not settled by negotiation or by the procedure expressly provided for in this Convention, shall, at the request of any of the parties to the dispute, be referred to the International Court of Justice for decision, unless the disputants agree to another mode of settlement." Saudi Arabia reserved its position by saying that it shall not be bound by the provisions of the article 22 of this Convention, since it considers that any dispute should be referred to the International Court of Justice only with the approval of the States parties to the dispute. Similarly, Saudi Arabia expressed its reservation on the article 9, paragraph 2 of the Convention on the Elimination of All forms of Discrimination Against Women which says that, "States parties (to the Convention) shall grant women equal rights with men with respect to the nationality of their children." Saudi Arabia also reserved the article 29, paragraph 1 of the same convention which reads, "Any dispute between two or more state parties concerning the interpretation or application of the present Convention which is not settled by negotiation shall, at the request of one of them, be submitted to arbitration. If within six months from the date of the request for arbitration the parties are unable to agree on the organization of the arbitration, any one of those parties may refer the dispute to the International Court of Justice by request in conformity with the Statute of the Court."[26]

Saudi Arabia ratified the Convention on the Rights of the Child with a general reservation which stated that, "The government of Saudi Arabia enters reservation into all such articles as are in conflict with the provisions of Islamic law."[27] Defending his country's general reservation on the Convention, a Saudi representative Mr. Al-Rassi said in a meeting at Paris in January 2001that:

> The Convention has been adopted by a very large consensus in the National Assembly and that its provisions were considered as minimum rather than maximum standards. The general reservation, therefore, had no practical

> repercussions and did not concern either the content or the objectives of the Convention. It was simply a precautionary measure to avoid interpretations of the Convention which might be inconsistent with the Sharia. Such position was not inconsistent with the Vienna Declaration and programme of Action, which provided for cultural differences between nations to be taken into account in the implementation of international instruments.[28]

Saudi Arabia abstained from voting in favour of the adoption of the Universal Declaration of Human Rights at the United Nations in 1948. Its abstention was based on two arguments. Firstly, it opposed the article 18 of the document which says of freedom of thought, conscience and religion. The article reads: "Everyone has the right to freedom of thought, conscience and religion; this right includes freedom to change his religion or belief, and freedom, either alone or in community with others and in public or private, to manifest his religion or belief in teaching, practice, worship and observance."[29] Secondly, for Saudi Arabia, human rights guaranteed by the Islamic-based law of the country surpassed those secured by the Declaration.[30] Saudi Arabia is a member of the United Nations whose purposes, as defined in Article 1 of its Charter, include "promoting and encouraging respect for human rights and for fundamental freedoms for all without distinction as to race, sex, language or religion." It is commonly held, therefore, that membership of the UN in itself carries with it the obligation to respect and promote human rights. This general obligation implies observance of recognized rules of international human rights law.[31] But Saudi Arabia has signed only a few international conventions citing its 'Islamic' reasons, and often stating that its domestic laws are good enough to protect the human rights of its citizens. By doing so, it is trying to stay aloof from any kind of external interferences or obligations in maintaining its domestic laws on human rights.

CONCLUSION

The recent initiatives on the part of the government towards a better human rights situation in the country are certainly a welcome step in many respects. But, all these moves have not come voluntarily from the government. People have had to fight hard to get these rights. There have been severe pressures on the King in the form of demands and petitions from different sections of society to opt for a more liberal human rights regime in the country. The King has been slow and cautious in undertaking the reforms as there are pressures on him from the religious establishment demanding greater Islamization of the society. The Saudi government is always under the pressure of the conservative elements of the society who feel that the issues of human rights should be dealt strictly within Islamic laws. They think that Saudi Arabia, being the birthplace of Islam, carries the moral responsibility of following and teaching Islamic principles, rights and duties. At the moment, it seems, the government is trying to strike a balance between demands for more liberal human rights, the Islamic responsibility of the government and the pressure from the conservative elements of the society. This has made the King strike a balance between the two opposite interests. Thus, though the King has initiated some reforms he still keeps the Sharia as the main point of reference for dealing with human rights issues.

The moves by the government regarding the education and employment of women, talking to the dissident Shia leadership, reforming the judiciary, giving some rights to the labourers, initiating press freedom, forming a national body to deal with the human rights abuses and to create awareness among the people and signing some international treaties etc. are highly lauded both inside and outside the kingdom. But it does not satisfy the aspirations of the people nor does it confirm to the established international human rights standards. Making the man made law subservient to the Islamic law and maintaining the Sharia law as the highest source of reference for dealing with human rights issues remain the foremost problem in the country.

NOTES

1. Abdulaziz O. Sager, *Reform in Saudi Arabia: Current Challenges and Feasible Solutions* (London: Gulf Research Centre, 2004), pp. 1-2.
2. For an elaborate discussion on women in Saudi Arabia see Mai Yamani, "Some Observations on Women in Saudi Arabia", in Mai Yamani (ed.), *Feminism and Islam: Legal and Literary Perspectives* (Reading: Garnet Publishing Ltd., 1996).
3. "Public Debate in Saudi Arabia on Employment Opportunities for Women", available at www.freemuslims.org/news/article.php?article=1803, accessed on 8 January 2007.
4. "Saudi Arabia: Women's Issues—Baby Steps and Individual Successes", available at www.wluml.org/english/newsfulltxt.shtml?cmd, accessed on 15 March 2007.
5. "Saudi Ministry is to Employ Women", available at http://newsvote.co.uk/mpapps/pagetools/print/news.bbc.co.uk/, accessed on 16 March 2007.
6. Faiza Saleh Ambah, "In Rare Public Dialogue, Saudi women Talk Rights", *Christian Science Monitor*, June 14, 2004.
7. Available at www.arabnews.com/page=7&section/, accessed on 7 September 2006.
8. Madawi Al-Rasheed also argues that now the Shias in Saudi Arabia are a minority in search of cultural authenticity. For an analysis of the changing perception of the Saudi Shias towards the government and the country see Madawi Al-Rasheed, "The Shia of Saudi Arabia: A Minority in Search of Cultural Authenticity," *British Journal of Middle Eastern Studies* (Durham), Vol. 25, No. 1, 1998.
9. Richard Dekmejian, "The Liberal Impulse in Saudi Arabia", *Middle East Journal*, Vol. 57, No. 3, Summer 2003, p. 412.

10. M.H. Ansari, *The Islamic Boomerang in Saudi Arabia: The Cost of Delayed Reforms* (New Delhi: Samskriti and ORF, 2004), p. 30.
11. Gulshan Dietl, *Saudi Arabia: People, Politics, Policies* (New Delhi: National Book Trust, 2006), pp. 51-52.
12. Available at www.english .aljazeera.net/NR/Exeres.htm., accessed on 22 May 2006.
13. F. Gregory Gause III, "Saudi Arabia: Iraq, Iran, the Regional Power Balance, and the Sectarian Question", *Strategic Insights*, Vol. 6, Issue-2, March 2007, available at www.ccc.nps/navy/si/2007/mar/gausemar2007.pdf, accessed on 31 March 2007.
14. See Human Rights Watch report on "The Ismailis of Najran", September 22, 2008, available at http://www.hrw.org/en/node/75197/section/7, accessed on 7 April 2009.
15. http://www.saudishia.com/?act=artc&id=108, accessed on 7 April 2009.
16. www.ilo.org/public/english.htm., accessed on 12 March 2003.
17. United States' Country Report on Human Rights Practices, 2001, available at www.state.gov/g/drl/rls/hrrpt/2001/htm, accessed on 12 March 2008.
18. Report of the Special Rapporteur on Civil and Political Rights, including the Question of Independence of Judiciary, Administration of Justice and Impunity, 14 January 2003, Commission on Human Rights, United Nations, available at, www.unhcr.ch/Huridocda/Huridocda.nsf/0/1fa4d2b31bb90 ce6c1256cd800372b43/FILE/G0310264.pdf, accessed on 11 May 2007.
19. Dietl, n. 11, pp. 47-48.
20. http://www.saudiembassy.net/ReportLink/Reform/pdf, accessed on 20 January 2007.
21. *Ibid.*
22. United States' Country Report on Human Rights Practices, 2003, available at www.state.gov/g/drl/rls/hrrpt/2003/htm., accessed on 5 February 2008.
23. www.saudiembassy.net/2004/News., accessed on 13 November 2005.
24. "Political and Economic Reform in the Kingdom of Saudi Arabia", Information Office, Royal Embassy of Saudi Arabia in Washington DC, 2006, Available at www.saudiembassy.net., accessed on 20 January 2007
25. Dietl, n.11, p. 57.
26. Available at www.arabhumanrights.org/en/ratification/viewarticle.asp?id=6&aid=29&pid=1, accessed on 20 April 2007.
27. Available at www.webcom.com/hrin/parker/0326., accessed on 11 March 2006.
28. Convention on the Rights of the Child, Summary Record of the 687th Meeting, 2001, Available at www.unhchr.ch/tbs/doc.nsf/(symbol)/, accessed on 11 March 2007.
29. Article 18 of the Universal Declaration of Human Rights adopted by General Assembly resolution 217 A (III) on 10 December1948.
30. Mohamed S.M. Eltayeb, *A Human Rights Approach to Combating Religious persecution: Cases from Pakistan, Saudi Arabia and Sudan*, (Oxford: Intersentia, 2001), p. 111.
31. *Torture in Saudi Arabia: No Protection, No Redress*, A report by Parliamentary Human Rights Group, London, 1997.

Part 4: Iran and Iraq: Ethnicity and Gender, Economy and Occupation

11

Political Discourses among Iranian Women since the Islamic Revolution

Beryl Anand

Political discourses among Iran's women can be grouped as Islamic and Marxist feminist discourses. The paper gives a brief historical account of the status of women in Iran before the Islamic Revolution in 1979. It then explains the policies adopted by the Islamists in Iran which led to the suppression of the Marxist feminist perspective, which had existed alongside the Islamist discourse. The latter part of the paper deals with how women in Iran have tried to evolve a distinct Islamic discourse for themselves which is within the Islamic context but still leaves political space to express their views.

Most women in Western and democratic countries created sustainable movements that have achieved remarkable outcomes. While it may be that many women under Muslim (and non-Muslim) authoritarian states do wish and indeed strive for building similar social movements, their struggles are often thwarted by the repressive measures of authoritarian/patriarchal states as well as the unsympathetic attitudes of many ordinary men.[1] Iran is one such example. Shari'a forms the basis on which laws regarding women are derived in Islamic societies. Iranian political discourses, whether secular or Islamic, regarded women as central to the future of the nation because of their role as biological reproducers, educators of children, transmitters of culture, and participants in national life.

The constitutional movement resulted in the Constitutional Revolution of 1906-11 and the establishment of a constitutional monarchy; it created a vision of Iran as a modern society capable of challenging Western intrusion and manipulation. In addition the movement provided a unique opportunity for women to gain political experience, particularly through the emergent women's movement which was supported by the constitutionalists (Bamdad, 1977). Despite varying degrees of clerical opposition to women's emancipation, and an absence of any real consensus concerning the precise nature and extent of these reforms, the constitutional movement did articulate a conceptual link between national independence and progress on the one hand, and women's emancipation on the other. Emancipation of women from the bondage of religion and culture was an important element in the constitutional revolution. Iranian society had, since the Constitutional Revolution of 1906-11, undergone considerable transformation. Women constituted a vital political force, and were organized into numerous leftist, socialist, nationalist and Islamic organizations.

During the Shah's regime, measures to modernize women were taken up by the State. Women, both individually and in groups, worked diligently to bring about these changes in laws concerning marriage, divorce, and voting rights. While some of these changes, such as the franchise for women (granted in 1963), could be accomplished relatively easily by constitutional amendment, changes in marriage and divorce laws were more difficult to bring about without contradicting the shari'a.

To overcome the resistance, women lawyers began to search, in close cooperation with sympathetic men religious leaders among them—for new interpretations of the shari'a that would be more in keeping with their demands. Each major law affecting women required several years of systematic and persistent negotiation and consultation with religious and lay jurists. The most important of these were the franchise in 1963 and the Family Protection Law in 1967.[2] With the effective support of the state and pro-western orientation of the shah's regime, women succeeded in spite of opposition from the clergy.

The dismantling of shah's regime entailed the support of social forces in Iran. Social forces—nationalists, Islamists and communists—could not envision the assumption of power without an agenda for the mobilization and organization of women. Ayatollah Khomeini, the leader of the revolution considered women's participation in the anti-Shah Revolution crucial. Women fought against the Shah and Western colonialism despite the fact that the shah had advanced Western-influenced dress and life-style for women. Hence it became imperative to defend women's rights in the face of opposition to the Shah's regime. The Islamic leadership took a nationalist position whereby shii'i modernism and Islamic culture were taken as examples to specify women's position in Iran. By problematizing cultural imperialism, a new 'revolutionary' and 'authentic' Muslim culture was constructed which appealed to wide sectors of the urban population.[3] In this context, far from returning to traditional Islam, the Iranian Revolution of 1979 represented both historical continuity in revisiting the political demands of twentieth-century Iran, and specificity in creating a new alliance between Islam and nationalism which became the cornerstone of the Islamic Republic's gender policies. It gave a prominent place to women, defining them as both mothers and citizens, and regarded the establishment of an Islamic nation as dependent on the Islamization of women's position.

The Constitution constructed the ideal Islamic woman in opposition to Western values of womanhood. It advocated a set of patriarchal relations which strengthened male control over women in the family while granting women the right to be active participants in society. It claimed that the new Islamic society would value women as upholders of family and nation and grant the right to fulfil their natural instincts as well as participate in social life. The same clerics who had in the 1960s objected to women's enfranchisement on religious grounds were, in the aftermath of the Revolution, prepared to grant women the right to vote in the name of Islam.

This discrimination in the name of Islam is significant in Iranian case because the building of the Islamic state depended on the negation of the idea of gender equality. The connection between the control of women and state building was frequently stressed by Khomeini and other leaders—women and law constituted both the targets and instruments of building the absolutist Islamic state. The architects of the Islamic state prioritized the Islamization of gender relations because 'women were the markers of the boundaries of the Islamic community and the markers of Islamic identity'.[4]

ISLAMIZATION OF WOMEN'S POSITION AND THE ENSUING DEBATE

When women's support was crucial for a political change prior to the Revolution, women were considered the pioneers to bring about this change. After the consolidation of the Islamic regime by the mullahs, existing gender relations were declared un-Islamic and western. To bring about another social change demanded a change in the status of women thereby restricting women's entry into technical, engineering and experimental sciences. While Khomeini repeatedly declared that women constituted the epicenter of the struggle against the shah's regime, a nation-wide regime of sexual apartheid was imposed largely through coercion. The dynamic nature of shari'a shaped feminist consciousness in Iran during this period. The imposition of hejab on women employees, segregation of male and female workers, silencing or sacking of non-Islamic employees, replacing secular employees in key posts with Islamic sympathizers, and installing Islamic societies in all state organizations as instruments of control and Islamization came to be called as the administrative revolution. One of the principal objectives of the leaders of the Iranian regime was to restore women to what they considered women's primary role in society: domestic responsibility, a role which was in keeping with the teachings of Islam.[5]

International political developments like the Iran—Iraq war (1980-88) demanded women to play a different role. Hence, Islamic authorities projected women as mothers and wives, who were to produce 'manpower for the war, for the glory of Islam and the nation'.[6] Any discourse about women's status during the war was suppressed. A nationalistic perspective on women's status demanded that women should produce manpower for the war and thereby serve the nation better. Hence any discourse which went against the larger agenda of the Islamist framework was suppressed by the clergy. Women became tools to accomplish social change and consolidate the changes that followed.

First, the discourse of Islamization was constructed as events developed in the post-revolutionary society. Historical conceptions of gender were drawn upon in the process of encoding the immediate social and political situation. Second, the discourse of Islamization did not develop in a unified manner. Although its framework was set in opposition to the Pahlavi system and related 'alien Western concepts of gender', the Islamization policy was formulated in a heterogeneous and adhoc manner by a variety of sources with different and sometimes conflicting interests. Political debate and power struggles between various Islamic factions led to the dominance of some Islamization concepts as opposed to others. Third, the discourse of Islamization faced a serious crisis not only in relation to policy formulation but also in relation to implementation.[7] Women were largely confined to their homes. Any debate on women's position was followed by oppression like the one on Marxist/leftist discourse on women.

MARXIST/LEFTIST POLITICAL DISCOURSE ON WOMEN

Prior to the Revolution in 1979, various schools of thought had joined together in opposition to the shah's regime. The dominant discourse which drew considerable support among the people was the Marxist/leftist perspective. Though there was no clear agenda concerning women, they participated in large numbers and did adhere to this school of thought. At the time of the 1978-79 revolution, most activist women belonged to revolutionary leftist organizations which had neither a clear objective for the revolution or a continuous presence in Iranian politics. Consequently, women's participation was disorganized and fragmented. The ideological orientation of the opposition was neither conducive to the establishment of autonomous feminist organizations nor to the development of a coherent feminist ideology."[8]

The changes introduced by the Islamic regime were regarded with cynicism by the Marxist supporters. The most vocal critics of the establishment were the Marxists and their sympathizers. They criticized these changes as mere efforts made by the regime to keep women from turning to the more radical solutions offered by Marx and Engels. They saw the efforts as means by which capitalists sought to exploit the masses of Iranian women by providing Western capitalism with cheap labour and markets for consumer goods. In their view, the lot of women could be improved only by a total overhaul of society, by the creation of a classless utopia in a communist state. Women revolutionaries were asked to join the larger struggle to overthrow the system. There was no separate women's movement associated with this school of thought. Rosa Luxembourg became a role model for these women.[9]

The Left addressed women's issues primarily through its defence of the rights of working-class and peasant women and women of national minorities. Though women had minimal participation in other women's organizations, their participation in working-class neighborhoods was quite remarkable. They worked in factories and explained capitalist political economy as well as the current social and political problems to working class women. Many of them joined the campaign against illiteracy.[10]

Iranian activists from the Left emphasized class and anti-imperialist characteristics of the revolution, and the struggle against sexual inequality took a backseat. Furthermore, they considered that "women's emancipation" would result from the socialist revolution in two ways. First, women's participation in the revolutionary movement would eradicate or at least weaken-stereotypes of women. Second, as a component of its social justice agenda, socialism would bring about sexual equality.[11]

Secular Marxist organizations attracted more women than religious ones, because Marxist organizations drew their membership heavily from colleges, urban intellectual circles, and professional centres. Marxist secular ideas were more attractive to these women than Islamic ideology.[12] An important reason for the higher political activism of urban women was that the Iranian Left was mostly "urbanized, educated, and youthful".[13]

The period of 1985 to the present comprises the exile years of the Islamic regime's opponents. Distance and exposure to a new environment shed a different light on women activists' past experiences. In exile, women activists analyzed the Left's defeat with reference both to the international feminist movement and to the mobilization of women by the Islamic Republic of Iran. Disenchantment with political organizations, especially because of their reluctance to address women's rights, has convinced many to end their affiliations with these groups and to concentrate on establishing women's organizations.

The immediate denial of women's rights by the Islamic regime caused public awareness about women's issues. However, the absence of an organized feminist movement, combined with the Left's limited vision of sexual oppression precluded a radical critique of Islam's patriarchal ideology and practice. Although numerous women's organizations quickly formed, most of them acted as auxiliaries for male-dominated political groups and focused their criticism on the abhorrent treatment of working and peasant women by Iranian capitalism.[14]

With the defeat of the Left in the 1980s came the ideological and organizational defeat and attempt to survive the persecution of the Islamic regime, for others, later, as they responded to the breakup of political organizations and their destruction in exile. Consequently, the Iranian Left did not consider the women's movement a worthy ally. Even among working-class women, the attention of the Left was focused on industrial workers, which left the revolutionaries relatively blind to the location of most working women who were peasants, handicraft workers, or service employees.[15]

ISLAMIC FEMINISM: THE DISCOURSE OF THE 1990s

Islamic modernism began in the 1960s for religious reform and revitalization of Shi'ism by a small number of educated laymen and became increasingly popular among the educated urban middle and lower class groups, especially in Tehran. Dr. Ali Shari'ati (d. 1977), a Sorbonne—educated intellectual and professor in his numerous lectures and writings, called for a return to the teachings and principles of Islam of the Prophet Mohammad's time.[16] He argued that much of the moral decadence and political corruption prevalent in the country was caused by the people turning away from real Islam embodied in Shi'ism. He ultimately placed the blame for the decline of Shi'ism on the ulema, who had allowed centuries of environmental and cultural influences to water down and render ineffective the central message of Islam, best exemplified in the life and teachings of the Shi'ite imams, such as the imams Ali and Hosayn. He repeatedly enjoined his readers to assume personal responsibility and strive for the revival of real Shi'ite Islam.[17]

Two important ideologues of the Islamic Republic, the late Ayatollah Morteza Motahhari and Ali Shariati, were part of the school of Islamic modernism. Their thinking on women was contradictory and problematical, but they claimed to espouse women's rights;" both men found it necessary to show that Islam did not stand in the way of women's education, work, and participation in social life or stunt the personal development of women" (Esfandiari 1993, p. 16).

After the Islamic revolution and the suppression of the discourses on women, agitation by activist Islamic women, restrictive barriers to women's educational achievement and their employment were removed. In 1992, the High Council of the Cultural Revolution adopted a set of employment policies for women. This new directive, while reiterating the importance of family roles and continuing to rule out certain occupations and professions as inappropriate, encouraged the integration of women in the labour force and directed attention to their interests and needs. The government also changed its policy on women and the legal profession, and during the 1990s the field of law became more open to women.[18]

Muslim women are contributing to the production of Islamic feminism. Iranian scholars like Afsaneh Najmabadi and Ziba Mir-Hosseini have presented the Islamic feminist rereadings of the Quran underway in the Islamic Republic of Iran since the early 1990s in which the non-gender egalitarian and misogynist constructions of Islam are being dismantled through interpretative methodologies that include classical Islamic and modern (secular) social science approaches.[19] Although writings on women and gender in the Islamic Republic were almost uniformly critical during the 1980s, a change of tone and style could be discerned after 1990.[20]

The discourse on Islamic feminism is attributed to the activism of a relatively small number of Iranian women who sought the amelioration of Islamized gender relations which was effected after the Islamic Revolution, mainly through arguing for legal reform within the framework of the shari'a. By emphasizing the historical context of the holy texts, challenging the clergy's monolithic interpretational power, and reformulating Islamic concepts and law from a "feminist" perspective, Islamic feminists in Iran are rethinking gender in Islam. Not only are Islamic feminists opening the doors of interpretation of sacred texts and debates on women's issues to groups other than Muslims but they have also broken with the reactive gender conservatism and West phobia prevailing among fundamentalists, connected themselves with Western feminism, and woven new connections between Muslim women and Western feminism.[21]

The major novelty of these gender sensitive theological debates was that, beyond a few enlightened clerics, women themselves were waging them, and they were doing so on the pages of the popular daily press.[22] Hammed Shahidian divides the women's participation in underground politics in Iran into four phases; the first period in the struggle for women's activism was during the Iranian revolution when women's participation was active. The second period (1979-81) includes women's involvement in the revolution and their semi-overt activism. The third period (1981-85) coincides with the steady retreat of the opposition to the Islamic regime and the rapid decline of overt political activism due to imprisonments, mass executions, and exile. During the fourth period (1985 to present), political activism in Iran has been scattered and marginal.[23]

The major challenge to post-Islamist feminism was to demonstrate that the claims for women's rights were not necessarily alien to Iranian culture or Islam.[24] As women's issues become an integral part of the modern Islamic discourses, Muslim and secular feminists, as well as those in political power, look for Islamic solutions for a very modern problem that is the result of the changed status of women. Women are increasingly calling for equality and participating in the politics of the Muslim world. Women are also working on religious and cultural levels to change women's situation in Islamic societies.

CONCLUSION

The Islamization of gender relations met strong resistance from the very beginning. By the mid-1990s, the Islamic regime was experiencing a serious crisis; it had failed to control women, workers, dissident nationalities, students, the print media, artists and secular intellectuals. The various discourses that were dominant after the Revolution can be classified as Islamist and Marxist discourses. The Marxist discourse was suppressed and later the followers were exiled. The predominant discourse since the 1990s has been the Islamic feminist discourse.

Though the etymology of Islamic feminism has been questioned by feminists worldwide, it is a commendable achievement as far as women's advancement in Iran is concerned as gender equality within an Islamic discursive framework has achieved remarkable strides. Can Islamic feminist really be called a feminist since it takes into account the *sharia* and tries to abide by that?

Women through their tacit struggle have accomplished changes with regard to laws and customs in Iran. Educated women from all walks of life and of all political persuasions have become more conscious of their identity as women and of their own special needs and interests. Yet since about 2001, there has been a recrudescence of conservatism, enforced in the streets especially by religious men and their organizations; this increased after the election of Mahmoud Ahmadinejad to the presidency in June 2005.

NOTES

1. Asef Bayat, 'What It Means to Be a Woman Activist in an Islamic State, Comparative Studies of South Asia, Africa and the Middle East Vol. 27, No. 1, 2007, p. 160.
2. Guity Nashat, "Women in the Islamic Republic of Iran", *Iranian Studies*, Vol. 13, No. 1/4, *Iranian Revolution in Perspective* (1980), p. 170.
3. *Ibid.*, p. 3.
4. Parvin Paidar, (1995) *Political Process in Twentieth-Century Iran*, (Cambridge University Press, Great Britain). p. 232.
5. Haleh Afshar, "Khomeini's Teachings and Their Implications for Iranian Women," in Azar Tabari and Nahid Yeganeh, eds., *The Shadow of Islam* (London, 1982), p. 75
6. *Ibid.*, p. 87
7. Nahid Yeganeh, "Women, Nationalism and Islam in Contemporary Political Discourse in Iran", *Feminist Review*, No. 44, Nationalisms and National Identities (Summer, 1993), p. 9.
8. Haideh Moghissi, "Women, Modernization, and Revolution in Iran," *Review of Radical Political Economics* 23:218 (fall 1991), p. 16.
9. *Ibid.*
10. Hammed Shahidian, " Women and Clandestine Politics in Iran, 1970-1985", *Feminist Studies*, Vol. 23, No. 1 (Spring, 1997), p. 36.
11. Ervand Abrahmian, *Tortured Confessions : Prisons and Public Recantations in Modern Iran*, (University of California Press,) p. 16.

12. Ali Mirsepassi-Ashtiani and Valentine M. Moghadam, "The Left and Political Islam in Iran: A Retrospect and Prospect," *Radical History Review*, no. 51 (fall 1991): 27-62.
13. *Ibid.*
14. *Ibid.*
15. Hammed Shahidian "The Iranian Left and the 'Woman Question' in the Revolution of 1978-79," *International Journal of Middle East Studies* Vol. 26 (May 1994), p. 10.
17. *Ibid.*
18. Valentine M. Moghadam, Islamic Feminism and Its Discontents: Toward a Resolution of the Debate, *Signs*, Vol. 27, No. 4 (Summer, 2002), p. 1140
19. Margot Badran, Understanding Islam, Islamism, and Islamic Feminism, *Journal of Women's History*, Vol. 13, no.1 (spring), 2001, p. 50
20. Representative of critical studies were Afshar 1985; Moghadam 1991; Tohidi 1991; Najmabadi 1994. For the tone and style of the 1990s, which emphasized resistance and empowerment, see Moghadam 1993b; Ramazani 1993; Afshar 1996; Tohidi 1997a, 1997b; Najmabadi 1998; Poya 1999.
21. Valentine M. Moghadam (2002), Islamic Feminism and Its Discontents: Toward a Resolution of the Debate, *Signs*, Vol. 27, No. 4 (Summer, 2002), p. 1136.
22. "*Fiqh* and Women's Human Rights," Farzaneh, no. 8, 22 December 1997, www.farzanehjournal.com
23. Hammed Shahidian, "Women and Clandestine Politics in Iran, 1970-1985, *Feminist Studies*, Vol. 23, No. 1 (Spring, 1997), p. 11.
24. Nayereh Tohidi, "The International Connections of the Women's Movement in Iran: 1979–2000," in *Iran and the Surrounding World*, Nikki Keddie and Rudi Matthee eds., (Seattle: University of Washington Press, 2002), 205–31.

REFERENCES

1. Ali Mirsepassi-Ashtiani and Valentine M. Moghadam (1991). "The Left and Political Islam in Iran: A Retrospect and Prospect," *Radical History Review*, Vol. No. 51: 27-62.
2. Azar Tabari and Nahid Yeganeh (1982). eds., *The Shadow of Islam* London., London: Zed Press; Wesport, Conn., U.S.A.: Distributor, Lawrence Hill, 1982.
3. Asef Bayat (2007). 'What It Means to Be a Woman Activist in an Islamic State, *Comparative Studies of South Asia, Africa and the Middle East,* Vol. 27, (1) p. 160-172.
4. Guity Nashat (1980). "Women in the Islamic Republic of Iran", *Iranian Studies*, Vol. 13, No. 1/4, Iranian Revolution in Perspective, pp. 165-194.
5. Haleh Afshar, "Khomeini's Teachings and Their Implications for Iranian Women," *Feminist Review*, No. 12 (1982) . pp. 59-72.
6. Hammed Shahidian (1997) . "Women and Clandestine Politics in Iran, 1970-1985, *Feminist Studies*, Vol. 23, No. 1 (Spring, 1997). pp. 7-42.
7. "The Iranian Left and the 'Woman Question' in the Revolution of 1978-79," *International Journal of Middle East Studies* 26 (May 1994): 223-47.
8. *Iran and the Surrounding World* (1987). Nikki Keddie and Rudi Matthee, eds., (Seattle: University of Washington, 2002).

9. Nayereh Tohidi, "The International Connections of the Women's Movement in Iran: 1979-2000," in *Iran and the Surrounding World*, Nikki Keddie and Rudi Matthee, eds., (Seattle: University of Washington Press, 2002).
10. Valentine M. Moghadam (2002). Islamic Feminism and Its Discontents: Toward a Resolution of the Debate, *Signs*, Vol. 27, No. 4, pp. 1135-1171.
11. "The Left and Political Islam in Iran: A Retrospect and Prospect," *Radical History Review*, no. 51 (fall 1991): 27-62.
12. Ali Mirsepassi-Ashtiani and Valentine M. Moghadam, "The Left and Political Islam in Iran: A Retrospect and Prospect," *Radical History Review*, No. 51 (fall 1991): 27-62.
13. Haideh Moghissi, "Women, Modernization, and Revolution in Iran," *Review of Radical Political Economics*, 23 (fall 1991): 218.
14. Margot Badran, Understanding Islam, Islamism, and Islamic Feminism, *Journal of Women's History*, Vol. 13 no. 1 (spring), pp. 47-52.
15. Nahid Yeganeh, Women, Nationalism and Islam in Contemporary Political Discourse in Iran, *Feminist Review*, No. 44, Nationalisms and National Identities (summer, 1993), pp. 3-18.

12

Flicker of Democracy in Iran? Assessing Freedom of Press under Khatami

Sujata Ashwarya Cheema

INTRODUCTION

The election of Syed Muhammad Khatami as the President of Iran in May 1997 ushered in a period of freedom for the press unknown in Iran since the Islamic Revolution. Khatami was elected on the platform of political and economic reforms. The foremost component of President Khatami's proposal for political reforms was to ease restrictions on civil liberties, particularly the right to freedom of expression. This right is one of the fundamental tenets of democracy and press is one of major channels through which citizens express their opinions on wide-ranging issues that concern their existence as citizens of the state. Thus, freedom of press became the test case for assessing the scale and success of political reforms pledged by Khatami during his election campaign. It also became the arena where the conflict between the conservative hard-liners and reformers was played out. In the first year of the reform movement, a large number of weekly and monthly publications received licenses. A variety of social, political and cultural issues was openly and vigorously discussed. In addition to discussions on secularism, role of religion in political life and democracy, there were lively discussions on the relationship with the United States, Britain, Russia, and even Israel. Those subjects previously considered taboo such as the power, position, and role of the Supreme Leader and corruption in important state institutions were brought into discussions in the public arena. However, Khatami's policy of granting greater freedom to the press was opposed by the conservative Islamists in the political establishment.

As President, Khatami found himself hamstrung by a system where the president holds the top elected post but not the highest executive power. He was outranked in authority by the supreme religious leader, Ayatollah Ali Khamenei, who along with his conservative allies controls most of the state institutions, including the parliament (majlis), the judiciary, the Army, the state media (radio and television), and the security forces. The conservatives sought, for the most part successfully, to impede the growing campaign for democratic change. The judiciary repeatedly stepped in to ban publications and order arrest of journalists. Hardline vigilante groups attacked and murdered writers and journalists under the benign eyes of the conservatives. It is, however, important to note that a number of editors and writers belonged to the clerical establishment (albeit they were middle-ranking clerics), revealing a clear disagreement among them over support for Khatami's reforms.

David Menashri observes that during the first three years of Khatami's presidency, 'there were in fact some signs of unprecedented criticism and free expression. At the same time, however, political repression also reached new heights.'[1]

FREEDOM OF PRESS: A HISTORICAL SURVEY

Freedom of press has always had a tortured history in Iran. There exists a remarkable similarity between the conservative clerics of the post-revolution period and the Pahlavi regime in their attitude towards the press. Both have exhibited hostility and derision towards the media. The press under the Shah was so tightly regulated that sycophancy was the order of the day. The domestic press was obligated to publish his photos and pronouncements daily and criticism of the much-flawed regime was almost non-existent. The gap was filled in by the foreign media, which frequently became the subject of his ire. The Shah once was particularly peeved when his regime was described as a 'dictatorship' and let out a volley of diatribe against the writer.[2]

In the post-revolution period, with the country closed to foreign media, the domestic press has come in for rigid censorship. With the pro-establishment media regularly churning out doctored information for the consumption of the general public, the liberal press in Iran has been accused of representing the views of foreign enemies bent upon destroying the Islamic Republic. Press freedom has always been at the centre of the tussle between the conservatives and reformists in the political establishment. It has been the focus of vibrant debates in the public sphere, especially in the universities across Iran. The right to express one's opinion freely has always been considered by the reformists as indispensable for the establishment of a modern state with legally regulated and transparent structures. The conservatives have construed this as an attempt to import foreign values that would lead to the subversion of the Islamic system.

The contestation between the conservatives and reformers over the issue of granting greater freedom to the press sharpened with the ascension of

Hashemi Rafsanjani to power in 1989. As a realist he found it expedient to allow for limited protection to the progressives and space for moderate debates. This helped him to beat down hardline opponents to his policies of economic liberalization and greater openness toward the West, particularly the United States. It also helped him to draft in competent cadre of administrative elites of the Shah's regime into his government. However, the openness sponsored by Rafsanjani led to a churning among the intellectuals and students in university campuses where the role of religion in politics, development of civil society, nature of synthesis between Islam and republicanism, and Islamic democracy were regularly debated.

Greater tolerance towards an independent press (from state control) was a natural corollary to this openness. Further, the death of Ayatollah Khomeini removed an extraordinary commander who gathered 'unquestioned authority' for the state after the revolution. The people of Iran were no longer willing to follow their leader uncritically. The situation was further built up by the fact that the veterans who emerged from the war were dissatisfied with the prevailing conditions and wanted a better deal from the government. Modern technology via satellite television and internet penetrated the life of the Iranian people in various ways, providing them with a peek into the world outside their country. In this general atmosphere of greater openness, Muhammad Khatami as the Minister of Culture and Islamic Guidance (1983-93) lifted many restrictions on the press, writers, artists, and films.

Khatami has been an unorthodox cleric, more exposed to the philosophical rather than juridical tradition of Islam. At Isfahan University, he was exposed to Western philosophy, which fuelled his understanding of the world as an integrative whole, famously expressed in his 'dialogue of civilization' thesis. His experience of living in the West while managing the Islamic Centre in Hamburg made him appreciate the achievements of Western culture and philosophical traditions. The Hegelian idea of history as a march of freedom through the world deeply influenced Khatami and constituted the force behind his advocacy of freedom for the press. He considered freedom to speak, assemble and criticize as inalienable rights of the people—a liberality that appalled and alarmed the conservatives. After a decade in the ministry he was forced to resign from his post, which brought back some of the old restrictions on the press.[3] Despite this setback the atmosphere had become sufficiently charged to spawn a trend towards freer and more forceful expression.

When Khatami ushered a liberal press regime upon his election as the president, the hardlines accused the local press of acting on behalf of the foreign enemies bent upon destroying the Islamic Republic. Ayatollah Khamenei went as far ahead to describe the non-establishment publications as bases of the enemy. This damning characterization of the press provided the conservative judiciary, whose head is appointed by the Supreme Leader, with a pretext to ban liberal newspapers and magazines. It also gave tacit permission to the judiciary to jail editors and journalists on ambiguous charges such as they were undermining the security of the state and insulting Islamic values. In these moves, the covert agenda of the conservatives was to frustrate Khatami's reform movement. However, it appears that they were genuinely apprehensive of the potential fallouts of a free press environment. They feared that open discussion of religious values by an independent press would undermine their sanctity and lead to the disintegration of the Islamic system. This fear was reinforced by the fear shared by both the conservatives and ordinary Iranians that a free regime for the press had the potential to fragment society, politically and culturally. Such a development would encourage foreign powers to interfere in the affairs of the state as they had done when the government of Muhammad Mossadeq was brought down in a military coup in 1953 amidst discord among the ruling elites. This argument borders on absurdity, even paranoia, but as a national myth it persists in Iranian minds.[4] This fear was exploited by the conservatives to clamp down on the reformist dailies and weeklies by labelling them as instruments of foreign intervention.

KHATAMI IN POWER: FREEDOM OF PRESS AND IMPEDIMENTS

When Khatami won the presidential polls on May 23, 1997 defeating the establishment-backed conservative candidate, Ali Akbar Nateq-Nuri, with 70 per cent of popular votes, it represented increased politicization of the masses over the question of reforms. During the election campaign Khatami promised comprehensive political and economic reforms. These included individual freedoms, civil society, political tolerance, social justice, increased economic opportunities for youth, greater rights for women, and rule of law. A free press was necessary if these conditions were to be met. The press channelizes public opinion, keeps a watch on governmental actions, and reports corruption in public institutions and abuse of power by public authorities. In Iran, as several publications served as mouthpieces for the hardline establishment, press reforms held the promise of greater governmental accountability and transparency.

Expectations of increased press freedom were, therefore, natural with the election of Khatami. After all he had been forced to resign from the post of Minister of Culture and Islamic Guidance during Rafsanjani's term over accusations that he was too lenient with the media. Signalling relaxation on freedom of expression, Khatami appointed Ataollah Mohajerani to the post he had to relinquish not long ago. Mohajerani's liberal credentials were certified by the fact that the conservative parliamentarians were extremely critical of his incumbency. Not surprising that the ministry issued licenses to more than 200 newspapers and magazines in the first year of Khatami's rule. These reformist publications were printed and distributed outside major cities and therefore had a wide reach.

A reinvigorated press reported corruption in the state institutions such as the conservative-packed Ministry of Intelligence and Secuirty (MoIS), whose officials were involved in the murder of dissident intellectuals and writers. Indeed, an era of freedom appeared to have dawned with newspapers publishing articles critical of the conservative clerical community. However, almost simultaneously, three counter trends were apparent. First, the conservative judiciary intervened to close liberal publications through the enforcement of vaguely worded rules and regulations. Editors and publishers were told there were 'red lines' that they must not cross, but those red lines were ill-defined, rendering the decisions of the judiciary arbitrary.[5] Secondly, the journalists were often beaten up by members of hardline vigilante groups and jailed. And thirdly, the banned newspapers regularly appeared under a different name by using up unused licenses to continue with their reformist programme.

Examples of a freer press regime were visible throughout the years 1998 and 1999. One of the notable publications was *Jameah*, which reported the Islamic Revolution Guards Corps commander's closed door speech in which he threatened to "cut the necks and tongues" of political opponents.[6] The daily also ran interviews with Abbas Amir Entezam, who had served 15 years in prison on charges of spying for the US. In his interviews he spoke of the extreme torture he suffered in prison. He also talked about the need to separate religion from politics in one of his other interviews. *Jameah* had its license suspended in June 1998 and the next month it resumed publication with the same staff under the name *Tus*. The judiciary ordered the closure of *Tus* in August for "publishing lies and disrupting public order"[7] and the members of hardline vigilante groups, of which Ansar-e Hizbullah is one of the better known, beat up the editor, Mashallah Shamsolvaezin. When the daily's license was revoked in September for initiating a debate on Tehran's policy towards the Taliban, it came out as *Neshat*.

In another event, the director of Iran's official news agency, IRNA, was charged with embezzlement, "mockery of public organizations", and "spreading lies, slander, and groundless accusations against others".[8] The accused, Fereydoun Verdinejad, was held in prison for six hours on May 29, 1999 on the orders of a special government employee's court and later released on bail. The complaint had been lodged with the court by the conservative-dominated Islamic Republic of Broadcasting (Iran's only broadcasting organization), the Judicial Organization of the Armed Forces, the Law Enforcement Forces and 20 right-wing members of parliament. The main purpose behind Verdinejad's arrest was to step up pressure on Mohajerani to him. The minister refused to bow to this demand but was forced to sack his deputy and moderate his reformist press policies. He also narrowly escaped an impeachment proceeding by the conservative-dominated parliament for "corrupting Islamic values".[9] Coming on the heels of this development was the closure of the flagship reformist paper *Salaam* in July 1999, which set in motion a 'rebellion' against the Islamic Republic.

Salaam was started nine years ago as a forum for liberal clergy and had become a leading reformist journal. The July 6 issue of *Salaam* published a top-secret letter from Said Emami, a former high-ranking official in the MoIS (and charged with gruesome murder of four intellectuals in Tehran in 1998), to his superior, outlining a policy of press repression with the aim of destablizing the Khatami government.[10] In the letter, Emami recommended that for survival, the hardliners should impose several restrictions on the freedom of writers, the press and artists, and place "plants" among reformist organizations to "create discord".[11] The letter was, perhaps deliberately, published one day before the Majlis approved the first reading of amendments to the press law, which required the journalists and publishers to reveal their sources and responsibility for published material went beyond the publisher to include photographers, journalists and editors. Further, it placed the press under the jurisdiction of the Revolutionary Courts, whereas article 168 of the Constitution only permits Press Courts to do so. The new amendments also stipulated that a complaint against a publication could be filed in an unlimited period. Granting of press accreditation was made more restrictive and it contained a proposal to ban 'anti-revolutionary' groups from the media, prohibit financial support to the media, and make incitement against 'national security' or 'foreign policy guidelines' a crime. "The press is a gateway for cultural invasion, so let us take measures," conservative parliamentary speaker Ali Akbar Nateq-Nuri said during debate on the bill, which was passed by 125 votes to 90 with 55 deputies absent.[12]

On the basis of a complaint from the Ministry of Intelligence and Security (MoIS), the Special Court of Clerics immediately banned *Salaam*, presumably giving itself jurisdiction to do so because the newspaper editor was cleric. Hojatoeslam Muhammad Aqsar Musavi-Khoeniha, who had impeccable revolutionary credentials, was tried by the clergy court on July 25, 1999. He was charged with publishing a confidential document without authorization, and fabricating lies and manufacturing public opinion. In the end, Khoeniha was banned from publishing activity for three years and *Salaam* was banned for five years.[13] In response to the closure of *Salaam* and the action of the Majlis, the students also frustrated over an earlier arrest of their fellows protesting the detention of officials from a weekly magazine, *Hoviat-i-Khish*, and galvanized by reformist rhetoric, held a protest demonstration outside the University of Tehran on July 8.[14] Vigilantes from Ansar-e-Hezbollah with support from some elements of the Law Enforcement Force attacked the demonstration in which at least one student died. They were also responsible for the attack on the student dormitories at Tehran University. These clashes led to a wave of protest throughout the country, carefully organized and coordinated through the use of internet and mobile phones.

The student demonstrations and the government crackdown that followed served as a wake up call for both the conservatives and reformists. Long used to having obedience from the people, the conservatives were at a loss of how to make sense of students' anger. The students' initial demands were for the repeal of the ban on *Salaam* and withdrawal of amendments to the press law. The mass protests soon became a comprehensive attack on the system of theocratic governance. The students demanded greater freedom of expression, association and relaxation of other social and political restrictions. The protestors' slogan, for the first time, included "Khamenei must go!"[15] The refrain was that Khamenei should stop interfering with the daily affairs of the state and facilitate the President in carrying forward the reform process. Both violence and breaking of taboo against attacks on Khamenei by name signalled that a new level in the struggle had been reached.

The Supreme Leader Ayatollah Khamenei was so perturbed by the student chants accusing him of creating problems for the government that he refused to make a formal announcement for days. Eventually when he emerged to speak, Khamenei, while deploring the attack on students, nonetheless condemned them for participating in a "foreign-instigated" plan to undermine the revolution. The pro-reform government press did not buy this line: 'This air of complacency is aimed at convincing public opinion that shadowy counter-revolutionary figures were behind the entire student protest,' editorialized the *Iran Daily*. 'This stratagem will not fly.'[16] Neither did the students, who responded to Khamenei's initiative to speak to them with shouts of derision: "Either Islam and the law or another revolution."[17]

The students' presented a serious dilemma for Khatami: on one hand while his core constituency, the youth, were urging him to take the reform forward, Khamenei and the Revolutionary Guards warned the President to stop the students or face a 'response'. Khatami owed much of his 1997 victory to student associations. They were the first to embrace his reformist agenda and had ardently campaigned for him. Ironically they were the first to become disenchanted with his slow and overly-cautious approach. The rebellion seemed to fuel a dire conservative response, possibly a potential coup against Khatami. *Keyhan*, the mouthpiece of the conservative Information Ministry, published a letter from 24 leaders of the hardline Revolutionary Guards (not including their top commander) to President Khatami on 19th July. It warned: "You [Khatami] either take now a revolutionary decision by stopping the unrest or tomorrow will be too late … ."[18]

While little was heard of the threat later, Khatami response to the turn of events was full of ambiguities. In an interview to the state television on the night of the protest, he condemned the event as an "insult to the university and to learning" sending shock waves among the reformers. Two days later he persisted that the "aim [of the events] was to inflict damage to the foundation of the system....The rioters aimed to inflict damage on public property and cause discomfort for the dear citizens," adding that there were "inflammatory slogans against the values of the system and our nation's belief."[19] His speech provoked renewed rioting by students. Whether Khatami was forced to adopt this line to save his presidency or genuinely believed that the Islamic regime was in danger is not clear. Ultimately, he adopted a purely legalistic approach towards the turn of events in urging the students to return to calm in order to avoid an unrestrained conservative backlash and instead prepare for the parliamentary elections in the following year. Extensive arrests followed as the conservatives tried to retrieve their monopoly over the use of violence, although the student leadership remained buoyant for having shaken the conservative establishment and in anticipation of the control of parliament in the forthcoming elections which would provide an opening to affect new reforms. However, the student protest of July 1999 marked the first sign of discontent between the reformist President and the younger generation who had voted for him.

Emboldened by the suppression of the student riots the hardliners proceeded to ban other reformist newspapers and incarcerate progressive journalists. In September 1999, the successor of *Tus*, *Neshat*, faced closure on charges that had origin in the publication of an open letter by Yadollah Sahabi, the 85 year old activist who had served long prison sentences because of his anti-Shah stance, to Khamenei urging him to distance himself from hardliners. In the letter, Sahabi also called for reducing the powers of the unelected Supreme Leader and transferring them to the elected President. The publication of the letter, in the eyes of the conservatives, was audacious enough. In another daring step a few days later, *Neshat's* lead editorial argued in favour of abolition of capital punishment and strict eye for eye vengeance law, or *qasas*. The managing director of the newspaper, Latif Safari, was hauled up by the Ministry of Justice to the Special Court of Clerics. The court ordered the closure of the newspaper and sentenced him to two-and-a-half years in jail on charges of the insulting the office of the *vilayet-e-faqih* (government by religious scholars), waging a propaganda war against the system and insulting Islamic sanctities.[20]

At heart of the closure of another popular reformist newspaper *Khordad* and the trial of its editor, former Interior Minister Hojatoeslam Abdullah Nouri in November 1999 before the Special Court of the Clergy was that the position and role of the Supreme Leader had been brought under question. Nouri faced charges of 'publishing reports that insulted officials and institutions of the system, reporting lies and waging a propaganda war against the system, insulting Father of the Revolution Ayatollah Ruhollah Khomeini and his views, publishing reports contrary to religious principles, and insulting religious sanctities. Other charges included backing ties with America, promoting dissident cleric Ayatollah Hussein-Ali Montazeri's views, and urging recognition of Israel.'[21] There was hardly any legal content in these charges, which were evidently political given that after his election to the Tehran Municipal Council in February 1999, he had announced his intention to run for the legislature and was seen a potential speaker of the Parliament.

Nouri's defence in the case became a cause célèbre, when he told the special court which tried him for insulting the Supreme Leader that the law of the land was equally applicable all and this did not exclude the leader. Citing article 107 of the Constitution, he argued that the Leader is equal with the rest of the people of the country. This implied that like any other person, "he has rights and duties and must obey the law, and had no power above those created for him by the constitution."[22] The trial also provided an occasion to question the aggrandizement of such wide judicial powers (vis-à-vis civil liberty) by the Special Court of Clerics as well as the legitimacy of theocratic rule. Though his trial earned him popular support, it did not help Nouri's case. The court found him guilty on 15 counts and rejected plea for leniency in sentencing. He was sentenced to five years in prison and was debarred from writing in newspapers for five years after that.

The closure of *Salaam*, *Neshat* and *Khordad* were clearly attempts to eliminate reformist newspapers and limit the influence of reformist leaders. It is pertinent to note here that the 'transgressions' of the hardline press easily passed muster under the benign eyes of the clergy court. As noted earlier, hardline publications—the weekly *Javan* and dailies *Kayhan* and *Jomhuri-yi-Islami*—printed copies of a letter from 24 Islamic Revolution Guards Corps Commanders to Khatami in which they threatened to take action if the President did not act against the demonstrators. The publications only received a warning from the Islamic guidance and culture ministry for publishing a classified document.

Besides the overtly reformist publications that suffered for their pro-Khatami leanings, other closures of 1999 and harassment of journalists on trumped up charges, has had serious implications for freedom of expression. The closure of Tehran's *Zan* daily by a decision of Tehran's Islamic Revolutionary Court for publishing a cartoon lampooning the Iranian interpretation of the principle of 'blood money' (In Iran, the compensation one must pay to a murdered woman's family is less than what must be paid to the murdered man's family) and for publishing letter from the former queen of Iran diminished the culture of openness on contentious issues being nurtured by the reform movement. The detention of weekly *Hoviat-i-Khish*'s editor-in-chief, Heshmatollah Tabarzadi, for his role as the leader of the radical Islamic Union of Students and Graduates was again an assault on the freedom of association and expression. Later, Tabarzadi and the director of the weekly, Hussein Kashani, were prosecuted by the Islamic Revolutionary Court for their participation in the July 1999 students' demonstration. The atmosphere of the provincial publications was vitiated too by the harassment and arrests of their editors and directors. Those associated with *Kosar Kavir Kerman*, Kurdish-language *Sirwan* weekly and *Payam-i Shomal* were some of worst sufferers.[23]

With the inauguration of reform movement under Khatami, the public debate over the office of the Supreme Leader chronicled a unique openness, unseen and unheard before 1997. The judiciary, dominated by the conservative clerics bent upon preventing the press from enjoying real freedom, also came in for severe criticism. Intellectuals, writers and journalists began debating the scope of Khamenei's power with alacrity, pointing out his increasing propensity to interfere with reforms as unconstitutional and unjust. The reformists argued that of late he had been exceeding his brief of a 'supervisor' and/or 'mediator' in times of conflict between various political factions on contentious issues. They repudiated 'the proposition put forward by religious traditionalists that the Supreme Leader is above the law and should not be subject to public scrutiny and criticism'.[24] The Constitution, they pointed out, ordains that the *faqih* should be selected by the 86-member Assembly of Experts (*Majles-e-Khabregan*), which in turn is elected from a government-screened list of candidates by direct public vote. Therefore, there is nothing in the Constitution which would indicate that the position of the Supreme Leader is divinely sanctioned or inspired and his actions could be as fallible as that of other leaders. What followed from this argument was that the actions of the *faqih* could be brought under public scrutiny.

Several prominent reformist theoreticians have rejected the notions of overarching power and infallibility of the Supreme Leader. One of the most well-known and forthright critics of Khamenei and the conservative Guardian Council, who see their jobs as defenders against the advance of a more liberal, modernizing trend in Iranian politics, has been Grand Ayatollah Hussien Ali Montazeri, once designated as the heir apparent to the leadership of Ayatollah Khomeini. In written answers to journalists' questions ahead of the February 2000 elections, Montazeri came out strongly against clerical interference in government—the key issue in the struggle between the reformers and conservatives in Iran. He upheld the principle of clerical supervision to ensure that legislation and government policy remain in line with Islamic principles. But he said Ayatollah Khamenei had overstepped his authority, and should submit himself to popular elections, curtail his power, and be accountable and open to public criticism for his actions.[25]

According to Montazeri, the conservatives' interpretation of the absolute guardianship of the *faqih* contradicts many articles of the constitution. For instance, Articles 6 of the Constitution says that the republic must be governed 'on the basis of public opinion expressed by the means of elections' and the word 'republic' expresses this meaning. He argues that people elect the members of the parliament to legislate and the President to implement the laws. Further, Article 56 specifies that no particular individual or group can subordinate the interests of another individual to 'master his own social destiny'.[26] Under the constitution, he says, the parliament and the executive branch are responsible to the people, but because the actual power of the state is monopolized by the members of the Guardian Council, these two branches are not able to carry out their constitutional duties and responsibilities. He also suggested that the Islamic republican constitution, of which he was a leading author, should be changed to give the reformist figurehead President Khatami control over the military and security forces. He warned that the silencing of the liberal press would result in rebellion and lead to disenchantment of the people with the principles of Islam.

Another prominent cleric who argued along similar lines was Alireza Alavitabar, a leading reformist intellectual and writer and the editor of liberal newspaper, *Sobh-e-Emrooz*. In his religious definition of democracy, he argues that people have received the right of self-rule from God and it is their prerogative to bestow this power upon whomsoever they choose. A leader who usurps more power than that granted to him by the will of the people is illegitimate. He circumscribes the faqih's power by stating that its boundary is defined by the constitution. If he oversteps these legal boundaries, he violates the contract with the people and can no longer expect their loyalty and support.

Mohsen Kadivar emerged as the most vocal critic of the stranglehold of clerical establishment in Iran. A philosopher of Islam, cleric and activist, Kadivar, presents a devastating critique of *velayat-e faqih* (guardianship of the *jurist*), the Shi'ite Muslim doctrine expounded by Khomeini that effectively grants the power of dictatorship to a top Shi'ite cleric. In his two books, *Nazariyeha-ye Dulat dar Fiqh-e Shi* (1997; Theories of state in Shi'ite law) and *Hukumat-e Velayi* (1998; Government by the Guardian), Kadivar has criticized the notion of *velayat-e faqih* by attempting to show the lack of Qur'anic, rationale, and *fiqh* grounds for the idea of political rule by the clergy headed by a supreme jurisprudent. As a result, the Special Court for the Clergy charged Kadivar with propaganda against the Islamic Republic, dissemination of lies, and creating confusion in public opinion, for which he served a prison term of eighteen months. He was released in July 2000.

PARLIAMENTARY ELECTION, CLOSURE OF PUBLICATIONS AND PRESS LAW

The parliamentary elections of February 2000 swept the reformists to power much to the chagrin of the conservatives. This moment of triumph not only raised their own expectations and that of their constituency but also galvanized the conservatives into quick retaliation. In the aftermath of the elections the conservative backlash resulted in an unprecedented crackdown on reformist newspapers. One of the first and perhaps the worst blow occurred on March 12, when Saeed Hajarian, publisher of the newspaper, *Sobh-e-Emrooz*, and the architect of reformists' victory in the recent polls, was shot, crippling him for life. Hajarian's newspaper had published investigative articles linking Intelligence Ministry officials to the murder of several leading intellectuals and dissidents in late 1998.

In March-April, the Supreme Leader and patron of the conservatives, Ayatollah Khamenei, made several pronouncements against the advocates of reform and castigated the reformist press specifically for promoting "Americanized reforms". The speech of 20 April 2000, in which Khamenei attacked the reformist press, triggered a sweeping crackdown: "There are 10 to 15 papers writing as if they are directed from one centre, undermining Islamic and revolutionary principles, insulting constitutional bodies, and creating tension and discord in society... Unfortunately, the same enemy who wants to overthrow the [regime] has found a base in the country. Some of the press has become the base of the enemy."[27] Such critical and disparaging labelling of the press gave a green signal to the judiciary to shut down publications and send journalists to jail. Shortly after the aforementioned speech, the conservative-dominated judiciary launched an open campaign of censorship, banning 16 newspapers and magazines on vague charges such as undermining the security of the state, insulting the Revolution, and offending Islamic sanctities. By May 2000 all but one or two of the reformist newspapers were closed down.

Several journalists were summoned to the notorious conservative-established Tehran Press Court and accused of ill-defined violations such as insulting Islamic principles in their writings. Prominent reformist editor Mashallah Shamsolvaezin lost his appeal and was sentenced to 30 months in prison because of a 1999 article in his newspaper *Neshat* that argued against capital punishment. The conservative crackdown also targeted investigative reporter Akbar Ganji, whose coverage of the 1998 murders of intellectuals in the daily, *Sobh-e-Emrooz*, had made him a celebrity in Iran. Ganji was arrested in April 22 for alleged Press Law violations and for participating in a conference in May in Berlin on the future of the Iranian reform movement. The next year he was sentenced to ten years in prison followed by five years of internal exile. Among the several reformist journalists, intellectuals and political figures who were arrested and tried because of their participation in Berlin conference, was a popular woman politician, Jamileh Kadivar. In the parliamentary election of 2000, Kadivar received the second highest votes in Tehran. She was brought before a Revolutionary Court for having participated in a 'conference that was held with the aim of changing Iran's system of religious government, insulting the [Islamic] sanctities and rejecting Islamic judgements'.[28] She tried to tell the court in vain that participation a conference held abroad was not a crime.

As the courts pursued their offensive, the new deputies to the majlis drew up a bill enshrining more freedom for the press. It was meant to amend the regressive press law of July 1999, which was passed by the previous conservative-dominated parliament. The new press law aimed at creating 'an open atmosphere for the press to work free of constricting supervision and control.'[29] However, no sooner had the *majlis* started debating the bill, than Ayatollah Khamenei in an unprecedented move on August 6, 2000 intervened and demanded its immediate withdrawal, describing it as a threat to national security: "If the enemies infiltrate our press, this will be a big danger to the country's security and the people's religious beliefs… The current Press Law has succeeded to a point to prevent this big plague. The [proposed] bill is not legitimate, nor is it in the interests of the system and the revolution."[30] Even his predecessor had refrained from publicly interfering with the functioning of the parliament, 'at least maintaining the fiction of an independent legislature'. Khamenei's step 'tore away this veil in an authoritarian gesture applauded by his supporters and derided by his critics.' It severely dented the power of the parliament to carry out meaningful reforms. In protecting their own interests, the conservative establishment 'had done incalculable damage to the credibility of the system.'[31] Given that the two levers of legal control—the judiciary that interpreted the law, and the Guardian Council, which vetted legislation for compatibility (politically defined/determined) with Islamic Law—were dominated by the conservatives and would have blocked the legislation anyways, the fact that Khamenei chose to prevent its ratification, sent out a clear message about who was really in command, despite the results of the popular elections.

With the Majlis being told to stop its deliberations on the new press law, the clerical establishment was emboldened to close down the last important reformist paper, *Bahar*, and arrest more journalists. As Said Arjomand rightly points out, 'the reformist Majles lost the first and best (and probably the only) chance it had for confronting the Leader, who had clearly stepped beyond his ample constitutional jurisdiction by telling parliament to shut up, to stand up as the legislative power against the judiciary. It was too timid to challenge the authority of the Leader and took the slap in the face without any vigorous reaction.'[32] He also considers that it was a grave mistake to elect a cleric, Mehdi Karurbi, as the speaker of the Majlis. This became evident when 'he confirmed the authority of the Leader, as the *vali-ye faqih*, to issue a "governmental order" (*hokm-e-hokumati*) to the Majles, and defended it as a constitutional exercise of the Absolute Mandate of the Jurist.'

The short-lived freedom experienced by the press in Iran, appeared to be a flicker as the conservatives got into their stride to suppress any democratic freedom of expression. The axing of the reformists' press bill mirrored the severe limitation imposed on Khatami's reform movement. The reformists by adopting a rigorous legalistic approach of working through the legislature helped the conservatives to seize initiatives to push through their own agenda. Khatami believed, or was persuaded to believe, that Khamenei would provide the backing he needed to implement the reforms and that the conservatives would eventually respect the will of the Parliament. These proved to be an illusion, as in the next four years, the Guardian Council and the Judiciary repeatedly blocked reformist legislation. The Supreme Leader indentified with the conservatives, frustrating many of the reformist policies. Khatami's disinclination for confrontation and his cautiousness in 'carrying out his reforms with a certain stealth, determined not to upset the apple cart by going too far or asking for too much'[33] left a highly politicized public frustrated and leaderless.

FREEDOM OF PRESS DURING KHATAMI PERIOD: AN ASSESSMENT

For a few years with the election of Khatami in 1997 and up to May 2000, the press in Iran was by far the freest and most dynamic in the region. In 1997, Khatami came to office promising Iranians freedom of expression, democracy, and respect for the rule of law. His first term saw the emergence of a new liberal press that quickly began to debate sensitive issues such as official corruption, the undemocratic behaviour of the ruling clerical establishment, Iran's theocratic form of government, and even the role of the Supreme Leader. While the press helped mobilize Iran's burgeoning reform movement, relying on their control of most of the state institutions—including the parliament, the judiciary, the Army and the security forces—the conservatives sought for most part successfully, to impede the growing campaign for openness by targeting the media. The Press Court closed down newspapers and prosecuted journalists for vague offences such as insulting the leadership and publishing lies, falsehood, slander, or propaganda against the system. Other courts, such as the Special Court of the Clergy and the revolutionary court system, were employed with similar effect against newspapers and journalists.

Both Khatami and the conservative opposition were brutally shaken by the events of July 1999 in Tehran—the student unrest and the brutal suppression of students by the vigilante forces. The conservatives, alarmed by the intensity of the protest, tried to suppress the demand for reforms, by further clamping down on the reformist press. To the great surprise of the reformists, Khatami joined forces with the conservatives in dampening the pro-reform demonstrations by reproaching the students for creating discord in society and adopted a legalistic approach by calling upon them to wait for changes through parliamentary action. Instead of leading this movement and turning it into an organized political power to force reform, Khatami tried to effect changes from within the establishment. Caught between public demands for change and the anti-reform posture of the conservative clergy, Khatami opted for a slow and cautious move towards his campaign goals.

After the parliamentary elections of February 2000, when the reformist candidates won two-thirds of the majority, there was a general feeling that the conservative forces were in retreat and Khatami's vision of establishing a society based on democracy and pluralism was within reach. However, such hopes were belied when within months of the decisive reformist victory, all the progressive publications were banned and several journalists and editors jailed by the conservative-dominated judiciary. Ayatollah Khamenei, in one of his speeches, termed the liberal publications as bases of the enemies, a label reserved for the US and Israel. He said that through these publications the enemies were trying to undermine the country's national interests and people's faith in Islamic values. This proved a green signal for the judiciary to clamp down the reformist press. Using the same argument, Khamenei took the unprecedented step of ordering the parliamentary deputies to stop discussing a press bill introduced by the reformists and demanded its immediate withdrawal. The bill was designed to secure freedom of the press and provide for the revival of banned publications. Had the legislators not complied, they would not only have created a constitutional crisis but also initiated demonstrations for and against the Supreme Leader. In all likelihood the demonstrations would have been larger and more violent than the ones that shook the Islamic Republic in 1999. Sensing such a scenario, Speaker Mahdi Karrubi, while withdrawing the bill declared that it was the duty of the deputies to obey the Supreme Leader.

It is worthwhile examining why President Khatami adopted a conciliatory attitude towards the conservatives in the implementation of democratic reforms. It appears Khatami had been aware of the limits of his power from the very outset. Realizing that the reform measures would be vetoed by the conservative centres of power in the Guardian Council and the conservative fifth parliament, he moved cautiously, attempting to forge a consensus wherever possible. He tried to elicit Khamenei's support for his policies, although the Supreme Leader sided with the conservatives on most occasions. As a result many of his policy goals suffered and this was particularly evident in the area of press reforms. Khatami's supporters often found it bewildering that he should step back without resisting the volley of onslaught on his reform measures and simultaneously solicit time and patience from his restless constituents.

On the other hand, the conservatives interpreted the president's attitude as 'lacking the nerve' to push through his agenda, which energized them to get into a repressive stride, especially where freedom of press was concerned. Eventually Khatami's governing style of taking one step forward and two steps backward left him with an empty coffer on democratic reforms which he tended to blame on 'systemic' forces, like all indecisive and unsuccessful politicians. None of his constituents were willing to grant him this line of defence and exonerate him for his weakness in confronting the conservatives, when he had the mandate to do so. Many argue that Khatami became part of the problem for not standing up early in his presidency, when challenged by the hardline judiciary and security services that shut down newspapers and jailed opponents.

It is also worth discussing why the conservatives took such an antagonistic stance against the reformist press. To begin with, the conservatives in the clerical establishment resented the fact that the liberal journalists and editors had begun to question the clerical rule in the country and power of the Supreme Leader. The reformists argued that the clerics including the Supreme Leader should respect the will of the people as evidenced in Khatami's victory in the elections. Therefore, they should allow Khatami's reform movement to take its course. The liberal press also reproached the partisan role of the Supreme Leader in leaning towards the conservatives. In other words, the reformist press was questioning the monopoly of power that the conservatives had held for nearly two decades. Secondly, to some extent correctly, they saw the reformist press as the reason for their defeat in the presidential, city council and parliamentary elections. However, even after electoral defeats, the conservatives continued to dominate the key centres of power such as the army, the judiciary, the Ministry of Intelligence, the police, and the radio and television networks. They, nevertheless, felt insecure so long as the free press continued to expose corruption in the system and demand an equal share in power for the reformists.

In the end Khatami proved that he was the loyal member of the clerical regime—a man who drew his legitimacy from it. His belief in the concept of *velayat-e faqih* tied his hands and left him incapable of making any radical or structural change in the Iranian system. Khatami failed to stand up for the ideals of his election campaign. His sophisticated words and fine demeanour were of no help when deeds were needed. The reform movement accomplished less than was originally hoped; setbacks for the reformers included crackdowns by conservative elements and blocked legislation. These resulted from a power structure weighted towards the conservatives, reformist leaders' weakness and reluctance to mobilize popular opinion, and the success of the conservatives in portraying dissent as a challenge to the entire state.

The conservatives continued to be uncompromising even after Khatami was re-elected in the presidential election of June 2001. He received 77 per cent of the votes, eight percent more than in the previous elections which indicated that majority of the people wanted him to push ahead with the reform agenda. Despite this, the conservatives continued to obstruct press freedom in the country. The spate of press closures continued throughout 2001, bringing Khatami idea of greater openness in Iranian society to its knees and further exacerbating the contestation between the reformists and the conservatives for greater dominance in the Islamic Republic. Here it is worth examining, with the benefit of hindsight, whether Khatami would have met with success had he pursued a more confrontational path in implementing reforms. In the light of the fact that most of his reforms were frustrated, it appears that riding the tide of reforms would have been more in tune with the aspirations of the people, rather than buckling under the onslaught of the hardliners. On the other hand, some of Khatami's reforms could have seen the light of the day had the conservatives relented on certain issues. He believed that they could be persuaded to support the path to reform. In this belief, he missed the determination of the conservatives to preserve their power and further entrench it.

NOTES

1. David Menashri, *Post-Revolutionary Politics in Iran: Religion, Society and Power* (Frank Cass, 2001), p. 142.
2. See Asadollah Alam, *The Shah and I: The Confidential Diary of Iran's Royal Court*, ed. Alinaghi Alikhani (New York: St. Martin's Press, 1991), p. 504.
3. For biographical information, see Muhammad Khatami, *Islam, Liberty and Development* (Institute of Global Cultural Studies, Binghamton University, 1998), pp. 155-6; and Daniel Brumberg, *Reinventing Khomeini: The Struggle for Reform in Iran* (University of Chicago Press, 2001), pp. 196-7.
4. See Ali M. Ansari, *Confronting Iran: The Failure of American Foreign Policy and the Roots of Mistrust* (New Delhi: Foundation Books, 2007), p. 30.
5. A.W. Samii, "The Contemporary Iranian News Media, 1998-1999+", *Middle East Review of International Affairs*, Vol. 4, No. 4 (December 1999), available at http://meria.idc.ac.il/journal/1999/issue4/samii.pdf (accessed on 5 March 2009).
6. A.W. Samii, "Sisyphus' Newsstand: The Iranian Press Under Khatami", *Middle East Review of International Affairs*, Vol. 5, No. 3 (September 2001), available at http://meria.idc.ac.il/journal/2001/issue3/jv5n3a1.html (accessed on 5 March 2009).
7. *Ibid.*
8. Vickie Maximova, "Middle East Iran's Conservative go on the offensive", available at http://news.bbc.co.uk/2/hi/middle_east/359251.stm (2 June 1999) (Accessed on 5 March 2009).
9. "Student power in Iran", available at http://news.bbc.co.uk/2/hi/middle_east/390974.stm (15 July 1999) (Accessed on 2 May 2009).
10. *Salaam* in Samii, 1999.

11. Quoted portions from Dr. John P. Nordin, "Iran Regime's Leading Reformers and Conservatives unite, Briefly, to put down mass protests", available at http://www.wrmea.com/backissues/1099/9910028.html (October/November 1999, pages 28, 104) (Accessed on 2 May 2009).
12. See "Iran closes down newspaper", available at http://news.bbc.co.uk/2/hi/middle_east/388635.stm (7 July 1999) (Accessed on 2 May 2009).
13. *Op. cit.*, Samii, September 2001.
14. *Ibid.*, Samii.
15. Quoted in Said Amir Arjomand, "The Rise and Fall of President Khatami and the Reform Movement in Iran", *Constellations*, Vol. 12, No. 4 (2005), p. 509.
16. *Iran Daily*, 26 July 1999, quoted in *Op. cit.*, Nordin, October/November 1999.
17. Rober Fisk, "Iran's old guard brings revolution upon itself," available at http://www.independent.co.uk/news/world/irans-old-guard-brings-revolution-upon-itself-1106322.html (14 July 1999) Accessed on 2 May 2009.
18. *Op. cit.*, Nordin, October/November 1999.
19. *Ibid.*
20. See Adam Tarock, "The Muzzling of Liberal Press in Iran", *Third World Quarterly*, Vol. 22, No. 4, pp. 585-602 (2001), pp. 591-92.
21. *Op. cit.*, Samii, 1999.
22. Nouri in *Op. cit.*, Tarock, 2001, p. 594.
23. *Op. cit.*, Samii, 2001.
24. *Op. cit.*, Tarock, p. 592.
25. "Profile: Iran's Dissident Ayatollah", available at http://news.bbc.co.uk/2/hi/middle_east/2699541.stm (30 January, 2003) (Accessed on 5 March 2009).
26. "Iran-Constitution", available at http://servat.unibe.ch/icl/ir00000_.html (Accessed on 5 March 2009).
27. Quoted in "Attacks on Press in 2000: Iran", available at http://cpj.org/2001/03/attacks-on-the-press-2000-iran.php dated 19 March 2001 (Accessed on 5 March 2009).
28. *Op. cit.*, Tarock, 2001, p. 594
29. Dariush Sajjadi, BBC News/Middle East, "Press caught in a power struggle," quoted in Ahmad Siddiqi, "Khatami and the Search for Reform in Iran", *Stanford Journal of International Relations*, available at http://www.stanford.edu/group/sjir/6.1.04_siddiqi.html 28 May 2006. (Accessed on 5 March 2009)
30. Quoted in "Attacks on Press in 2000: Iran", available at http://cpj.org/2001/03/attacks-on-the-press-2000-iran.php dated 19 March 2001 (Accessed on 5 March 2009).
31. *Op. cit.*, Ansari, 2007, p. 175.
32. *Op. cit.*, Arjomand, 2005, p. 510.
33. "The people against the mullah", *The Economist*, 17 February 2000.

13

Subsidies in Iran: Impediments to Democratic Experience

Sameena Hameed

The impediments to democracy in the Gulf are largely understood in the framework of the relation between the state and the citizen as determined by the rentier economies. The relationship in the rentier economies of the Gulf has been 'no taxation, no representation'. The governments in most of these states do not have popular representation through democratic electoral process. The regimes earn their legitimacy through their welfare measures financed through oil revenues. They hardly impose any financial burden in the form of taxes.

But, what is less comprehended is the threat emanating from the erosion of economic space and the existing inequalities in these economies, which inhibits the generation of creative skills and self-reliance. An egalitarian society facilitates larger economic participation and the flourishing of economic democracy. It is due to the lack of economic democracy that political democracy has failed to take firm roots in the rentier economies. More noteworthy is the fact that Iranian society has been practically losing its century old democratic heritage and the essence of the most popular revolution to the autocratic State. Taking a cue from Arrows' proposition of 'Learning by Doing'[1] and the discussions of 'Unlearning by not doing' by Amartya Sen in his book *Social Exclusion: Concept Application and Scrutiny,* one can get some insight into the question why the Iranian society has not been able to consolidate its century old democratic heritage.

Iranian politics over the last century has unraveled itself as the jumble of paradoxes. The country has experienced considerable success in state building and development. The political history of Iran in the modern era reveals that democracy has been an old idea with a complex history, one that is tightly interwoven with the main forces that have shaped the Iranian society, politics, institutions, identities, and interests. Iran's first attempt to set up a democratic constitutional government was during the Constitutional Revolution 1905-07. At that time, a coalition of secular intellectuals, enlightened *Shia* clergy, traders, workers, and even some members of the landed aristocracy came together to topple the despotism of the Qajar kings and replace it with a monarchy, whose power was limited by a constitution.[2] It was the same coalition of forces, much stronger than before that staged a successful revolution overthrowing the Shah in 1979. Scholars and experts consider it as the most 'popular revolution' in modern times with almost 10 percent of the population participating in it, while the French and Russian revolutions had the estimated participation of 2 percent and 1 percent of their citizens.[3]

Nevertheless, the most popular of all 'modern revolutions' then led to the creation of a state, where the constitution places absolute power in the hand of an unelected, unimpeachable man Vilayet-e-faqih, and where the basic political philosophy considers people as subjects rather than citizens. Inspite of elected governments, the democratic functions are still missing. Nevertheless, the Iranian society is still full of vibrant democratic elements poised to produce an indigenous democratic movement in the Muslim world. The emerging demand for functional democracy in Iran is neither a sudden development nor a western import. This is seen by the innovative ways the people are resorting to live their civil liberties and express their will. Many found a new 'virtual' space for free speech by creating one of the largest communities of bloggers in the world, inspite of the onslaught against the internet.[4] They expressed the voices of a burgeoning generation of educated young people. Iranian officials have announced that they have blocked or filtered more than 10 million websites. It is therefore, important to understand why democracy fails to grow roots in Iran.

ECONOMIC ROOTS OF DEMOCRACY

Political democracy is incomplete without economic democracy. Political democracy gives space to citizens to exercise their will in the formation of government, which is their representative and is responsible to them. Economic democracy would involve the participation of a larger public rather than a small official or corporate group in economic decisions and opportunities. It gives space for the exercise of one's creativity. It is through the articulation of individual creativity, that the fullest development of any individual as well as that of society takes place. An egalitarian society provides larger opportunities of economic participation and is the generative of creative skills. Political democracy has shown greater resilience in a society, which develops by harnessing the creative potential of its people. Once democracy is created, it is more likely to consolidate in an egalitarian society.[5]

The reason for failure of Iran to consolidate its democratic traditions lies in erosion of opportunities of private participation in its economic space. The Iranian economy is rentier economy based on oil revenues. It is world's second ranking owner of oil and gas reserves. During 2000-05, oil revenue constituted about 79 of total export earnings and about 58 percent of government budget (Table 13.1). About 11 percent of Gross Domestic Product (GDP) came from the oil exports. There has been high correlation between petroleum export revenues and GDP.

Table 13.1: Contribution of Oil Revenues to the Iranian Economy

Variable	*2000-05 Average Percent*
Oil Export Revenues as % of GDP*	10.9
Oil Export as % of Total export	79.1
Oil Export Revenue as % of total Government Revenue	57.6
Correlation between Oil Export Revenue and GDP	0.98 (0.97)

*GDP taken at current prices.
The figure in the bracket is for non-oil GDP

Source: Computed from Data from Central Bank of Iran.

The correlation is high between oil revenues and GDP as well as with non-oil GDP as shown in Table 13.1. This shows that the resources for the growth of the other sectors of the economy also come from the oil revenues. The export revenues enabled the government to spend on capital accumulation and development expenditure.

The common malaise of un-diversified economies in oil rich West Asian and North African (WANA) countries, has also affected Iranian economy. They provide low employment opportunities and have high inflationary pressures. The onus of growth and development in the rentier economic is on the state, where the regime secures legitimacy through the distribution of rent, collected from the ownership of natural resources. This rent is distributed through the provision of subsidized goods and social services. But, the Iranian state faced a more difficult task in post-revolution period. Economic growth suffered because of the debilitating effect of the Iran-Iraq war and negative terms of trade. Besides, Iran was not only marginalized on the regional platform by the Arabian neighbourhood but also faced sanctions by the United States (US). Most of the US measures concerned blocking all the Iranian government and Central Bank assets, banning US import of Iranian oil and limitations on US exports to Iran. In 1993, the US Congress passed the Iran-Libya Sanctions Act (ILSA) threatening non-US companies with sanctions if they invested more than $40 million per year in Iranian oil and gas sectors. This ceiling was eventually reduced to $20 million.

The fiscal policy of the government has been the main source of investment, capital formation and development. After the Islamic Revolution, the government was extensively involved in the manufacturing sector. It owned and operated most of the important manufactures, allocated domestic and foreign credits to the sector and regulated international trade by setting quotas and tariffs. The state controlled oil, gas, steel companies, petrochemical plants and public utilities (water and electricity), metal processing, the car manufacturing, shipyards and aircraft construction.

The government is also obliged to provide employment and access to basic amenities. The thrust of the government has been more towards development than growth. The public expenditure on development has been high in comparison to other developing economies. The poverty level of the war torn economy was very high. In the beginning of the 1990s, about 28 percent of the urban households and 32 percent of the rural households were below the poverty line.[6] Further, Iran's double-digit inflation eroded the purchasing power of the common man. High inflation hurts the poor households. The government regulated the prices of common household goods below their market prices to make them affordable.

Table 13.2: Socio-economic Indicators of Selected Countries in West Asia

	Unemployment 2007 (%)	*Inflation 2007 (%)*	*Poverty HPI 2005*
Saudi Arabia	13	4.1	—
Iran	11	18.4	12.9
UAE	2.7	11.1	8.4
Kuwait	0.7	5.5	—
Bahrain	15	3.4	—
Jordan	17	5.4	6.9
Lebanon	18	4.1	8.5

Statistical, Economic and Social Research and Training Centre for Islamic Countries (SESRTCIC) *OIC Member Countries Economic Performance and Human Development 2000-2007,* Ankara.

But Iran continued to face the problems of unemployment, poverty and inflation more than other countries in West Asia as seen in table 13.2.

IRAN: ONE OF THE MOST SUBSIDIZED ECONOMY

Besides other external factors, Iran's larger socio-economic predicament was because of another malaise that has been affecting its economy disproportionately more than the other oil-based economies of the WANA region. Iran has been giving huge subsidy to its citizens. The total subsidy as percent of GDP was about 15.5 percent in the year 2004.

Subsidy and transfer payments form an important channel for the distribution of oil rent among the different sectors of the economy and therefore earn legitimacy for the regimes. The wide-ranging subsidy has been given by the

Iranian government to enable the common household to have access to basic needs and to shield them from high inflation. The inputs to productive sectors like agriculture and industries have been subsidized to promote their growth. Table 13.3 shows the coverage of direct subsidies in Iran. There were many other implicit subsidies in the financial market, which go unaccounted in the various estimates.

Table 13.3: The Coverage of direct Subsidies in Iran

Type of Subsidy	*Coverage*
Social	Housing, Food grains and other basic edibles, Health, Education, Electricity, water, Fuel
Productive sectors	Capital, Electricity, water, Fuel

Source: Hossein Askari, (2006), *Middle East Oil Exporters: What happened to Economic Development?* Edward Elgar Pub.

Subsidy has been an important tool used by the governments in the developing countries to promote the consumption of 'merit goods' among the people to socially desirable level. The merit goods usually comprise of basic needs and other goods like energy to enable tolerable standards of life. But subsidy to non-merit goods adversely affects the economy and the society. While some subsidies have helped in raising the development indicators in Iran but their scale and coverage have eroded the economic space and set up a 'vicious circle' of perpetual dependence on subsidy.

The government expenditure on the wages and salaries as well as on subsidies and social security payments is very high as shown in Table 13.4.

Table 13.4: Hossein Askari (2006), Middle East Oil Exporters: What happened to Economic Development? Edward Elgar Pu.

Variables	*2007*
Wages & Salaries as % of Govt expenditure (2000)	52
Subsidies and current transfers as % of Govt Expenditure (2000)	10.3
Total Subsidies as % GDP (2004)	15.5

SOCIAL IMPACT OF SUBSIDY

Subsidised food, education, water, household cooking and lightening energy have raised the living standards of the poor households. Subsidy given to kerosene and LPG had saved millions of poor households in Iran from indoor pollution related diseases (Fig. 13.1). About 2 billion people round the world are suffering from indoor pollution due to burning of solid fuels like firewood, cow dung etc.

Fig. 13.1: World Distribution of Indoor Pollution Related Diseases

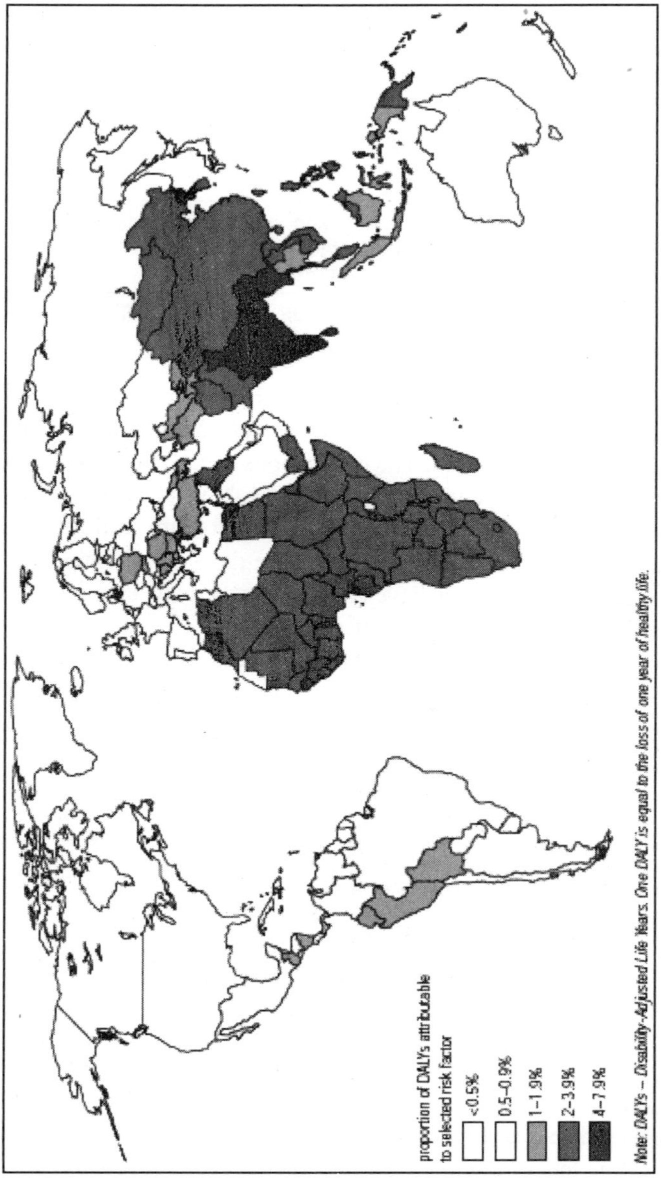

Source: United Nations Environment Programme (UNEP) (2006) *Global Energy Outlook Year Book* 2006, Nairobi: UN Pub.

Subsidy to an abundant resource tends to be more equitable in distribution and benefits the poor sections of the society if it caters to the basic needs. This can be seen in the relative distribution of kerosene and gasoline subsidy in Iran among the different income brackets in the rural and urban areas Figs. 13.2 and 13.3.

Subsidy for kerosene (Fig. 13.2) was relatively evenly distributed. The wealthiest urban decile received only 12 percent of the kerosene subsidy. The poorest decile received 6 percent. The comparatively equal distribution was due to two reasons. First, there has been no fuel supply constraint and second, according to Engel's law the consumption of necessities like cooking fuel has low income elasticity. Beside, kerosene is an inferior good, consumed by the poor for cooking and heating. Similarly, the distribution of LPG subsidy has been comparatively equitable. The consumption of the rich households for 'necessity goods' does not increase proportionately with their income. Hence, there was relatively less incidence of appropriation of subsidy by the rich and consequent inequality in distribution of subsidy among different income groups.

Fig. 13.2: Distribution of Kerosene Subsidy among the Iranian Households by Income Decile

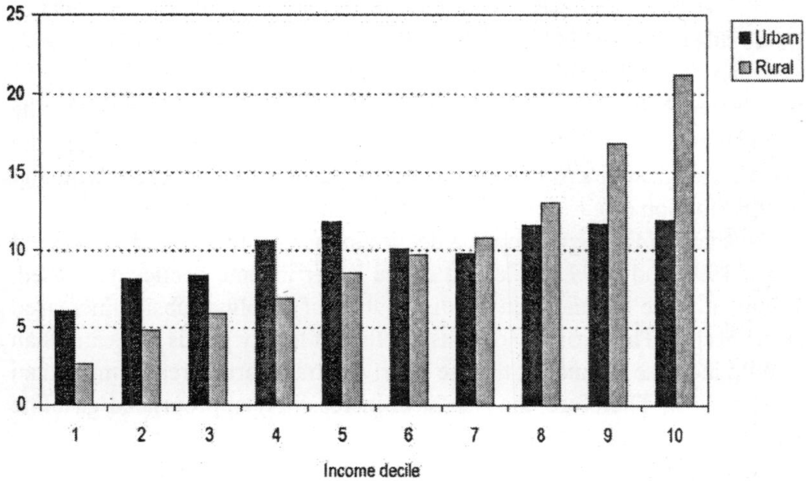

Source: Ministry of Energy, Islamic Republic of Iran cited in Mostafa Tavanpour Paveh, (2004), in Trevor Morgon, edts *Energy Subsidies: Lessons Learnt in Assessing their Impact and Designing Policy Reforms*, New York: UN Pub., p. 107.

Fig. 13.3: Distribution of Gasoline Subsidy among the Iranian Households by Income Decile

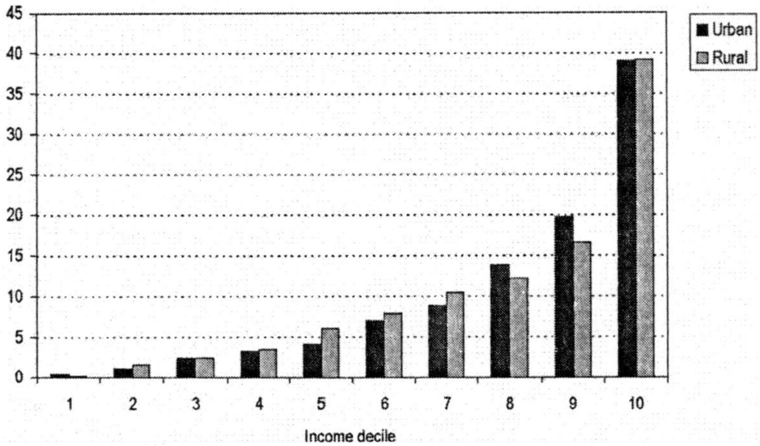

Source: Ministry of Energy, Islamic Republic of Iran cited in Mostafa Tavanpour Paveh, (2004), in Trevor Morgon (ed) *Energy Subsidies: Lessons Learnt in Assessing their Impact and Designing Policy Reforms*, New York: UN Pub., p. 106.

The distribution of gasoline subsidy among the Iranian households was more inequitable. The lowest income decile received less than one percent of gasoline subsidy; the wealthiest received about 39 percent (Fig. 13.3). In 1996, the amount of gasoline subsidy that went to the highest income group was 57 times greater than that received by the lowest income group. By 2000, the ratio had increased to 78 percent. The appropriation of gasoline subsidy by the upper income group increased during the 1990s resulting in larger inequality in the distribution of gasoline subsidy as seen in Fig. 13.4.

The share of the higher income deciles in the gasoline subsidy increased between 1996 and 1999, while that of the lower income deciles decreased. Consequently, the inequality in the distribution of gasoline subsidy increased over the period. The elasticity of consumption of luxury goods is greater than one. With increase in income, the use of private transport increases more than proportionately. Therefore, the rich have increasingly appropriated gasoline subsidy.

The cost and benefit analysis of Iran's subsidy reveal that the adverse effects have been more due to the large scale and universal coverage. The distortions and the wastage especially due to energy subsidy have hampered growth and consequently eroded the economic space. Their adverse effects have operated through multiple channels in the economy. The petroleum subsidy has adversely affected Balance of Payments and fiscal position of the government.

Fig. 13.4: Distribution of Gasoline Subsidy in Urban Area

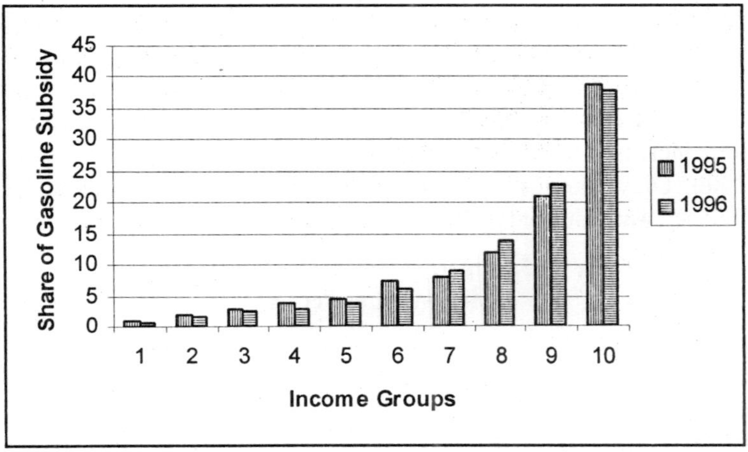

Source: Mostafa Tavanpour Paveh, (2001), "Socio-Economic Impact of Energy Subsidies: Challenges and Opportunities (The Case of Iran), paper presented in Energy Subsidy Reform Work Shop. 16-17 January 2001 in Bangkok, He was from Ministry of Energy, Tehran.

EFFECT OF ENERGY SUBSIDY ON BALANCE OF PAYMENTS

Huge energy subsidy led to inefficient consumption. The production became energy intensive and the share of the residential sector has been the second highest in the final energy consumption. In oil exporting countries, oil revenues play a vital role in capital accumulation. The excess domestic consumption reduced the exportable surplus, since Iran's total petroleum production was regulated by OPEC's quota. Between 1995 and 1999, the increasing domestic consumption squeezed the exportable oil surplus from 1,002.8 million barrals of oil equivalent (mboe) to 810 mboe in 1999. This had put Iran in severe Balance of Payments constraint during the oil price crisis in 1998-1999. The current account deficit in 1998 was $2,140 million. Reduction of exportable surplus entailed a heavy economic burden in Iran. There had been insufficient funds to finance investment. The non-oil GDP growth rates as well as per capita income had close relation with the oil revenue.

Besides, Iran had to import middle and light petroleum distillates to meet the burgeoning domestic demand. Subsidy to goods that are income elastic like gasoline inflicted a much larger burden. The demand for gasoline had outpaced the domestic supply. The imports increased over time. It has been estimated that if the domestic price of a representative barrel[7] were increased to half the world level, Iran could have saved about 13 percent of its domestic demand between 1994 and 2005.[8] The country had achieved self-sufficiency in fuel oil and lubricants but it imported diesel, kerosene and gasoline. Table 13.5 shows the imports of the petroleum products in Iran. Gasoline import rose at an increasing rate in the first half of 1990s, though it reduced in the second half and stabled afterwards. Kerosene import declined in 1990s and self-sufficiency was achieved only by 2000. LPG imports increased from 1.2 million litres/day to about 2.9 million litres/ day in 2000. Diesel imports had significantly declined in 1990s and self-sufficiency was achieved in 2000.

Table 13.5: Import of Petroleum Products in Iran (Million Litres Per Day)

Products	*1990*	*1995*	*2000*	*2005*
Gasoline	0.9	3.4	2.9	2.9
Kerosene	6	5.2	0	0
Diesel	12.8	3.8	0	0.3
L.P.G.	0	1.2	2.9	2.9
Total	**19.7**	**12.6**	**5.8**	**6.1**

Source: NIOC.

Importing petroleum products due to lack of sufficient refining capacity adversely affected BoP in two ways. It transferred to a foreign country the refiner's margin, which was usually more during low crude oil price. This was due to the asymmetric movement[9] of prices of crude oil and that of petroleum products during periods of increasing and decreasing crude oil prices. According to National Iranian Oil Company (NIOC), Iran needed to add about 200,000 b/d refining capacity every two to three years to keep pace with the domestic demand.

The refining capacity shortage has deprived Iran the opportunity to export value added petroleum products rather than crude oil. The refiners earned a larger margin in middle and lighter petroleum distillate owing to their demand in the light of environmental concerns. Further, the exports of petroleum products would have exposed Iran to less risk in the international oil market. The price fluctuations of gasoline have low correlation with that of the crude oil.

But Iran imported gasoline. By the end of the decade, it nominally exported diesel and kerosene (Table 13.6). Thus, petroleum subsidy affected the BoP in two ways. It reduced the exportable surplus and constituted the 'opportunity cost'[10], which was the investment in the refining capacity. The refining capacity would have further improved Iran's terms of trade and mitigated the risk in the international petroleum market.

Table 13.6: Export of Petroleum Products in Iran (Million Litres per Day)

Products	*1990*	*1995*	*2000*	*2005*
Fuel oil	9.4	25.1	43.9	36.9
Kerosene	0	0	0.8	0.3
Diesel	0	0	2.3	1.5
L.P.G.	0	0	0.1	0
Total	**9.4**	**25.1**	**47.1**	**38.7**

Source: NIOC.

Subsidy has hampered energy conservation. Conservation of petroleum could be achieved through more efficient energy consumption and substitution by renewable sources of energy. Due to availability of cheap energy, efficiency was not taken into account while selecting technologies and appliances. The available technology had low energy efficiency. Table 13.7 shows the gap in the energy use efficiency. In many sectors like textile, metal, the energy efficiency gap was about 40 to 50 percent.

Table 13.7: Comparison of Energy Consumed in Iran and Industrialized Countries

Industry	*Unit*	*Modern Technology*	*Available Technology In Iran*
Cement	kWh/t	85-110	130-161
Textile	kWh/t	3,500-5500	7,400-12,600
Glass products	kWh/t	70-95	120
Metal products	kWh/t	8-12	30
Primary metal Industries	Gcal/t	5.7	9
Chemical products	TOE*/US$1000	0.28	0.71-0.94

Source: Ministry of Energy (1998), *Energy Balance Year Book* 1997-1998, Islamic Republic of Iran, Tehran

The onus of taking the energy efficiency measures is on the government. Till 1993, there was hardly any attempt in the field of energy conservation in the country. Gradually, some attention was paid and the office of Energy Efficiency was established in 1994. Iran Energy Efficiency Organization (SABA) was established in 1995. This along with the SUNA, (the organization for the development of renewable sources of energy) was semi-government organizations. Later, they became government organizations. About $ 9 millions were given to SABA to promote energy efficiency measures.

The adoption of power saving home appliances led to some energy conservation. In the transport sector, petroleum conservation was hampered by low gasoline price. Fuel efficiency was not a major consideration and majority of the cars were over 20 years old with poor fuel efficiency. The rate of return on investment for energy efficiency and fuel substitution were significant. For cement industry, it was 70 percent and 50 percent for iron and steel.[11] But the government expenditure was constrained by short-term goals rather than long term planning. The government incurred high social expenditures on subsidies and other current transfers to maintain its legitimacy. Besides, the investments in energy efficiency projects, awareness programmes and research were required to save energy.

The abundance of oil and gas led to the neglected of renewable sources of energy in Iran. Considerable thrust was given towards development of renewable sources of energy in the second half of 1990s. The Organization for Renewable Energy (SUNA) was established in 1995. Solar water heaters were developed even in the rural areas. Renewable energy was new to Iran and needed research and investment for its exploitation. In 1990, the share of renewable energy was nil in the primary energy supply. In 2000, it increased to 0.06 percent.[12] The overall budget for the renewable energy and energy conservation in the country was about US$ 76 million.[13] This attempt was remarkable for a country with abundant fossil fuel resources and was under financial constraint. But, cheap availability of petroleum and natural gas discouraged the consumption of alternate sources of energy.

The production base of the economy in spite of being energy intensive could neither adequately meet the essential needs of the people nor could contribute to the non-oil exports. The non-oil exports were carpets, fruits, nuts, hides and agricultural products, which were from the less energy intensive sectors. The import basket of Iran comprised essential items like food, medicines and machinery etc. Food imports were about US $ 3,050 m in 2005 at current price.[14] The imports of essential consumer and capital goods put further pressure on BoP.

ON FISCAL POSITION

Oil export contributed about 50-58 percent to the total government revenues. Reduction in oil export constrained the government revenues. Subsidy put a heavy fiscal burden on the government in the form of large budgetary deficit. The budgetary deficit has been monetised, which increased money supply. Inflation increases, when there is an increase in money supply through monetization of budgetary deficit. Since the Islamic revolution, the governments had to contend with deficit. The share of borrowing from the Central Bank in financing the budgetary deficits between 1986 and 1990 increased to over 90 percent.[15] The government expenditure and monetary policy had a tremendous impact on the variation of money base and was the main cause of high inflation. Money supply growth was largely determined by the growth of private and public sector credit. Inflation, in turn had caused the government expenditure to rise faster than the revenue.[16] This further enhanced the budgetary deficit.

Growth in Iran had been adversely affected by high inflation. There has been a strong correlation between rate of inflation and economic growth. Elasticity of GDP growth rate with respect to the inflation rate has been estimated 0.5.[17] Though, the government tried to control inflation by keeping the energy cost low to the productive industries and administering the prices of essential commodities, yet inflation remained above 20 percent.

The universal subsidy to non-merit goods increased the cost of the programme. The gasoline subsidy, which was about 17.8 percent of the total petroleum subsidy not only imposed a direct burden but also an indirect one in terms of pollution. It had imposed an economic cost of health hazards, global warming, etc. Due to the large price differential the oil products were also smuggled into the neighbouring countries.

IMPACT OF ENERGY SUBSIDY ON SOCIAL CAPACITY

Subsidy to basic human needs helped to improve the development indicators with respect to health and literacy in Iran. Subsidy to cooking fuel, which has income elasticity, benefited the lower and middle-income groups. Hence, there was low incidence of disease from indoor pollution. But the high-income groups largely appropriated the subsidy to luxury goods with high-income elasticity of demand like gasoline and diesel. The share of subsidy accruing to the non-poor was about 94 percent in urban areas and 89 percent in rural areas.[18]

The government subsidised the essential household consumption like food, fuel, medicine, sugar, edible oil, etc. to shield the poor from the adverse effect of inflation. Even though, subsidy had prevented their cost of living from increasing yet it generated inflationary pressures in the economy. This was socially undesirable. Inflation restricted growth and employment. It therefore, adversely affected the poor through many other channels in the long run by impeding their capacity to sustain themselves. Thus, subsidy generated causative factors operating in 'vicious circle' to perpetuate them.

Subsidy to luxury goods had harmful social impact. It increased the income inequality, and reduced the fiscal capability of the government to invest in pro-poor growth strategies. If the subsidy on gasoline were withdrawn and distributed to the poor under various assistance programme, their per capita income would increase multiple times.[19]

Thus, the impact of energy subsidy on the social welfare was two folds. It supported the consumption of clean energy for the basic needs of the poor households but the universal subsidy spelled a double jeopardy for them in the long run. Excess domestic consumption was at the cost of export revenue. It deprived the government of the investment capital. Besides, it fuelled inflation by widening the budgetary deficit. In the long run it hampered the capability of the common household, depriving them of opportunities of growth and gainful employment. It reduces the profitability of domestic production as well as competitiveness of the country's export in the international market. This hampers the diversification drive in the economy and the dependence on oil sector remains large. Restricted avenues for growth and private participation have perpetuated the society's dependence on the State for employment and other social security transfer payments.

The adverse effect of subsidies operating through diverse channels as discussed above led to the erosion of the economic opportunities as can be seen in Table 13.8.

Table 13.8: Growth Performance in Iran (GDP at PPP US $)

Economies	*1990*	*2000*
Iran billion US $	1258.14 (1043)	223.92 (193.98)

Figures in the bracket are for non-oil GDP

Sources: Calculated from using PPP exchange rate given in World Bank (2002), World Development Indicators, Washington D.C.

Between the year 1990 and 2000, GDP in Iran at PPP contracted nearly five times from $1258.14 to 223.92. The non-oil GDP also contracted from $1043 in 1990 to $193.98 in 2000. Thus, the inadequate expansion of economic space in Iran and the existing inequalities due to mismanagement of oil rent have perpetuated their dependence on state employment and other welfare measures. The working environment in the government enterprises has not been conducive to the generation and articulation of creative skills given the nature of recruitment process and structure of financial incentives. All these have cumulatively inhibited the Iranian society to consolidate its century old democratic tradition.

But, the elements of democracy remain vibrant in the society and are making increasing demand for functional democracy. The people have successfully backed Khatami against the candidate supported by the supreme leader Ayatollah Ali Khamenei during the presidential elections in 1997. But, these outbursts of 'people's will' get lost in a consumerist economy, which provide little venues for broader economic participation. It is the 'Schumpeterian innovator' that can promote growth in an economy and the 'citizen's will' learns to transform itself into effective demand. Thus, one of main challenges for ensuring a functional political democracy in Iran is to transform the economic space to allow greater participation and skill generation. This is only possible if the government takes bold initiative to streamline the subsidy and eliminate the inefficient and distorting ones. The government has to generate larger economic opportunities through diversification to redress the issues of inequalities rather than rely on subsidy.

CONCLUSION

The impediments to democracy in the Gulf emanate from the erosion of economic space and the existing inequalities in these economies, which inhibit the generation of creative skills and self-reliance. An egalitarian society facilitates larger economic participation and the flourishing of economic democracy. It is due to the lack of economic democracy that political democracy has failed to take firm roots in the rentier economies. The inadequate expansion of economic space in Iran and the existing inequalities due to mismanagement of oil rent have inhibited the Iranian society to consolidate its century old democratic heritage. Huge amount of oil rent have been given in the form of subsidies. Though subsidy to merit goods ensured citizen's accessibility to essential needs of development but those to luxury goods hampered their capabilities to sustain themselves in the long run by depriving them of growth and gainful employment. The huge subsidy in Iran has restricted growth, fuelled inflation and increased disparities. Besides, it has contributed to the widening of disparities.

But the elements of democracy remain vibrant in the society and are making increasing demand for functional democracy. These outbursts of 'people's will' get lost in a consumerist economy, which provide little venues for broader economic participation. Thus, one of main challenges for ensuring a functional political democracy in Iran is to transform the economic space to allow greater participation and skill generation. The government has to generate larger economic opportunities through diversification to redress the issues of inequalities and poverty rather than rely on subsidy.

NOTES

1. Kenneth J. Arrow, (1962). "The Economic Implications of Learning by Doing." *Review of Economic Studies* 29: 155-173.
2. Ali Gheissani and others (2006). *Democracy in Iran: History and the Quest for Liberty*, Oxford Press.
3. Charles Kurzman, (2004). *the Unthinkable Revolution,* Harvard University Press.
4. Alavi Nasrin (2005). *We are Iran,* Soft Skull press.
5. Daron Acemoglu and James A. Robinson (2006). *Economic Origins of Dictatorship and Democracy: Economic and Political Origins,* Cambridge Univ. Press.

6. Statistical Research Center (2002). *Poverty Index Measurement in Iran 1984-2000*, Tehran.
7. Representative barrel of petroleum product has the share of different petroleum products in the same proportion as that in domestic consumption.
8. F. Birol (1995). "The Economic Impact of Subsidy Phase Out in Oil Exporting Developing Countries: A Case Study of Algeria, Iran and Nigeria, *Energy Policy*, 23(3), p. 213.
9. The prices of petroleum products increase with the price of crude oil but do not fall proportionately when the latter falls. Thus, the refiner's margin increases, when the price of crude oil falls.
10. Opportunity cost is the next best use of the resource.
11. A.R. Karbassi and M.A. Shafizadeh (2005). "Energy Efficiency Indicators in Developed and Developing Countries", *Iranian Journal of Energy* Vol. 23, p. 22.
12. Ministry of Energy of Iran (2004). *Energy Balance of Islamic Republic of Iran* {online} URL:http://www.iranenergy.org.ir/english/Statistical%20Info/bxlalance.
13. M.A. Abduli and E. Mahin Abdollahzadeh (2007). "Sustainability of Energy Production and Use in Iran", *Energy Policy* 35(10):5177.
14. SESRTCIC (2007). Agriculture: Information Series of OIC Countries 15, Ankara.
15. Alavirad Abbas and Sanhitha (2005). "The Impact of the Budget Deficits on Inflation in the Islamic Republic of Iran", *OPEC Review*, 3(1):39.
16. Alavirad Abbas (2003). "The Effect of Inflation on Government Revenues and Expenditure: The Case of Islamic Republic of Iran', *OPEC Review*, 12(4):339.
17. A.R. Jalali-Naini and M. Mir-Hoseini (1997). "Review of Trend of Inflation Rate and Monetary policies". Institute for Research in Planning and Development, Tehran.
18. World Bank (2003). "Energy and Health for the poor", *Indoor Air Pollution Newsletter* Energy Sector Management Assistance Programme (ESMAP).
19. Jesper and Tarr David (2002). *Trade, Foreign Exchange, and Energy Policies in the Islamic Republic of Iran: Reform Agenda, Economic Implications, and Impact on the Poor*, World Bank.

14

Democratizing Iraq: Parliamentary Election January 2005

Angela Gangmei

INTRODUCTION

Democratization of the state that has collapsed or been toppled through violent conflict is an intrinsically difficult and protracted process that requires a huge commitment from both Iraqis and international actors. As in Iraq, a war that lacked broad international sympathy and support created a host of post-war problems, and tended to weaken the international consensus behind democracy promotion as an endeavour. While US constructed Coalition Provisional Authority (CPA) with the military and administrative participation of many countries, the occupation was in its design and structure overwhelmingly American. Also what the Washington leadership ignored to the great misfortune of both Iraqis and the United States was that the US needed to prepare in advance for a major commitment with adequate resources.

From the day Baghdad fell on 9 April 2003, it was clear that the US didn't have enough troops on the ground. Not only did the US leadership fail from the beginning to deploy sufficient military resources to secure the country, to deter and face down potential spoilers, and to seal the borders to prevent Al Qaeda and other foreign jihadists from pouring in from neighbouring countries—it also didn't have in place enough resources for the civilian component of post-invasion phase, including the capability to move civilians about the country while adequately protecting them. These failures led to a situation in which the US could not effectively implement either the economic reconstruction plans or the political and civic reconstruction plans. Moreover if a country moves from a political vacuum very rapidly to election for the sake of conducting the election, it does not have a level playing field. In Iraq it resulted in an overwhelming advantage for the recently surfaced Islamist movements and parties, whose democratic credentials or commitments were at best ambiguous and at worst entirely absent.

The occupation forces agreed to the holding of election on 30 January 2005 in an attempt to create an authority that would have enough legitimacy to suppress the Iraqi and insurgent resistance and to legitimize their presence internationally. The insurgents recognized the threat and pledged a bitter war of violence to undermine them. Despite continuing violence and resistance, Interim Prime Minister Ayad Allawi insisted that elections had to proceed for it was the key to defeating the insurgency. The main moderate Sunni Muslim party withdrew from the election, citing violence as inhibiting a fair vote. The party headquarter of Allawi and several polling stations were bombed. Despite these attacks, the election began, with Iraqis living abroad being the first to cast ballots in the country's first free election in five decades. Iraq thus went into election in January 2005 facing not only a virulent Sunni-based insurgency, but also increasingly muscular and ambitious Shiite militias on the streets as well. Question arises as to why there was need to create legitimate authority? Why were the Iraqis resisting their liberators? And why did the coalition occupation want to be seen as legitimate to the international community? Does it mean that Iraqis were against the occupation and its collaborators? If so, what were the reasons for their resentment forcing them to resort to violent means?

The paper would examine how different scholars conceptualised the evolution of the notion of democracy in West Asia and particularly in Iraq, and would focus on how election became the necessity and the goal of democracy promotion in Iraq. Also it will look in to the ways and means adopted to attain the desired ends of electoral politics. It would further examine how election was an attempt to create an authority that had enough legitimacy to resist the Iraqis resistance. Another aspect of study which needs attention would be the focus on the participation level of various ethnic groups in the election and their apprehensions, demands and interests. Moreover the study would explain how the elections gave flight to their aspirations and wish to sustain their regional interest at the cost of national identity and how far their interests were met. And the pattern how Iraqis voted, the outcome of the elections, the emergence of political trend that followed and the repercussions of the changed political order would also be studied. Last but not the least the election would be scrutinized in its spatial-temporal background.

CONCEPTUALISING THE EVOLUTION OF THE NOTION OF DEMOCRACY IN WEST ASIA

The US's notion and mission of democracy led to the overthrow of Saddam Hussein as he had become the threat to their security and to their regional interests. Different scholars conceptualised the evolution of the notion of democracy in West Asia and Iraq in particular. By mid 2003, only one justification for the Iraq War remained with the US administration and it was its claim that the United States could bring democracy to Iraq and that Iraq then would become a model, and perhaps even a base, for the spread of democracy to other countries in West Asia, particularly Syria, Iran, and Saudi Arabia.[1]

The Bush administration's democratization policy was the product of a grand coalition of two of the contemporary American major ideological groupings: the neo-liberals and the neo-conservatives. The central interest of the *neo-liberals* is America's role in the global economy and society. They wanted to establish a global order characterized by liberal democracies, free markets, open societies, and the 'democratic peace.' The neo-liberals are self-consciously and self-confidently carrying on the Wilsonian tradition of 'making the world safe for democracy'. And the *neo-conservatives'* central interest was America's role in global security. They wanted to eliminate threats to the security of America and its allies, especially Israel. They were also carrying Wilsonian tradition of making the world safe for democracy, with emphasis on "safe". The neoliberals and neoconservatives each had a special interest in West Asia, lying between democratic Europe and democratizing East Asia, as the next great arena for democratization. (They also knew that stable oil exports from the Gulf were crucial for smooth functioning of the global economy.) The conservatives saw rogue states in West Asia if they became armed with WMD and allied with Islamic terrorists, as the greatest threat to US (and Israel) security. Both therefore saw the overthrow of Saddam Hussein's regime which ruled in Iraq that might acquire WMD, which was rich in oil reserves, and whose relatively well educated population seem ready for democratization to be a fulfilment of their own central interest in the region.[2]

The primary focus of the neo-conservative discourse was West Asia as a potential threat to US hegemony and military power. Pressure to remove Saddam Hussein from power and undermine the regime in Iran were the enduring themes of the neo-conservatives' focus on the West Asia.[3] The Bush doctrine espoused a strong and proactive neo-conservative focus on the aggressive use of US power, including military power, to spread liberal democracy to make the world safe for the United States, with particular emphasis on West Asia and the removal of its 'rogue' regimes.[4]

US foreign policy had always contained a powerful idealist element, and promoting democracy abroad had been one of its goals, in one way or another since the time of Woodrow Wilson and gained particular salience in the Cold War context under Ronald Reagan. It was then re-emphasized in the euphoria of the Post-Cold War period under Bill Clinton. But after 11 September 2001 the US administration focused on promoting democracy in West Asia especially, and with unprecedented forcefulness. There were both ideological and practical reasons for this. Democracy was a key principle in the neo-conservative world-view which had come to dominate the Bush administration of 2000 to 2005; and the policy consensus in the Bush administration had been that fostering democracy in West Asia would drain the pool from which terrorist Organizations drew recruits in their "global struggle" against the US. It would also contribute to the peaceful resolution of disputes in the region because 'democracies do not go to war with one another'.[5] Thus the concept of democracy and democratization came into being in US's agenda towards Iraq.

Iraqis increasingly viewed the post-Baathist occupation of their country not as vehicle for democratization and progressive change, but as a mechanism for the domination of Iraq by United States and its allies. For many Iraqis, "democracy" had become a code word for using Iraq to remake West Asia in the United States image. They feared that through this "domino democracy,"[6] the United States was actually seeking to enhance its strategic interests in West Asia: that it was using this pretext to put pressure on neighbours such as Syria and Iran, to enhance Israel's power in the region, and to control Iraq's oil.[7]

At a popular level in West Asia and elsewhere democratization had also assumed negative connotations through its association with the regional policies of the Bush Administration. This was not because the people of the region think democracy was a bad thing, but because they saw the Bush Administration's promotion of it as a cover for more nefarious aims.[8]

Democracy promotion thus became an integral part of an interventionist US foreign policy in the Arab West Asia, epitomized in the invasion and occupation of Iraq. It was argued by the US administration that democratic Iraq would be a natural American ally and that its example would encourage political reform in the Arab world as a whole. Whatever the American motive in effecting the regime change in Iraq and in spite of the ease with which it was accomplished the American actions in Iraq from the very beginning lacked legitimacy and credibility. The failure to find any WMD in Iraq after the war and the fact that the National Commission that enquired into the September 2001 terrorist attacks in the US absolved Iraq of any involvement in the same completely undermined the American credibility. Then US contended that though no WMDs (Weapons of Mass Destructions) were found in Iraq, the overthrow of Saddam's regime freed Iraqis from tyranny and brought them democracy and human rights.

POLITICAL LEGITIMACY OF THE OCCUPYING FORCE

The removal of Saddam Hussein proved to be the beginning of a long and highly uncertain process of occupation and state-building. For the Bush administration, a combination of ideological vigour, insufficient planning and misperception about Iraqi society meant that the aftermath of war had been far more troublesome than regime change itself. The lawlessness and looting that greeted the seizure of Baghdad on 9 April, 2003 had evolved into an organized, self-sustaining and politically motivated insurgency. Against this background, the failure of US attempts to replace Saddam's regime with stable, sustainable and hopefully liberated government had major consequences far beyond Iraq, the region or the US itself.[9]

The task of the occupation was the building of the new political order that would be stable and legitimate yet also in broad agreement with US foreign policy aims. The US wanted to create a space within which new, pro-US elite could be nurtured. However, this policy objective clashed with the needs and demands of the Iraqi population. Legitimising a new government both internationally and even more importantly domestically needed the involvement of Iraqi governing elite that were either popularly elected or could at least mobilize a significant section of Iraqi popular opinion to support its rule.[10]

The US—led occupation, however, moved swiftly to implement its pre-determined concept of removing all traces of the Baathist regime in order to have a clean slate on which to start building the new 'free and democratic' Iraq. Instead of identifying and strengthening capable and legitimate elements of the existing state, it moved to dismantle it by removing key institutional and human resources. It was important to recognize that legitimacy could not be based solely on re-establishing security and authority, but should have been earned through advocating reconstruction policies that were inclusive and accountable. Rather than demilitarizing Iraqi society and promoting civil governance, the disbanding of the army promoted the rule of the gun, thereby restricting not enhancing the participation of civilians in public life.[11]

L. Paul Bremer arrived in Iraq on May 12, 2003, as President Bush's new presidential envoy and head of Coalition Provisional Authority. Four days after Bremer arrived in Iraq he issued Coalition Provisional Authority Order Number 1: DeBaathification of Iraq. It eliminated as many as 85,000 members of the Baath Party. This was because implementation of the policy was handed over to Iraqi politicians who had a long list of grievances against the old regime.[12] Bremer ordered Coalition Provisional Authority Order Number 2 on May 23, 2003, which officially eliminated Iraq's security apparatus.[13] The DeBaathification order implemented a declaration "of eliminating the party structures and removing its leadership from positions of authority and responsibility in Iraqi society." It intended to ensure that the new representative government of Iraq was not threatened by Baathists returning to power.[14]

IRAQI GOVERNING COUNCIL (IGC) AND THE SIGNIFICANCE OF THE EXILES

The initial political planning process focused heavily on Iraqi exiles. From the beginning the coalition authority wanted to anoint Ahmed Chalabi, an exile as Iraq's future leader. In fact, the first American Viceroy, Jay Garner, later claimed that it was his own alleged support for free elections (and opposition to fast privatization) that led to his being replaced after one month. Rather than teaching democracy by example Bremer came to be known for his "imperious and authoritarian ways". His "unwillingness to handover power to Iraqis further fuelled resentment" while it was hard to imagine that the pretence of legitimization through democratic procedures would have been avoided, it seemed that the original plan for Iraq was to install Ahmed Chalabi in power.[15]

Iraq was formally occupied for a year without a concrete timeline for the withdrawal of foreign troops or the holding of elections. The decision on the timing of elections, drafting of the constitution, and transfer of power to the Iraqis was not taken until a year after the fall of the Saddam Hussein regime. A US—led CPA and a US Administrator, Paul Bremer, ruled the country from May 2003 until June 2004. Following a UN recommendation, a 25 member IGC[16] (Iraqi Governing Council) with no significant powers and dominated by exiles was appointed by Bremer in mid-July 2003. Originally, the US administration envisaged that the CPA would stay in place until a permanent constitution was drafted and a government elected. However, this plan underestimated the importance of Iraqi leadership in steering the country's transition as well as of negotiation and consensus building among Iraqis.[17]

IGC held their first meeting on 13, July 2003; their assigned tasks under the American supervision were to prepare budget and approve a constitution.[18] From the beginning Bremer stated that it would be Iraqis who were to write the constitution, but he also emphasized some of the principles that a constitution should embody. But then the CPA was forced to adopt a lower profile in the constitutional process. On 30 June 2003 the senior spiritual Shia leader, Grand Ayatollah Ali al-Husseini al-Sistani, issued a religious edict (a fatwa) demanding that the drafters of the constitution be elected. Bremer wanted to push forward with his plans, but members of the IGC were afraid of falling out with the Grand Ayatollah and refused to support Bremer's plan.[19]

Transitional politics was led by the USA and a number of Iraqi political parties, many of them dominated by exiles. The US—appointed IGC had merely an advisory role since the head of the CPA, Paul Bremer, could veto any of its decisions. This inevitably undermined the body's public legitimacy as well as its ability to agree on a transitional framework. Furthermore, only allies and supporters of the US occupation were allowed in the IGC. Importantly, this narrow elite group was not only maintained without efforts to create a more representative and legitimate body, but also drafted the TAL[20] (Transitional Administrative Law) behind closed doors and with minimal, if any, consultations with relevant actors who were not in the IGC.[21]

The CPA seemed to be unwilling to involve seriously either the Iraqi people or international community. They lived in virtual isolation, unable to communicate effectively with the Iraqi population. Also De-Baathification heightened suspicion and anger in Iraq and part of the Moslem world where many viewed CPA as a part of Washington's agenda to reshape the region. The IGC was considered as an attempt by the US to develop an interim authority that would have legitimacy in Iraq and abroad and also would have appeased the population and deflected criticism of the occupying forces. It also lacked credibility in the eyes of many Iraqis and much of the outside world. Their members were chosen so as to mirror Iraq's sectarian and ethnic makeup. The occupying power granted UN only an advisory and wholly subordinate role.[22]

THE TRANSITIONAL GOVERNANCE

On 15 November 2003, the Americans proposed transferring sovereignty on 30 June 2004 to a government selected indirectly via a series of regional caucuses. This government would rule under a TAL until a constitutional assembly elected in March 2005 completed its work. Al-Sistani rejected this approach as undemocratic; his rejection was congruent with Iraqi suspicion that such a system would be rigged by the occupying powers and GC (Governing Council) they had created. Al-Sistani opposed the GC from the beginning, declining even to recommend names for the GC in June 2003. He also issued a religious decree, a *fatwa*, which called for elections because "there is no guarantee that the (US—backed) council would create a constitution conforming to the greater interests of the Iraqi people."[23]

The American plan to rely on a network of "caucuses" was also revealing of their resistance to allowing democracy. It was the adamant opposition of Ayatollah Ali al-Sistani in 2004 that resulted in dropping of this plan to choose representatives and instead, to holding elections. Such caucuses were designed to constitute a "well-choreographed process" whereby candidates would be chosen by the "hand-picked" Iraqi Governing Council or by local officials collaborating with the occupiers, that was, essentially a process of indirect election by the occupation authority. These caucuses, in turn, would select a number of delegates proportionate to the province's share of national population to a newly formed interim national assembly. This was a undemocratic proposal to create a government "based on co-optation and potentially clientelism meant to be closed meeting of notables, rather then open ones of citizens," representing a rejection of democratic procedures "just because of one side would lose" if they occurred, which, "was certainly the wrong way to begin a democracy".[24]

Faced with increasing pressure from the UN Security Council for sovereign power to be delegated to an Iraqi governing body, the increasing alienation of the Iraqi population from the CPA and a rising tide of political violence, the more cautious and incremented constructions of Iraq's administration and governing institutions was abandoned. The Bush administration set 30 June 2004 as the deadline for transferring sovereignty to Iraq. Sistani, painfully aware of Iraq's history and the tendency of 'temporary' unelected government to transform themselves into permanent dictatorships, demanded that any future sovereign government be directly elected. Sistani's ability to influence events and the highly mobilized nature of the Iraqi polity were highlighted by the 100,000 people who demonstrated in Baghdad in January 2004 to convince the CPA that their objections could not be ignored.[25]

The appointment in June 2004 of the IIG (Iraqi Interim Government), with the blessing of the UN, gave some managerial responsibilities to the Iraqis, but did not change the central premise of the political process, namely that the transition to elections and constitutional drafting was to be managed by the USA and a select political grouping. The IGC then more or less reproduced itself in the IIG. Significantly, the CPA did not initiate or encourage a process of broad consultation and negotiation aimed at reaching agreement on the interim government and then on the transitional framework. Rather than an Iraqi consultative process leading to the appointment of the IIG, the UN was invited to give its approval.[26]

The UNSC (United Nations Security Council) Resolution 1546 stated that coalition forces were there at the consent of the IIG. The handover arrangement was endorsed through UN Security Council Resolution (SCR) 1546 of 8 June 2004. It declared that the occupation would be over and Iraq would regain 'full sovereignty' by 30 June. The handover actually took place two days early and with no prior announcement, to avoid insurgents' attack. Bremer immediately left the country and the CPA was dissolved. SCR (Security Council Resolution) 1546 approved the presence of Coalition forces and their use of 'all necessary measures' for security and stability, but stated that they were there only with the consent of the Iraqi government and should coordinate with it. However, Washington made it clear that the previous structure of the multinational force, with a US military commander taking the primary decision-making role in the security sphere, would remain in place.[27]

THE MOTIVATION OF THE INSURGENCY AND THE RESISTANCE

There were several distinct motivations for the insurgents. Some were intangible, such as the traditional tribal reluctance to submit to any kind of authority—Saddam often had trouble with Sunni Arab tribes—and the conservative Islamist and nationalist reluctance to submit to foreign infidels. Others were material grievances that the coalition could have addressed. These included not only the lack of security and economic opportunities, but also American missteps and alleged boorish behaviour; trampling on tribal honour and customs when searching private homes and individuals, and withholding information about and access to detainees for months.[28]

The disbanding of the Baath party and the army made several hundred thousands of Iraqis unemployed—a significant part of the country's professional middle class. The decrees were compounded by Bremer's decision not to pay their pensions. Unrewarded and humiliated, these men resented the 'guilt by association' which implied that every army officer or party member was implicated in repression, torture, or murder. Their economic plight and their alienation from the Americans were bound to seep through the networks of the extended family and the tribe, into the attitudes of millions of other Iraqis who were never Baathists or army officers themselves. It did not, of course, follow that they would become insurgents or even take part in funding or organizing insurgents. But it might well mean that they supported the insurgent efforts to end the occupation and would only work with the Americans with extreme reluctance.[29]

The trauma of war and a rapid decline in living standards and social structure led to strengthening of a militant Iraqi nationalism. The state-inspired credo of Arab nationalism had historically found support among a population that thought that Iraq was unjustly treated by the west and international system. The 12 years of suffering under sanctions fuelled the rise of a powerful nationalism, born of a stubborn pride that Iraq had managed to survive despite everything that occurred. The situation could not but exacerbate such perceptions. The failure of Baghdad's liberated population to offer the ecstatic welcome to US troops as predicted in Washington was indicative of the power of nationalism in Iraq.[30]

Iraqi leaders (both former exiles and internals) were warning of potential resistance if an interim government was not established soon. "This gave fuel to all those extremists who said the US had secret agenda to occupy Iraq and exploit its oil resources", one Iraqi warned. Shiite religious leaders loyal to militant young cleric Muqtada al-Sadr brought out some ten thousand protesters on the street of Baghdad on May 19. Chanting "no for foreign administration" and "yes, yes to Islam," the protesters called on the US to surrender power to an elected government and criticized Americans for favouring exiles groups (particularly Chalabi).[31]

The offensives against Fallujah and the Mahdi Army made the Coalition into a common enemy for many Sunnis and Shi'a. Shi'a involved in the Mahdi uprising found common cause wit the insurgents fighting against the Coalition in the Sunni Triangle. Shi'a empathized with images of wounded women and children in Fallujah. Shi'a mosques called people to help the Sunnis in Fallujah. Similarly, certain Sunni neighbourhoods in Sadr City actively assisted the Mahdi Army. Graffiti in one Sunni neighbourhood of Baghdad signified the moment of common cause: "Long live the resistance in Fallujah"; and "Long live the resistance." The United States faced international political pressure as well, although the bulk of it appears to have transpired after the unilateral cease-fire. Lakhdar Brahimi, UN special representative to Iraq, disapproved of the offensive and threatened to quit his mission to construct a plan for the selection of an interim government.[32]

THE COMMENCEMENT OF THE ELECTION

The delay of elections was not acceptable to the Iraqis as they were under foreign rule not under UN. At each stage the occupying authorities, the Coalition Provisional Authority, would supervise the process, giving them the right to weed out candidates they did not like. If the country were under an impartial UN administration or trusteeship, delay might have been acceptable. As long as the election delay was being imposed by foreign occupiers with no announced limit to their own term in the country, it was bound to arouse suspicion.[33]

In the run-up to the election, Americans and Iraqi planners put into operation a programme to enhance security for the day of the election itself. The numerous measures included border closures, tight curfews and the banning of private vehicles from roads. US military forces conducted a series of major convoys operations prior to election to ensure that in the election period itself there would be little need for the movement of vulnerable convoys.[34]

IRAQI POLITICAL PARTICIPATION

The countdown to the elections started on 1 November 2004, with voter registration. The electoral roll was based on existing information collected for the ration distribution system. An audit of this data indicated that it was up to 83 per cent accurate. From the beginning of November 2004, the heads of all households in Iraq were asked to confirm the names of those in their families old enough to vote. If the rationing information proved to be incorrect, they were directed to one of the 545 electoral registration centres across the county to update the register of voters. The Independent Electoral Commission of Iraq employed 6,000 local staff to run the registration centres, and managed to open all but 90 of them. The Transitional Administrative law set stringent standards of eligibility. Candidates had to have a 'good reputation', had no criminal convictions 'involving moral turpitude' and must not have been senior members of the Baath Party or the old regime's secret services. Candidates had to sign a declaration certifying that they met these terms, and collect 500 signatures in support of their application. By the election, a total of 7,785 candidates had registered to take part, loosely organized in 111 parties and coalitions.[35]

Iraqis were also receiving contradictory messages on whether or not to vote. Ayatollah Muhammad al-Ya'qubi, an influential anti-occupation cleric, had said that the voting was Islamic obligation like fasting or Zakat. Even representatives of radical Shiite preacher Muqtada al-Sadr, who was yet to participate in the elections, had encouraged their congregations to sign up their names to the voters' lists. Sunni Arab voters were receiving mixed messages. The influential Muslim Scholars' Board had urged a boycott. The Islamic Iraqi Party, which worked with the interim government while distancing itself from its policies, had also expressed reservations about election under occupation, but it said that it would participate none the less to avoid Sunnis being marginalized. Many parties were also reportedly reluctant to test their popularity in a contested election, preferring to maintain a presence in government through backroom deals then to risk all in an open vote. Talks were going on the ethnic/sectarian lines. The two Kurdish parties had thrashed out the bases of an arrangement to present their unified list, while representatives of Ayatollah Sistani were reportedly trying to deal between the two main Shiite parties, al Dawa and SCIRI, to merge their lists. Any Sadrist political activity, independent or in coalition with other groups, was hampered by the movement's failure to put forward a political manifesto, although it had promised to do so.[36]

The head of the electoral mission in Iraq and the director of the UN global programme of electoral assistance, Carina Perelli, was finally able to broker an agreement for the electoral modalities for Iraq. The agreement established a framework and an electoral commission to oversee the up coming election. Perelli and the UN electoral commission established that the best electoral system for the National Assembly that could be implemented under the current circumstances was List Proportional Representation (LPR). "It was determined," Perelli announced "that the best for these elections would be the system of proportional representation, using the whole country as a single national district." Under LPR, parties would be able to run their national lists that may consist up to 275 candidates, but shorter list of 12 candidates could be established. Each candidate would have to gather 500 valid signatures to be placed on the ballot and may require a 26,000 threshold vote to win a seat in the National Assembly. Votes could be counted in a ranked order as the highest ranked candidates win. Independent candidates might establish individual lists.[37] One of the shortfalls of LPR in Iraq, as proposed by the UN, was the long party candidate lists that added to voters' confusion and frustrations. Each candidate had to win approximately 26,000-27,000 votes in order to win a seat in the National Assembly.[38]

The major actors of the electoral game were grouped along two dimensions. The first dimension was the subcultural group the party was identified with: Kurds, Shia Arabs, Sunni Arabs, Turkomen, or Christian: this was an easy determination. The second dimension was labelled informally as "moderate" or "liberal/secular" and "other". There was gradation of support for democratic principles among the parties, and few Iraqis wanted to be called "secular" in the western sense. Furthermore the parties labelled as "other" did not necessarily have much in common politically. Explicitly religious parties were assigned to this group on the ground that they were more likely to push for Islamic law that would seem counter to democratic notions of equal rights, though Shia Arab and Sunni Arab religious parties supported very different notions of Islamic law. The "other" group also included parties associated with the aspects of insurgency, and Chalabi's INC, who after having his party offices raided in 2004 had moved close to Moqtada Al-Sadr and Iran.[39]

In January major Sunni parties and organizations declared they would boycott the elections. Muqtada al-Sadr, the militant Shi'i Cleric, head of the Mahdi army, said that his organization was also thinking of boycotting the elections. Even Adnan Pachachi, the leader of a Sunni secular party and a former U.S. favourite to head the IIG instead of Iyad Allawi, wrote a long piece in the *Washington Post* giving many reasons as to why the elections should be postponed in order that the Sunni regions of the country be given more time to consider participating in the elections. Mas'ud Barzani, the leader of the KDP, also said the elections should be postponed to allow additional time for negotiations with the Sunnis, although he did say that the Kurds would participate in the elections. On 30 January, the Kurds were also to elect a 111 member Kurdish Parliament with voters limited to the provinces of Dohuq, Arbil, and Sulaymaniya. Kurds outside of this area, such as Kirkuk, were not eligible to vote.[40]

POLITICAL ENVIRONMENT DURING ELECTION

The elections took place under conditions of extreme insecurity and political turmoil that made it all but impossible for every eligible voter to freely make choice, but the indications were that something like 8 millions voters, or 60 per cent of those eligible, turned out. In human rights terms, voters in many areas faced a quandary: they had to risk their lives to participate in the elections or forgo the historic chance to cast their ballot. It was therefore all the more credible that so many voted. But it was hard to say that the elections were free and fair. An election is free when it reflects the full expression of the political will of the people concerned. Freedom in this sense involves the ability to participate in the political process without intimidation, coercion, discrimination, or the abridgement of the rights to associate with others, to assemble, or to receive or impart information. The 'fairness' of an election refers to the right to vote on the basis of equality, non-discrimination, and universality. No portion of the electorates should be arbitrarily disqualified, or have their votes given extra weight.[41]

The security situation in Iraq had overshadowed every aspect of the election. The violence and threat of attacks by insurgent groups had severely restricted Iraqi citizens' right to assemble, association, movement, and expression. Significant parts of electorate were unable to participate because of violence and intimidation. Given that many political entities could not campaign freely and many voters were afraid or unable to register or vote, these elections did not measure up to the usual international criteria.[42] Sixty million ballot sheets were flown to Iraq days before the election for an estimated 15 million eligible voters. Some 7500 candidates were scattered among 257 lists. Twenty-five Iraqi towns and cities boycotted the elections. According to Reuter's news agency, while there were 63000 polling booths throughout Iraq, there were only 33763 Iraqi election monitors.[43]

Despite continuing violence, Interim Prime Minister Allawi insisted that elections had to proceed, as they were the key to defeating the insurgency. On 27 December the main moderate Sunni Muslim party withdrew from the election, citing violence as inhibiting a fair vote. The party headquarter of Allawi and several polling stations were bombed. Despite these attacks, the election began on 28 January, with Iraqis living abroad being the first to cast ballots in the country's first free election in five decades.[44]

Table 14.1: Iraqi Voter Turnout by Province

Province	*Total Vote Turnout*	*% of Eligible Voters*
Anbar	13,753	2
Babil	501,331	71
Baghdad	1,866,021	48
Basra	738,243	72
Dohuk	393,655	89
Dhi Qar	531,211	67
Diyala	204,155	34
Ebril	657,030	84
Karbala	302,641	73
Misan	253,156	59
Muthanna	189,429	61
Najaf	368,338	73
Nineveh	201,477	17
Out-of-Country	263,685	—
Qadisiyya	338,717	69
Salah al-Din	144,598	29
Suleimaniya	743,120	80
Tamim	397,224	70
Wasit	348,482	66
Total	**8,456,266**	**58**

Source: Article—Toensing, Chris (2005), "Iraqi Elections", *Middle East Report*, No. 234, spring, pp. 8-9.[45]

Iraq thus went into election in January 2005 facing not only a virulent Sunni-based insurgency, but also increasingly muscular and ambitious Shiite militias on the streets as well. In the north was the country's most powerful Iraqi armed force, the Kurdish *Peshmerga*. Due to division among various communities in Iraq the electoral area became polarised along ethnic and identity lines. The January 2005 election, for all of its deeply moving characters and successful elements was largely an identity referendum. The two main identity and sectarian blocs (Shiites and Kurds) were the winners in the elections. The losers were the parties representing secular centre, who preferred to take a position of opposition in the parliament. And Sunnis boycotted the election.

The Result of the Elections

The January 2005 election produced two main winners. The first was the United Iraqi Alliance (UIA), an umbrella group of Shia candidates including several other religio-political parties (the Supreme Council for Islamic Revolution in Iraq [SCIRI], the Dawa, the Sadrist trend, Fadila, and a number of independents), which won a slight majority of seats. The second was the Kurdish list consisting of two main Kurdish parties the (KDP {Kurdistan Democratic Party} and PUK {Patriotic Union Kurdistan Party}) and a smattering of others. The main losers were the most secular parties of the centre, notably the Iraqi List, led by Ayad Allawi, a former Baathist opponent of Saddam. In this election the Sunni population was virtually absent, either because Sunnis refused to vote or because they were intimidated.[46]

Election Result, January 2005

Slate/Party	*Seats, Janurary 2005*
United Iraqi Alliance (Shi'ite)	140
Kurdistan Alliance (PUK and KDP)	75
Iraqis List (secular, Allawi)	40
Iraqi Concord Front (Sunni)	—
Dialogue National Iraqi Front(Sunni)	—
Iraqis Party (Yawar, Sunni; was part of Iraqis Lis in Dec. Vote)	5
Iraqi Turkomen Front (Turkoman, Kirkuk based)	3
National Independent and Elites (Jan)/Risalyun (Dec) (pro-Sadr)	3
People's Union (Communist, non-sectarian)	2
Kurdistan IslamicGroup (Islamist, Kurd)	2
Islamic Action (Shi,ite Islamist, Karbala)	2
National Democratic Alliance (secular)	1
Rafidain National List (Assyrian)	1
Liberation and Reconciliation Gathering (Sunni, secular)	1
Ummah Party (secular)	0
Yazidi List (Kurdish)	—

Source: Kenneth, Katzman, "Iraq: Election, Constitution, and Government," CRS Report for Congress, March 30, 2006.[47]

Following the January 2005 elections, the Shiite list and the Kurdistan Alliance formed a coalition. In exchange for making Dawa leader Ibrahim Jaafari prime minister, the Kurdish leader Jalal Ṭalabani became president. The coalition divided up the key ministries with the Shiite list taking interior, oil, and finance and the Kurds foreign affairs. A Sunni Arab, Sadoun Dulaimi, became defence minister while a Kurd, Babkir Zebari, remained chief of staff of the Iraqi Army and another Kurd, Bruska Noori Shaways, served as the ministry's top civil servant. Ahmad Chalabi and the former speaker of the Kurdistan Parliament, Rowsch Shaways, became Iraq's two deputy prime ministers. SCIRI's Adel Abdul Mehdi became the Shiite vice president and former President Ghazi al-Yawar (who refused to vacate the presidential residence) became the Sunni vice president. A Sunni Arab from California, Hajim al-Hassani, was elected speaker of the National Assembly.[48]

The outcome of the election, the most significant political trend in Iraq had been the shift form a relatively unified country with a nationalist orientation (under the Baathists) to an emerging political dynamic based on ethnic and sectarian identity. An overall Iraqi identity, which should form the basis for the newly constructed state, was not absent, but it was weak and rapidly diminishing.[49] Elections and installation of the rulers under foreign military occupation was bound to have dangerous implications for the creation of democratic institutions and a tolerant society. Imposition of the elections on the pretext of democracy had not only weakened the opposition forces but also structured the system of 'client states' to serve the interest of 'strong'.[50]

CONCLUSION

30 January 2005 election was an instrument organized by the coalition occupation and some political Organizations and individuals with vested interest to attain their desired ends. The Coalition wanted to create an authority that had enough legitimacy to resist the insurgents' resistance against the occupation. Also some exiles and some worried leaders like Ayatollah Ali Sistani, wanted election to take place as soon as possible so that the Shiite majority would prevail. The exiles had their own share of spoils to capture the power before the Iraqis fully understood "democracy" and its values, electoral process and the candidates running for the election. It was clear that the aim of the 30 January 2005 election was to form a government that would free US—led occupation from the criticism of the domestic and international community to cover up the resistance against the occupation by putting up a client regime through an election.

There were varied reasons for the resistance against the coalition forces; the most important was the way America and its allies handled the reconstruction of the post-Saddam Iraq. The reconstruction programmes and policies were more of destructive nature than of reconstruction as it disbanded the Iraqi military which could have helped to restore law and order and deal with the insurgents. Some of the disbanded army personnel felt humiliated and took to armed resistance against the occupation. 30 January 2005 election took place against the backdrop of the rising civil and insurgent resistance against the occupation. Due to division among various communities in Iraq, the electoral area became polarised along ethnic and identity lines. The January 2005 election was largely an identity referendum. It was clear that the steps taken by the US in Democratizing conflict ridden Iraq had not only been inadequate but also revealed the lack of seriousness on US's part in conducting the election and the method followed in the same. Though it formed institutions of democracy, it failed to bring true spirit of democracy as it divided the Iraqi society on the ethnic and sectarian lines.

NOTES

1. Kurth, James (2005), "Ignoring History: US Democratization in the Muslim World", *Orbis: A journal of World Affairs,* spring, Vol. 49, No. 2, p. 305.
2. *Ibid.*, p. 311.
3. Ritchie, Nick and Roger, Paul (2007), *The Political Road to War with Iraq: Bush, 9/11 and the Drive to overthrow Saddam*, Routledge, London, p. 146.
4. *Ibid.*, p. 156.
5. Dalacoura, Katerina, 'US Democracy promotion in the Arab Middle East since 11 September 2001: A critique', *International Affairs,* October 2005, Vol. 81, no. 5, p. 963.
6. Eric Davis's concept of domino democracy means that the invasion of Iraq constituted the first step in larger and audacious process of reshaping the political and economic terrain of West Asia. It envisioned the transformation of Iraq into a democratic polity with open market and a technocratically and non-ideologically oriented government a model to West Asia states, particularly Iraq's neighbours.
7. Davis, Eric, 'History matters: Past as Prologue in Building Democracy in Iraq', *Orbis: A Journal of World Affairs*, spring 2005, Vol. 49, No. 2, p. 240.
8. Heazle, Michael and Islam, Iyanatul (ed) (2006), *Beyond the Iraq War: The Promises, Pitfalls, and Perils of External Interventionalism*, UK, p. 59.
9. Dodge, Toby (2005), *Iraq's Future: The After Math of Regime Change*, Routledge, New York, p. 25.
10. Fawn, Rick and Hinnebusch, Raymond (2007) *The Iraq War: Causes and Consequences*, Lynne Rienner Publishers, Inc., p. 220-1.
11. Barakat, Sultan (2005), "Post-Saddam Iraq: Deconstructing a Regime, Reconstructing a Nation", *Third World Quarterly*, Vol. 26, No. 4/5, pp. 579.

12. Cordesman, Anthony H (2008), *Iraq's Insurgency and the road to Civil Conflict* Westport, Connecticut, London 2008, p. 47.
13. Barakat, no. 11, p. 49.
14. Bremer, L. Paul and McConnell, Malcolm, *My Year in Iraq: The Struggle to Build a Future of Hope*, New York, 2006. p. 39.
15. Glenn E. Perry (2006), 'Imperial democratization: Rhetoric and Reality', *Arab Studies Quarterly*, Vol. 28, No. 3&4, Summer/Fall, pp. 69-70.
16. The Iraqi Governing Council (IGC) was a 25-member group of Iraqi leaders approved by L. Paul Bremer in July 2003 and charged with transitioning the country to democracy.
17. Papagianni, Katia (2005), "Transitional Politics in Afghanistan and Iraq: Inclusion, Consultation, and Public Participation", *Development in Practice*, Vol. 15, No. 6, Nov, p. 750.
18. Polk, William R. (2005), *Understanding Iraq: A Whistlestop Tour from Ancient Babylon to occupied Baghdad,* I.B. Tauris, London, p. 180
19. Klitgaard, Peter Kurrild (2004), "Blood, Baath and beyond: The Constitutional Dilemma of Iraq", *Public Choice*, Vol. 119, No. 1/2, Apr, p. 14.
20. TAL is the formal name for the Iraqi interim constitution under the Nov.15 agreement and signed on March 8, 2004.
21. Diamond, Larry (2004), 'What Went Wrong in Iraq', *Foreign Affairs*, September/ October, vol. 83, no. 5, p.
22. Middle East Report No. 11 (2003), "War in Iraq: Political Challenges after the Conflict", *International Crisis Group,* 25 March, Amman/Brussels.
23. Mowle, Thomas S (2007) (ed.) *Hope is Not a Plan: The war in Iraq from Inside the Green Zone*, Westport, Connecticut, London, p. 89.
24. Perry, n. 15, pp. 69-70.
25. Dodge, Toby (2005), 'Iraqi Transitions: from regime change to state collapse', *Third World Quarterly*, vol. 26, no. 4-5, pp. 715-6.
26. Papagianni, n.17, p. 753.
27. Herring, Eric and Rangwala, Glen (2006), *Iraq in Fragments: The Occupation and its Legacy*, London, p. 32.
28. Hashim, Ahmed (2005), "Iraq from Insurgency to Civil War", *Current History*, January, pp. 12 & 13.
29. Steele, Jonathan (2008), *Defeat why they lost Iraq,* I.B. Tauris, London and New York, p. 68.
30. Dodge, n. 9, p. 47.
31. Diamond, Larry (2005), *Squandered Victory: The American Occupation and the Bungled Effort to bring democracy to Iraq*, times books, New York, p 37
32. Mahnken, Thomas G. & Keaney, Thomas A. (ed.) (2007), *War in Iraq: Planning and execution*, New York, pp. 174-5.
33. Steele, n. 29, p. 104.
34. Rogers, Paul (2006), *Iraq and the War on terror: Twelve month of insurgency 2004/2005,* I.B. Tauris, London, p. 99.
35. Dodge, n. 9, p. 37.
36. Steve Negus (2004), "Iraq: of insurgency and elections", *Middle East International*, 5 November, p. 14.

37. Salamey, Imad and Pearson Frederic (2005), "The Crisis of Federalism and Electoral Strategies in Iraq", *International Studies Perspectives*, p. 202.
38. *Ibid.*, p. 203.
39. Mowle, N. 23, p. 94.
40. Olson, Robert (2005), *the Goat and the Butcher: nationalism and State Formation in Kurdistan-Iraq since the Iraqi War*, Mazda Publishers, California, p. 186.
41. Harold walker and Sir Terence Clark (2005), *Asian Affairs journal of the Royal society for Asian Affairs*, Vol. 23, no. 2, July, pp. 187-8.
42. *Ibid.*, pp. 187-8.
43. Ismael, Tareq Y., and Ismael, Jacqueline S. (2005), "Whither Iraq? Beyond Saddam, Sanctions and Occupation", *Third World Quarterly*, Vol. 26, no. 4-5, p. 624.
44. Fawn, and Hinnebusch, n.10, p. 16.
45. Toensing, Chris (2005), "Iraqi Elections", *Middle East Report*, No. 234, spring, pp. 8-9.
46. Bouillon E.Markus, Malone M. David and Rowswell Ben (ed.), *Iraq: Preventing a New Generation of Conflict*, New Delhi, 2007, p. 42.
47. Kenneth, Katzman (2006), "Iraq: Election, Constitution, and Government," CRS Report for Congress, March 30, pp. 1-6, http://cpa-iraq.org/goverment/TAL.hmtl
49. Bouillon, Malone and Rowswell, n. 46, p. 42.
50. Khan Arshi, American Style Elections in Iraq, *Mainstream*, February 11-17, 2005. p. 3.

15

Democratic Experiment in Iraqi Kurdistan, 1991-2003

LungthuiYang Riamei

INTRODUCTION

The Kurds are an ancient race who inhabited the contiguous mountain regions that fall under the eastern part of modern Turkey, the northern and eastern part of Iraq and north-western part of Iran for some 3000 years (or longer, as some historians insist), retaining their own language, customs and culture. Following World War I and break-up of the Ottoman Empire, President Woodrow Wilson's support for the principle of national self-determination for the non-Turkish nationalities living under the Ottoman control caused upheaval amongst the Kurdish people. The Versailles Peace Conference of 1919 provided the first forum whereby Kurdish national aspirations were acknowledged by the international community, but this acknowledgement proved to be short lived. Upon the break-up of the Ottoman Empire, an ancient race composed of tribes, tribal confederations and feudal groups with martial traditions was promised for the first time in the long history an independent state in their own mountainous homeland under the Treaty of Sevres, 10 August 1920. But a vigorous nationalist uprising under the Turkish leader Mustafa Kemal Ataturk forced the allies to accept a revised agreement, the Treaty of Lausanne 1923,[1] which omitted all references to an autonomous or independent Kurdish state. The Sevres-Lausanne period presented what might be called a tragic incident in the Kurdish struggle and aspirations. Unimpressed by the Kurds' many bloody uprisings for independence, France and Britain divided up the Ottoman Empire among Turkey, Syria, Iraq and Iran. British imperialism provoked Kurdish nationalist aspirations for an independent Kurdistan. The problem was compounded by the viewpoints of neighbouring states refusing to acknowledge the existence of a contiguous Kurdish geographical entity.

Traditionally Kurdish life was nomadic, revolving around sheep and goat herding throughout the Mesopotamia plains, the highlands of Turkey and Iran. Although the Kurds lived in Kurdistan for centuries, they never had a state of their own nor formed an independent political entity. In the modern times they achieved two short-lived semi-independent entities: the Kingdom of Kurdistan in Iraqi Kurdistan under Sheikh Mahmoud (1922-1924), and the Mahabad Republic under Qazi Mohammed (January-December 1946), which is now Iranian Kurdistan. Throughout their history they have been ruled by outsiders, including the Armenians, the Persians, the Byzantines, and later the Turks, British and Arabs.

Since the end of the First World War when the great powers imposed their ill-suited solutions to the problems of West Asia, the Kurdish people have constantly suffered from various forms of national oppression in each of the newly constituted states. In some cases this oppression was brutal and denied the existence of Kurdish identity, as in Kemalist Turkey[2] while in others it was cunning, suppressed as in Iran. Iraq, on the other hand, has allowed the existence of a Kurdish nationality, allowed a limited use of Kurdish language and provided for at least a nominal degree of autonomy in Kurdish inhabited areas which also included a policy of Arabization involving the mass deportation of Kurds and implantations of Arabs on their lands.

IRAQI KURDISTAN

Kurdistan in Iraq is often referred to as Southern Kurdistan but in fact it occupies a more or less central position in the Kurdish territories. It is the link between what is variously known as Turkish, Northern or Western Kurdistan to the north and north-west, and so-called Eastern or Iranian Kurdistan to the east and south-east, and also borders Kurdish areas of the Syrian Jezireh. This part of Kurdistan is a rich country which extends over a partly wooded region of mountainous terrain curving from the River Zagros in Iranian Kurdistan to the mountains of Turkish Kurdistan. Iraqi Kurdistan is well endowed with a broad spectrum of natural resources, in particular oil and water. However, the control of such resources, whether in terms of dams, oil refineries or mines has rarely been in the hands of the Kurds. The peoples of Kurdistan have never directly benefited from the exploitation of the resources but have only received its benefits indirectly through the Government of Iraq.

The area of northern Iraq where the Kurds predominate is a region of about 83,000 square kilometers to the north of Hamrin Mountain (see Fig. 15.1). The area is roughly the size of Jordan or Austria.[3] Smaller ethno-linguistic communities of Assyrian Chaldeans, Turkomans, Arabs and Armenians are also found in Iraqi Kurdistan. The Turkomans share the same religious belief as the Kurds, but the Christians display a different religion, as well as a different ethnic origin. The Christian community in Iraqi Kurdistan used to be the Armenians but after assimilation with the surrounding people and conversion to Islam, the development of a Kurdish identity in the late nineteenth century and the mass deportation and massacre of Armenians in the Kurdish region in 1915, there are few Armenians left in Iraqi Kurdistan. The largest Christian communities are the Assyrians. Other Christian community includes the Chaldeans. Both of these speaks the Aramaic language and have a strong cultural identity. There are about 3.7 million Kurds in the Kurdish northern safe haven area and between 1 and 2 million in the rest of Iraq, which comprises roughly 16 to 20 percent of Iraq's population.[4]

Fig. 15.1: The Iraqi Kurdistan

Source: "An introduction to the Kurdish People of Iraq and elsewhere", http://www.eurolegal.org/neoconwars/kurdsiraq.htm

Since the creation of the modern state of Iraq, the history of Iraqi Kurdistan has been one of underdevelopment, political and cultural repression, destruction, ethnic cleansing and genocide. Saddam Hussein's regime implemented large scale nationalization and land distribution programme after crushing the 1975 Kurdish insurgency which was followed by Arabization of the regions around Kirkurk and Mosul. Beginning in the mid-1970s and continuing until the eve of the 2003 war on Iraq, Baghdad expelled hundreds of thousands of Kurds, Turkomans and Assyro-Chaldean Christians from areas around Mosul, Kirkurk and Khanaqin. Sunni and especially Shiite Arabs from south were then brought in with economic incentives.[5] The major saga affecting the Kurds was the Iran—Iraq War (1980-1988). Both countries subverted and used the other's Kurdish factions. Kurds were also conscripted into the armies of both sides, and generally gave a good account of themselves in battle. When the war ended through military exhaustion, both the governments settled accounts with their rebellious Kurdish factions. In Iraq, the government launched punitive military expeditions into its northern Kurdish mountains, but only met with partial success. In Iran, the revolutionary guards who were responsible for internal security strove to bring rebellious Kurdish factions to heel, while a covert assassination campaign was mounted against insurrectionary Kurdish political leaders in exile. Both in Iran and Iraq, Kurdish factions fought against each other on their home ground. During the later stage of the war, Saddam Hussein used chemical weapons against Iran, but these were deployed with greater intensity against his own rebellious Kurds, then fighting in the pay of the Tehran government. *Al-Anfal*[6] was the codename given to an aggressive, planned, military operation against Iraqi Kurds. It was also a part of an ongoing, larger campaign against Kurds because of their struggle to gain autonomy from the Republic of Iraq. The main attack was against the Kurdish town of Halabja in March 1988, where thousands of Kurds perished from chemical weapon effects. Arabization programme and *Anfal* campaign led to the greatest number of Iraqi internal displaced persons (IDPs) and refugees in the country's history. The problem of displacement in Iraq, at its core, stems from an authoritarian state and a fascist, exclusionary Arab nationalist state ideology (Ba'athism).

When Saddam Hussein invaded Kuwait in August 1990, an Allied coalition was formed under UN authority to oust him, a task accomplished by March 1991. Kurds played no part in the Gulf War except as conscripted soldiers. Anticipating the defeat of Saddam Hussein and his fall, an impromptu Kurdish uprising occurred in Iraq in March 1991. This had not been anticipated by Kurdish leaders, who were carried along with it. However, it was a popular uprising in which the people and not the factional or tribal leaders led the way. Soon after Saddam Hussein had dealt with a southern Shii revolt, he moved northwards to wreak vengeance on Kurds, causing mass exodus from cities, towns and villages.

THEORETICAL ANALYSIS

Many of the Kurds, Assyrian Chaldeans and Turkomans suggested that a new sense of Kurdish identity is taking root precisely because it accommodates pluralism or cultural diversity by not threatening deep-rooted ethno-linguistic identities. The Kurdish Democratic Party established in 1946 and renamed the Kurdistan Democratic Party in 1953 supported a broad-based political platform for all people in the region regardless of ethnic identity. The Patriotic Union of Kurdistan Party advocated the same view since its creation in 1975. It was therefore, expected that a possible interim solution would be a variant of a consociational model of multi-party elite, political accommodation within a divided administrative and territorial system.

The theories of consociational political system can be used as a basis to analyze the reasons behind political instability in Iraqi Kurdistan, in the first half of the 1990s and the subsequent stability that has been apparent particularly towards the end of the 1990s. With its clearly divided society and political structure, between the factional areas of the KDP and PUK, as well as older tribal and linguistic divisions, a model attempting to analyze the political structures of deeply divided societies, with a proscriptive element for future sustainable political development, obviously has a significant value. The multi-ethnic, multi-cultural and multi-religious people inhabit the Kurdish region.

The model of consociational political system was developed in the 1960s in relation to the Third World by Arend Lijphart to describe how a culturally diverse country ensured that all significant groups were incorporated into the government without any being frozen out by a crude majoritarianism. He defined his model as 'government by elite cartel designed to turn a democracy with a fragmented political culture into a stable democracy'. The role of leaders of rival groups is therefore of paramount importance in societies where political culture is deeply fragmented. The elite must possess the ability to accommodate divergent interests which exist within the society, and also understand the perils of political fragmentation. The elite must also have the ability to transcend cleavages.[7] The system recognizes society as consisting of these distinctive groups based on language, race, culture and religion. Therefore, future development of the political system of the Iraqi Kurdistan could be achieved by adopting a consociational model.

STRUCTURE AND PROGRAMME OF THE KURDISTAN REGIONAL GOVERNMENT

The Kurdistan Regional Government exercises executive power according to the Kurdistan Region's laws as enacted by the democratically elected Kurdistan National Assembly. The government coalition consists of several political parties. The coalition reflects the diversity of the region's people who are Chaldeans, Assyrians, Turkomans, Yazidis, Kurds and others living together in harmony and tolerance.

The KRG determined to establish strong constitutional institutions to support the democratic process in Iraq. Its main task was to form a system of good governance through the participation of all groups with transparency and accountability which means a modern professional government. The cabinet worked at all socio-economic levels of Kurdistani society. The KRG looked forward to a democratic federal system in Iraq, based on agreement and respect for all nationalities and religions.[8] It therefore, supported democratic consensus in the political process.

The Kurdistan Regional Government, 1992-1996

In the absence of a negotiated autonomy agreement with the Iraqi Government, the KIF (Kurdistan Iraqi Front) organized elections to a 105 member Iraqi Kurdistan National Assembly. It was hoped that the elections would result in the establishment of a legitimate, constitutional and legal entity embodied in a council that would represent the Kurdish people and would be the political decision making body in the Iraqi Kurdistan. Kamal Fuad, the official in charge of foreign relations in PUK, added that "the only solution to Iraqi Kurdistan is through parliamentary elections for the people of Kurdistan. The Kurdish parliament will form the civil administration and will act as the Kurdish northern government".[9] Faced with the administrative vacuum and double embargo, the Kurdistan Iraqi Front—an alliance of diverse political groups in the Kurdistan region—held a general election. The internationally supervized election was held on 19 May 1992 in which virtually an estimated 1.1 million strong electorate participated in the Kurdish areas. Their goal was to establish an administration to provide for essential public services and to meet the basic needs of the people. The people expressed a strong desire to choose their representatives. Men and women over the age of 18 were eligible to vote. The legislative candidates had to be citizens and residents of Kurdistan for at least 30 years. Barzani and Talabani were the two leading candidates for the supreme leadership position. However, the election for an overall Kurdish leader was inconclusive. Massoud Barzani, the leader of the KDP, received 50.22 per cent of the votes cast and Jalal Talabani, the leader of the PUK, 49.78 per cent.[10] This regional election led to the formation of the first Kurdistan National Assembly and the establishment of the Kurdistan Regional Government. The leadership and the people of Kurdistan decided to remain part of Iraq, adopt and abide by all national laws except for those that violated human and universal rights. And after decades of dictatorship, the people in Kurdistan were able to vote for their representatives.

The two socialist parties, the Kurdish Socialist Party (KSP) and the Party of Socialism in Kurdistan (PASOK), both of which called for an independent Kurdish state, ran on the same ticket in the 1992 elections garnering 2.6 percent of the total vote; they did not win any seat in parliament since a party must receive 7 percent of the vote to be represented. A few months after the polling, the parties merged with Abdulrahman's Kurdistan Popular Democratic Party (KPDP) to form the Kurdistan Unity Party, under the leadership of Abdulrahman and Mahmoud Osman. The Islamic Party of Kurdistan which believed that Iraq should become an Islamic state captured 5.1 percent of the vote in the election and sent no members to parliament. The northern branch of Kurdish Communist Party received 2.2 percent. The number of Christian Assyrians in northern Iraq was in dispute, but to forestall international criticism and local disapproval, the Iraqi Kurdistan Front (IKF) allocated the Assyrian Democratic Movement five seats in parliament regardless of the party's electoral showing; theoretically these were the swing votes in the body.[11]

Apparently only seven of the eight reputed members of the Iraqi Kurdistan Front participated in the elections. On the other hand, the Iraqi National Turkoman Party (IMTP), which was not a member of the Kurdish Front, decided not to participate in the elections.[12] None of the smaller Kurdish parties achieved representation. After much negotiation, the Kurdish Front decided that the KDP and the PUK would be given 50 seats each in the National Council. The remaining five would be given to the Christian minority with four of them going to the Assyrian Democratic Movement. The elections contributed to the KDP and PUK working even closer together. As a part of the agreement, it was decided that the chairman of the National Council would be from the KDP, while his deputy would be from the PUK. Conversely, the chairman of the Executive Council would be from the PUK and his deputy from the KDP. The design adopted, which effectively divided all executive and legislative positions equally with real power being unofficially vested in the political bureaus of the PUK and KDP which came to be known as the 50 : 50 system.[13]

The First Cabinet of the KRG

The first cabinet of the KRG was presented with the unenviable task of attempting to govern the newly formed *de facto* state. Within the territory, UN sanctions and the GOI embargo were creating immense socio-economic problems, in addition to the unease created by the tense political environment. Furthermore, the first cabinet had managed several internal and structural problems.

The first cabinet targeted the problem of massively over-staffed and under-skilled personnel in the administration. However, its achievements have often been overlooked due to the subsequent breakdown of inter-party relations and the formation of the second cabinet under the premiership of Kosrat Rasoul of the PUK. The greatest problem the first cabinet presented to the decision making process was the equality of power which existed between ministers and their deputies, creating an administration effectively hamstrung by the contrary political motivations of its highest executive members. The actual decision making process of the cabinet therefore appears to have been managed by some form of coordination between the two political bureaus. However, there was a problem with achieving a balance within the governmental structure with regard to the inclusion of civil servants trained by the GOI, and those Kurds who had spent their lives fighting in the *peshmerga* brigades.[14] The attempts at achieving a balance between these two groupings created the first signs of tension between the KDP and PUK, with both sides accusing the other of placing *peshmerga*[15] personnel into positions which required a technocrat.

The Second Cabinet of the KRG

Towards the end of 1992, the first cabinet of the KRG became increasingly embattled. Faced with increasing partisan problems caused by the seemingly inextricable difficulties of revenue control, the leadership of the cabinet attempted to become more technocratic in the face of the politicization of the governmental structures by the KDP and PUK. In March 1993, the Kurdish cabinet elected in 1992 was dismissed by the Iraqi Kurdistan National Assembly for its failure to deal effectively with the crisis in the region. An important shift in government positions saw the PUK place some of its senior leaders into the cabinet. Korsrat Rasoul Ali, a leading member of the PUK politburo, replaced Faud Massoum who was more a technocrat as Prime Minister. Tension began to rise as the government became more partisan. Moreover, in the summer of 1993, Sami Rahman's Kurdistan Unity Party—an alignment of three smaller parties that had previously all been members of the Iraqi Kurdistan Front-joined the KDP.[16] The change in Kurdish politics in favour of KDP sent shock waves in the PUK camp.

The second cabinet of KRG included members only from the KDP, PUK and one Christian. There was no representative from the newly combined three leftist parties (SPKI, KPDP and PASOK, a group that began as the 'Unity Party of Kurdistan') because they had unsuccessfully demanded one of the three main ministries namely, Interior, *Peshmerga* Affairs or Humanitarian Aid as well as one governor, several districts officers and sub-district directors.[17]

The partisanship of the governmental structures was considered a primary reason of the subsequent fall into conflict which occurred in 1994. As a renowned *peshmerga* commander with an infamous fighting reputation, Kosrat Rasoul remained an easy task for members of the KDP to describe him as uneducated and volatile. However, he proved able to mobilize public support behind his cabinet and his premiership far more effectively than the more technically minded Fu'ad.[18] But the KDP had deep-rooted feelings regarding Kosrat Rasoul and attributed much of the failures of the 50 : 50 system of government to him.

THE ESTABLISHMENT OF POWER-SHARING SYSTEM

Under Allied and then United Nations encouragement and help, the Kurds held elections within the safe haven zone in 1992. The two main groups-Patriotic Union of Kurdistan (PUK) and its rival, the Kurdistan Democratic Party (KDP) jointly formed an administration to govern which became known as Kurdish Regional Government. They began to build a *de facto* state and government. However, this cooperation did not last long. The KDP and PUK broke up in 1994 and a civil war which ensued threatened the very existence of everything that they had achieved. It is undeniable that the conflict in 1994 and 1996 resulted in the division of the administration into two separate factions based in Arbil and Suleimaniyah, dominated by the KDP and PUK respectively. It could be argued that the weakness in the political system stems from the rivalry which exists between the PUK and KDP. Until 1997, neither party displayed the ability to manage rivalries in a peaceful manner and therefore resorted to military options, often with the assistance of foreign national governments making the possibility of any stable joint government unlikely. When they separated into a divided political system, they were paradoxically strengthened due to the increased efficiency in the activities of the *de facto* governmental institutions.

The Division of Iraqi Kurdistan

In August 1996, the combined forces of the KDP and the Iraqi government invaded Arbil, expelling the PUK from the city. A further round of serious fighting took place in 1997 before a ceasefire was reached and the division between the KDP and PUK reverted to the status quo *ante*. Particularly after the 1997 conflagration, the two political areas of Iraqi Kurdistan developed into two administrative zones, dominated by the KDP in Arbil and Dohuk Governorates and by the PUK in Suleimaniyah and New Kirkurk Governorates. Both sides claimed legality for themselves and scorned the illegality of the other, with the political system of Iraqi Kurdistan becoming characterized by two separate, almost identical, political and administrative systems.[19]

This system proved to be a stable alternative to the previous power-sharing arrangement. It managed to preserve the influence of the political elite of both parties and allowed governance and administration to take place with less consideration for party politics than when all political groupings were located in Arbil. Furthermore, the divide in the system implied that the overt potential for the *de facto* state becoming more institutionalized was somewhat diminished, thereby reducing the necessity for neighbouring states to promote stability within a unified structure. However, it was argued that the cabinets of the divided administration were the most effective of the Kurdish political institutions formed since 1991. The ability of the two main factions to dominate the administrations within their strongholds enabled both entities to relax somewhat and promote a more effective system of governance.

Iraqi Kurdistan was therefore divided geographically and politically between a KDP dominated axis of Arbil-Dohuk and a PUK dominated axis of Suleimaniyah-Kirkurk. The creation of this system enabled smaller parties to enjoy more political power as both the KDP and PUK realized the dangers of being seen to be too overly dominant, both to the Iraqi Kurdistan populace in particular and the international community at large. Whilst the administration remained divided between Arbil and Suleimaniyah, the judiciary remained unified and was headed by the Supreme Court of the Iraqi Kurdistan region based in Arbil.[20] It was the presence of this unified institution and unwritten agreement not to alter the interim status of the position of President that seemed to exist between Jalal Talibani and Massoud Barzani, which provided a small degree of unity to Iraqi Kurdistan.

The emergence of Kurdistan's *de facto* autonomy forced the Kurds to set up their own administrative and legislative organs to avoid chaos and a further decline in public security. But the Kurdish experiment in freedom has revealed deep-seated differences and splits within the Kurdish movement and attracted the intervention of their Turkish and Iranian neighbours.[21]

Washington Agreement of 1998

Despite some disagreement between PUK and KDP, there were some positive political developments in the late 1990s. In January 1998, the PUK leader Jalal Talabani proposed peace and reconciliation and the establishment of a transitional government, in which both the PUK and KDP would be represented to assume sole responsibility for customs duties on cross-border trade. However, the KDP did not respond following its military success against the PUK. Iran continued to offer some support to the PUK, but appeared unwilling to become more directly involved in the Kurdish enclave.

Under the auspices of the Ankara peace process the two parties met again. The first meeting took place on 12 February 1998 in Shaqlawa (territory controlled by the KDP). The KDP delegation was led by Sami Abdul Rahman, and also included Jawher Namiq Salim (Speaker of the KNA), and Bruska Nuri Shawaise (Central Committee). The PUK delegation was led by Kamal Fu'ad and also included Omar Sa'id Ali and Arsalan Bayaez (all Political Bureau). This meeting formulated confidence-building measures, including the enforcement of ceasefire, ending of media attacks, the release of prisoners, ending of the expulsions, establishment of a joint committee to ensure the implementation of SCR 986, and the promotion of increased coordination between public service ministries. The specialized sub-committees formed to coordinate the public service sectors proved to be reasonably successful and resulted in the reduction of checkpoints between cities and the easing of travel restrictions between Arbil and Suleimaniyah.[22] By mid-1998, the fragile peace process between the PUK and the KDP appeared to be holding and after a number of meetings between representatives of the two factions, agreement was reached on exchange of prisoners and the establishment of a joint committee to promote co-operation in public health, education and energy. Meanwhile, the issue of KDP control over customs duties on cross-border trade from Turkey which had thwarted previous attempts to reconcile the rival factions remained unresolved. Nevertheless, the two factions continued to hold regular meetings and both parties pledged to cooperate to secure a permanent settlement with Baghdad leaders and stated that all Kurdish factions were prepared to make peace with the Government of Iraq. The Washington Accord reached in September 1998 between Barzani and Talabani, halted their infighting and obligated both to prevent the PKK from using northern Iraq as a base from which to attack Turkey. The Iraqi Kurds conceded to the accord because they needed Turkish acquiescence for their own local administration.[23] United States support gave the Kurds increased security against potentially destructive policies of the governments of Turkey and Iraq. The agreement was expected to draw the two political parties into closer cooperation and in the formation of an interim administration in Arbil followed by multi-party elections to unify the KNA and the KRG.

The United States brokered a formal peace agreement between representatives of the PUK and KDP in Washington which provided for a unified regional administration, the sharing of local revenues and cooperation in implementing the UN sponsored 'oil for food' programme (UNSCR-968).[24]

Re-convening of the Kurdish National Assembly

A major step in the implementation of the 1998 Washington Agreement was taken on 4 October 2002, when all members took their seats in the Iraqi Kurdistan National Assembly in Arbil for the first time since 1994. Roj Nuri Shawaise, President of the Parliament opened the session. Massoud Barzani and Jalal Talabani addressed the Parliament where both stated in clear and unequivocal terms, their total commitment to making the Iraqi Kurdistan National Assembly function for the benefit of all the people in the region. New members of Parliament were sworn in during the session. Members unanimously voted to accept the terms of the Washington Agreement. They reaffirmed their position on the future of Iraq. All parties remained in agreement that Iraq should be a free, democratic, federal and pluralist country.

Free and fair local elections were held in dozens of municipalities in the KDP administered areas in May 2001. According to KDP sources, to select 571 officials, KDP candidates received 81 percent of vote cast and the rate of voter participation was recorded at 79 percent. A second session of Assembly was held on 8 October 2002 in Suleimaniyah, further strengthening solidarity and unity. Government and party officials of KRG remained very positive and people in the local community were very pleased that the Parliament was unified again. More steps were taken aimed at normalising the situation in the Kurdish area. At a further session held on 12 November 2002 a joint committee was established with the aim of preparing for parliamentary elections, scheduled to be held in Iraqi Kurdistan within nine months. However, these elections were postponed following the US—led campaign to oust the regime of Saddam Hussein.[25]

The reconvening of the Kurdish National Assembly in 2002 was a clear indication of the growing cooperation between the KDP and PUK. In particular, the KDP and PUK are unified in asserting the Kurdish right to self-determination in a future democratic Iraq. Despite various internal difficulties and constraints, including a strong opposition of neighbouring countries and both external and internal embargoes on the region by the Iraqi government, all basic services were provided to the extent the resources permitted. Freedom of speech and free movement was respected. According to Human Rights Watch, the leadership of the region made notable progress in promoting and protecting the basic rights of the people of liberated Iraqi Kurdistan.[26]

CONCLUSION

Despite differences, the Iraqi Kurdistan experienced self-rule in democratic form of government. This emerging democratic form allowed Kurds, Assyrian Chaldeans and Turkomans to maintain their respective ethno-linguistic identities, while simultaneously establishing a wider sense of collective identity based on three key factors: first, common geography, second, the ongoing experiment in self rule, democratization and cultural tolerance and last, their shared experience as non-Arab Iraqis who have all known repression and marginalization within the modern state of Iraq.

The KRG developed from a united Organization at the beginning of the 1990s into two separate administrative systems till 2002. The joint system of the First and Second Cabinets brought together two political parties which were separated by the quest of power. Furthermore, the joint system was of concern to neighbouring states, and not least the Government of Iraq, as the *de facto* state possessed a structure of governance which had the potential to promote the Kurdish national movement in a unified manner. Until 1997, at least, neither party displayed the ability to manage these rivalries in a peaceful manner, and therefore resorted to military options. However, the reconvening of the KNA in October 2002 presented a clear growing cooperation within the Iraqi Kurdistan. But a unified administration presented a regional geopolitical instability, particularly to Turkey and Iran. These countries and other powers pursued active destabilizing policies with their own national interests in mind, prompting tensions within the *de-facto* state. The government of Turkey in particular referred to the Iraqi Kurdish region as being a power vacuum with no effective government and therefore characterized by lawlessness

Between 1997 (the year of the last major round of PUK-KDP fighting) and mid 2002, Iraqi Kurdistan enjoyed a period of enhanced political stability, economic development and growing international recognition. It further benefited from the United States containment policy against Saddam Hussein. Relations between the KDP and the PUK generally improved following the Washington Agreement of September 1998.

The increased unification could be achieved in a more technically oriented manner under a consociational approach of elite accommodation with more focus on the coordination of the activities of the separated local authorities. With its clearly divided society and political structure between the factional areas of the KDP and PUK as well as the older tribal and linguistic divisions, a consociational model of attempting to analyze the political structures of the deeply divided societies. For instance the first two cabinets of the Kurdistan Regional Government between 1992 and 1996 can be said to have the consociational system with shared ministerial portfolios.

However, notions of Kurdish democracy (proving that Iraqis are not alien to democratic concepts), apparent improvements in human rights and the belief that Kurdistan could be the flicker of democracy in Iraq which lights the Iraqi beacon of democracy in West Asia now appear to be a part of the discourse surrounding the regime change. Moreover, Iraqi Kurdistan has benefited from the establishment of a unified system of governance since 2002. The history of the Kurdish *de facto* state will be a constant reminder that Iraqis and Kurds are not alien to the democratic ideal.

NOTES

1. For detail of the Treaty *see*, Eagleton, William (1963), *The Kurdish Republic of 1946,* London: Oxford University Press: pp. 11-12, also see, Ali, Othman (1997), "The Kurds and the Lausanne Peace Negotiations, 1922-23", *Middle Eastern Studies*, 33(3): pp. 521-534.
2. Kirisci, Kemal and Gareth M. Winrow (1997), *The Kurdish Question and Turkey: An Example of a Trans-State Ethnic,* London: Frank Cass & Co., p. 1.
3. "An Introduction to the Kurdish People of Iraq and elsewhere", (Online: web), Accessed 7 February 2007, URL: htt://www.eurolegal.org/neoconwars/kuridisiraq.htm.
4. Mcdowall, David (1992), *The Kurds: A Nation Denied,* London: Minority Human Rights Publications: p. 12.
5. Romano, David (2007*), The Kurdish Nationalist Movement: Opportunity Mobilization and Identity,* Cambridge: Cambridge University Press: p. 432.
6. The word is religious in origin; it is name of eighth *sura*, or chapter of the Koran. In this *sura* the Arabic word 'al-anfal' means 'spoils' as in the spoils of battle.
7. Lijphart, Arend (1969), 'Consociational democracy' *World Politics*, vol. 21(2): p. 218.
   Also see Lijphart, Arend (2003), 'Consociational Democracy', in Dahl, Robert, Shapiro Ian, et al. (ed.) *The Democracy Source Book,* Massachusetts: MIT Press: pp. 142-143.
8. See, Kurdistan Regional Government (KRG), "About the Kurdistan Regional

Government", (Online: web), Accessed 5 June 2007, URL: hhtp://www.krg.org/articles/article_detail.asp?RubricNr=93&AricleNr=48& LangNr=12&L....

9. Gunter, Michael M (1993), "A de-facto Kurdish state in Northern Iraq", *Third World Quarterly*, 14 (2): p. 297.
10. For detail see, Kurdistan Regional Government (4 July 2005), "A Brief History of Iraqi Kurdistan: The Kurds and Kurdistan", (Online: web), Accessed 22 October 2006, http://www.krg.org/articles/article_detail.asp?
11. Prince, James M (Jan.1993), "A Kurdish State in Iraq?" *Current History,* 92 (570): p. 19.
12. Gunter, no. 9. p. 298.
13. Stansfield, Gareth R.V. (2003), *Iraqi Kurdistan: Political Development and Emergent Democracy*, London: Routledge Curzon: p. 145.
14. *Ibid*., p. 149.
15. Peshmerga in Kurdish means 'those who face death'.
16. Gunter, Michael M (Spring 1996), "The KDP-PUK Conflict in Northern Iraq", *Middle East Journal*, 50 (2): p. 232.
17. *Ibid*., p. 302.
18. Stansfield., no.13, pp. 150-51.
19. *Ibid*., pp. 153-154.
20. *Ibid*., p. 155.
21. Hashim, Ahmed (Jan.1996), "Iraq: Fin de Regime?" *Current History*, 95(597): p. 13.
22. Stansfield., no.13, p. 100.
23. Gunter, Michael M (Dec.2001), "Bane of Kurdish Disunity", *Orient,* 42 (4): p. 609.
24. For detail see, UNSCR 986(1995), Adopted by the Security Council at its 3519th meeting on 14 April 1995, (Online: web), Accessed 29 May 2008, URL: http://www.world press.org/specials/Iraq/unscr986.htm.
    Also see, UNSRC 686 see, United Nations (1996), The United Nations and the Iraq-Kuwait Conflict, 1990-1996, Department of Public Information vol.9, New York: pp. 182-183.
25. O'Leary, Carole A. (December 2002), "The Kurds of Iraq: Recent History, Future Prospects", *Middle East Review of International Affairs,* 6 (4): p. 3. Also see, Kurdistan Regional Government" (15 October, 2002), *Kurdistan Today*, (Online: web), Accessed 8 June 2007, URL: http://www.old.krg.org/docs/KT021015_full.asp.
26. For detail see the Human Right Watch (January 1995), *Human Rights Watch World Report 1995-Iraq and Iraqi Kurdistan,* (Online: web), Accessed 15 March 2007, URL: http://www.unhr.org/refworld/docid/467fcab51e.html.

REFERENCES

Ali, Othman (July 1997). "Kurds and the Lausanne Peace Negotiations, 1922-23" *Middle Eastern Studies*, 33 (3): 521-34.

Eagleton, William (1963). *The Kurdish Republic of 1946*, London: Oxford University Press.

Gunter, Michael M (Spring 1996). "The KDP-PUK Conflict in Northern Iraq", *Middle East Journal*, 50 (2): 225-41.

——, (Dec. 2001). "Bane of Kurdish Disunity", *Orient,* 42 (4): 607-16.

——, (1993). "A de-facto Kurdish state in Northern Iraq", *Third World Quarterly*, 14 (2): 295-319.

Hashim, Ahmed (Jan. 1996). "Iraq: Fin de Regime?" *Current History*, 95 (597): 10-15.

Kirisci, Kemal and Gareth M. Winrow (1997). *The Kurdish Question and Turkey: An Example of a Trans-State Ethnic,* London: Frank Cass & Co.

Lijphart, Arend (1969). 'Consociational democracy' *World Politics*, vol. 21(2): 206-225.

Lijphart, Arend (2003). 'Consociational Democracy', in Dahl, Robert, Shapiro Ian, *et al.* (ed.) *The Democracy Source Book,* Massachusetts: MIT Press, 142-146.

Mcdowall, David (1992). *The Kurds: A Nation Denied,* London: Minority Human Rights Publications.

O' Leary, Carole A. (December 2002). "The Kurds of Iraq: Recent History, Future Prospects", *Middle East Review of International Affairs,* 6 (4): 1-13.

Prince, James M. (Jan. 1993). "A Kurdish State in Iraq?" *Current History,* 92 (570): 17-23.

Romano, David (2007*). The Kurdish Nationalist Movement: Opportunity Mobilization and Identity,* Cambridge: Cambridge University Press.

Stansfield, Gareth R.V. (2003), *Iraqi Kurdistan: Political Development and Emergent Democracy*, London: Routledge Curzon.

United Nations (1996). *The United Nations and the Iraq-Kuwait Conflict, 1990-1996,* Department of Public Information: vol. 9, New York.

Websites

"An Introduction to the Kurdish People of Iraq and elsewhere", (Online: web), Accessed 7 February 2007, URL: htt://www.eurolegal.org/neoconwars/kuridisiraq.htm

Human Right Watch (January 1995). *Human Rights Watch World Report 1995-Iraq and Iraqi Kurdistan,* (Online: web), Accessed 15 March 2007, URL: http://www.unhr.org/refworld/docid/467fcab51e.html.

"Kurdish Regional Government", (15 October 2002). Kurdistan *Today* (Online: web), Accessed 8 June 2007, URL: http://www.old.krg.org/docs/KTO21015_full.asp.

Kurdistan Regional Government (4 July 2005). "A Brief History of Iraqi Kurdistan: A Decade of Evolution", (Online: web), Accessed 22 October 2006, URL: http://www.krg.org?articles/article_detail.asp?show secondimage=&RubricNr=93

Kurdistan Regional Government (KRG) "About the Kurdistan Regional Government", (Online: web), Accessed 5 June 2007, URL: http://www.krg.org/articles/article_detail.asp?RubricNr=93&AricleNr=48& LangNr=12&L...

UNSCR 986 (1995), Adopted by the Security Council at its 3519th meeting on 14 April 1995, (Online: web), Accessed 29 May 2008, URL: http://www.worldpress.org/specials/Iraq/unscr986.htm.

PART 5: KUWAIT, OMAN, BAHRAIN, QATAR AND THE UAE

16

Trajectory of Political Democracy in Kuwait

Anwar Alam

INTRODUCTION

The history of parliamentary democracy in Kuwait has defied the dominant western paradigm of 'Middle East exceptionalism' and 'thesis of rentier economy' that sought to explain the absence of democratic rule in Muslim West Asian countries, particularly in the Gulf. Except for two short breaks: 1976-1981 and 1986-1992 Kuwait has been a functioning democracy since 1961, irrespective of debate over the nature and scope of its democracy. This paper attempts to sketch out an historical account of the gradual progression and institutionalization of democratic rule in Kuwait. While doing so the paper will highlight the gradual transfer of power from monarchy, Al-Sabah family, to the elective representatives, the National Assembly (NA) or parliament—a trend that continues even today. Given the partyless nature of Kuwaiti democracy, most of the political activities are organized around the structure of National Assembly. Hence scholarly debates and discussion on the issue of democracy in Kuwait have dominantly revolved around the role of National Assembly in Kuwait's political process. As Crystal wrote, "the Kuwaiti National Assembly has succeeded in being the democratic tool through which all find a chance to express inside it their stances and orientations. It has given a chance to all trends to express their political approaches without exception. This covers the bedouins coming from the desert, and the town dwellers such as merchants, businessmen, intellectual nationals, qualified graduates and those of political and advanced specialized expertise in Kuwait."[1] In this sense the scope of the paper is limited and does not reflect on the issue of socio-economic reform as a part of democratization of Kuwaiti society.

Following the promulgation of the Constitution in November 1962, periodic national assembly election has been taking place with the exception of 1976-1981 and 1986-1991. The election process has generally been free and fair and marked by intense media and public debate. Despite the fact that Kuwaiti democracy is partyless and organized on the basis of individualized politics, the cluster of groups that is formed around certain political and ideological lines is often visible both inside and outside of National Assembly. Within this parameter the paper will not reflect upon minute details about the election process but highlight the broad socio-political and ideological trends and the nature of the conflict and compromise between the ruling al-Sabah and the oppositions that has marred the Kuwaiti democracy since its inception.

THE HISTORICAL TRADITIONS: IMPLICATIONS FOR KUWAITI DEMOCRACY

The roots of political democracy in Kuwait lie in the historical pattern of relationship between the ruling Al-Sabah family and the elites of the country, particularly the merchant community. The informal alliance between the two institutionalized the political culture of governance. Any breach or attempt by the ruling family to disrupt this historically evolved political culture has been historically resisted. The subsequent analysis of this paper will reflect this pattern. The alliance was based on the division of labour: the al-Sabah controlled political and military matters while the merchants dominate the economic life. Overall, the al-Sabah were not absolute rulers. Their power was constrained by tribal customs, Islamic Law, the century's old practice of Shura (consultation), and the influence of prominent merchant families. To maintain the support of merchant and tribal elites, they needed to consult widely before making critical decisions. This political arrangement worked well as long as al-Sabah lacked their own financial autonomy and was depended on the revenue generated through tax on the pearl diving, fishing, and boat building—the most dominant economic activities that were controlled by the merchants.

However towards the end of nineteenth century the revenues generated through commercialization of dates that the al-Sabah family acquired in southern Iraq and its agreement with Britain in 1899 that resulted in making Kuwait as 'protectorate' of British kingdom provided the financial, military and political freedom to al-Sabah ruling family to assert its authority over the entire nation and ignored the practice of consultation with tribal and merchant elites for the purpose of governance. The political distance of al-Sabah alienated the section of merchant elites who demanded the establishment of elected consultative councils throughout 1920s and 1930s. The combination of economic crisis generated by the collapse of pearl industry in view of the then worldwide economic depression and sustained socio-political mobilization over the two decades by the elites, particularly the merchant community, forced the al-Sabah to recognize the short lived National Legislative Council (June-December 1938), which they had already formed.

The Council, among other things, laid down the Basic Law of Kuwait. It consisted five articles, and is therefore sometimes called the first constitution of Kuwait. The document was approved by the emir on July 2, 1938. It stipulated that the nation is the source of all authority and that it should be represented by an elected assembly authorized to legislate on all matters of concern to the country, including security, foreign policy, the budget, and social policy (particularly in the areas of education, health, and housing). Furthermore, Article Three of the New Basic Law stated that internal concessions, leases, and monopolies, as well as agreements and treaties with foreign powers, could not be considered legal and binding unless approved by the Assembly. During its short duration of existence, the Council passed far-reaching legislation. It revamped the tax and the judicial systems, launched important construction projects, expanded educational facilities and introduced public health regulations.[2] These articles along with measures of Council had potential to curtail the prerogatives of Emir and harm the interest of the British and the oil companies who were eyeing the vast oil resources of the Kuwait. Hence when the Council, in December 1938, demanded that it, rather than emir, decide how to allocate the money the Kuwait received from the oil companies, the Emir reacted by disbanding the Assembly and forcefully crushed the ensuing opposition. Though the phenomenal rise in the oil revenues (from $ 760,000 in 1946 to $169 million in 1953[3]), enabled the Emir to launch the social services and expand state related opportunity structure that helped him in winning over social support of large segment of society and co-opting a section of merchants and tribal leaders over last two decades, the intelligentsia in the context of rising tide of Arab nationalism continued to raise the issue of political democracy and convening of the Assembly during these decades. In fact the short lived National Legislative Council gradually became a part of national democratic tradition and therefore a very critical barometer for judging the emir's rule as legitimate or not.

It is in this context that that Emir Abdallah al-Salim al-Sabah decided to issue a decree calling for the election of Constituent Assembly to draft a constitution for the nation immediately after gaining independence in 1961. The other considerations behind this political move were as follows: First, Emir Abdallah al-Salim al-Sabah was known for his liberal and democratic sensibilities (As Crown Prince, he had chaired Kuwaits first legislative assembly in 1938 before it was dissolved by the Emir). Second, he correctly perceived the importance of having an elected parliament to provide avenues for political expression. By the 1960s, Kuwait had a very significant and politicized intelligentsia. Third, the decision to create representative institutions was heavily influenced by long standing Iraqi claims to Kuwait. An elected parliament was intended to help muster support in the face of serious regional threat. Finally, a representative assembly would foster national integration, establish Kuwait as a nation-state, and legitimize the rule of al-Sabah.

The 1962 Constitution

The Constituent Assembly deliberated and produced a constitution for Kuwaiti nation in November 1962. The details of the deliberations in the Constitution Committee, which were made public only recently, leave no doubt that the participants were aware of the fact that they were about to institutionalize the relationship between the ruling family and the "citizens", a term replacing the traditional "subjects".[4] The emir signed the document within three days of its submission. Some of the salient features of the Constitution are as follows: a political system that combines hereditary monarchial rule with representative government; that country's head of state must be chosen by the ruling family from among the male descendants of Mubarak the Great; that Emir selects and appoints the Prime Minister as well as the entire cabinet and a provision for a 50 member National Assembly for a term of four years to be elected by male citizens over the age of 21, whose families had lived in Kuwait since at least 1920. The Assembly was given significant power of discussing and approving budget as well as ratifying the treaties related to war and peace, alliances, the use of natural resources and financial obligations. It can override the Emir's vote to a particular legislation by passing it again by two-third majority.

SOCIO-POLITICAL CLEAVAGES, IDENTITY AND IDEOLOGICAL TRENDS IN WEST ASIA

There are three main identity groups that make up the Kuwaiti electorate: the Sunni *hadar* (as the settled townspeople are known, 35%) the Shi'a (17%) and the bedouin (45%). Many Sunni *hadar* families claim descent from a tribe, but do not organize themselves politically by tribe—indeed, there is a sharp social, political and economic divide between the h*adar* and the bedouin tribes in Kuwait. The merchants make up the traditional elite of Kuwaiti society, and are drawn from the Sunni *hadar*. These merchant families dominated the assemblies of 1938 and 1939, and pressed for the resumption of parliamentary life at independence. While the Sunni *hadar* settled in Kuwait town long ago, most of the bedouin settled only in the second half of the twentieth century, as oil drove a strong process of urbanization across the Arabian Peninsula and along the Gulf. Thus it is not so much tribal descent as the timing of settlement in Kuwait that distinguishes the tribes from many of the Sunni *hadar*. Yet the distinction remains very real and politically important. In the tribal districts, tribal affiliation is at least as important as ideology in determining who wins elections. In early parliaments, deputies from tribal districts tended to support the government, and the ruling family naturalized many tribal members in the 1960s and 1970s in order to counterbalance the demographic and electoral weight of the Sunni *hadar*, long the core of opposition to the ruling family in Kuwait. Kuwait's Shi'a are mostly Persian in origin, and their families migrated to the emirate in the first part of the twentieth century. A smaller part of Kuwait's citizen population of the Shi'i sect is Arab, hailing from Saudi Arabia's Eastern Province, Bahrain, or southern Iraq. Shi'i immigration had led to sectarian hostility among Kuwait's Sunnis. The Sunnis did not allow Shi'a to vote in elections of 1938 and 1939 assemblies, and no members were Shi'i. The Shi'i, not surprisingly, supported the ruling family's efforts to shut down the *Assembly* in 1939, and this history explains the Shi'i support of the ruling al-Sabah family up to 1979.

There were three main politico-ideological blocks that dominated the Kuwaiti political process during 1960s and 1970s. The first consisted of tribal supporters of the ruling family. During the 1960s, the regime granted citizenship to large numbers of bedouins and offered them various advantages—low-income housing, social services, and jobs in the state bureaucracy and the army. In effect, the monarchial regime used material incentives to turn tribes into political allies. As a result, representatives of these tribes became the back bone of support for the ruling family in parliament. The second group in parliament comprised of Kuwait's merchant class. Although this group was not homogenous, it included primarily independent and moderate reformist elements intent on pressing the government to become more accountable and to open up the political process. The third and most vocal group consisted of representatives of pan Arabism, Nasserism and leftists. Arab nationalist deputies in the Kuwaiti parliament came almost exclusively from one social group: the Sunni *hadar*. The Shi'a did not support the Arab nationalists, in part because many Kuwaiti Shi'a are of Persian origin, and because Arab nationalists were often hostile toward the Shi'a. This block served as a mouthpiece for the aspiration of many intellectuals, university professors and professionals. It mounted severe criticisms of government policies and Kuwait's social and political order. It vociferously pushed its agenda for internal reforms and advocated support for the Palestinian cause and 'anti-imperialist' forces in the region.

Along with the above trends, the Kuwiti political process has been marked by rise of Islamist forces within Sunni as well as Shii segments of the population since 1980s. In the elections of the 1960s and 1970s Islamists won only two seats, in Sunni *hadar* districts. By 2003 their's number increased to 16 out of 50 in the Parliament. About two thirds of these seats came from tribal districts, while the remainder coming from Sunni *hadar* areas. The election of 1981 showed the extent of the change among the Shi'i voters. They rejected, in whole, the traditional pro-government deputies who had represented them in Parliament and replaced them with a new group of opposition deputies, some of them Islamists with sympathies for the 1979 revolution.

The Role of Oppositions and National Assembly

In the early 1970s, opposition members forced the government first to put ceiling on the country's oil production in 1972 and then to nationalize the Kuwait Oil Company two years later. Subsequently oppositional members in parliament demanded more accountability of Emir's Council of Ministers including right to control and supervise over the ruling family's expenditure. The al-Sabah, backed by the revenue generated through oil boom of early 1970s, saw the assertion of parliament as intended to undermine the privilege of al-Sabah family and breach of informal trust that was historically built between the family and the rest of the society. As a result the al-Sabah ruler dissolved the National Assembly in 1976.

The Assembly remained suspended till 1981. In between Kuwait city witnessed the periodic demonstration demanding the restoration of the Parliament. The ruler also received several petitions and memorandum to convene the Parliament or hold fresh election or to set up a committee to recommend the measures so as to end the political impasse. Under mounting criticism from oppositions and threat of Islamic revolution of Iran (1979) the al-Sabah ruler finally announced in 1980 to hold the fresh election of National Assembly in 1981. To ensure a favourable outcome to the regime the government hurriedly passed a new electoral law that involved substantial gerrymandering. Until then, the country had been divided into 10 districts, each sending 5 members to the national assembly. As per new law there were 25 districts, each electing 2MPs. Most of the new districts had been created in predominantly tribal areas, a stronghold of the regime. On the other hand, the seats allotted to predominantly Shiite districts had decreased from 10 to 4. Most important, the liberal and leftist opposition remained competitive in only 15 districts; even there, it faced strong rivals. Predictably the parliamentary election result of 1981 proved disaster to liberal-leftist alliance. They could manage only 3 seats while the strength of pro-regime deputies from tribal areas went up from 22 in 1975 to 27 in 1981. At the time of the 1981 elections it was estimated that these eligible voters comprised only 6.4 per cent of the total population.[5] In 1996 naturalized citizens were given the right to vote, but only after they had been naturalized for at least 30 years.

However the 1985 parliamentary elections reversed the fortunes of oppositional forces. Candidates with liberal, reformist, pan Arab or leftists leaning captured 13 seats, Suni Islamists, 6, while pro regime block consisted merely 13 tribal MPs. Some of the important reasons for impressive comeback of oppositional forces are: first, the opposition had endeavored to present only one candidate in those districts where it stood a chance to win. Second, it had run tribal candidates with liberal-leftist leaning in pre-dominantly tribal districts. Third, it had been able to capitalize on mounting discontent with governmental corruption. Finally, it had benefited from the public outcry generated by the

1982 crash of an informal stock market known as the *Suq al-Manakh*. From the very beginning, the 1985 parliament proved very assertive. To the surprise of many observers, the Islamists, pan-Arabists and leftists often found common ground in blocking governmental bills and in sponsoring legislation or resolution against the cabinet. They kept raising the highly sensitive issue of corruption in high places. The combined oppositional forces forced the Minister of Education and Minister of Justice to resign. Finally in July 1986, the prime minister (Crown Prince) submitted the resignation of his cabinet to the Emir, citing the non-cooperative behaviour of members of NA and oppostion's relentless attack on the ministers. Further, the country had witnessed the rise of political violence during 1985-1986 that also included an attempt on the life of Emir himself. Given this precarious political situation the Emir once again decided to dissolve the Parliament in 1986 and censored the press, suspended parts of the constitution, and outlawed public meetings of more than five people. The Emir ruled by decree and greater number of cabinet positions were given to the members of al-Sabah ruling family.

However the regime's authoritarian turn and its repressive policies faced strong resistance from several sections of the society, particularly the merchant class. There were several reasons why merchant class, which was politically lying low since 1950s, took the lead in opposing the regime's authoritarian measures. First, the collapse of oil prices led to reduction in government contracts and benefits. Second, the merchants were disturbed by the increasing presence of members of the ruling family in commercial activity. After all, the implicit bargain between the al-Sabah and the merchants had been that the former would leave business to the latter, in exchange for which merchants would accept the ruling family's political dominance. The agitation of merchants was soon joined by sections of professionals, intelligentsia, former parliamentarians etc. making the oppositional movements broad based. The movement soon focused on the restoration of parliament, the full implementation of 1962 constitution and the lifting of restrictions on free speech and on the right to peaceful assembly. The movement resurrected the traditional Kuwaiti institution known as *diwaniyya*[6] to exchange views and ideas, mobilize support for change and coordinate its actions. By 1989, the pro democracy movement was engaged in a protracted battle with ruling family. The Kuwait City, the capital of Kuwait, witnessed the largest ever pro-democracy public demonstrations in January 1990 despite regime's stern warning and repression. It was this growing public sentiment for parliamentary democracy that forced the Emir in January 1990 to invite the opposition to participate in a national dialogue. The Crown Prince was entrusted the task of opening negotiations with the leaders of political reform. However even before the commencement of such national dialogue or negotiation with opposition could take place, the Emir unilaterally announced the setting up an advisory National Council of 75 members (50 elected and 25 nominated by Emir) for a term of four years for the purpose of deliberating on the feasibility of a restoration of Parliament and suggesting the constitutional changes, if required any.

Leaders of the pro-democracy movement immediately denounced the proposed council on several grounds. First, they criticized this move as delaying tactics and called instead the immediate restoration of parliament. Second, given the consultative and advisory character of the Council, it will fail to check the power of executive. Third, the opposition rightly feared that Council will propose radical changes in the 1962 constitution with the purpose of curtailing the democratic rights of Kuwaiti citizens and further strengthening the executive at the cost of national assembly. Accordingly the opposition called for a boycott of the elections to the proposed Council. Though the election for the Council did take place in June 1990, but it lacked legitimacy in view of poor turnout of the voters. Within the two months of this election Iraq under late Saddam Hussein invaded Kuwait and annexed it as 19th province of Republic of Iraq.

The Iraqi invasion changed the national-political context of Kuwait. The ruler, al-Sabah, fled to Saudi Arabia. However the invasion proved a boon for pro-democracy movement in Kuwait. It exposed al-Sabah's failure to defend the country and therefore pro-democracy movement demanded that the ruling family could no longer claim exclusive controls over matters related to national security, defence and foreign affairs and the management of the country's financial asset. By the fall of 1990 the ruling family was under intense pressure to promise a radical political reform after the liberation of Kuwait.[7] It was in this context that the Emir sponsored a highly publicized three day conference in Jiddah in October 1990. The conference brought together twelve hundred representatives of all major Kuwiti political groupings, including key opposition figures that had long been at odds with the al-Sabah. After protracted negotiations a deal was struck between al-Sabah and the opposition: the latter agreed to stand by the emir, reaffirm its loyalty toward him, and acknowledge him as the legitimate ruler of the country, while the former promised that liberation of the country would be followed by far—reaching political reforms that would include the restoration of parliament.

Following the liberation of Kuwait in 1991, election to National Assembly was announced to be held on October 5, 1992. In between six main opposition parties, including both the secular and Islamic groups, signed a manifesto demanding a free press, an independent judiciary, legalized political parties and anti-corruption measures. The election process saw vigorous campaign by the oppositions and the ruling family including the periodic public meetings and lively open media debate. Even though only about 81, 400 were allowed to vote, very large number of those not eligible (including women and naturalized citizens) made their voices heard throughout the campaign. The oppositions, though united on the issue of political reform, consisted broadly of the following politico-ideological trends. First, the Kuwait Democratic Forum consisting mostly of former Arab nationalists was formed in March 1991, immediately following the liberation of Kuwait. The Forum included well known personalities such as Ahmad al-Khatib, Abdullah-al Nibari and Jasim al-Qottammi. The thrust of their campaign was to resurrect dying idea of pan-Arabism and to demonstrate its relevance in the democratic functioning of the government. The second group consisted mostly of reformists that itself was broadly divided into three factions: the Constitutional Block, the Independents and the Parliamentarian group. The Constitutional Block was dominated by wealthiest merchants of Kuwait, heads of Kuwait's major corporations, banks and insurance companies. The Independent Block comprised mostly of professionals, intelligentsia, lawyers and academicians. The Parliamentary group consisted mostly of former MPs. It was heterogeneous coalition ranging from militant secular to religious. The third was Islamists that itself was divided into three main factions: the Islamic Constitutional Movement (ICM), the Islamic Popular Alliance (IPA) and the National Islamic Coalition (NIC). The ICM developed out of Association of Social Reform which had gained prestige and credibility in the course of resisting the Iraqi occupation. In ideological terms it represented contemporary Muslim Brotherhood of Egypt in Kuwait consisting mostly of Sunni moderate Muslims. A highly organized group, it maintained generally good relations with the government and sought to reform the system from within. The IPA was a conglomeration of various Sunni fundamentalist organizations that stood for the implementation of the Sharia and Islamization of Kuwaiti society and politics and was in general opposed to governmental policies. It had participated in the 1981 and 1985 elections. The NIC represented predominantly the Shitte group and included both fundamentalist and liberal-secular elements. Its electoral agenda mostly centred on promoting civic equality and creating more opportunities for the Shiite in the governmental sector. On the other hand the al-Sabah regime tried hard to influence the electoral process in its favour by such measures as writing of billion of dollars in mortgage and consumer loans, giving $2,000 grants to every individual who had been in Kuwait during the occupation, boosting monthly child allowances by 75 percent; raising by 50 percent state assistance to widows, orphans and the poor and implementing a 5 percent across the board salary increase for all public employees.

However these material incentives did not help the regime to convert the electoral result in its favour. In Kuwait City and its surrounding areas, opposition and independent candidates made a clean sweep. Together they captured thirty-five out of the 50 seats in Parliament. The ICM, IPA and NIC got three seats each, while KDF could manage only two. The election result demonstrated that various segments of the urban middle class—businessmen, professionals, intellectuals—were united in their desire for greater governmental accountability. In view of Jeddah pact and decisive victory of opposition in the election the emir was left no alternative but allotted six crucial ministries to the members of national assembly. These were oil, justice, commerce and industry, education, Islamic affairs, labour and social affairs. Five of these ministries went to the opposition—the highest ever since 1962. With new mandate the parliament asserted its prerogatives most forcefully in matters related to the use of public funds and the management of the country's overseas investments. It launched an investigation into what came to known as the Kuwaiti Investment Office (KIO) scandal. The KIO is a London-based Kuwaiti government agency in charge of investing the country's oil revenues. Another crucial investigation by parliamentary committee involved the Kuwaiti Oil Tanker Company (KOTC). Through this investigation the national assembly exposed the corruption in highest echelon of Emir's administration. The former investigation implicated the involvement of Shaikh Fahd Mohammad al-Sabah, the KIO's chairman for more than twenty years and a cousin of the emir and the former oil minister, Shaikh Ali Khalifa al-Sabah (who had been finance minister between1982 and 1985 and from June 1990 until April 1991). These investigations were bold attempts to seek the accountability of emir's financial and expenditure policy, that was hitherto beyond the domain of public scrutiny, and therefore challenged the very foundations of power and authority of the emir. In 1993 and 1994, the Parliament passed several laws that intended to review all expenditures by state-owned companies. One such law required all corporations in which the government holds 5 percent or more of the share to report any changes in investment policies or investment portfolios to official auditors. Furthermore, financial transactions by companies in which the state owns at least 25 percent of the shares must now be ratified by the National Assembly. More recently in March 2009, the Assembly insisted on questioning the Prime Minister over his management of the global financial crisis, and alleged misuse of public funds. The disputes had held up passage of a proposed $5 billion fiscal stimulus and financial guarantees programme to address economic weakness and the severe decline in Kuwait's stock market, which had triggered protests from investors who saw much of their savings wiped out.

The 1990s witnessed the rise of Islamist force both within and outside of parliament. The issue of Islamization of Kuwaiti society and political empowerment of women dominated the decade. The Islamists tried hard to push the agenda of Islamization by demanding *Sharia* as a main source of legislation and segregation of educational institutions on gender lines. The 1996 parliamentary elections reflected this trend. While women were still not granted the right to vote, they took advantage of the campaign to agitate for women's rights. The Islamist bloc increased its share from 15 to 20 MPs while

KDF could win only 2 seats. The July 1999 parliamentary election saw the polarization of Kuwait society on the issue of grant of right to vote and contest an election to Kuwaiti women. Two weeks before the election the Amir through a decree granted full rights to women to be implemented in 2003. However Islamists opposed this move and called it un-Islamic and un-constitutional. Finally new elected parliament in 1999 rejected the Amir's decree by a margin of two votes. All the groups won seats, with the ICM winning six, the KDF three, the IPB two, the SM (Salafi Movement) one, the NIA two, and the NDB three. The main losers were the pro-government candidates, with 11 major incumbents losing what had been considered "safe", secured seats. The election results were a clear indication of public dissatisfaction with both the government and the previous Parliament. Only 48 per cent of the incumbents were reelected. The government lost 11 of its valued supporters from the previous Parliament, and 11 of the new members were candidates who had lost in the 1996 elections. Women were given the right to vote and run for office only in 2005.

Under pressure from the opposition the Emir in July 2003 separated the posts of prime minister and crown prince for the first time since independence. In 2006 the Emir also reluctantly endorsed the National Assembly legislation to divide Kuwait to 5 electoral districts only, which was a major issue in the preceding election campaign. The voter now can cast votes for 4 candidates and in each district the highest 10 candidates earn seats. It is hoped that this would make vote buying more difficult and decrease the importance of tribe, family and sect in elections. In the June 2006 election over 340,000 Kuwaitis, including about 195,000 women, were eligible to vote for 253 candidates. The opposition won 34 out the 50 parliamentary seats. Though 28 women contested the election but failed to win a single seat. This was also the case in the election held in May 2008. However, in May 2009 parliamentary election there were 19 women among the 280 candidates and four women were elected to the National Assembly for the first time in Kuwait's history.

CONCLUSION

It is clear from the above analysis that democratic governance and its values are taking deep root in Kuwaiti, though in gradual and incremental manner. When Kuwait became independent the 1962 constitution set down certain guidance which could facilitate political participation: elections for the selected few, a national assembly and so on. Whatever the deficiencies of those processes they did represent a definite move towards a participatory democracy involving the gradual transfer of power from ruling al-Sabah family to the elected representatives. This is also clear from the gradual increase in the number of registered voters and voter turn out. Thus number of registered voters increased from 42,005 (1981-1986) to 56,848 (1985-1986) to 81,440 (1992-1996) to

107,169 (1996-2000). The voter turnout during the same period was 37,689 48,368 67,724 and 89,387 respectively.[8] The constitution has remained in force from 1992 to the present, the longest uninterrupted span of constitutional life in Kuwait. The constitution today has a great deal of support across the Kuwaiti political spectrum, and among many members of the ruling family itself. While the prospect of another suspension has receded, the possibility remains as Amirs of Kuwait have, on several occasions used their power to dissolve the Assembly when it aggressively challenged the government.

NOTES

1. Jill Crystal, *Oil and Politics in the Gulf: Rulers and Merchants in Kuwait and Qatar* (Cambridge: Cambridge University Press, 1990), pp. 21.
2. Abdo Baaklini, Guilian Denoeux and Robert Springboard, *Legislative Politics in the Arab World: The Resurgence of Democratic Institutions*, Lynne Rienner Publishers, Boulder London, 1999, pp. 173-174.
3. Rosemarie Zahlan Said, *The Making of the Modern Gulf States*, London: Unwin and Hyman, 1989, p. 30.
4. Ghanim Alnajjar, 'The Challenges Facing Kuwaiti Democracy', *Middle East Journal*, Vol. 54, No. 2 (Spring, 2000), pp. 242-258, p 244, quoting Majalat al-Huquq (Kuwait University Special Edition, November 1999).
5. Heather Deegan, *The Middle East And Problems of Democracy* Open University Press: Buckingham, 1993, p.42.
6. Diwaniyyat are informal gatherings of men who are relatives, friends, or close associates. These meetings typically take place once a week, in the home of one of the members of the group. They provide opportunities for individual to socialize; exchange views and find ways of helping each other. Diwaniyyat discussions frequently turn to business or politics. See, Abdo Baaklini, Guilian Denoeux and Robert Springboard, op.cit, foot note number 10, p. 200.
7. On the impact of Iraqi occupation of Kuwait for democratic movement in Kuwait, see, Steve Yetiv, 'Kuwait's Democratic Experiment in Its Broader International Context', *Middle East Journal*, Vol. 56, No. 2 (Spring, 2002), pp. 257-271.
8. Jill Crystal and Abdallah al-Shayeji, "The pro-democratic agenda in Kuwait" in Rex Brynen, Bahgat Korany and Paul Noble, ed; *Political Liberalization and Democratization in the Arab World*, Vol 2, (Lynne Rienner, Boulder: 1995), p. 117.

17

Building Representative Institutions in a Traditional Society: The Political Reform Process in Oman

Shelly Johny

The political reforms in Oman have gained added attention in the context of increased political liberalization efforts in the Arab Gulf countries during the 1990s. Most of the works make a comparative study of Oman's political reforms with the political developments in the other Gulf countries. The problem with this approach is that it does not take into consideration certain unique characteristics that differentiate Oman from the other countries in the region. Even in the few works that take into account the uniqueness of Oman, the vital aspects of Oman's history and culture that have an influence on the building of representative political institutions in that country are not looked at in depth. The aim of this paper is to not just merely chart the course of Oman's attempts to introduce political liberalization but also to identify the major factors that influence this process and make Oman's experience unique in the Gulf region.

THE POLITICAL REFORM PROCESS IN OMAN

The political reform process in Oman has been described as evolutionary in nature with the government gradually expanding or increasing representation with each stage. This is reflected in the increasing number of members throughout the years in the Consultative Council or *Majlis al-Shura* and the Council of State or the *Majlis al-Dawla*. While elections are held for the *Majlis al-Shura*, the members of the *Majlis al-Dawla* are appointed by Sultan Qaboos. The responsibilities of these bodies have also gradually increased over a period of time. The evolutionary nature of the *Majlis al-Shura* is especially noticeable. The predecessor of the Consultative Council was the State Consultative Council (SCC) which was created in 1981. The fact that the SCC itself was established after the earlier Council on Agriculture, Fisheries and Industry was abolished[1] have led to opinion by seasoned observers that the SCC was part of an evolutionary process of building representative institutions which began in the

1970s.[2] The SCC had limited powers as compared to the *Majlis al-Shura*. While the SCC was purely a consultative body with no legislative powers,[3] the *Majlis al-Shura* has broader jurisdiction including some authority over development policy, social welfare, education and environmental issues. Except the Ministers of Foreign Affairs and Defence, all the other ministers have to submit annual reports to the *Majlis* regarding their past performance and future plans. The members of the Consultative Council have the right to question the ministers either on a specific issue or the overall performance of a particular ministry. Apart from ensuring a level of accountability from the ministers, the *Majlis* also performs certain legislative responsibilities, notably reviewing and recommending amendments to the draft legislation pertaining to economic development and social services before its becoming law.[4]

The *Majlis al-Dawla,* whose members are appointed by the Sultan from former ministers, ambassadors, judges, retired military officers, dignitaries and businessmen, serves as an advisory body that reviews draft laws proposed by the government and presents its opinions to the Sultan and his ministers in cooperation with the Consultative Council. The *Majlis al-Dawla* serves as a source of expertise to the government for the implementation of development plans and programmes and economic and administrative reforms. This Council also provides the opportunity to the Sultan to promote women.[5] During the course of its political reform process, Oman has achieved certain milestones in the general context of the political environment in the Gulf. For example Oman empowered women to be nominated for all the seats in the *Majlis al-Shura* in 1993. Until then, women had little representation in the administrative bodies in Oman. Oman thus became the first GCC state to grant women the right to vote and stand for elections.[6] In 2003, the Sultan granted universal suffrage to all Omanis over the age of twenty-one.[7]

In 1996, along with the announcement of the creation of the *Majlis al-Dawla,* Sultan Qaboos presented the "The Basic Statute of State" which defines the type of government as *Sultanate* and enshrines the succession among the male descendents of Sayyid Turki bin Said bin Sultan. This statute has laid down the rules of succession according to which the Royal Family Council (RFC) will select a new Sultan within three days of the throne falling vacate. If the RFC fails to nominate a successor, the Defence Council will confirm the appointment of the person designated by Sultan Qaboos in his letter to the RFC.[8] Members of the Defence Council include the Sultan (chairman), the director of the office of Supreme Commander, the minister of the palace staff, the inspector-general of police and customs, the chief of staff of the Sultan's armed forces, the commanders of the air force, the navy and the army, the commander of the royal guard, and the head of the internal-security.[9] The statute also guarantees a range of personal freedoms including freedom of religion, assembly and expression, freedom of association, and freedom of press.[10]

Besides the political reform process itself, it is important to understand the factors that led to the process.

CONDUCING FACTORS FOR THE POLITICAL LIBERALIZATION PROCESS IN OMAN

The introduction of political reforms in many of the West Asian countries during the 1990s have been attributed to economic crisis or internal political disturbances which forced ruling authorities to introduce reforms to secure the stability of the regime. In the specific context of the Gulf countries, apart from domestic demands for greater political liberalization[11] other factors have been described as having influenced the governments to liberalize their political systems. Governments in West Asia have had to face external pressure, mainly American and European, to liberalize their political systems. The first phase when American pressure was applied on the countries in the region to introduce political reforms was in the period following the Gulf War of 1990-1991. The aftermath of the 2001 terrorist attacks in the US can be seen as a second stage where the US government believed that democracy was the only panacea to the problems of the region including religious radicalism and vigorously conducted a campaign to promote the same. This campaign has slackened down its pace due to the political problems in Iraq and Afghanistan and also perceptions of an Iranian threat.

Oman's political reform process cannot be attributed to exactly the same reasons as in the cases of other countries of the region. Oman definitely shares some of the characteristics especially of the other states in the Gulf region. Along with the other GCC states, Oman does not have the political vibrancy of states in the West Asian region like Egypt, Syria and Iraq which have been influenced by different political trends by the virtue of being intellectual centres of the Arab world and also being caught up in the circumstances related to the creation of Israel and the emergence of the issue of Palestine. While there is mention of some type of civil society initiatives in countries like Saudi Arabia by virtue of the internet and blogging websites, Oman is not seen as a part of this phenomenon. The process of building representative institutions in Oman had begun in the aftermath of the Dhofar insurgency which was put down in 1975. It was only after the new ruler, Sultan Qaboos, had tided over the biggest internal challenge to his authority that he could launch a process that sought greater participation of the people in matters of governance. At the same time, it cannot be denied that Oman's political reforms received a major fillip during the 1990s. Oman did not face as much pressure from its population calling for political liberalization as in the other Gulf countries. Here it is important to digress a little bit and see why domestic pressure was not an important factor in Oman's political development since 1970.

OMAN'S UNIQUE POLITICAL-ECONOMY IN THE GULF REGION

While Oman like the other Gulf countries gains a major portion of its revenue from the sale of oil, the amount of revenue generated is much less than that of states like Saudi Arabia and Kuwait. Also, Oman began production of oil later than the other Gulf countries. In spite of oil revenues, the Omani government has had to fend for a larger and more diverse population than the smaller Gulf states and it has had to distribute development projects in a wider area than the limited areas of the Gulf city states. Aware that it did not have much oil reserves, it began to carefully manage its spending from the 1980s itself.[12] It can also be seen as part of deliberate attempt to bring about development gradually so as not to bring about a backlash from the conservative forces in the interior. This should be seen as a priority of the ruling authorities keeping in mind the long history of animosity between such forces and the Sultanate.

As a result, Oman has not seen the kind of rapid modernization and infrastructural development that the other Gulf countries have witnessed. This factor has in one way protected the Omani political system and society from the after effects of rapid change in a short period of time. That rapidly modernizing Gulf states were facing problems due to the clash between opposing forces of modernization and conservatism was proved during the siege of the Mecca Mosque in 1979. Oman's gradual development helped in preserving the unwritten understanding between the ruler and the ruled in that the citizenry would not demand political accountability in return for benefits handed out by the government to the different segments in society.

The conditions in which Sultan Qaboos assumed power in Oman has also helped in earning the loyalty of the Omani people. When Qaboos took over the rule of the country, the southern province of Dhofar was embroiled in an insurgency waged by a pro-Marxist guerrilla movement with help from the communist government of the then South Yemen. There were signs that the insurgents were trying to spread the rebellion into northern Oman and it appeared as if the very unity of the country was under threat. In 1975, the rebellion was put down and Oman entered a period of modernization and economic build-up. His early challenges and his success in putting down the rebellion albeit with massive external help have helped in creating an image of Qaboos as one capable of providing political stability. At a more personal level, his education abroad[13] has created an image of a person who has got an exposure of the outside world as compared to his contemporaries ruling in the other Gulf countries. The Omani people are ultimately very well aware of what could happen in the absence of Al Busaidi rule, a theme that will be looked at closely later on as having greater significance in the future.

The Omani government's political reform initiatives are not then introduced in response to immediate threats to regime stability. In comparison to many democratic countries where only the issues vital during the term of a government are considered worthy of attention, the Omani government's initiatives are taken in the light of the long-term stability of the Sultanate. Therefore, it is natural to come around to the understanding that external factors were alone responsible for the beginning of political reforms in Oman. Likewise, Oman under Qaboos has sufficiently demonstrated its capability of following an independent foreign policy both in the region and at the international level as compared to its compatriots in the GCC. This is in spite of the fact that it shares strong military relations with the US and Britain and continues to host US military bases on its territory. We need to look at Oman's heritage and history in order to understand the factors that influenced Oman's political reform process.

THE SULTANATE AND THE CONCEPT OF IMAMATE

Ibadi Islam is considered as the national religion of Oman even if there continue to be Sunnis and Shias among Muslims in present day Oman. More than being a national religion promoted at the expense of other faiths, Ibadi Islam is seen as an essential component of Omani socio-cultural identity. The Ibadis are seen as a sect separate from the Sunnis and the Shias whose origins can be traced to the Khawarij who were the first dissenters from the main body of Muslims. Therefore, it can be said that Ibadi Islam can be traced back to the early Islamic period itself. The Ibadis are more moderate as compared to the zealous Khawarij. The main centres of Ibadi Islam in Oman were in the interior regions of the north in the present day nation-state of the Sultanate of Oman. One of the important characteristics of Ibadi Islam is its concept of government which Ibadi Muslims considered to be as the one most identical to the system of government that existed during the early Islamic period immediately after the death of the Prophet Muhammad. This system of government was also seen as the one most suited to the requirements of mankind.

According to this system, the Imam who was the ruler of the Muslims was elected from among worthy candidates by a group of learned religious scholars with support from the chiefs of the major tribes.[14] In this manner, the Imamate system of government of Ibadi Islam did not sanction hereditary succession to the position of Imam.[15] In practice though, there have been whole periods in the history of Oman when a particular dynasty continued to hold the position of Imam as during the rule of the Yaariba dynasty during the seventeenth and early eighteenth century Oman. After a period of civil war, which broke out due to a succession dispute after the death of the last Yaariba Imam, and occupation of the coastal areas by the Persians, Ahmad bin Said, the first ruler of the presently ruling Al Busaidi dynasty, was declared Imam after he drove out the foreign occupiers and unified the country. But Ahmad bin Said's successors could not hereditarily retain the title of Imam. This led to a situation where a Sultan ruled in Muscat and the surrounding coastal areas while the tribes enjoyed autonomy in the interior. There was no Ibadi Imam during most of the eighteenth century and certainly none at Muscat. It was only once that an Ibadi Imam, Azzan bin Qays, who was a descendent of Ahmad bin Said, could capture Muscat with help from tribal forces and install a theocratic government which lasted for a short time.

The twentieth century saw a revival of the Ibadiyya and two Imams in succession were elected and they governed in interior Oman separate from the Sultanate. When the Imamate began to be a threat to the Sultanate, the Sultan's forces with considerable help from the British defeated the interior tribes during the 1950s and the last Imam fled to Saudi Arabia where he found refuge.[16] The Sultanate finally managed to bring under firm control all the territory in the northern parts of the present day Oman. Since then, the Ibadi Imamate has become dead issue in Oman and there has been no sign of an attempt to revive this system of government especially in the period since Sultan Qaboos came to power in 1970.[17] This does not mean that the Ibadi concept of Imamate has become completely irrelevant. The concept of Imamate has evolved over a very long period of time and has survived in a variety of situations and challenges. This concept has envisaged a variety of responses to different kinds of circumstances.

According to Ibadi concepts, there are different grades or types of Imams who can function according to the prevailing circumstances. There are *shari* Imams who enjoy absolute powers and have the right to wage holy war for the spread of Islam when the Ibadi community is in a strong position. There are *daif* Imams who do not have as much authority as *shari* Imams, do not have the right to wage holy war and they lead the community when it is under external threat or does not have complete autonomy.[18] There are also circumstances in which the community is in concealment or *kitman* and does not have an Imam.[19] The importance here is for the survival of the Ibadi Muslim community rather than the personality of the Imam.

The Ibadi concept of Imamate can become especially relevant in Oman if it passes though political turbulence resulting from a situation where there is no clear successor after the demise of the present Sultan. It can be seen as the only solution, by at least some, to the threat of political instability that will affect Oman in case of a succession dispute. At the same time, there are strong arguments against the possibility of such an occurrence. The transformation that has taken place in Oman since the past thirty to thirty-five years have affected interior Oman in the same manner as the other parts of the country. The Imamate functioned in a highly tribal environment with the ulema having their own influence. These social structures have been affected by the transformation and the old tribal equation where specific tribes had their own territorial influences have been altered. As mentioned earlier, there are no signs that there is an Ibadi revival in the interior. Even though the government has made pronouncements in favour of Ibadi Islam, describing it as an important part of the national identity, it has actually preferred adopting a more generalised version of Islam. The Qaboos mosques with their domes and minarets resemble those in other parts of the Muslim world rather than the Ibadi tradition of mosques consisting of plain square buildings without domes and minarets.[20]

While this was the situation in the initial period of Qaboos's rule, new circumstances placed added emphasis on the promotion of Ibadi Islam in Oman. In 1987, the Wahhabis attacked the authenticity of Ibadi Islam and commented that it could not be regarded as a true version of Islam. This accusation resulted in a counter-reaction by the Omani government where it resolved to defend Ibadi Islam as a vital part of Omani heritage in the context of a pre-dominantly Sunni Muslim Gulf region. The government began to establish Ibadi-oriented 'Islamic cultural institutions'. The government's efforts were spearheaded by the Grand Mufti of Oman, Sheikh Ahmed bin Hammeed al Khalili. These efforts has had it impact on Omani society especially in terms of defining the role of women in Omani society.[21] Most of the members of a clandestine group who were arrested by Omani security forces in 2005 and accused of plotting against the government were Ibadi Muslims and were from the interior areas.[22]

This is not to say that there is a general revival of Ibadi Islam in Oman. Nor is the attempt here to state that the kind of tribal Ibadi political activism that took place in the earlier times is making a comeback. But there have been precedents where traditional Islamic belief systems have inspired radical political movements in a contemporary setting. An example of this is how Khomeini's anti-Shah revolutionary movement emerged from a pre-dominantly 'quietist' Shia tradition. While gathering inspiration from Ibadi history, any new movement calling for a revival of Ibadi ideals would look very different from the old and would be functioning in a completely new environment.

A great deal of thought has gone into the attempts by the regime into introducing political reforms in Oman. Considering the past history of antagonism between the Imamate and the Sultanate, Sultan Qaboos and his advisors could have weighed in the possibility of a neo-Ibadi movement challenging continued Al Busaidi rule in Oman. Apart from the concept of Ibadi Imamate, there are other factors that could work against Al Busaidi interests in Oman. The most vital issue here is the absence of a male heir to succeed Sultan Qaboos. By the mid 1990s, it had been twenty five years since Qaboos had become king. The insecurities associated with the lack of a successor could have prompted Qaboos to introduce more substantial political reforms during that period. Another factor that weighs into political calculations is the fact that Oman's oil reserves are limited and a conversion from an oil-based economy into a more diverse one is rife with consequences for Oman's political stability.[23] This is where strong representative institutions can play an important role in offsetting potential threats to the succession process after the time of Qaboos. These institutions can be a strong source of support for a successor of Qaboos in the face of challenges to his political legitimacy. Ironically, the future of the democratization process itself in Oman depends on the smooth transfer of power after the time of Sultan Qaboos.

A word has to be put in here about descriptions of Oman's political reforms being influenced by the local culture and heritage. Oman's recent political developments have been described as adhering to the Ibadi practice of consultation. It is true that the process has been influenced by unique Omani characteristics as the reluctance to overtly criticize one's political competitors during elections to the *Majlis al-Shura* and bring forth accusations personally against ministers as it is considered as not polite in Omani society to do so.[24] At the same time, only the religious and tribal elite had a role in the election of the Imam and the consultation process that took place before making major decisions. Ultimately, the kind of representative institutions that are being created in Oman albeit with Omani characteristics are without precedent in either Imamate or Sultanate Oman.

CONCLUSION

Most of the studies on the political reform process in Oman have not taken into consideration Oman's historical and cultural aspects. Rather than the reform process itself, it is important to look at the domestic factors that have influenced Oman's political liberalization efforts. Oman's political reform process has passed through various evolutionary stages during which it has gradually increased its scope of representation and the responsibilities of the representative institutions. Oman has also achieved several milestones like allowing women to vote and contest in elections and providing universal suffrage. There has actually been less domestic pressure for democratization in Oman because of Oman's unique political economy in the Gulf region. Relatively less oil revenues, large population and area, and careful spending has brought about a more gradual transformation of Oman's economy and society. This has meant less demands for political representation from below. But the concept of Ibadi Imamate, complications due to lack of a successor to Qaboos and dwindling oil resources can create problems for Al Busaidi rule in Oman. It is here that representative political institutions can help in smooth transfer of power after the time of Sultan Qaboos.

NOTES

1. Joseph A. Kechichian, *Oman and the World: The Emergence of an Independent Foreign Policy*, (Santa Monica, CA, RAND, 1995) Joseph A. Kechichian, "Democratization in Gulf Monarchies: A New Challenge to the GCC", *Middle East Policy*, Vol. 11, No. 4, (Wniter, 2004), p. 52.
2. Jeremy Jones and Nicholas Ridout, "Democratic Development in Oman", *Middle East Journal,* Vol. 59, No. 3, (Summer,2005), p. 385.
3. Calvin H. Allen Jr., *Oman: The Modernization of the Sultanate,* (Boulder, Colorado, Westview Press, 1987), p. 84.
4. Aswini K. Mohapatra, "The Sultanate of Oman-A Liberalized Autocracy", *Journal of Indian Ocean Studies*, Vol. 15, No. 1, (April, 2007), pp. 83-4.
5. *Ibid.*, pp. 84-85.
6. *Ibid.*, p. 82.
7. *Ibid.*, p. 384.
8. Francis Owtram, *A Modern History of Oman: Formation of the State since 1920*, (London, I.B. Tauris and Co. Ltd., 2004), p. 183.
9. Calvin Allen, Jr. and W. Lynn Rigsbee, II, *Oman under Qaboos: From Coup to Constitution, 1970-1996*, (London, Frank Cass Publishers, 2000), p. 79.
10. n. 2, p. 389.
11. Joseph A. Kechichian, "Democratization in Gulf Monarchies: A New Challenge to the GCC", *Middle East Policy*, Vol. 11, No. 4, (Wniter, 2004), n. 1, p. 38.
12. Marc J. O' Rielly, "Omanibalancing: Oman Confronts an Uncertain Future", *Middle East Journal*, Vol. 52, No. 1, (Winter, 1998), p. 76.
13. n. 12, p. 72.
14. Patricia Risso, *Oman and Muscat: An Early Modern History,* (London, Croom Helm Ltd., 1986), p. 28.
15. John C. Wilkinson, *The Imamate Tradition of Oman*, (Cambridge, Cambridge University Press, 1987), pp. 169, 187.
16. n. 1, p. 70.
17. n. 8, p. 190.
18. n. 15, pp. 158-60.
19. *Ibid.*, p. 155.
20. n. 9, p. 176.
21. Khalid al-Aziri, "Gender, State and Culture in Oman (1970-2005), in Valeria Fiorani Piacentini and Elena Maestri, *From Tribe to State: Perspectives on Identity, Social and Cultural Dynamics in Eastern Arabia,* Crissma Working Paper, Vol. 1, ISU Universita Cattolica, 2007, pp. 23, 24.
22. n. 2, p. 381
23. n. 12, p. 70.
24. n. 2, p. 384.

18

Political Reforms in Bahrain: Initiative from Above

Rajiv Kumar

Authoritarian regimes in the Gulf demonstrated a remarkable degree of resilience over the past two decades. The stagnation in the world oil prices that appeared in the mid 1980s prompted a wide range of responses by Governments of the Gulf States.[1] The six authoritarian states, Saudi Arabia, Kuwait, Qatar, Bahrain, and United Arab Emirates (UAE) of Gulf Co-operation Council (GCC), are hereditary monarchies with little or no scope for genuine participatory governance. These monarchies rely on a combination of coercive and administrative institutions i.e. the National Guard and the bureaucracy to maintain power. For these states, historical tradition is an important source of legitimacy. This legitimacy is further reinforced by the state's access to oil riches and royal benevolence towards society. Consequently, these states have by and large been able to placate societal demands for major political changes.[2] The question of political reform in the kingdom of Bahrain has come to be an integral part of assessing progress made in this regard. Bahrain, in comparison to other states of the GCC is the poorest and less endowed. The wealth from hydrocarbons historically served to stifle widespread demands for political reform. Nevertheless, the change is occurring in the kingdom, albeit in a controlled manner and imposed from the top.

With the end of the Cold War, the 1990s heralded the onset of a new world order which brought with it new challenges and winds of change.[3] Serious questions have been raised regarding the legitimacy of the GCC rulers, fuelled by issues like political exclusion, lack of accountability, economic and demographic problems, ethnic and religious discriminations, religious extremism, external interferences, unemployment and unusual reliance over migrant labour and so on.

Understanding the potential for reform in Bahrain requires a clear appreciation not only of the nature of change, but also of how such change fits in with the socio-political structure of the country and external issues influencing reforms. The power structure within the kingdom determines the origins of reform and influences its potential for the future. Historically, power has been held firmly by the ruling family, and their control over society means that top-down reform is the only viable course. The ruling family's tendency is to retain their traditional hold on power over the long term and to liberalize rather than implement substantive reforms challenging the power structure.[4] It is, therefore, prudent to examine how far the kingdom of Bahrain has progressed on the path of political transition.

POLITICAL ENVIRONMENT

Bahrain is a small archipelago located between Saudi Arabia and the Qatar peninsula. The largest island contains the capital, Manama. The population of Bahrain is the smallest of the Gulf states, about 727,785 (includes 235,108 non-nationals).[5] The population is primarily Arab. Bahrain's ruling family, the Al-Khalifah, has ruled Bahrain since 1783, which is the longest in the Gulf, and is a branch of the Bani Utub tribe that rules Kuwait.[6] Although, they are Sunni, some 70 per cent of Bahrainis are Shia. Unlike Kuwait, where the ruling family is generally accepted, in Bahrain it has been opposed by the majority of the Shia population. As a result, Bahrain's movements in the direction of political liberalization have been much more cautious.[7]

The historical process of state formation has been decisive in the current institutional characteristics and determining the pattern of rule. The British colonial heritage and tribalism are the major elements which have influenced in shaping the political developments in Bahrain. By the time of independence of Bahrain in 1971, the ruling family had already established their supremacy over the tribal areas that later became the independent state. British support was a critical factor in transforming ruling class into royal family. Up until the 1950s and the 1960s, the ruling family governed through a combination of British material and diplomatic protection, traditional and tribal legitimacy. The discovery of oil changed the political equation considerably, resulting in a steady bureaucratization of the monarchy and the development of a modern civil service. A pyramidal power structure emerged, with the royal family at the top, supported by the civil service and the armed forces. The ruling family created institutions and patterns of rule that have considerably cushioned their vulnerability against popular uprising or other similar domestic threats.

At the level of political institutions, the monarchy has become highly institutionalized. Tribal practices such as *Shura* (consultation) and institutions such as the *Majlis* (advisory council) continue to remain important symbolic elements in the state's *modus operandi*. The state also offers—education, medical treatment, subsidized food, housing and employment—to reinforce the strength of the royal family. Further, royal family monopolized all important bureaucratic, military and provincial institutions. In Bahrain, the offices of

Prime Minister, foreign minister, interior minister, and the defence minister are all occupied by members of the royal family. Moreover, in Bahrain, where the royal family is not as wealthy as in the other states of GCC, Princes and Princesses are deeply involved in a variety of commercial and business activities. This strengthens their ability to maintain clientalistic ties with wealthy merchants, and with the larger society in the country.[8]

The Al-Khalifah family enjoys a monopoly of political power at the top in the social stratification. They are supported by their tribal allies, originally from the Nejd region of what today is Saudi Arabia. The Hawla merchant class constitutes the second stratum and is the principal economic elite. These families migrated to Bahrain from Iranian coast over the last several centuries but claim to be Arab, Sunni. The largest stratum is formed by Baharina, concentrated in Bahrain's villages. They are presumed to be original inhabitants of the Island and are entirely Shia. The Persian population forms the fourth stratum in the social stratification. Nearly all Persians in Bahrain today were immigrants during 20th century. They came to Bahrain first as small merchants and then especially as workers in the oil fields during 1930s and 1940s.[9]

Bahrain has a long history of political dissent. The combination of political domination by the Al-Khalifah and their allies and the economic deprivation of the Shias produced the root cause of dissidence, that marked much of the 20th century. The divisions between rich and poor, powerful and powerless are sharper than anywhere else in the Gulf. It is more because of Bahrain's paucity of oil and income opportunities.[10] Bahrain, the poorest of the oil producing countries in the Gulf, depends on oil for 50 per cent of its immediate national income. Petroleum production and refining account for over 60 per cent of Bahrain's export receipts, over 70 per cent of government revenues, and 11 per cent of GDP (exclusive of allied industries).[11] During the 1970s, the tremendous growth in oil wealth successfully built up the infrastructure and other manifestation of the state and provided citizens with wide range of services for free. When the oil prices fell in the 1980s, the whole region was adversely affected and this reflected in economic and political difficulties. Bahrain, the poorest and less endowed of the Gulf states suffered most from economic distress. It translated into a violent sustained uprising demanding political reform.[12]

In Bahrain, there is an extremely high unemployment rate accounted 15 per cent of the local population by the end of the year 2007. Unemployment is reported to be particularly high among the Shia population. The Shia population, who account for up to two thirds of the Bahraini national population, feel excluded from jobs, both in government and the private sector. From time to time, Shia protests have been put down severely by the government forces. They feel discriminated against both politically and economically by the government.[13]

Bahrain has a long history of political activism. M. Fakhro (1998) has divided the democratic movement into six phases: Administrative Reforms (1919-20), the growth of political awareness (1938-52), the popular uprising (1953-56), the uprising of March 1965, the first National Assembly (1972-75), and The Shura Council, 1992. Apart from these, there were anti-government demonstrations in 1994, demanding employment, freedom of expression, restoration of parliament. Since then, demonstrations and arrests have continued intermittently.[14] In December 2007, the Al-Haq Movement of Liberties and Democracies, a non-sectarian movement group pursuing a campaign for democratic reform, launched a petition calling for the dismissal of the Prime Minister Sheikh Khalifah bin Sulman. He has held the post for 37 years. It also rejects the constitution of Bahrain, and will boycott the National Assembly elections due in 2010. The opposition groups want "true constitutional monarchy" not the removal of Al-Khalifah monarchy.[15]

Before oil, Bahrain's economy was largely dependent on pearling. Oil was discovered in commercial quantities in Bahrain in the late 1930s, but the scope of its reserves has always been modest, the lowest in the GCC. Bahrain was both the first Gulf state to develop an oil industry and also the first oil producer in the region to begin to run out of oil. The modest scope of Bahrain's oil made it the first country to make serious efforts to diversify its economy. Bahrain undertook several industrial projects. The largest was Aluminium Bahrain. Other projects included the Arab Shipbuilding and Repair Yard (ASRY) and the Arab Iron and Steel Company (AISC). Another diversification effort was the establishment of offshore banking units. These sources generated significant income for Bahrain.[16] Despite attempts at diversification, hydrocarbons still account for about 60 per cent of Bahrain's export receipts, 65 per cent of government revenues, and 27 per cent of gross domestic product.[17]

DRIVERS OF REFORMS

In order to address the question of the reasons behind political reforms in Bahrain, it is important in the first instance to look into the impact of the power structures within the Kingdom. Historically, the ruling tribal elites have held a monopoly of power in the state. This position has been buttressed by the availability of effective and loyal armed forces and internal security forces to quash any domestic challenge. Adding to this, the activities of social groups are constrained through legislation. Political parties are prohibited but political societies are legalized as per July 2005 law.[18]

The entrenched power structure in the Gulf states is the widely held belief among the ruling families that they could rely on support from the other GCC ruling tribes if the internal situation became too difficult to manage. Such regional support networks are based on the view that if one ruling tribe were overthrown, this would foster political activism in the other monarchies, and so their survival is commonly held to be interlinked. The nature of this power relationship within the oil monarchies is crucial to understanding the character of current reform and prospects for the future. The ruling families have historically been in firm control of the reins of power, and civil society simply lacks the capacity to force change onto the political agenda. While the elites hold power too tightly, change will come only if those in power choose to implement it.[19]

The ruling family of Bahrain see themselves as the 'owners' rather than 'rulers' of the country, and reform which shifts the balance of power is seen as leading to a loss of such traditional tribal rights.[20] Any departure from the *status quo* is thus seen as leading to a fundamental change in the balance of power which could open the way for an uncontrollable challenge to their position. It is, therefore, viewed by them as a highly risky strategy especially in Bahrain where civil society is highly assertive. Nevertheless, it is generally recognized that stability and maintenance of power can be linked with the level of legitimacy held by the elites. Increasing legitimacy is thus seen as a means to stifle opposition and cement the staying power of the regime. However, by enacting reforms to achieve this objective, the ruling family of Bahrain is seeking to maintain their position of power for the long term.[21]

In GCC states, it is generally a motley group with little or no shared characteristics is at the forefront demanding reforms. Some of them are political groups often referred to as societies, some are conservative clerics, technocrats, minority groups, expatriates and sometimes even members of the royal family. Apart from these internal players, external pressure has also been wielded at times calling reforms. Conservative groups, active in all the countries, are in the vanguard of reformist movements in some of the states like Bahrain and Kuwait, though their major concern is opening up of political system.

In Bahrain several NGOs have been set up since the endorsement of the national charter of action in February 2001, including the Bahrain Human Rights Society and the Supreme Council for Bahraini Women. The Arab Islamic Wasat Society, the Democratic Progressive Forum, the Islamic National Accord, the National Action Charter Society and the National Democratic Action Society are the major political societies.

External pressures are considered as significant factors for embarking on the reform process. Some of it is coming from the US, declaring its intentions of democratization of the region by any means. At the same time, the US invasion of Iraq, objections regarding American presence in the Gulf, its backing for Israel, and its patronage for the monarchs have led to a backlash against the GCC rulers in their own states. The effects of globalization through the growth of Information and Communication Technology and Internet access are likely to result in greater political awareness. The impact of satellite-based media and the increasing use of Internet is likely to foster a better understanding among the younger generation of political and social practices on an international level.[22]

POLITICAL ECONOMY FACTOR

The process of political reforms in the GCC states is based first and foremost on an analysis of the political economy of these states. In view of the grave economic difficulties and social tensions that confront the ruling families, they have had little choice but to consider the introduction of economic and political reforms.[23] Pointing to the rentier nature of the GCC societies and political economy persuasion enduring authoritarian regimes, Giacomo Luciani states:

> A state that economically supports society and is the main source of private revenues through government expenditure, while in turn supported by revenue accruing from abroad, does not need to respond to society. On the contrary, a state that is supported by society, through taxes levied in one form or another, will in the final analysis be obliged to respond to social pressure.[24]

The oil monarchies in the GCC are detached from their socio economic liability by virtue of rent. They have acquired relative autonomy from society, which gives them the ability to pursue national goals without accountability.[25] Beblawi, one of the main theorists of rentierism, extended the argument that 'with virtually no taxes, citizens are far less demanding in terms of political participation'.[26] Huntington relates the failure of oil-rich states to democratize to windfall from hydrocarbons, which discards its need for introducing tax system. He further says that these states are comfortable with *status quo*, that is, non-competitive polities in which there is neither representation nor taxation.[27] Luciani was arguing in the mid 1990s:

> "Rentier nature of the state is a strong factor in discouraging democratization in all the countries that have access to oil rent, and I would be surprised if any of the rentier states were to democratize; but the presence of a fiscal crisis creates the expectation that a country may embark on a process of democratization".[28]

Despite declining oil revenues beginning in the 1980s and the shock of Gulf war in 1990-91, Bahrain continues to placate domestic pressure for liberalization. It was just because of the state's institutional strength, which is a result of the rentier nature of economy.[29]

The rise of petrodollar economic system in the early 1970s and the massive influx of capital resulting from rapid increases in the price of oil had enabled the ruling families to buy off their population and to depoliticize them. This was made possible because the ruling families tried to satisfy their material needs without additional costs to the population, in other words, without taxing them for the privileges. The offering included the provision of services as health care, education, housing, food, electricity, and a wide range of other important services, a high-tech infrastructure and employment. The way in which the state deployed their oil income not only cushioned them against political upheaval; not only made much of society dependent on the ruling family, but also led the emergence of powerful state machineries and allowed the elites to undertake a form of social engineering by creating state-reliant middle class.[30]

CONSTITUTIONAL REFORMS IN BAHRAIN

In his speech on the occasion of Bahrain's independence in 1971, the Emir stressed the necessity of establishing a constitution. He stressed that, Bahrain's modern polity should be based on a constitution the function of which would be (a) to protect the unity of the country and the cohesion of Bahraini society (b) to define the guarantee of basic individual freedoms such as education, health, work and expression, and (c) to establish a framework in which the people would by right participate in the governance of the country.[31]

A Constitution Assembly was established in 1972 with 22 elected and 8 appointed members. After many elaborate discussions, a constitution for the country was established and it called for a National Assembly.[32] The constitution consist of 109 Articles and of five major chapters, which are the State; the basic principle of society; general rights and duties; Branches (the Emir, the legislative, the executive and the judiciary); and general rules and procedures, was drafted. The constitution called for a National Assembly, a unicameral body (article 43), the members of which were to be elected by the people by secret ballot. On 7 December 1973 about 27,000 Bahraini male citizens went to the polls to elect the 30 member of the first National Assembly in the history of Bahrain.[33] In absence of political parties, the clubs and societies have played the essential function performed by political parties in the other political systems. However, continuing protests against the government prompted the ruler to issue a state security law in 1975, granting the government wide powers to detain and hold dissidents. The law was never submitted for the approval of Assembly which was united in opposition to this law. In 1975, the government suspended the Assembly and the constitution.[34]

Since the 1990s, the GCC states have significantly emerged with some political reforms establishing limited parliaments and regular elections (as in the case of Bahrain and Kuwait). With the exception in Bahrain, rest of the GCC states do not have legal political parties. There were growing demands for political participation. In an attempt to appease and divert the demands for reinstating the constitution, in 1992, the government announced plans for a Consultative Council whose members would be drawn from business, professional, religious and academic backgrounds.[35] A Consultative Council (*Majlis al-Shura*) was established in 1993 in Bahrain with 30 appointed members by emir, most of them representing the merchant community and the private sector, and none belonging to any political movement. Fifteen members were merchants, three were building contractors, two were religious preachers, two property landlords, one academic, one from the workers committee of Bahrain Petroleum Company (BAPCO), five professionals and one editor-in-chief of a local daily. In 1996, the Council was expanded to 40 members.[36] In terms of importance and national role the new council was a mere shadow of the directly elected, 30 member national assembly which was suspended in 1975.[37] The main function of this council was to express its opinion and advice on bills before they become law, on the general policy of the state, matters of general and municipal services, and economic development. Furthermore, all members were appointed and had no legislative or supervisory authority. In other words, it was a powerless consultative body. The emir was empowered to dissolve the council if the interest of the state so demanded.[38] However, this Council as well as proposed Municipal election did not measure up to the demands for real democratic political rights, and opposition remained adamant in its demand for a constitutional parliament, expansion of employment opportunities for Bahrainis and end to corruption in the government.[39]

The situation changed with the death of Amir Shaykh Isa bin Salman in early 1999 and the accession of his son Shaykh Hamad bin Isa Al-Khalifah. He was heir apparent since 1964 and succeeded his father as Amir on 6 March 1999, promised a new era of reform. A National Charter (*mithaq*) for the country was announced in December 2000, with the provisions of creation of a bicameral legislative body including an elected body (lower house) by 2004, the independence of the judiciary and the provision that Bahrain would become a monarchy (*mamlaka*) and the Amir a King.[40] In summary, the principal provisions of the charter were as follows:

Chapter One sets out the social and legal responsibilities of the state and the people, including: (a) an emphasis on justice and the sovereignty of the law; (b) stipulations on how personal freedom and equality were to be guaranteed; (c) the freedom of religion; (d) the freedom of expression and publication; (e) the freedom of institutions of civil society; (f) protection for the family and the state's responsibility to care those in need; (g) the right to work; and (h) the right to education and to academic freedom.

Chapter Two defines the structure of the state. Bahrain is defined as a hereditary constitutional monarchy with the Amir as head of state and supreme commander of the armed forces. He appoints and dismisses the Prime Minister and the ministers. Islam is the religion of the state and Islamic jurisprudence as a principle for legislation; the people are the source of all powers; the democratic principle depends on the separation of power between the three branches (legislative, executive, and judiciary), but Amir is the head of the three branches; the sovereignty of the law is the basis of rule and therefore the independence and the immunity of the Judiciary are two essential warranties to protect rights and liberties; and the people, including both men and women, have the right to take part in public affairs, including voting and candidacy for office.

Chapter Three defines the economic foundation of Bahrain; private property is guaranteed; economic justice is secured through legal adherence to contractual relations; the diversification of economic activities in Bahrain has promoted economic development and offered employment opportunities; Bahrain seeks to protect the environment and wildlife; public funds should be protected and the state must safeguard natural wealth and resources; and citizens should receive support for training in order to enhance their employment opportunities.

Chapter Four details the responsibilities and requirements for national security. These include supporting the Bahrain Defence Force to allow it to carry out its mission, as well as the National Guard. The role of the Amir as the BDF's founder is emphasized.

Chapter Five sketches the background to parliamentary activities, with emphasis on the role of the *Majlis al-Shura*. It asserts that many long-standing democracies have adopted a bicameral legislative system, with one council to represent the trends and thoughts of the people on contemporary issues, and other to operate as a council for competent and experienced members.

Chapter Six affirms Bahrain's commitment to the Gulf Cooperation Council and pledges to work for more coordination within the GCC in such areas as economic complementarity, defence cooperation and information coordination, as well as for the improvement of GCC institutions for popular participation.

Chapter Seven emphasizes Bahrain's Arab identity, its membership in the organization of Islamic Conferences and the United Nations, and its belief in the peaceful settlement of disputes and international free trade.[41]

The release of the text of the National Charter was accompanied by the holdings of several public meetings to discuss its provisions and implications in the light of the government's announcement that the charter would be put to vote in a national referendum. For the first time, the atmosphere in the country was open and talk of democracy was everywhere. The Heir Apparent, Shaykh Salman bin Hamad, was appointed to head the committee charged with implementing the Charter.[42] The National Charter was put to referendum on 14-15 February 2001 and approved by 98.4 per cent of the eligible electorate.[43] Soon after the referendum, the Emir underlined his commitment to reform by abolishing both the hated State Security Law and State Security Court, which had been used extensively to suppress all opposition. A new constitution was framed on its basis and was released approximately one year after the referendum. On 14 February 2002, Bahrain was declared as the Constitutional Monarchy, Shaykh Hamad proclaimed himself King of Bahrain and designated his son, Salman, crown Prince. The new constitution also provided for elected Municipal Councils and a bicameral legislature (*Majlis al Watani*) consisting of an appointed Consultative Council (*Majlis Al Shura*) and the elected Chamber of Deputies (*Majlis Al Nuwab*). Both houses of Parliament comprise 40 members each, who serve for four-year renewable terms of office. However, the move towards Constitutional Monarchy has not eliminated the tribal source of legitimacy.[44]

2002 Elections for Municipality and Parliament

Following the adoption of the constitution, Municipal elections were held in May 2002-the first since 1957, and the parliamentary elections in October 2002 respectively.[45] In the Municipal elections, 306 candidates, including 34 women competed for 50 seats in five governorates.[46] Voter turnout amounted to 51 per cent of the registered electorate, but the significance of this poll was that it was the first election in Bahrain's history which was conducted on the basis of universal suffrage. Women were allowed both to vote and to stand as candidates. They accounted for 52 per cent of all voters, but no female candidates were elected. Nevertheless, the Islamists, primarily from the main opposition party, Al Wefaq National Islamic Society gained a major victory. Although Al-Wefaq National Islamic Society participated in the Municipal elections, it opted to boycott the October 2002 parliamentary elections as a protest against the provisions in the constitution on the role of the appointed *Majlis al-Shura*.[47] However, the results of the 2002 parliamentary elections saw majority of seats go to Sunni Islamist candidates, winning 20 seats with most leading Shia societies boycotting the election. The Shia societies that did take part won only four seats. With no women elected out of 174 candidates which included 8 women competing for 40 seats.[48]

The Most Recent Elections in 2006

The latest round of parliamentary elections in Bahrain was held on 25 November 2006 for the Chamber of Deputies (*Majlis Al Nuwab*). Municipal elections were also held simultaneously. In parliamentary elections voter turnout was 72 per cent of the electorate.

In this election, only one woman won a seat out of 18 women candidates registered, from a total of 207. A pro-government independent named Latifa al-Qaud, who ran unopposed. Her opponent dropped out of race just a few weeks before the first round. Both Shia and Sunni Islamists dominated the poll, while liberals and nonsectarian lost their seats. The Shia bloc (with 17 seats) and Sunni bloc (with 12 seats) gained majority of seats, securing a total of 29 seats between them in parliament. King Hamad bin Isa A-Khalifah has named Jawad bin Salem al-Oraied, a Shia Muslim and a former cabinet minister as a deputy Prime Minister in Bahrain.[49]

The new constitution deprived the national assembly of the right to directly introduce legislation, gave preponderant power to unelected upper house, and gave the king nearly limitless power.[50] The 2002 constitution safeguarded the traditional rule of the Al-Khalifah and prevented the parliament from asking any change towards fulfilling the opposition's demand that the *Majlis al Shura* have not legislative capacity if comprised of appointed officials. According to the 'Article 120', no constitutional amendment was permissible by the Parliament on the provision for a bicameral system under hereditary rule. The king has the right under the constitution to dissolve Parliament, but although he retains the power of veto on legislation, the National Assembly may overturn this by two-thirds majority vote. Given that this would require a number of the appointed *Majlis al Shura* to vote against the King, such an eventuality is unlikely.[51]

Bahraini legislature along with Kuwaiti and Qatari are more empowered and effective than the rest of the GCC states. The Chamber of Deputies (lower house) which consists of 40 members, are elected by direct, secret general ballot. Ministers are responsible to the Chamber of Deputies. The Prime Minister presents bills to the Chamber of Deputies, which is entitled to pass, amend or reject them. If the Consultative Council does not approve a bill passed by the Chamber of Deputies, it shall be returned to the Chamber for reconsideration. If the two Chambers differ twice over any bill, a joint session (National Assembly) is convened to discuss. If the National Assembly does not reach a decision the King may issue the bill as a Decree that has the force of a law. All financial and budgetary bills shall first be submitted to the Chamber of Deputies. The constitution provides the Chamber with powers of interpellation. The Chamber of Deputies may question any Minister on matters coming within the sphere of competence. The Chamber can move a no-confidence motion against a minister upon an application signed by at least ten members of the Chamber of Deputies following the debate on the question put to him. If the motion is passed by a majority of two-thirds the Minister shall be regarded as having withdrawn from the ministry. However, the Chamber is not empowered to move such a motion against the Prime Minister. Only the National Assembly can consider such a move. If the National Assembly decides by a two third majority that the Prime Minister has to be changed, the matter is submitted to the King. He may either remove the Prime Minister and appoint a new government, or dissolve the lower house.

REFORM FROM ABOVE

The main purpose of reform from above is system maintenance in a situation of socio-economic crisis.[52] On close inspection, it is clear that change has consistently been initiated by the ruling elites themselves and has taken a character of controlled liberalization rather than a substantive shift in power relationships. A process of democratization, therefore, has not been established. This may be explained by the simple lack of power on the part of civil society to act as a driver of change. The key motivation of any reform lies in the elites desire to safeguard their position of power through enhanced legitimacy. The ruling family still maintains a clear hold on the reins of power and is carefully implementing reform initiatives to bolster their own positions. The ruling family is the firm masters of the political domain and are able to control the pace and direction of reform. Although civil society is increasingly politically energized, it simply does not have the ability to force reforms. Reform essentially remains a top-down, controlled process. Moreover, most of the reforms taking place in Bahrain are a result of the willingness of the rulers to implement reforms, perhaps for their own advantage, as a strategy of system maintenance.[53]

Despite the government's interest to maintain the status quo, change is happening. The reforms that accompanied the accession of a new ruler in 1999 have set in place an expectation of democratic progress. Reform was effectively stagnant until King Hamad bin Isa succeeded his father. While it is tempting to believe that international pressure was the driving force behind the reforms enacted by the rulers, their own desire to safeguard their own positions have been the main motives for introducing reforms. It is understood to be the King's attempt to craft its own legacy.[54] As Ehteshami and Wright suggest that, until the locus of power in the Gulf monarchies shift substantively away from the elites towards civil society, generational succession will prove to be the single most important factor in ushering in new reforms by the GCC ruling families.[55]

IMPLICATIONS FOR THE REFORM PROCESS

One strong conclusion emerging from the survey outlined above of the Kingdom of Bahrain is that the country is far from being a stagnant political activity, and in fact characterized by a great deal of dynamism. Although Bahrain has been more cautious and has preferred a more gradualist approach, it has managed to keep some of its traditional political features while adapting to the forces of modernization. In 1973, even circumscribed forms of representative assembly which was created in Bahrain proved too much of a threat to the ruling family and it was dissolved. Yet today, Bahrain, along with Kuwait and Qatar are in the vanguard of a new wave of reforms.

Bahrain also badly needed to create the stability if it was to establish itself successfully as new financial hub of the region. One of the main factors driving a reform process has been fiscal crisis of the state. During the 1970s, the massive influx of capital from oil had enabled the ruling family to depoliticize the population by providing them privileges without taxing for the facilities. The state provided certain level of economic security, in exchange for which society grants the ruling elites considerable political legitimacy. In other words, in a rentier economy, state-society relations seem predicated on the principle of 'no taxation, no representation.'[56]

Recent studies have demonstrated that strains in the rentier economies of the Gulf countries have prompted some states in the region to embark on liberalization processes.[57] It may have forced the pace of reform, but have not dictated its content, which has increasingly been set by the need to reform the socio-economic relations of society. As Gause III notes:

> As the role of the state in these countries has grown, it has begun to call forth new demands for representative institutions and responsible government from society. The recent (1990s) upsurge in political activity in the Gulf monarchies is not only consistent with the realities of the rentier state and its relationship to society, but is in fact generated by those realities.[58]

In Bahrain, the march towards constitutional development already started, but the process of reform is being guided from above. It is the rulers themselves who are emerging as very agents of political change. On the broader level, many problems remain. Critics of the GCC ruling families point to the wider governance issues. They argue that, for all the reform measures adopted or proposed, power continues to rest in the hands of a family group embedded in the structures of the state. In the absence of the decision making bodies outside the ruler's circle, and of political parties, an accountable and responsive government, transparency in the working of the government and its agencies, more powerful Shura Councils, an effective legal framework for rights, a free press and the conditions conducive to the free flow of ideas, these societies remain far from being on a democratic or pluralistic path. Nevertheless, reform as a process is now firmly on the agenda of the GCC states, albeit at a measured pace.[59]

Despite its shortcomings, Bahrain transition to Constitutional Monarchy has attracted international plaudits. The Kingdom has been referred to as a "beacon of democracy" in the Gulf by its Western allies, which are keen to promote Bahrain as a model for others in region to follow.[60]

Taking into account the above discussion, it can be concluded that Bahrain along with other GCC states have to go a long way in attaining effective levels of political reform. However, a beginning has been made in this direction in almost all the GCC states, including Bahrain. In most cases, they are not the result of any natural movement, but imposed from the above, depending on the convenience of the ruling families. For reforms to succeed there has to be an overall restructuring of the political, judicial, legal, legislative and administrative apparatus. And they also require bold and imaginative leadership and cooperation from citizens.

NOTES

1. Fred H. Lawson, 'Economic liberalization and the reconfiguration of authoritarianism in the Arab Gulf states', *Orient* 46:1, 2005, p. 19.
2. Mehran Kamrava, 'Non-democratic states and political liberalization in the Middle East: a structural analysis', *Third World Quarterly*, 19: 1, 1998, p. 75.
3. Anoushiravan Ehteshami and Steven Wright, 'Political Change in the Arab oil monarchies: from liberalization to enfranchisement', *International Affairs* 83:5, 2007, p. 913.
4. Ehteshami and Wright, 'Political Change in the Arab oil monarchies', p. 914.
5. The World Fact Book: Bahrain, May 8, 2009, URL:https://www.cia.gov/library/publications/the-world-factbook/geos/ba.html#top
6. Rosemarie S. Zahlan (1989), '*The Making of the Modern Gulf States: Kuwait, Bahrain, Qatar, and the United Emirates and Oman*' (London: Unwin Hyman), pp. 82-83; Rosemarie S. Zahlan (1979), '*The Creation of Qatar*' (London: Croom Helm), pp. 26-28.
7. Jill Crystal (2007), "Eastern Arabian states", in David E. Long, Bernard Reich and Mark Gasiorowski (eds), *The Government and Politics of Middle East and North Africa* (Colorado: West View), p. 168.
8. Kamrava, 'Non-democratic states and political liberalization in the Middle East', pp. 75-79.
9. J.E. Peterson, 'The nature of succession in the Gulf', *Middle East Journal* 55:4, Autumn 2001, pp. 587-89; Zahlan (1989), '*The Making of the Modern Gulf states: Kuwait, Bahrain, Qatar, and the United Emirates and Oman*', pp. 46-49.
10. J.E. Peterson, 'Bahrain's first steps towards reform under Amir Hamad', *Asian Affairs*, 33:2, June 2002, p. 217.
11. The World Fact Book: Bahrain, May 8, 2009, URL:https://www.cia.gov/library/publications/the-world-factbook/geos/ba.html#top
12. Peterson, 'Bahrain's first steps towards reform under Amir Hamad', p. 218.
13. MEED (2008), 'Special report on Bahrain', *Middle East Economic Digest*, 25-31 January 2008, 52:4, pp. 30-32.
14. Munira A. Fakhro (1997), 'The uprising in Bahrain: An Assessment', in Gary G. Sick and Lawrence G. Potter (eds), *The Persian Gulf at the Millennium*, (London: Macmillan), pp. 168-181.
15. MEED (2008), 'Special report on Bahrain', *Middle East Economic Digest*, 25-31 January 2008, 52:4, pp. 30-32.
16. Jill Crystal (2007), 'Eastern Arabian states', p. 168.

17. MEED (2008), 'Special report on Bahrain', *Middle East Economic Digest*, 25-31 January 2008, 52:4, p. 37.
18. The World Fact Book: Bahrain, May 8, 2009, URL:https://www.cia.gov/library/publications/the-world-factbook/geos/ba.html#top
19. Ehteshami and Wright, '*Political Change in the Arab Oil Monarchies*', p. 915.
20. Ibid., p. 915.
21. Gudrun Kramer, 'Liberalization and democracy in the Arab world', *Middle East Report*, January-February 1992, pp. 24-25.
22. Ehteshami and Wright, '*Political Change in the Arab Oil Monarchies*', pp. 914-916.
23. Anoushiravan Ehteshami, 'Reform from above: the politics of participation in the oil monarchies', *International Affairs* 79:1, 2003, p. 54.
24. Giacomo Lucuani, 'Resources, revenues and authoritarianism in the Arab world: beyond the rentier state', in Rex Brynen et al. (eds), *Political liberalization and democratization in the Arab world: Theoritical perspectives* (Boulder: lynne Rienner, 1995), p. 211.
25. Ehteshami, 'Reform from above: The politics of participation in the oil monarchies', p. 57.
26. Hazem Beblawi, "The rentier state in the Arab world', in Hazem Beblawi and Giacomo Luciani (eds), *The rentier state*, (London: Croom Helm, 1987), p. 53.
27. Samunel Hutigton (1991), "*The third wave: Democratization in the late twentieth century*", (London: University of Oklahoma Press), p. 65.
28. Giacomo Luciani, 'The Oil rent, the fiscal crisis of the state and democratization', in *Ghassan Salame*, (ed.), *Democracy without democrats: the renewal of politics in the Muslim world* (London: I.B. Taurus, 1994), p. 152.
29. Kamrava, 'Non-democratic states and political liberalization in the Middle East', p. 79.
30. Ehteshami, 'Reform from above: the politics of participation in the oil monarchies', pp. 58-59.
31. Emile A. Nakhleh (1997), 'Political participation and the constitutional experiments in the Arab Gulf: Bahrain and Qatar', in Tim Niblock (ed.), *Social and economic development in the Arab Gulf*, (London: Croom Helm), p. 166
32. Fakhro (1997), 'The uprising in Bahrain', p. 175.
33. Nakhleh (1997), 'Political participation and the constitutional experiments in the Arab Gulf', pp. 167-169; Zahlan (1989), 'The making of the modern gulf states', pp. 50-60.
34. Jill Crystal (2007), 'Eastern Arabian states', pp. 168-169.
35. Ibid., 169.
36. Fakhro, 'The uprising in Bahrain', p. 175.
37. Ehteshami, 'Reform from above', p. 66.
38. Fakhro, 'The uprising in Bahrain', p. 175.
39. May Seikaly (2001), 'Kuwait and Bahrain: The appeal of globalization and internal constraints', in Joseph A Kechichian (ed.), *Iran, Iraq and the Arab Gulf states* (New York: Palgrave), p. 189.
40. J.E. Peterson (2002), 'Bahrain's first steps towards reform under Amir Hamad', *Asian Affairs*, 33:2, p. 218.
41. *Ibid.*, pp. 220-221.

42. *Ibid.*, 221.
43. Voting was based on universal suffrage for Bahraini citizens, including women, aged over 20 years. According to election monitoring committee, 217,579 individuals were given the vote, of whom 196, 262 chose to participate in the ballot: 191,790 people supported the charter, www.arabicnews.com (17 Feb, 2001).
44. Nakhleh (1997), '*Political participation and the constitutional experiments in the Arab Gulf*', p. 161.
45. The municipalities have no political role and are merely geared toward the provision of social services.
46. Bahrain was divided into twelve municipalities with five governorates. Each governorate has an elected ten-member council; oversight and control are exercized from the Ministry of Municipal Affairs.
47. The other key political societies which called for a boycott are the Arab Nationalist Democratic Society; the Secular National Democratic Action Society; and the Islamic Action Society.
48. Ehteshami and Wright, '*Political Change in the Arab Oil Monarchies*', pp. 920-921; Ehteshami, 'Reform from above', pp. 66-67; Jill Crystal, 'Eastern Arabian states', p. 169.
49. F. Gregory Gause III (2007), 'Bahrain parliamentary election results: 25 November and 2 December 2006', *International Journal of Middle East Studies*, 39:2, pp. 170-171; Ehteshami and Wright, '*Political Change in the Arab Oil Monarchies*', pp. 920-921.
50. Jill Crystal, 'Eastern Arabian States', p. 169.
51. Ehteshami and Wright, 'Political change in the Arab oil monarchies', p. 119.
52. Kramer, 'Liberalization and democracy in the Arab world', p. 24.
53. Ibid., 24-25.
54. MEED (2008), 'Special report on Bahrain', *Middle East Economic Digest*, 25-31 January 2008, 52:4, p. 31
55. Ehteshami and Wright, '*Political Change in the Arab Oil Monarchies*', pp. 930-931.
56. Giacomo Luciani, 'Economic Foundation of Democracy and Authoritarianism: The Arab world in a comparative perspective', *Arab Studies Quarterly* 10, 1988, p. 463.
57. Jill Crystal, 'Authoritarianism and its adversaries in the Arab World', *World Politics*, 46, 1994, pp. 262-289. See also, Rex Brynen et al. (eds), *Political liberalization and democratization in the Arab world: Theoritical perspectives*, Vol. 1, (Boulder: lynne Rienner, 1995); Augustus Richard Norton (ed.), *Civil Society in the Middle East*, Leiden: EJ Brill, 1995.
58. F. Gregory Gause III, 'Oil monarchies: Domestic and security challenges in the Arab Gulf states', New York: Council on Foreign Relations Press, 1994, p. 81.
59. Ehteshami, 'Reform from above', pp. 74-75.
60. MEED (2003), 'Special report on Bahrain', *Middle East Economic Digest*, 30 May 2003, 47:22, p. 20.

19

Democratic Reforms in Qatar

Basir Ahmed and Marshal Gao

Many nations in the Arab world are making efforts to address the issue of democratic deficit. Democratic reforms figure high on the agenda of these governments. The 8th Doha Forum on Democracy, Development and Free Trade held in the Qatari capital, demonstrated a deep keenness to continue moving ahead along the path of democracy. It demanded that the path of democratization be cleared from all political, economic, media and social impediments. Qatar, though a latecomer in this regard, has gone far in this direction. Within a short span of time, since 1971, Qatar has made tremendous progress on the democratic front. Yet much remains to be done. This study focuses on democratic reforms enacted or underway by the Qatari political setup, the pace of such reforms and how far those reforms have been able to meet existing expectations. Lastly, this study tries to map the extent to which the Qatari state has, or has not, been able to successfully address the problem of democratic deficit.

The title of a conference held at an Ivy League University sometime back was 'Democracy in the *West Asia**. Is it possible?' The tone is almost incredulous: it is as though someone had just caught sight of a phenomenon so unexpected, so unlikely, that they could hardly believe their eyes. It is widely held, that, West Asia is a region of the world that remains untouched by democracy.[1] Since 1970s, the absolute number of democracies in the world has nearly tripled, while the percentage of the world's states that are democratic has doubled. Democracy has expanded significantly in every other major region of the world. Only in the West Asia it has failed to expand. Overall, the 19 states of West Asia have by far the lowest average levels of freedom. On the 7-point combined Freedom House scale of political rights and civil liberties, with 1 being most free and 7 the least free, the states of the West Asia have an average score today of 5.53. Not only is this the least free region of the world—by more than a full point on the Freedom House scale, as compared to the

*Italics are of authors.

next most repressive region—but it is also the only region where the average level of freedom has declined since 1974. Moreover, if we examine only the 16 predominantly Arab states of the region (excluding Israel, Turkey, and Iran), the picture is even more uniformly authoritarian. Among the 16 Arab states, there are no democracies, and the average level of freedom in 2002 was 5.81, compared to an average of 3.16 for the other 176 states of the world. This gap (2.65 points on the 7-point scale) has doubled since 1972 (when it was 1.34).[2]

Autocrats generally do not willingly commit political suicide. In Qatar, particularly autocracy has repeatedly outlived predictions of its demise. This is not to underestimate the struggles of democrats within the state. Nor does it support the idea that, Islam is a stumbling block to democracy.[3] It is the concentration of economic and political clout in the hand of emir, and the existence of weak opposition, which is financially and institutionally dependent on the state, that gives ruler enough power to scuttle the democratic agenda and thereby delay the march of democracy. In short, both the ruler and opposition lack the means or incentive to negotiate a political accommodation or pact that would ease their exit from a deeply rooted legacy of autocratic rule.[4] There is very limited room for reforms and especially for political reforms. The social, economic and political structure is such that, it hardly permits any scope for political contrive.

The Head of the State has stuck a "Ruling Bargain" by which the state provides jobs, subsidies, and a modicum of social order in return for political quiescence. The Head of State controls and distributes economic resources in order to buy it political survival. In short, State's control over economic resources has made autocratic social pact possible. The oil rents that flow to state elites have fused political and economic power in ways that magnify the risks of reform. State control of the economy allows rulers to fund huge patronage systems that turn workers, professionals, intellectuals, and business people into dependents. While in recent years some of these client groups have pushed for democracy, the porous boundaries between business and the state powerfully promote an unhealthy collusion between commerce and autocracy.[5] Thus, economic factor plays a very vital role in survival of autocracy in Qatar. It is through, economic incentives that the ruler buys political allegiance. In Qatar, autocracy and economic interests reinforce each other, thereby scuttling the scope, or creating difficulties for real democracy there.

However, there is also a cultural dimension to the continuation of autocratic rule in Qatar. It is not just confined to religion or Islam, it goes beyond these elements. It's a mix of both, traditional and charismatic elements of authority. The rulers and their opponents invoke, shape, reinterpret, and sometimes even distort a myriad of religious, tribal, or ethnic symbols to defend or challenge each others' authority. The cultural norms and traditions do not give enough space for democracy, at least on the lines of Western democracy. No doubt, often the authority of the ruler is challenged and people's rule is invoked, but in a limited space within the domains of religion and culture.

Another factor which contributes to the survival of autocracy in Qatar today is "Depoliticization". It remains one of the most pernicious cultural and ideological legacies of autocratic rule. Culturally, its patrimonial nature encourages excessive deference to hierarchical authority while harnessing symbols and traditions rooted in rural Islamic structures. Ideologically, it pushes totalitarian ideologies with decidedly *Western* roots. Rulers have paid a high price for "normalizing" these patrimonial visions of authority. The state's dissemination of religiously inspired statist ideologies has crowded out secular, ethnic, or liberal Islamic alternatives, thus reinforcing the influence of illiberal Islamists.[6] Thus, in Qatar we found that there is a deliberate attempt to depoliticize the society by invoking religion and other religious symbols. The Head of State sometimes knowingly, and sometime for sheer political survival promotes it. As a result, the polity is depoliticized and the scope for democratic reforms or for a vibrant civil society is scuttled.

Yet, the persistence of autocracy cannot be reduced to Islam or to its manipulation by rulers and opposition alone. Instead, the more fundamental cultural impediment to democracy lies in the failure of both the rulers and oppositions to forge a democratic solution to the question of national identity.[7] Divided societies in giving one or more ethno-religious groups the power to marginalize opposing groups (absent strong constitutional guarantees and a culture of constitutionalism), democratic elections generate risks for minority groups. These risks of democracy are especially great for minority groups that have long monopolized power by authoritarian means, and the more abusive their rule has been, the greater the risk they will suffer retribution under democracy.[8] Hence, we found a kind of hidden fear among ruling family towards democracy. The ruling classes do not support the idea of democracy, not because the power will be taken away from their hands, but they feel that once it is done, they will be marginalized economically and politically both. Because they are a minority, they fear that, in democracy, they may not gain power and loose the same kind of clout that they enjoy today.

A LIBERALIZED AUTOCRACY

Since the ruling elite do not want to loose control over political power, and at the same time they also have to meet popular demand for democracy, they have devised a new technique of political survival called as "Liberalized autocracy". The central problem with Qatari political order is not unfamiliarity with the process of political competition, that democracy may entail, but entrenched elite that is determined to retain power. The Qatari elite is aware of the need for change and adaptation, hence, they have found a technique (Liberalized Autocracy) which seems to offer authority without displacing any of the political prerogatives of the ruling regime.

A liberal autocracy is a non-democratic government that follows the principles of liberalism. The existence of real liberties in these autocracies is very questionable. Such autocracies often abolish medieval institutions like privileges for the nobility, and inequality before the law. However, freedom of speech and freedom of association are at best limited. Liberal autocracies are much more open than monarchies but less free than modern liberal democracies. Liberal autocracy is certainly an improvement over politically repressive, economically stagnant regimes, but they are not, and cannot be equated with, functioning democracies.

In Liberal Autocracies, the rulers may eschew full-scale authoritarianism for a system that offers periodic openings in response to a variety of social, political and strategic challenges. Despite its tolerant pretensions, the governing structure lays down clear "red lines", ensuring that the prerogatives of the executive are not circumscribed by legislation and judicial oversight. A liberal autocracy may hold elections and countenance critical media, but all actors must agree to the rules promulgated by leaders who remain unaccountable. Far from challenging the reigning autocrats, the partnership actually complements their survival strategies.[9]

Qatar, in this context is also a case of "liberalizing autocracy". Despite the mix of socioeconomic, political, cultural, and ideological forces that have encouraged rulers to hold on to power, it has initiated a measure of political liberalization while trying to retain the essential elements of autocracy. Liberalized autocracies not only tolerate but depend on a limited, state-managed pluralism of ideas and organization as a strategy for legitimation and hence survival. Often adopted in response to various pressures, internal as well as external, limited liberalization and greater political participation are methods by which the ruling elite in Qatar hope to offset popular pressure for democratic reforms.[10]

The main idea behind this is to ensure that such political openings never get out of hand. The rulers in Qatar, therefore, it could be said, look to liberalization as a way to divide the opposition even while letting it blow off steam. The proliferation of civil society groups, a somewhat open press, and access to the Internet and satellite television can create a feeling of virtual democracy without opening the doors to dramatic reforms. State-monitored political parties and even state-managed elections can also serve these purposes, so long as the key "ministries of sovereignty" remain under regime control. Liberalization without popular sovereignty or political accountability is thus the essence of liberalized autocracy—a form of hybrid regime that produces "elections without democracy".[11] While it remains true that, Qatar has undertaken certain political reforms to quell domestic opposition, it cannot be said with the same certainity, that those measures will be successful in maintaining the institution of autocracy. Once people have tasted a certain amount of freedom it will be difficult for the state to hold it back. Soon there will be more demand for democracy and constutional reform. Hence the most important issue is, whether the so called "liberalizing autocracy" in Qatar can hold back the onset of real democracy? And for how long. However, before reaching any definite conclusion, let us examine in detail, how the ruling autocracy in Qatar has chosen to liberalize itself. What are those democratic reforms that, it has undertaken, in an attempt to retain autocracy.

CONSTITUTIONAL REFORMS

Qatar's constitution has passed through transitional stages starting in 1970 when the first provisional system of governance was enacted. This system was revised in 1972 after the national independence and amended to address the requirements and responsibilities of the new age. Thereafter, a number of amendments and additions were included in the constitution. For instance various articles relating to the executive authority and inheritance to the Head of State's post were included.

The Drafting Committee of the Permanent Constitution

On the 13th of July, 1999, Emir Sheikh Hamad Bin Khalifa Al-Thani issued decree no. (11) stipulating the formation of a drafting committee of the permanent constitution. In his decree, the Emir maintained that the Constitution would be the basic document and will contain principles relating to country's sovereignty and functioning of its political system. He stressed on peoples participation in governance. Therefore, Drafting Committee of the Permanent Constitution was formed. It was headed by a chairman and thirty members. The committee drafted the constitution within a span of three years. On the second of July, 2002, the Emir received the manuscript of the permanent constitution. The drafted Constitution consisted of five chapters and 150 articles. It stipulated the establishment of a parliament to be called as "The Advisory Council" of which two-thirds of its members will be elected via free direct elections whereas the remaining members shall be appointed by the Emir. The Advisory Council shall be entrusted with the legislative authority, the endorsement of the public budget and accountability of the ministers and the executive authority.

Referendum on the Constitution

A referendum to approve a new constitution was held in Qatar on 29 April 2003. The Ministry of Interior and the Public Committee of the referendum formed one hundred committees to oversee the referendum on the permanent

Constitution and define the centres where the referendum would take place. These committees were distributed among work places at the ministries, establishments and residential areas. In addition, a number of mobile committees were set up to cover certain schools, work places in the State, commercial malls, clubs, Doha International Airport, Abu Samra Centre, hospitals and other health centres of the Ministry of Public Health. The requisite terms and conditions that qualify citizens to cast their votes on the draft constitution were defined as, being a citizen holding a natural Qatari nationality and at least eighteen years of age by the 29th of April. The constitution was overwhelmingly approved, with over 98 per cent in favour. Although the population of the country was estimated to be around 790,000 at the time of the referendum, there were only 85,000 registered voters. The voter turnout was 84.3 per cent and there were 533 invalid votes (0.7% of the total).[12]

Table 19.1

Registered Voters	*85,000*	*(2003 approx.)*
Votes Cast	71,665	84.31% of registered voters
Valid Votes	71,132	99.26% of votes cast
Invalid Votes	533	0.74% of votes cast
Type of Vote	*Valid Votes*	*% of Valid Votes*
'Yes' Votes	69,987	98.39
'No' Votes	1,145	1.61

Source: IFES Election Guide (Guide, 2003).

On the 29th of April 2003, the Qataris dawned a new era, where they could soar high in the horizons of freedom, nearly after thirty years of living under the umbrella of the amended Provisional Constitution which had fallen short of being convenient to the requirements of contemporary life. This new era was marked with setting up of a permanent constitution that upholds personal liberty, safeguards the principle of equal opportunities for all citizens, protects private proprietorship, deems all people equal in rights and duties and prohibits the expulsion of any citizen from the country or preventing him from returning to it. Furthermore, the Constitution strives to create a free atmosphere whereby all types of expression are allowed and it enhances the freedom of press and publication. Likewise, it enshrines the freedom of religion, worship and conviction for all people. It also contains a provision that, all legislations are hitherto to be exercised through an elected legislative council.

On 29th of April, 2003, as it was believed Qatar made a shift from a group of totalitarian states to democratic countries. It was also said that, Qatar has moved from being a closed country to the world of liberties and cultural openness. The result of the referendum in which the percentage of popular turnout was high showed a general consent to the Constitution. The heavy turnout to the ballot boxes evidently reflected the extent of the Qatari people's response and their willingness for change. It also reflected their growing urge to have a say into the decision making process.

On 8th June 2004 Sheikh Hamad bin Khalifa Al-Thani, the Emir of the State of Qatar, issued a statement on the occasion of the ratification of the Permanent Constitution of the State of Qatar. The statement stated the following:

> "We, Hamad bin Khalifa Al-Thani, the Emir of the State of Qatar, have decreed the following: In implementation of our objectives to complete the premises of democratic rule in our beloved homeland through ratification of a permanent constitution for the country that consolidates the basic foundations of society, reflects people's participation in decision-making and guarantees the rights and freedoms of citizens, and recognizing our Arab and Islamic affiliation of which we are proud, and having been familiarized with the results of the Referendum on the Permanent Constitution of the State of Qatar on 9th April 2003 and the approval by the overwhelming majority of citizens of this constitution, and having read Article 141 of the Permanent Constitution, we have issued this Constitution" to ourselves.[13]

According to the provisional constitution adopted on 2nd April 1970, executive power was vested in the Amir, as Head of State, and exercised by the Council of Ministers, appointed by the Head of State. The Amir was assisted by the appointed Advisory Council of 20 members (increased to 30 in 1975 and 35 in 1988), whose term was extended for six years in 1975, for a further four years in 1978, and for further terms for four years in 1982, 1986, 1990, 1994 and 1998. All fundamental democratic rights were guaranteed. In 1975, the advisory Council was granted the power to summon individual ministers to answer questions on legislation before promulgation.

The constitutional development in Qatar graduated from one phase to another. Since 1970s, Amendments were made on some provisions of the provisional basic statute in regard to the executive authority and hereditary rule so as to conclude the constitutional arrangements in the country. The Judicial Acts and other basic laws, which were enacted to regulate civil and commercial interactions, were other steps that were taken in pursuit of democratic reforms. The Emiri Decree, which was issued in July 1999, to form a high level committee to draft a new, permanent constitution for the country, aimed to meet the democratic aspirations of Qatari citizens. Much before 2003, in 1999, free elections were held to form the Central Municipal Council for the first time in the history of Qatar. The historic event marked the country's first step towards democracy in its civic sense. In a pioneering move, women were allowed both to vote and run as candidates in this initial step towards popular participation in decision making in the country.

THE NEW CONSTITUTION

The Amir formally adopted the new constitution following a referendum held on 29 April 2003. Under the new constitution, the Amir was to remain head of the executive, a 45 member unicameral parliament, of which two thirds was to be directly elected (the remainder being appointed by the Amir), was to have the powers to legislate, review the state budget, monitor government policy and hold ministers accountable for their actions. The parliament was to have a four year mandate. Suffrage was to be extended to all citizens, including women, aged 18 years and above. Elections to the new legislature, after which the Advisory Council was to be abolished, were initially expected to be conducted in 2004, but were subsequently deferred. The constitution guarantees freedom of association, expression and religious affiliation, and provides for the establishment of an independent judiciary; however it does not authorize political parties.

Qatar is developing into a constitutional monarchy, but it doesn't allow political parties nor elections on a national level yet. Suffrage is currently limited to municipal elections (for both males and females aged 18 years or more). Expatriate residents are excluded. The elected Municipal Council has no executive powers but may offer advice to the Minister. The State is gradually increasing popular participation in public affairs. The draft constitution envisages a partially elected Advisory Council, to review legislation and advise the Amir.

Head of State

At the top is the Head of State, Amir Sheikh Hamad bin Khalifa Ath-Thani. He assumed power on 27 June 1995. He is assisted by the prime minister Hamad ibn Jaber Al Thani, (3 April 2007). In Qatar, the ruling Al Thani family continue to hold power following the declaration of independence in 1971. The head of state is the Emir, and the right to rule Qatar is passed on within the Al Thani family. Politically, Qatar is evolving from a traditional society into a modern welfare state. Government departments have been established to meet the requirements of social and economic progress.[14] The Basic Law of Qatar 1970 institutionalized local customs rooted in Qatar's conservative Wahhabi heritage, granting the Emir preeminent power. The Emir's role is influenced by continuing traditions of consultation, rule by consensus, and the citizen's right to appeal personally to the Emir.[15] The Emir, while directly accountable to no one, cannot violate the Sharia (Islamic law) and, in practice, must consider the opinions of leading notables and the religious establishment. Their position was institutionalized in the Advisory Council, an appointed body that assists the Emir in formulating policy. There is no electoral system. Political parties are banned.

The Consultative Assembly

The Consultative Assembly (*Majlis as-Shura*) has 35 appointed members with only consultative tasks. Qatar's constitution, approved in April 2003 by popular referendum, has created a legislative body elected by universal suffrage, excluding fifteen appointed by the emir. According to the constitution, the legislature will have three powers: to approve (but not prepare) the national budget; to monitor the performance of ministers through no-confidence votes; and to draft, discuss, and vote on proposed legislation, which becomes law only with the vote of a two-thirds majority and the Emir's endorsement.

Apart from various institutional mechanisms, Qatar's constitution includes various Articles in tune with democratic norms. For instance, Article 8 says that, the Rule of the State shall be hereditary within the Al Thani family and by the male successors. In Qatar women are allowed to vote but are denied the opportunity to rule. Article 48 deals with Press freedom, printing and publishing is assured in accordance with the law. Article 44 grants the right of assembly in accordance to the provisions of the law. No doubt that Qatar has one of the freest press in West Asia, but the phrase "in accordance with the law" is unclear and confusing, especially in a context when "law" is not clearly defined. The issue is what "Law" and whose "law". Is that "law" commonly agreed and given to themselves by the people? Is it debated, discussed and then agreed on. Any law or constitution, which does not have sanction of the people, lacks legitimacy. Article 50 says that, freedom to worship is assured to all, in accordance with the law and the requirements of protecting the public system and public behaviour. And Article 1 says that, Islam is the State's religion and the Islamic Shariah is the main source of its legislations. Articles 19 provides that, the State shall preserve the principles of the society and maintain security, stability and equal opportunities to the citizens. There is a basic contradiction between the two. If Islam is the State's religion, and Shariah is the main law, then how Qatari government can provide equal opportunities to its citizens. In short the "Law" does not recognize differences diversities, one of the fundamental pillars of democracy.

These Articles, when viewed in a holistic manner, suggests that, the state expects Islam to be the religion that is freely worshipped. Because, Islam is the state's religion and the state shall preserve the principles of the society. There is no problem, if religion is integrated with the affairs of the state, but it should not be so tightly integrated, that State appears to be advocating a particular religion. In Democracy, there should be space for secularism, pluralism and coexistence. The state should not associate itself with any particular religion.

No doubt, it is also true that, the new constitution adopted in 2003, is not the ultimate constitution. It does not intend to satisfy all sections and all interests, but it is indeed a major step towards responsible government. 20

years ago, women were not allowed to sit on the front seat, but today Qatari women can drive a car. This is here, where the relevance of constitutional reforms matter. True, that the women cannot be rulers as per the new constitution, but at least, they can vote, they have rights like any other citizens, they can move freely. The most interesting fact, which keeps the hope for democracy alive in Qatar, is that, 98 per cent of the Qatari citizens voted for the new constitution. This adds a degree of legitimacy to the constitution. It would be unrealistic to expect Qatar to move into democracy in one big step. Qatar must take small steps towards democracy. The movement towards democracy should be a gradual process, in stages, a process of experimentation and learning. Democracy brought in one big step may not sustain itself, and soon it will degenerate. However, it must be ensured that, the new constitution should herald genuine democracy. It is not used for scuttling the real demands of the people. The new constitution must not serve as a tool in the hands of the ruling family to further strengthen autocratic rule. For this to happen, citizens, civil society, pressure groups, and international stakeholders must be vigilant.

There are several credits to the new constitution which came into force on June 9, 2005. It is a landmark development in the history of democratization of the Gulf region. Written over a two year period, it replaces the provisional constitution of 1970. Jamal Yahya, a renowned Egyptian constitutionalist involved in drafting the document, told *Gulf News*: "The new constitution... is one of the most modern in the Arab world. The new charter marks a new beginning for Qatar, as the country embraces democratic reform, gender equality and a new modern judiciary".[16]

The Qatari constitution may have sanctioned Islam as the State religion for a country whose predominant population is Muslim. However, religion is not the sole source, it is only one among several sources inspiring the new legislation. The beauty of the new settlement is that, the new constitution derives much from Shariah (Islamic Law) yet it is not based on it. The constitution beautifully blends democratic norms with religious principles. There is a strong desire to ensure public participation in decision making and state administration. It sanctions establishment of a parliamentary chamber which is elected on the basis of universal suffrage. The constitution strongly advocates the protection of private property while giving an equal consideration to the public sector.

The new constitution has brought drastic reforms into the judicial system. It replaces the Shariah and Civil tribunal and establishes a single court to decide on all matters. Equality before law is the guiding principle in any judicial settlement. However, a detailed legislation is required to protect women. For instance, there is no proper family law with regard to issues such as divorce, inheritance and child custody. In short, we can safely conclude by saying that, the new constitution, though insufficient, is a bold attempt to bring the Qatari society on the path of democratization. It is an attempt to bring in democracy, while avoiding the pains, as history tells us, is associated with it. Democracy cannot be established in one go, by one franchise, in a single year. It takes several years of evolution and experimentation. If that is true, then Qatar has taken, by drafting the new constitution, advocating universal adult franchise, popular participation and judicial reforms, a small step in the right direction.

However, this is not to deny the hidden intentions and motives of its rulers. The ruling family of Qatar would not like to give away its privileges, just for the sake of some ideal or ideology. There is a definite self interest of the ruling family behind its articulation of democratic reforms and launching of the new constitution. The family wants to protect its authority and perpetuate its rule. During the 1990s, the proliferation of civil society organizations in Qatar made the state go for democracy. Unable to cope or being threatened with the challenges posed by these groups the State started to take the issue of democratic reforms seriously. Therefore, democratic reforms in Qatar are an act of survival. No doubt, the referendum was held, the new constitution was launched but this does not signify any real political change. with greater freedom of the press, assembly, and association, improved transparency, and an opening up of the political process to allow for the partial inclusion of forces hitherto excluded from it, still it is a matter of great debate whether the regime actually believed in democracy, because the institution of kingship is not only firmly protected but it is also effectively saved from any encroachment.

CONCLUSION

The goal of tactical political opening is to sustain rather than transform autocracy. Yet what we are witnessing in Qatar today is probably not a return to full authoritarianism, but rather an attempt in which the ruler is widening the boundaries of political participation in response to various socio-political challenges facing his regime. This is a much more dangerous stage in comparison to, when Qatar was a wholly autocratic state, because it endangers the formation of a robust political society. In short, it depoliticizes the polity.

While the solution to the problem of democratic deficit in Qatar lies in gradualism, any reform must ensure not only strengthening of the political society, but also should aim at promoting effective political parties, independent judiciary and legislature that represent citizens rather than a chamber that merely reflects the will of the ruler. Such changes call for bold initiative from the Qatari ruler, new thinking from mainstream groups and a readiness on the part of international agencies.

At the same time we must be aware of the fact that, there is nothing called as a common destination in the form of Western Model of Democracy. There is a certain view in the academia and other circles which assumes a finishing line demarcated according to the values, institutions and social practices of existing, mainly Western, democracies. It does not accommodate the possibility that the process of political development currently underway in the countries of the region may be going in different directions. If one size is not enough for all, then neither is one finishing line. In some cases, the process of political development is both gradual and experimental, and therefore there may be no specific finishing line in mind. While it would perhaps be wrong to characterize such gradual and cautious processes as continual revolution, it might be equally misleading to suppose that each is headed towards a common goal, and, further, that the common goal in question is either identical to or even closely resembles the kind of democratic systems with which we are familiar in the West.[17] Political development is an organic process arising out of interactions between people in specific social and cultural environment. We must respect the uniqueness of the country engaged in the process, and imagine ourselves promoting and protecting a kind of political biodiversity. In that sense, whether democracy is possible in Qatar, has become an irrelevant and outdated question. What is important is its present status. And if that is true then we can safely say that, it is already under construction. In the diverse institutions and conversations, the traditions and experiments with which the people of Qatar conduct their daily lives, manage their social relations and organize their politics there are a number of practices which could be called democratic in nature. There is ample scope within Qatari tradition for democratic practice to evolve itself. Democratization is a process, a journey it is not a condition.

NOTES

1. Jones, Jeremy (2007) *Negotiating Change: The New Politics of the Middle East,* I.B. Tauris & Co Ltd, London, p. 1.
2. Diamond, D.B. (2003). *Islam and Democracy in the Middle East,* The Johns Hopkins University Press, London, p. xi.
3. Saikal Amin and Schnabel Albrecht, (2003), *Democratization in the Middle East: Experiences. Struggles, Challenges,* The United Nations University Press, Tokyo, Japan, p. 2.
4. Diamond, no. 2, p. IX.
5. *Ibid.*, p. ix.
6. *Ibid.*, p. xii.
7. Kechichian A. Joseph, (1993) *Political Dynamics and Security in the Arabian Peninsula Through the 1990s,* Published by RAND, Santa Monica, p. 73.
8. Diamond, no. 2, p. XII.
9. Ray Takeyth, "Democracy or Autocracy", *The National Interest,* Feb/March 2005, The Nixon Centre, Washington D.C.
10. Diamond, D.B. no. 2, p. 2.
11. *Ibid.*, p. xiv.

12. Guide, I.E. "Election Profile: Qatar" Retrieved June 18, 2009, from A publication of IFES' F. Clifton White Applied Research Center for Democracy and Elections, 2003, April 29, http://www.electionguide.org/results.php?ID=341
13. Orr Tamra, (2008), "Qatar", Publisher, Marshall Cavendish, New York, Page 20.
14. Zahlan, Rosemarie Said (1989), "*The Creation of Qatar*" Routledge, London p. 34.
15. Tamra, n.13, Page 12.
16. Yahya, J. " Qatar: Qatari Democracy" *APS Review Oil Market Trends*, 19 September 2005, pp. 1-2.
17. Jones, Jeremy (2007), *Negotiating Change: The New Politics of the Middle East*, I.B. Tauris & Co Ltd, London, p. 2.

20

US Initiative of Political Liberalization and Democracy in UAE: A Myth

Syeeda Khatoon

POLITICAL AND ECONOMIC LIBERALIZATION INITIATIVES IN WEST ASIA POST 9/11

United States initiated political and economic liberalization in West Asia only after the 9/11 incident, mainly due to the fact that the 9/11 attackers came from the region. Taking the 9/11 incident as the pivotal point on the issue, the 9/11 Commission Report[1]—among other things—very explicitly stated: "A comprehensive U.S. strategy to counter terrorism should include economic policies that encourage development, more open societies, and opportunities for people to improve the lives of their families and to enhance prospects for their children's future." Going further, President George W Bush termed the reform in West Asia in the national interest of United States. He stressed using trade as a tool for fighting terrorism on the understanding that political, social and economic development will solve the problem of Islamic terrorism. Robert Zoellick (2004)[2] stated that "piece by piece, the administer is building a mosaic of modernizers with a plan that offers trade and openness as tools for Muslim leaders looking towards the rebirth of an optimistic and tolerant Islam." The 9/11 commission report[3] further considered economic openness essential for fighting terrorism. The report states that

> *The policies that support economic development and reform also have political implications. Economic and political liberties tend to be linked. Commerce, especially international commerce, requires ongoing cooperation and compromise, the exchange of ideas across cultures, and the peaceful resolution of differences through negotiation or the rule of law. Economic growth expands the middle class, a constituency for further reform. Successful economies rely on vibrant private sectors, which have an interest in curbing indiscriminate government power. Those who*

> *develop the practice of controlling their own economic destiny soon desire a voice in their communities and political societies.*

In line with the spirit of 9/11 Commission Report, Middle East Free Trade Area (MEFTA) was proposed by President George W. Bush. MEFTA was slated to be completed by 2013 and was part of Washington's long-term policy shift. Its long term policy would then engage country by country through Free Trade Areas (FTAs) under MEFTA. These FTAs would then be melded into one regional grouping called MEFTA.[4]

The MEFTA "would link 22 Arab nations, Israel and the United States by 2013", as per the Whitehouse news release.[5] Hence MEFTA captured the idea of using trade as a tool to fight terrorism. It drew its strength from the reasoning that trade will lead to opening of political systems which otherwise would breed resentment and extremism aimed against the United States of America, the West and generally the entire World.

Robert Zoellick,[6] US Trade Representative, proclaimed that the "U.S. agreements—for example, with Jordan, Morocco, and Bahrain—will serve as models for their neighbors that need to embrace openness". Drawn on the similar lines, the Greater Middle East Initiative is the US proposal towards political liberalization and democracy in West Asia that is nothing but the strategy of freedom by which the political rights and political participation in the Muslim world is expected to combat the call of Islamist extremism.[7]

Immediately after the incidence of 9/11, a plethora of economic and political liberalization initiatives were initiated from Washington.

US POLITICAL AND ECONOMIC LIBERALIZATION INITIATIVES: THE CASE OF THE UAE

Taking the case study of United Arab Emirates, the UAE economic freedom score is 64.7 on economic freedom index, making its economy the 54th freest in the 2009 Index and can be one of the parameters to judge the economic freedom index. Signifying improvements in five of the 10 economic freedoms the score though is 2.2 points higher than the previous year as well as overall score being higher than the world average, taking the UAE's ranking at position 7 out of 17 countries in the Middle East/North Africa region.[8] However, contrary to this, Freedom House 2008 ranked the UAE "Not Free" in terms of political rights and civil liberties.[9] The fact remains that U.A.E. is now the only country in the Gulf that offers no elections for its citizens. This becomes further conspicuous after the municipal elections in Saudi Arabia, also a politically closed regime. None of the United Arab Emirates—Abu Dhabi, Dubai, Sharjah, Ra's al Khaimah, Umm al Qaiwan, Ajman, Fujarah.—has a provision for elections.

UAE has authoritarian monarchies as political structures with considerable bureaucracies. The population by and large is offered almost no participation over the decision-making processes. UAE also does not ensure its government officials being held accountable for their actions in a region whose policies are subjugated by ruling families. The UAE's authoritarian monarchies readily check against any political factors that might turn its populace against their governments by identifying potential events that might form chain reaction leading to the shift in general attitudes and hence balancing the potential threat to violence by using various ways to prevent violence, promote stability and impede anti regime political organization.[10] The state nevertheless maintains elaborate system of controls that encompass many aspects of life within the country despite the fact that UAE does not suffer from highly oppressive social atmosphere as well as almost no level of general opposition to the regime.

The federal government controls the internet access as well as controls the press by requiring all publications to be licensed by the Ministry of Information and Culture—the direct controls being exercised over mass communications and publishing. The absence of a free press or free government in the UAE further restricts its citizens to know the exact facts. UAE further limits any autonomous political organization. The civil society groups can never go for open members' recruitment or seek open financing as this would bring the police action on the group. The people assemble usually in small local gatherings as the large gatherings are either monitored or prohibited. Even the mosque and Islamic organizations are monitored and regulated by the state, thus leaving political activity to happen in private homes and in private gatherings. UAE does not have formal political institutions or organization but is also devoid of strong civil society where political opposition might develop. The Federal Ministry of Justice and Islamic Affairs employs all Sunni imams. It even issues weekly advice regarding what topic is appropriate for sermons. The state's control over public spaces such as mosques and Islamic charities is justified on the ground that political discourses in other Arab authoritarian regimes are often destabilizing. The state not only monitors its own population but also extends its regulations to the expatriate workers. It must be noted that expatriate workers constitute nearly 70 per cent of the population of UAE, another possible threat to the stability of regime in the country.

Deducing from the facts presented above, UAE can be simply said to be an economically liberalized country but lacking political liberalization. It contradicts the US assumption that political and economic liberalization initiatives and democracy occur simultaneously or they supplement each other. This has definitely not happened in case of UAE. Democracy as the concept is developed and grown internally rather than being imposed externally; and democracy according to current definitions requires that the states must not only hold free and fair elections but must also guarantee such civil liberties such as freedom of speech, assembly and association. Political liberalization is therefore a second feature of political reform, stressing on the expansion of the civil and political rights. Democratization and political liberalization generally happen hand in hand but they are two distinct processes that do not necessarily cross each other[11] as has happened in the case of most of West Asian countries and also in UAE.

Looking back once again at the statement of Robert Zoellick stated above, the statement seems to imply that Islam is intolerant and violent and that the trade and openness will reduce the aggression. The literature generically claims that Arab and Islamic culture is violence-prone and not conducive to economic growth. The thesis is not supported by the facts on the ground in the case of UAE, as it has achieved a high degree of economic liberalization. The actual attitude of the state and the populance is notedly different in case of UAE if we go by the theory that Arab and Islamic identities of UAE leaders and populance would have led to internal violence and being Arab Muslims, would have tended to reject greater links with the world economy due to their traditionalism and contempt for risk-taking. The UAE as the state and its population have displayed a high degree of unity and a willingness to hold arm in arm the economic liberalization, instead of being characterized by infighting between them.

POLITICAL LIBERALIZATION AND UAE RULING ELITES

The UAE is in the top 50 list of best countries on human development index. UAE is also ranked 27 overall out of 55 countries included in the global ICT survey that shows even its information, communication and technology (ICT) scores are outstanding. Literacy always stands for the indicator or measuring political culture in a society. UAE if evaluated in terms of literacy has exhibited that the monarchies have used oil money to improve education that has boosted educational enrolment at the primary, secondary and university levels.[12]

Literacy however could not change the nagging issue of press freedom and political liberty. These are the areas where the UAE lags behind hopelessly. The question remains unanswered as to why the UAE is not at its best when it comes to political liberalization. The onus for subdued state of press freedom in the UAE rests with the government, the society, the media establishments, the journalists and the writers at large who can voice effectively against press freedom limitation in the society.

The UAE government is no exception with other governments in the world, who never like to be accountable. It has done all possible acts to gently contain the media, yet keep it happy; keeping under its tight watch yet trying to be caring. All these have been done to ensure that the media does not develop an independent mind of its own. The UAE society is very cautious with regards to demand for democracy, transparency, political reform and press freedom despite as progressive as it looks to the outsiders. Democracy, transparency, political reform, press freedom, etc. are hardly the issues of serious discussion or challenges in the UAE.[13] Moreover, the state has learned the best art of keeping the critics at bay by providing positions in government, financial incentives and other rewards for cooperating. Government also divides the potential oppositionists by playing on tribal, regional, religious and class distinctions; and creating an unmarked divide in the population at large, and among elites to keep all opposition weak. At the same time, the regime often champions opposition causes, nominally supporting a wide range of agendas in order to weaken and divide the opposition and boost support for the regime. The governments have even allowed citizens limited voices in order to defuse political estrangement.[14]

United Arab Emirates joined the league of Bahrain, Oman, Qatar, Saudi Arabia for establishing consultative councils as a way to increase representation without holding elections. Even as their power remains fairly circumscribed in most states, these councils in theory allow increased popular input into the policymaking process. They generally serve in an advisory capability, without any institutional checks on the executive, and are appointed directly by state monarchies. Membership has become increasingly varied in recent years, as rulers reach out to business leaders, academics, and other key constituencies, but it remains limited to elites who probably will not challenge government policies. Consultative councils perform an important cooptive function, which may make them an attractive strategy of democratization for rulers concerned about their power base. As council membership expands, an increasing number of groups have at least nominal input into the decision-making process. They can no longer claim to oppose the government, since they now have acquired the status—albeit nominally—as the stakeholders in the political system. Rulers often do try to reach consensus with the councils on policy decisions but they have the choice to disregard council advice whenever they consider it necessary. Consultative councils therefore enable rulers to increase popular representation without sharing any significant decision making power.[15] UAE ruling elites and monarchies also know how to satisfy the population so as to avoid any revolt.

The state ruling monarchies started the economic diversification plan by the early 1960s as they have been aware of the limited nature of their oil supplies since the discovery of the same. The kind of economic vitality created by new forms of rent for the ruling elites further helps consolidate ruling elite positions and hence helps them in maintaining their status quo. Once their modern economy had been built up the ruling elites required these new forms of income like rent as the government bureaucracy very well understood that it would not be able to survive without continuous revenue inflows from the diversified channels considering the limited oil supplies as opposed to other Arab regimes. They established these new sources of rent mainly in two ways, namely, by leasing property and by renting plots within the Emirates' free zones. Foreigners were not permitted to hold land as it was discouraged by UAE law and customs. Taxation was never considered a preferred option as it happens with every authoritarian regime, that taxation typically brings with it popular demand for representation and demand for sharing in to the economy building. UAE leaders arranged for fresh sources of rent which would allow for the maintenance of the political status quo and at the same time putting aside the threat to stability of the government. Summarily speaking thus the oil economy has developed a rent seeking ruling class who have developed another kind of rent seeking sources in order to enjoy the political power structure with the declining oil revenues thus ensuring to maintain their status quo on their power grip on the state.

At this juncture, it is important to understand as to how the rent seeking class has developed in UAE in the light of the above backdrop. It is hence imperative to give a glance to the history of ruling family in UAE in order to understand it. There is no rule of primogeniture for deciding the successive ruler. The rulers are chosen by the elders and there is always fear of being jettisoned by family members. Hence installing them on key positions and distributing to them the oil revenues is one sure way of pleasing them. However, they need to look for other rent seeking incomes for maintaining their current power status in the face of the declining oil revenues, and at the same time also avoid taxation which will only give rise to demand for increased political participation.

Further the rent against the UAE's 100 year leases to foreigners provide the ruling families profits from development contracts. The rents are also sought from leasing parcels of land for office spaces. These new sources of rent appear to be sustainable for the anticipated future and will certainly contribute as the very ready and sustainable alternative to oil for the continued survival of the ruling regime. A high degree of political unity is exercised by these rulers although there were internal divisions and conflict during the British rule and prior to British rule.[16] But the discovery of oil and the wealth which came along with it allowed UAE to emerge as rentier state adding to the ruling family consolidation. Discordant family members are brought back into the fold of unison with government posts that allowed them a degree of power. Their succession mechanism is also one of the key factors leading to political unity wherein crown princes are appointed by elders within the family and most display a substantial amount of recognized personal authority, instead of simply following primogeniture patterns. Family members have an incentive to go along with the appointed crown prince as a result of prisoner's dilemma that can arise in inter family succession negotiations. There might be instances of certain members preferring to increase their own power more than that of the family as a whole but most family members will rationally choose collective support for the family over supplementing their own authority to the ruling dynasty as they in end always live up to safeguarding the dynasty's control of the state.

Moreover state has very well developed a habit in the population to be dependant on state by taking care of needs of the population by various social welfare programmes like education and health care. This balance of care and control is very well maintained by ruling elites in UAE in order to avoid any kind of unrest among the ruling population. These state run welfare programmes have led to a pacified public generally satisfied with its ruling class. The rentier model involves an implied exchange between material well-being and political calmness. As long as the state maintains independent sources of revenue it does not need to be very receptive to its population. Logically speaking hence as long as independent sources of revenue are stable in place the political opposition becomes naturally subdued, and the state has the choice to exercise coercive structures to shut down the opposition altogether.[17] The monarchical rulers will not tend to achieve democracy albeit may allow for calculated and limited increases in participation, generally care about maintaining power, and will necessarily strengthen their survival prospects in the future.

UNITED STATES AND POLITICAL LIBERALIZATION IN UAE

Although UAE is a US ally in the Gulf, it does not station United States troops. However, the port of Dubai has become the most visited US Navy Port of Call outside the continent, wherein the US troop presence can get increasingly high and can total more than 30,000 in times of crisis.[18] Hence it needs to be probed as to whether US backed Western style democracy package is workable in UAE, in the light of the above background.

The United States has multiple and often conflicting interests at stake in the Gulf in general and UAE in particular. It prefers the UAE ruling class firmly holding to its monarchical ruling stakes. The impact of US initiatives on UAE can be very conflicting. The quick reform in UAE may increase regional instability and it could make friendly ruling regimes much more sensitive and averse to their cooperation with the United States, particularly to the fact that UAE ruling class is not easily ready to give up its power stakes. Moreover, as discussed already, democracy is a concept evolving internally hence any attempt by external pressure for internal political change is always difficult. No doubt US initiative even clarified as a partnership initiative.[19] It seeks to undermine the anti-American sentiment common throughout the Gulf with the security alliance with the United States is still increasingly unpopular. Security cooperation also displays that current regimes cannot provide security for their own people without depending on external powers. Empowering citizens' right to express their opinions more effectively shall lead to ruling regimes turning more against U.S. policy and could be forced to reduce their security cooperation with the United States.

The change in government in US to President Obama's administration has presented US moderate image. However it is too early to judge the president Obama policies in the Gulf region; particularly regarding democracy, Palestinian Israel conflict and above all fighting war on terrorism. United States president Obama Administration's West Asian Policy is still to get clarity. Although President Obama explicitly called for a two-state solution for the Israeli Palestinian conflict and mellowed down the West's perceived conflict with Islam. The positive signals were sent when Washington sent the CIA Chief Leon Panetta to Tel Aviv to deliver warnings against Israel's unannounced attack on Iran. It is however clear that other issues concern Obama more than maintaining relationships with Israel ranging from possible Iranian rapprochement to newly discovered Hizbullah activity in Egypt, to soften relation with Syria, or the divided state of Palestinian political establishment. Therefore, a definite shift is expected in US Foreign Policy with regard to West Asia.[20]

The resolution of Israeli Palestinian conflict and US policies in West Asia is the solution to combat the problem of terrorism in West Asia. No doubt President Bush proposed a US backed "road map" to solve the Israeli Palestinian problem. President Bush proposed establishment of independent Palestinian state, living side by side in peace with Israel.[21] But he did not mention road maps 2005 target date for Palestinians statehood. It is also conditioned that they stop violence and follow the path of peace, reform and democracy.[22]

US traditionally has supported authoritarian and autocratic regimes towards fulfilling its hegemonic ambitions. In the late 1940s US started involving itself more actively in the local politics of West Asia. The US supported all that has been in its national interest; from fighting communists during the Cold War to maintaining a steady supply of oil and above all ensuring that no single power dominated the region and fighting terrorism in the current times. Further, US has supported those whom it considered as stable allies, like the Saudi Royal family, Israel and Egyptian governments since Anwar Saadat. During the Cold War period the US continued to supply arms to Israel, Lebanon and Saudi Arabia not only to counter Soviet arms sales in the region but also to cut down on any building of the Soviet influence in the region. United States tends to forget that the anti-American sentiment runs strong through out the region, this sentiment is particularly strong among those most likely to use violence resulting in radicals often criticizing or attacking the United States.[23]

The United States has to understand the stable existence of various religious groups in West Asia. A survey by the Jordan Centre for Strategic Studies (CSS) conducted in five Arab countries found that West is associated with individual liberty and wealth whereas West Asian societies are linked with religion and family. They also did not find religion as exacerbating divisions between Arabs and the West. The findings of the Centre also included that what Arabs' see of Western social and cultural values do not decide their attitudes toward Western foreign policies. Hence, US positions on issues such as the definition of terrorism, the Arab-Israeli conflict, and the war on Iraq remain challenged in theory by the Arabs.[24] General religious groups have shown more advanced organizational skills than have other oppositionists in West Asia. Religious groups have an advantage as they can work through existing channels that receive the support or at least the tolerance of the regime. Religious organizers often exploit existing religious and social meeting halls that are meant for day to day religious activities.[25] Religious groups often are stronger because they are in a better position to muster support from people and willing to work for the ideology in the name of Islam. Moreover religious groups have provided social services in West Asia marked with the lack of basic amenities because of economic problems thus becoming more popular among the masses.

CONCLUSION

From United States initiatives in West Asia it can be believed that United States understood that political, social and economic development is necessary for fighting terrorism so that it can engage growing young population in developmental activities. United States remains baffled on the implementation of its own initiatives in the wake of its other strategic considerations. It also tends to forget that the dissatisfaction of US policies in West Asia is the root cause of Islamic terrorism along with the resentment towards the US support of Israel and to a lesser extent US hostility towards Iraq and Iran. Much of the West Asian populace are angered by large US presence in the region. United States is the focal point of attack of this resentment in West Asia. Therefore even if democracy comes to UAE, there are more chances of Islamist groups winning the elections that are not willing to cooperate with United States. United States itself is not interested in implementing its own agenda which it has announced in haste after the 9/11 incident or in depth analyzes of its repercussions on United States itself.

Therefore for bringing democracy in UAE, population of UAE should act with well defined objectives and coordinate their actions towards democracy to be evolved internally. The UAE rulers' interests in preserving their monarchical set up on one hand and US more concerned about its strategic and hegemonic interests on the other hand. The clash of interests may lead to public desperation and at the same time any coercive response by the ruling regime may also fuel the determination of the opposition groups to continue resisting the regime. Political exclusion sometimes proves lethal because even peaceful citizens may become frustrated and come to believe that only violence will move the regime to action. Moreover, the students of the Gulf countries studying abroad after experiencing the democratic institutions get inspired when they come back. The thrust to democracy and liberalization can come from within the UAE as the US interests and its hegemonic ambitious alliance with the ruling regimes can only produce conflicting interests fuelling the myth of its initatives of political liberalization and democracy.

NOTES

1. Commission Staff (2004), National Commission on Terrorists Attacks, The 9/11 Commission Report, p. 379.
2. Robert Zoellick (2004), When Trade Leads to Tolerance, *The New York Times*, June 12, Washington DC.
3. Commission Staff (2004), The 9/11 Commission Report, *op cit.*, p. 378.
4. Antonia Juhasz (2004), Ambitions of Empire: The Radical Reconstruction of Iraq's Economy, (2003/04 Project Censored Award Winner) LeftTurn Magazine
5. News release (2003), Proposed Middle East Initiatives, Promoting Economic Growth, (http://www.whitehouse.gov/news/releases/2003/05/20030509-12.html), (downloaded on June 7, 2006).
6. Robert B. Zoellick (2003), "Our Credo: Free Trade And Competition" *The Wall Street Journal*, (http://www.ustr.gov/speech-test/zoellick/2003-07-10_WSJ.htm), (downloaded on June 7, 2006).
7. Tamara Cofman Wittes (2004), *The New U.S. Proposal for a Greater Middle East Initiative: An Evaluation*, Saban Center Middle East Memo #2, The Brookings Institution.
8. Ambassador Terry Miller & Kim R. Holmes (2009), 2009 Index of Economic Freedom, The Heritage Foundation, Washington, DC.
9. Report (2008), Freedom in the World 2008, Freedom House, Washington, DC.
10. Daniel L. Byman & Jerrold D. Green (1999), *Political Violence and Stability in the States of the Northern Persian Gulf*, Prepared for Office of the Secretary of Defense, RAND National Defense Research Institute, Washington, DC, p. xiv.
11. Nora Bensahel and Daniel L. Byman (2004), *The Future Security Environment in the Middle East*, Prepared for the United States Air Force, RAND Project Air Force, Washington, DC, p. 16.
12. UNDP & Arab Fund for Economic and Social Development (2005); *Arab Human Development Report*, p. 288.
13. Abdulkhaleq Abdullah (2008), Press freedom in the UAE, Gulf News, UAE, (http://www.gulfnews.com/opinion/columns/nation/10200299.html) (Accessed on May 13, 2009).
14. Nora Bensahel and Daniel L. Byman (2004), *op cit.*, p. 54.

15. *Ibid.*, p. 18.
16. Rosemarie Said Zahlan, The Origin of the United Arab Emirates—A Political and Social History of Trucial States, Macmillan Press Ltd, London 1978, p. 34-38.
17. Nora Bensahel and Daniel L. Byman (2004), *op cit.*, p. 20.
18. Daniel L. Byman & Jerrold D. Green (1999), *op cit.*, p 5.
19. Tamara Cofman Wittes (2004), *op cit.*
20. Jeremy Walker (2009), U.S.—Israel partnership: fraying at the edges, *The Hindu*, New Delhi (May 18, 2009).
21. Office of the Press Secretary (2006), President Bush Attends World Economic Forum, Sharm el Sheikh International Congress Center, Egypt.
22. DEBKA file Exclusive Report (2003), Middle East Road Map—A Useful Cover Story, DEBKA file, (http://www.debka.com/article.php?aid=485), (Accessed on August 20, 2008).
23. Global Connections (2002), What have been the role and effects of US policies and actions in the Middle East; WGBH Educational Foundation, (http://www.pbs.org/wgbh/globalconnections/mideast/questions/uspolicy/index.html), (Accessed on April 14, 2009).
24. Maggie Mitchell Salem (2005), Bush and the Arab street, *Asia Times*, June 2, 2005.
25. Daniel L. Byman & Jerrold D. Green (1999), *op cit.*, p. 51.

Contributors

Ajish P. Joy is an Associate Fellow in the Eurasian Studies Division at the Observer Research Foundation (ORF), New Delhi. At ORF, he focuses on democratic reforms, constitutional evolution and the political aspects of the energy policies of the Eurasian countries. He has done his MPhil on *Minority Rights and State Responses in Israel and Turkey*. Presently, he is a doctoral candidate working on the topic *Political Reforms in the Gulf Co-operation Council States*.

Angela Gangmei is a research scholar at the School of International Studies, Jawaharlal Nehru University. She has written her M.Phil dissertation on *Parliamentary Election in Iraq, January 2005* and is now working on her Ph.D thesis. Her research interests include Iraq's polity and foreign policy.

Anwar Alam is currently Professor and Director of the Centre for West Asian Studies, Jamia Millia Islamia, New Delhi. Earlier he has served Aligarh Muslim University, Aligarh and Jawaharlal Nehru University, New Delhi as lecturer and Assistant and Associate Professor respectively. He has been awarded several long and short term scholarships including the prestigious Alexandor von Humboldt post doctoral fellowship. His major publications includes *Religion and State: A Comparative Study of Egypt, Iran and Saudi Arabia* (1998), *India and West Asia in the Era of Globalisation* (ed; 2008), *Iran and Post 9/11 World Order: Reflections on Iranian Nuclear Programme* (ed; 2009) along with several chapters in the edited books and articles in the national and international academic journals.

Basir Ahmed is an IFS officer. He wrote his M.Phil dissertation on *The Changing World Energy Market: Emerging Issues in Gulf* Security and working on *Gulf-Asia Energy Trade: Implications on Maritime Security* for his Ph D. He has had a brief stint as an Executive Officer at the Associated Chamber of Commerce and Industry of India (ASSOCHAM).

Beryl Anand wrote her M.Phil dissertation on *Israel's Perceptions of Iran's Nuclear Programme* and is currently working on her Ph.D thesis on *Israel's Policy toward Iran, 1979-2005*.

Dietrich Jung is a Professor and Head of Department at the Center for Contemporary Middle East Studies, University of Southern Denmark. He holds a MA in Political Science and Islamic Studies, as well as a Ph.D. in Political Science from University of Hamburg, Germany and has large field experience in the Muslim world. He has published numerous scholarly articles on causes of war, peace and conflict studies, political Islam, modern Turkey and on conflicts in the Middle East. His most recent books are: *Religion, Politics, and Turkey's EU Accession*, New York: Palgrave Macmillan (ed. with Catharina Raudvere, 2008) and *Orientalists, Islamists and the Global Public Sphere,* (London: Equinox, forthcoming 2010).

Gulshan Dietl is a Professor at the School of International Studies, JNU. Her publications include *The Dulles Era: America Enters West Asia* (Lancer International, New Delhi, 1985), *Through Two Wars and Beyond: A Study of the Gulf Cooperation Council* (Lancer Books, New Delhi, 1991), *Saudi Arabia: People, Politics and Policies* (National Book Trust, New Delhi, 2006), and *Contemporary Saudi Arabia and the Emerging Indo-Saudi Relations* (Shipra Publications, New Delhi, 2007; Co-edited).

Hussein Solomon is a professor in the Department of Political Sciences at the University of Pretoria and is currently Visiting Fellow at the Mackinder Programme for the Study of Long-Wave Events. He is also a former Nelson Mandela Chair in African Studies at the Centre for West Asian and African Studies at Jawaharlal Nehru University in New Delhi. His research interests include Islam and Political Democratisation and the rise of Political Islam in Africa.

Jajati K. Pattnaik is an Associate Professor in the Department of Political Science, Indira Gandhi Government College, Tezu, Arunachal Pradesh. He wrote his M.Phil dissertation on the *Political System in the Kingdom of Saudi Arabia* and his Ph.D thesis on *Political Development in the Kingdom of Saudi Arabia: A Theoretical Study*. He has contributed a number of articles to edited volumes, journals, national dailies and weeklies. He specializes in Comparative Politics, International Relations, Foreign Policy and West Asian studies.

Lungthuiyang Riamei is a research scholar at Jawaharlal Nehru University. He wrote his M.Phil dissertation on the *Political Developments in Iraqi Kurdistan 1991-2003*. He is now pursuing Ph.D on the topic the *Kurdish Issue in the Post-Cold War Period, 1991-2007: Domestic and Regional Implications*. He has been participating and presenting papers on the Kurdish issue.

M.H. Ilias is an Associate Professor in the India Arab Cultural Centre and the Centre for West Asian Studies, Jamia Millia Islamia. His main areas of research include Culture and society in the Arab Gulf; film and popular culture in West Asia; Hadrami Diaspora on the Malabar Coast; Islam and Globalization. His publications include: *India-West Asia Relations: Understanding Cultural Interplays* (co-editor); *Space, Memory and Jewish National Identity*; *Society and Change in the Contemporary Gulf* (co-editor, forthcoming) and *Hadrami Diaspora in India: History, Society and Culture* (forthcoming).

Marshal Gao is working on the issues relating to the natural gas with special emphasis on the Qatari gas.

Omair Anas has done his M.Phil on *Globalization and Media Regimes in the GCC Countries*. He has been presenting papers and publishing on Arab media. His research interests include globalization, modern Islamic thought and culture in addition to the issues related to media. He blogs on www.easternmedia. wordpress.com

Prasanta Kumar Pradhan is an Associate Fellow at the Institute for Defence Studies and Analyses, New Delhi. He wrote his M.Phil dissertation on *The First Majlis of Saudi Arabia, 1993-97: An Assessment*. A revised version of his Ph.D thesis on *Human Rights in Islam: The Case of Saudi Arabia* is under publication. His areas of research are foreign policy, security and strategic issues in the Gulf region and in West Asia.

Rajiv Kumar is a senior research fellow in Jawaharlal Nehru University. He wrote his M.Phil dissertation on *India's Relations with Bahrain, 1913-1936.* Currently, he is completing his Ph.D thesis on *Political Liberalization in the Kingdom of Bahrain: Search for Legitimacy*. His research interests include Liberalization and Democratization in the GCC region. He has published on the subject and has taught in Jesus and Mary College, Delhi University.

Rushda Siddiqui is currently working as a Research Fellow with the Indian Council of World Affairs, New Delhi on the project: *Development of Socio-political movements in West Asia and North Africa*. Prior to this, she worked with the National Maritime Foundation, New Delhi, where she was also the Associate Editor of its bi-annual journal *Maritime Affairs*. She was awarded a Ph.D in 2005, from the Centre for West Asian and African Studies, Jawaharlal Nehru University for her thesis on State and Political Islam in North Africa.

Sameena Hameed is an Assistant Professor in the India Arab Cultural Centre and the Centre for West Asian Studies, Jamia Millia Islamia. She wrote her M.Phil dissertation on "Market and the Cartel: A Critique of OPEC Decision of 26 March 1999" and her Ph.D thesis on "Domestic Petroleum Subsidy and Oil Resource Management: A Comparative Study of India and Iran in 1990s". Her areas of interest are behavioural and cultural aspects of public policy.

Shelly Johny is a research scholar at the Jawaharlal Nehru University. He wrote his M.Phil dissertation on *Islamic Revolutionary Guards Corps as an Actor in the Iranian Political System: The Khomeini Era* and is now in the process of submitting his Ph.D thesis on *The Decline of Oman's Maritime Empire during the late Nineteenth Century*.

Stanly Johny is working on his Ph.D thesis on *Hezbollah and the Asymmetric Warfare in Lebanon*. He has been publishing in several newspapers and magazines on security and defence issues.

Sujata Ashwarya Cheema is an Assistant Professor in the Centre for West Asian Studies, Jamia Millia Islamia, New Delhi. She was awarded the Government of Israel Graduate Fellowship (2002-03) to conduct research at Hebrew University of Jerusalem and Hermes Post-Doctoral Fellowship (2007) at Maison des Sciences de l'Homme (MSH), Paris. She was also awarded a visiting fellowship (2009) at the MSH under the Indo-French Cultural Exchange Programme. Her research specializations include Israeli politics and foreign policy, Arab-Israeli conflict, and politics in West Asia. Her publications include *Structures of Political Violence in Palestinian-Israeli Conflict* (New Delhi, 2005), research papers and book articles.

Syeeda Khatoon is senior lecturer in the Department of Economics in MMH College, Ghaziabad. She has been working on *Bilateral Free Trade Agreements between the US and Israel, Jordan and Bahrain* for her Ph D, in pursuance of which she has done field work in the US.

Index